Perspectives on
ORSON WELLES

Perspectives on
FILM

RONALD GOTTESMAN
University of Southern California
and
HARRY M. GEDULD
Indiana University

Series Editors

F for Fake: Welles as Orson Welles.

Perspectives on
ORSON WELLES

edited by

MORRIS BEJA

G.K. Hall & Co.
An Imprint of Simon & Schuster Macmillan
New York

Prentice Hall International
London   Mexico City   New Delhi   Singapore   Sydney   Toronto

G.K. Hall & Co.
An Imprint of Simon & Schuster Macmillan
866 Third Avenue
New York, NY 10022

Library of Congress Catalog Card Number: 94-33581

Printed in the United States of America

Printing number

1 2 3 4 5 6 7 8 9 10

Library of Congress Cataloging-in-Publication Data

Perspectives on Orson Welles / edited by Morris Beja.
p.   cm.—(Perspectives on film)
Filmography: p.
Includes bibliographical references and index.
ISBN 0-8161-7344-3
1. Welles, Orson, 1915– —Criticism and interpretation.
I. Beja, Morris. II. Series.
PN1998.3.W45P47 1995
791.43\0233\092—dc20

94-33581
CIP

The paper used in this publication meets the minimum requirements of American National Standard for Information Sciences—Permanence of Paper for Printed Library Materials. ANSI Z39.48-1984 ∞ ™

For Eleni Rachel Beja, who also loves films

Contents

ESSAYS

Illustrations Follow Page 160

Series Editors' Note

M ORRIS BEJA'S kaleidoscope of selections reveals many facets of Welles the man and his productivity. The selections also point up his unparalleled influence as writer, director, producer, and actor for radio, stage, and screen. No one volume, of course, could hope to do full justice to either the person or his creative legacies, and Professor Beja has, in keeping with the series concept, kept his eye on Welles's contributions to film history, the full dimensions of which, he is right to remind us, are only now beginning to be understood. Anyone who sees the recently released documentary devoted to *It's All True* will register both the wonder of what Welles did achieve and the acute sense of deprivation over what he was unable to bring to unmediated completion.

Many of the items chosen for representation will be agreeably familiar to those who know the abundant body of opinion, interpretation, criticism, and scholarship devoted to Welles. The reviews, interviews, and essays here selected range from the shock of recognition of John O'Hara's early response to *Citizen Kane* to the deeply meditative, arm's-length assessment by William Johnson. Welcome, too, are the contributions by Robert Carringer, who has demonstrated in many articles and books that it is how scholarship procedes, not what its subject is, that counts—or that should count. And precisely because of the sharp disparities of evaluation they represent, the commentaries of David Bordwell, Dudley Andrew, Michael Anderegg and Robert Stam, all of whom rank among the most thoughtful of those who consider film within the academy, greatly enrich the volume.

Finally, Professor Beja is to be applauded not only for his own essay and elegant introduction, but also for providing fresh perspectives from such distinguished scholar-critics as Professors Geduld, Naremore, and Mulvey—perspectives that enlarge our understanding of Welles's mind and art and the continuing pertinence of his achievements. And who more than Welles could fully appreciate the ironies of Director Henry Jaglom's moving tribute to the man behind the masks? For in peeling back layer after layer of these disguises Jaglom reminds us, as Emerson (and Welles) knew, that "around every circle another can be drawn: that there is no end in nature, but every end is a beginning; that there is always another dawn risen on mid-noon, and under every deep a lower deep opens." This is another way of saying that this fine collection is a milestone, not a finish line.

Ronald Gottesman
Harry M. Geduld

Publisher's Note

PRODUCING A volume that contains both newly commissioned and reprinted material presents the publisher with the challenge of balancing the desire to achieve stylistic consistency with the need to preserve the integrity of works first published elsewhere. In the *Perspectives* series, essays commissioned especially for a particular volume are edited to be consistent with G.K. Hall's house style; reprinted essays appear in the style in which they were first published, with only typographical errors corrected. Consequently, shifts in style from one essay to another are the result of our efforts to be faithful to each text as it was originally published.

Acknowledgments

I WOULD LIKE to thank the general editors of the series of which this collection is a part, Ronald Gottesman and Harry M. Geduld, for their encouragement, valuable advice, and active participation at all stages of the preparation of this volume. I am also grateful to them for careful and keen readings of drafts of the Introduction—as I am, as always, to my wife, Ellen Carol Jones.

For locating and especially for helping to select the illustrations, I owe a major debt of gratitude to my daughter, Eleni Rachel Beja.

INTRODUCTION

Introduction

MORRIS BEJA

The biggest mistake we have made is to consider that films are primarily a form of entertainment. The film is the greatest medium since the invention of movable type for exchanging ideas and information, and it is no more at its best in light entertainment than literature is at its best in the light novel.

Orson Welles[1]

THE BIGGEST mistake we can make about Orson Welles is to consider that he did not take his art seriously, to fail to realize that he regarded himself as an artist. To him, movies may have been the greatest train set a child ever had, but he also realized that they are a form of great power, to be treated with profound respect. The twenty-five-year-old who made *Citizen Kane* was young—very young; but he was not a naïf. Asked almost a quarter of a century later if he had had "the sensation of making such an important film," he asserted confidently that he "never doubted it for a single instant."[2]

Welles was passionate about film, but it was not the only world he knew. Before he went to Hollywood he had made important contributions in radio and drama, as a producer, director, writer, and actor, and he would continue to do so. He was extremely well-read, a fact that always had an enormous impact on his filmmaking. He could be impressively articulate both within and about his art, and he regarded himself as "above all else" a "man of ideas," reflecting once, "I am even more a man of ideas than a moralist, I suppose" (Cobos, 532). But not more so than an artist, again. In all his comments over many years, his passion for the art of film

3

never blurred. Reminded that he had once written that "the film itself is a dead thing," he quickly explained that "it's as dead as a book. And, potentially, as everlastingly alive."[3]

Many controversies surrounded Welles while he was living and active—all too active, it often seemed, as an actor in sometimes embarrassingly awful movies, as a guest on television talk shows, in commercials, engaged in seemingly endless ephemera while often not being able to complete his own film projects. Welles was frequently criticized during his career for such activities, which were felt to be beneath the dignity of a great director. No doubt at times he compromised his own ideals by taking part in some lesser projects, but he never abandoned those ideals in the realm that meant most to him, his own films. He knew—how could he not?—that he had to earn a living, but after directing *The Stranger* (1946) he rarely worked as a director within the Hollywood system, and never at all made a movie that wasn't his own, that didn't reflect his personal vision; as he put it, "I decided that I'd rather do what I didn't like very much as an actor than what I didn't like very much as a director. So I've kept my virtue slightly less sullied in the megaphone-holding department" (*TIOW*, 174).

The controversies centering on Orson Welles can be viewed with a bit more distance since his death in 1985. Even now, however, we cannot truly see his whole career: several major film projects were never completed, but substantial portions of them could still be made available to us, as has recently been done with footage from *It's All True* (see the essay by Robert Stam in the present volume). In any case, we need no longer be distracted by the trivial and transient aspects of the life of a professional trying both to make a living and, sometimes desperately, to raise enough money to start or continue one of his own films.

As a young man Orson Welles became famous for being the force behind the radio broadcast "The War of the Worlds" (1938); soon he was famous for being the boy wonder who took on William Randolph Hearst; for a time he was famous for being Rita Hayworth's husband; eventually he was famous for being Harry Lime, for having enormous bulk, for appearing on those talk shows, for pitching wine in those commercials, or for acting in other people's movies. And for not finishing his own films—a bitter twist of fate for the director of a dozen feature films. The myth of Orson Welles has yet to be overcome by some version of the "real" Orson Welles, in an irony that conceivably might have bemused or even pleased the creator of *F for Fake*—but that did not.

Welles's career was a full one—it is my profound conviction that he deserves his current image as a towering figure in film history—despite paradoxes entailed in a mixture within his career of the transient and the enduring. Of course, any artist will produce work that is of varying value. In Welles's case, the superb triumph of his first film has tended to overshadow his other genuine achievements. Those achievements were in varied film genres: an enduring cop thriller in *Touch of Evil*, for example; several of the most cinematically interesting Shakespeare adaptations ever filmed, and in *Chimes at Midnight* one of the most artistically successful of them all; at least two of the most fascinating novel adaptations ever made—one from a book hardly anyone still reads, and only then probably because of Welles's movie (*The Magnificent Ambersons*), and the other from one of the great, timeless works of twentieth-century literature (*The Trial*). And he did, after all, make that totally uncategorizable movie called *Citizen Kane*.

Let us acknowledge right off that Welles never surpassed or equalled the achievement of that first film. But let us also keep in mind that it has become a commonplace that *Citizen Kane* will be at or near the top of any and all polls of the world's "greatest films": that it is not just Welles's finest work in film, but arguably *anyone's*. Nor is there serious doubt of Welles's central role in the creation of that masterpiece; yet somehow for a long time there was far from universal agreement that the director of what many people regard as the greatest film in cinema history was in fact a great filmmaker. It was as if the magnificence of *Middlemarch* were so to eclipse all of George Eliot's other novels as to make one wonder about her overall mastery. Or one might try to imagine arguments in which the achievements inherent in *Moby-Dick*, the *Messiah*, or *Sunday Afternoon on the Island of La Grande Jatte* would somehow lead to the conclusion that in the rest of their careers Melville, Handel, and Seurat were artists of distinctively limited attainments.

Of course, there are artists whose other works never match their crowning achievements: in literature, one could mention Mary Shelley and *Frankenstein*, or Ralph Ellison and *Invisible Man*—a work he never equalled but which one would readily give at least an arm to have been able to write; in film, one could cite Robert Wiene and *The Cabinet of Dr. Caligari*. Welles himself defended Greta Garbo when Peter Bogdanovich remarked that she might not be regarded as a great star if it were not for *Ninotchka* and *Camille*: "If it hadn't been for *Don Quixote*," Welles replied, "I don't think you could say that Cervantes was the greatest writer in Spanish literature" (*TIOW*, Kane, 106).

Before *Citizen Kane*, Welles had already attained fame—and notoriety—in both drama and radio; the essays by Phyllis Goldfarb, Robert Hapgood, and Harry M. Geduld in this volume deal particularly with those aspects of Welles's career, of which he remained justifiably proud. He occasionally played down the importance of his original contributions to filmmaking in *Citizen Kane*, but even as he did so he would claim that "my big inventions were in radio and the theatre. Much more than in movies. Nobody knows that. I invented the use of narration in radio."[4] His experience of working in the theater and on the radio clearly affected his work in film; he adapted Shakespeare for several of his films, and his use of sound in his film work has long been seen as pioneering.

Welles's early fame, notably but not exclusively the result of his radio dramatization of H. G. Wells's *The War of the Worlds* (which caused a famous panic among people who did not realize it was a fictional program), brought him offers from Hollywood that he at first resisted. But he accepted unprecedented creative freedom from the RKO studio, and after an abortive attempt to direct an adaptation of Joseph Conrad's *Heart of Darkness*, he began work on *Citizen Kane*.

The history of the production of that film, and of the controversies surrounding its "authorship," are keenly dealt with in Robert L. Carringer's *The Making of "Citizen Kane."*[5] Carringer corrects Pauline Kael's extreme claims that Welles had little or nothing to do with the writing of the screenplay,[6] stressing instead that "*Citizen Kane* is not only Hollywood's greatest film, but it is also . . . Hollywood's single most successful instance of collaboration. In a very real sense, the two propositions are synonymous" (Carringer, x). Welles's own attitude toward the script work of others on his projects had probably already been encapsulated in a remark he had made about the work of those who wrote the radio plays he directed: "It is not expected of Pharaoh that he build with his own hands, his own pyramids."[7]

The question of authorship was only one controversy surrounding *Citizen Kane*, and for years after its release in 1941 a much more prominent one centered on the correlations between the lives of Charles Foster Kane and the newspaper publisher William Randolph Hearst (1863–1951). Those correlations are touched on in several essays in this volume; they led Hearst and his newspapers to bring pressure on the film industry to suppress the film. RKO had difficulty both exhibiting it in theaters, which at that time were often controlled by other studios, and even publicizing it, since Hearst newspapers refused to carry ads for the film, much less print reviews of it. And after the novelist John O'Hara's enthusiastic review, with which the present volume begins, was printed in *Newsweek*— he called *Citizen Kane* "the best picture" he had ever seen, and attacked those who, he claimed, were trying to make sure that audiences would "never see the picture"—O'Hara was fired, or so at least the story goes (Brady, 305).

O'Hara was far from alone in immediately recognizing the film's importance, but even the extraordinarily enthusiastic reviews did not produce success at the box office, probably because of the pressures to keep the film out of the chain theaters. Thus, *Citizen Kane* was financially disappointing. Soon the film was basically withdrawn from circulation, merely resurfacing occasionally for brief runs during the rest of the 1940s and the 1950s. In a 1952 poll taken by the film journal *Sight and Sound* that attempted to determine the ten best films ever made, *Kane* did not make the list at all. Yet something happened during the next decade, and in 1962 *Kane* was in first place. It is not easy to pin down all the complex sources of the changed perception, and obviously many forces were at work. Among them was the increasing attention being paid to the film by cinema scholars and critics, both in the United States and Europe. In France the writings of André Bazin and those of the critics and auteurists (and future film directors) of the journal *Cahiers du Cinéma*, most notable of whom was François Truffaut, were particularly influential (see Truffaut's review and Bazin's essay in this collection). Andrew Sarris publicized the auteur movement in the United States, and by the mid-1950s was declaring *Kane* an auteurist masterpiece. Then in 1961 the critic and scholar—and future filmmaker—Peter Bogdanovich helped to arrange an Orson Welles retrospective at the Museum of Modern Art in New York.[8]

The 1961 MoMA retrospective was not restricted to *Citizen Kane*, for by then Welles had gone on to make other films—excellent, even major ones. His movies *The Magnificent Ambersons* (1942), *The Stranger* (1946), *The Lady from Shanghai* (1946), *Macbeth* (1948), *Othello* (1952), *Mr. Arkadin* (or *Confidential Report*, 1955) and *Touch of Evil* (1958) had all already appeared. He had also acted in a large number of other films, most famously in *The Third Man* (1949), but also notably in *Jane Eyre* (1943), *Moby Dick* (1956) and *Compulsion* (1959). Yet to come among his own films were a number of his finest and most important works, including *The Trial* (1962) and *Chimes at Midnight* (or *Falstaff*, 1966). Such a record hardly supports the legend of the wunderkind who never went on to do very much after *Citizen Kane*, and the 1975 Life Achievement Award he received from the American Film Institute could well have seemed overdue.

Welles never did complete some major projects, notably *It's All True*, *The Other Side of the Wind*, and *Don Quixote*, the title of which he contemplated changing to *When Are You Going to Finish Don Quixote?* But artists must be judged by their accomplishments, by what they actually have done, not by what might have been. Moreover, Welles's body of work is that of a single artist who put his unique stamp on every one of his films. Truffaut claimed in his foreword to André Bazin's book on Welles that "the sound cinema has given us only one, one single filmmaker whose style is immediately recognizable after three minutes of film, and his name is Orson Welles."[9]

Truffaut's exaggeration suggests how influential Welles's work has inevitably been on later filmmakers (as it has also been on written literature, for that matter.)[10] One of the enviable things Steven Spielberg has been able to do with the fortune he has made from his films was to buy the original Rosebud sled.

It was a special point of gratification to Welles late in his career that "*Citizen Kane* has influenced more movies in the last years than it did before" (*TIOW*, 88). But an especially interesting aspect of the homage paid to Welles by later generations of directors is that it frequently takes the form of allusions to films other than *Kane*. Often the homage is fairly explicit, as when Robert Altman's *The Player* opens with a complicated long shot while two characters discuss the famous tour-de-force long shot at the start of *Touch of Evil*, or when Woody Allen's *Manhattan Murder Mystery* concludes with clips from—and, within Allen's own film, an imitation of—the "Crazy House" scene at the end of Welles's *The Lady from Shanghai*. (Welles himself, ironically, once observed that "the more film people pay homage to each other, and to films rather than to life, the more they are approximating the last scene of *The Lady from Shanghai*—a series of mirrors reflecting each other" [*TIOW*, 258]).

In other instances the homage is relatively oblique. For example, in Neil Jordan's widely acclaimed *The Crying Game*, both early in the film and at its end he uses a fable that Welles frequently liked to tell, and that the title character played by Welles himself in *Mr. Arkadin* (also known as *Confidential Report*) recounts in that movie. The tale is often seen, with justice or (in my own view, certainly) crude injustice, as a reflection of some of Welles's own allegedly self-destructive traits.

In the fable a scorpion is unable to cross a stream and asks a frog to carry him across. Fearing that the scorpion might sting him and cause him to drown, the frog refuses. That is absurd, the scorpion points out; if he were to sting the frog, he would drown too. The frog sees the logic in that explanation and agrees to help the scorpion; yet in the midst of the stream he feels the scorpion's sting after all. As they both are drowning, the frog cries, "Is that logic?" The scorpion, acknowledging that it is not, replies "But I can't help it. It's my character." (In Jordan's *The Crying Game*, the last words of "Mr. Scorpion" are, "I can't help it, it's in my nature." When another character asks, "So what's that supposed to mean?" the teller of the tale replies, "Means what it says. The scorpion does what is in his nature." At the end of *The Lady from Shanghai*, Michael O'Hara [played by Welles himself] says to Elsa Bannister [Rita Hayworth] that "one who follows his nature keeps his original nature in the end. But haven't you heard ever of something better to follow?" "No," she replies.) However we may view the trajectory of Welles's career, it reflected his own character; his own nature.

As part of the effort to indicate that trajectory, ten contemporary reviews of a number of Welles's films are reprinted at the start of this volume to provide a brief but telling sampling of the varied reactions (opinionated or awed, confident or uncertain) to a disconcertingly disparate and challenging body of work that spans over thirty years.

I have also included two interviews: one with Welles, and one with Charlton Heston, who has interesting remarks about the filming of *Touch of Evil*. But readers should be aware that the single most important source for Welles's comments on his own work is the compilation of interviews he conducted over several years with his friend Peter Bogdanovich, collected as *This Is Orson Welles* (1992).

The rest of the present volume consists of critical studies of Welles's work, and one memoir. Five of the essays were commissioned for this book and appear here for the first time. The basis of selection for all the others is fairly straightforward: I have tried to present an array of some of the most valuable and interesting essays published on Welles, while also attempting to reveal the diversity of his achievements, although inevitably his central role as a filmmaker is foregrounded. I have decided to present the essays chronologically according to their publication date, without attempting to impose upon them an immediate context (such as "Orson Welles's Shakespeare," or "The Early Orson Welles").

I have also deliberately limited the number of essays on *Citizen Kane*, given the fact that a number of collections center on that masterpiece (including one in the series in which this volume appears). But no anthology on Orson Welles could fail to include several such pieces; those here by David Bordwell, Robert Carringer, Morris Beja, and Laura Mulvey approach the movie from quite varied perspectives.

Some essays discuss a number of films, such as William Johnson's exploration of key elements of Welles's filmmaking style, and Phyllis Goldfarb's analysis of his use of sound. André Bazin's influential essay concentrates on the techniques of *Citizen Kane* and *The Magnificent Ambersons*, while Dudley Andrew's essay considers many films, though with special attention to the adaptations of Shakespeare and *The Magnificent Ambersons*. Other essays examine individual works: in addition to those essayists concentrating on *Citizen Kane*, Peter Cowie looks at *Touch of Evil*, Mark Graham and Karen Marguerite Radell at *The Lady from Shanghai*, and Robert Hapgood and Michael Anderegg at *Chimes at Midnight*.

Harry M. Geduld and James Naremore consider aspects of Welles's career other than his work as a director—his most famous radio production and his acting, respectively. Two essayists focus on major projects Welles never completed: Kevin C. Brechner on *The Other Side of the Wind*, and Robert Stam on *It's All True*. Welles believed the "tragedy" of the *It's All True* project produced "the basis of the whole enormous anti-Welles edifice": "It cost me many, many other pictures which I never made; and many years in which I couldn't work at all" (*TIOW*, 134, 150). The volume ends with a moving tribute by Henry Jaglom, who knew Welles closely both personally and professionally.

Welles always resisted connections between himself and the lives and personalities of the characters in his films, or the ones he portrayed as an actor.[11] In fact, he didn't even like most of the people he played (with good reason). Still, I hope it is not perverse of me to end this introduction to a book devoted to Orson Welles with another of his own fables.

Welles's career was fitful, turbulent, inconsistent, often chaotic, never neat and predictable; but it was also creative, intriguing, and fascinating. One may be reminded analogously of the one bit of dialogue he wrote for his Harry Lime character in Graham Greene and Carol Reed's *The Third Man*: "You know what the fellow said . . . In Italy for thirty years under the Borgias they had warfare, terror, murder, bloodshed—they produced Michelangelo, Leonardo da Vinci and the Renaissance. In Switzerland they had brotherly love, five hundred years of democracy and peace, and what did that produce . . .? The cuckoo clock."

Notes

1. "The Third Audience," *Sight and Sound* 23 (January—March 1954): Reprinted in Peter Cowie, *A Ribbon of Dreams: The Cinema of Orson Welles* (South Brunswick, N.J.: A.S. Barnes, 1973), 226.

2. Juan Cobos, Miguel Rubio, and José Antonio Pruneda, "Orson Welles," trans. Rose Kaplin, in *Interviews with Film Directors*, ed. Andrew Sarris (New York: Avon, 1969), 556; hereafter cited in text as Cobos.

3. Orson Welles and Peter Bogdanovich, *This Is Orson Welles*, p. 214, ed. Jonathan Rosenbaum (New York: HarperCollins, 1992), hereafter cited in text as *TIOW*.

4. *TIOW*, 88. During another conversation Bogdanovich made the connection between Welles's radio work and the use of narration in *The Magnificent Ambersons*, and Welles remarked that although narration is supposedly uncinematic, "I'd like to do more of it in movies. . . . I think words are terribly important in talking pictures" (*TIOW*, 103). Whatever the truth of his claim that he "invented" radio narration, in the same volume Jonathan Rosenbaum's "Welles' Career: A Chronology" (*TIOW*, 323–453) presents ample evidence that Welles's "work in theatre and radio represents by far the most prolific part of his career" (*TIOW*, 491n).

5. (Berkeley: University of California Press, 1985); hereafter cited in text as Carringer.

6. Pauline Kael, "Raising Kane," in Herman J. Mankiewicz and Orson Welles, *The "Citizen Kane" Book* (New York: Bantam, 1971), .

7. Quoted in Frank Brady, *Citizen Welles: A Biography of Orson Welles* (New York: Doubleday, 1989), 144; hereafter cited as Brady.

8. Welles's own views on auteurism were apparently ambivalent. Reminded that "the French" argue that there are "no works, only authors," Welles "heatedly" replied, "I believe there are only *works*." But he could also claim to "have a theory that the *success* of a movie" always depends on one person—who, however, "may very well be the cutter or the actor or the writer instead of the director" (*TIOW*, xxix, 257).

For more-detailed run downs of the critical reception of *Citizen Kane*, see the introduction to Ronald Gottesman, ed., *Focus on "Citizen Kane"* (Englewood Cliffs, N.J.: Prentice-Hall, 1971), and, more recently, Carringer, *The Making of "Citizen Kane"*, 115–20.

9. André Bazin, *Orson Welles: A Critical View*, trans. Jonathan Rosenbaum (New York: Harper & Row, 1978), 27.

10. Welles's influence on literature has been as global as his impact on film; in Latin America, for example, both Carlos Fuentes and Gabriel García Marquez have testified to the effect on their novels of Welles's films (see Brady, 600).

11. In a notable exception, he regarded *The Trial* as "the most autobiographical movie that I've ever made, the *only* one that's really close to me. And just because it doesn't speak in a Middle Western accent doesn't mean a damn thing. It's much closer to my own feelings about everything than any other picture I've ever made" (*TIOW*, 283).

REVIEWS

Citizen Kane

JOHN O'HARA

IT IS with exceeding regret that your faithful bystander reports that he has just seen a picture which he thinks must be the best picture he ever saw.

With no less regret he reports that he has just seen the best actor in the history of acting.

Name of picture: *Citizen Kane*.

Name of actor: Orson Welles.

Reason for regret: you, my dear, may never see the picture.

(From now on, it's *I*.)

I saw *Citizen Kane* the other night. I am told that my name was crossed off a list of persons who were invited to look at the picture, my name being crossed off because some big shot remembered I had been a news-paperman. So, for the first time in my life, I indignantly denied I was a newspaperman. Nevertheless, I had to be snuck into the showing of *Citizen Kane* under a phony name. That's what's going on about this wonderful picture. Intrigue.

Why intrigue? Well, because. A few obsequious and/or bulbous middle-aged ladies think the picture ought not to be shown, owing to the fact that the picture is rumored to have something to do with a certain publisher, who, for the first time in his life, or maybe the second, shall be nameless. That the nameless publisher might be astute enough to realize that for the first time in his rowdy life he had been made a human being did not worry the loyal ladies. Sycophancy of that kind, like curtseying, is deliberate. The ladies merely wait for a chance to show they can still do it, even if it means cracking a femur. This time I think they may have cracked off more than they can chew. I hope.

The story is that of a publisher, from his whippersnapper to his doting days. His origin is humble, and most likely not acceptable to the quarrel-ing ladies, whose origin is not for a second in question here. A fresh punk out of various colleges, the publisher walks into a newspaper office as a not quite legitimate heir, and thereupon enjoys himself and power. At a rather late date it is shown that his sybaritic pastimes and his power are incomplete, for he can buy or produce everything but love. He doesn't give love; he lacks love. With everything in the world that you and I might expect to bring happiness, the publisher is a lonely, unwanted, feared, tragicomic man. He dies, speaking one mysterious word, a female name. At the end of this wonderful picture you get to know what the name was. You also (later) realize how silly women can be, especially obsequious women.

Look in vain here for any but obscure hints as to the story of *Citizen Kane*. My intention is to make you want to see the picture; if possible, to make you wonder why you are not seeing what I think is as good a picture as was ever made. Up to now I have thought that the very best talking picture ever made was *M*. I have seen *M* at least eight times. As a movie writer and press agent I used to have them run off the attack sequence in *The Big Parade*, the one in the woods where the boys don't know where the sharpshooter's going to hit next, everytime I had a chance. One of my very favorite silents was that beautiful job *The Great Gatsby*. And if you want to settle bets on any phase of *The Birth of a Nation*, call me. But *Citizen Kane* is Late 1941. It lacks nothing.

And aside from what it does not lack, *Citizen Kane* has Orson Welles. It is traditional that if you are a great artist, no one gives a damn about you while you're still alive. Welles has had plenty of that. He got a tag put to his name through the Mars thing, just as Scott Fitzgerald, who wrote better than any man in our time, got a Jazz Age tag put to his name. I say, if you plan to have any grandchildren to see and to bore, see Orson Welles so that you can bore your grandchildren with some honesty. There never has been a better actor than Orson Welles. I just got finished saying there never has been a better actor than Orson Welles, and I don't want any of your lip.

Do yourself a favor. Go to your neighborhood exhibitor and ask him why he isn't showing *Citizen Kane*. *Then* sue me.

Kane Case [*Citizen Kane*]

ANONYMOUS

A s IN some grotesque fable, it appeared last week that Hollywood was about to turn upon and destroy its greatest creation. That creation was *Citizen Kane*, the film which Orson Welles and his Mercury Players had spent more than a year talking and thinking about and 70 days shooting, with $750,000 of Radio-Keith-Orpheum's money.

The film was in the cans. A magazine advertising campaign had begun. But no release was set by R. K. O. for the picture to be shown to the public, and it seemed very likely that none would ever be. Old Mr. William Randolph Hearst, who had only heard reports of the picture through his cinematic eyes, ears and tongue, columnist Louella Parsons, thought the life of Kane was too close a parallel to the life of Hearst.

THE PICTURE.

The objection of Mr. Hearst, who founded a publishing empire on sensationalism, is ironic. For to most of the several hundred people who have seen the film at private showings, *Citizen Kane* is the most sensational product of the U. S. movie industry. It has found important new techniques in picture-making and story-telling. Artful and artfully artless, it is not afraid to say the same thing twice if twice-telling reveals a fourfold truth. It is as psychiatrically sound as a fine novel but projected with far greater scope, for instance, than Aldous Huxley was inspired to bring to his novel on the same theme. It is a work of art created by grown people for grown people.

THE STORY.

The story begins with the death of Charles Foster Kane (Orson Welles), at one time the world's third richest man, overlord of mines and factories and steamship lines, boss of newspapers, news services and radio chains, possessor of a vast castle in Florida, a staggering agglomeration of art, two wives, millions of enemies. The MARCH OF TIME is running off rushes of its Kane biography in its projection room. But when they are shown, the editor does not think the facts reveal the man. "It might be any rich publisher—Pulitzer, Hearst or John Doe," he complains. "Get me something that will show it is Kane. Find out his last words. Maybe they meant something."

Kane's last word was "rosebud." Thompson (William Alland), the newsreel reporter, spends two feverish weeks in interviewing five people. Thompson talks to Kane's trollopish second wife (Dorothy Comingore), whom he tried to make a singer, finally established in the castle. There she passed the years assembling jigsaw puzzles until she walked out in boredom. Then there is Kane's rich guardian (George Coulouris) whom Kane hated; Kane's general manager (Everett Sloan), the sad, loyal, philosophical Jew who stuck by to the end; his former drama editor and best friend (Joseph Cotten) with whom Kane broke after Kane's disastrous try for the Governorship of New York; Kane's butler (Paul Stewart). None knew the meaning of "rosebud." But each in his way understood a little of the man: he was not cruel, but he did cruel things; he was not generous, but he did generous things; he was willful, capricious, and he wanted to be loved—on his own terms. The MARCH OF TIME never finds the meaning of "rosebud," nor the key to Kane's frustrations, but, almost by accident, the audience does.

So sharply does *Citizen Kane* veer from cinema cliché, it hardly seems like a movie. There are some extraordinary technical novelties through which Welles and wiry, experienced little photographer Gregg Toland have given the camera a new eloquence—for example, the "stolen" news-reels, the aged and streaked documentary shots. When Susan makes her disastrous operatic debut, the camera tells the story by climbing high up among the flies to find two stagehands—one with his hand pinching his nose in disgust. Always the camera seems to be giving the narrative a spe-cial meaning where it will help most: picturing a small bottle beside a tum-bler when Susan Kane is lying drugged with an overdose of sedatives, exploring the love nest and the family breakfast table like a pair of prying eyes and ears.

Orson Welles treats the audience like a jury, calling up the witnesses, letting them offer the evidence, injecting no opinions of his own. He merely sees that their stories are told with absorbing clarity. Unforgettable are such scenes as the spanning of Kane's first marriage in a single conver-sation, the silly immensity of the castle halls which echo the flat whines of Susan.

HOLLYWOOD. Hollywood claimed Welles never would make the grade. From the moment he arrived there its citizens resented him and his Martians and his youth and his talent. When he grew a beard for his first film, a sporty press agent sent him a bearded ham for Christmas; while he was dining out one evening, a playful actor cut off his tie with a table knife; columnists dubbed him with nicknames like "Little Orson Annie." At announcements that his first two productions had been called off, the town nodded knowingly. He was just a big bag of publicity.

But whatever Orson Welles did do, Hollywood was pretty sure it would break all the rules. Hollywood was right.

Citizen Kane

JOY DAVIDMAN

*C*ITIZEN KANE is a magnificent if unfinished portrait. Orson Welles went to Hollywood to break conventions, and he has succeeded in finding new and splendid ways of casting, writing, directing, photographing, and cutting motion pictures. He has united an admirable group of actors with a vigorous script and a startling technique. The result makes most experienced Hollywood directors look sick. There is only one fly in the ointment; Welles has not escaped one Hollywood convention, the smirking thesis that the important thing about a public figure is not how he treats his country but how he treats his women.

In consequence *Citizen Kane* is content to achieve a murderous study of the private life of a public egoist. Alleged (we take no chances) to concern a newspaper publisher whom we will not name, the film is calculated to stab its prototype in all his softest spots. Kane's character, built up in what one of the actors calls a jigsaw puzzle method, is presented by sending a reporter, after Kane's death, to interview those who knew him. We see first, a brilliantly handled March of Time sequence of Kane's life as it appears to the general public; then we see him through the eyes of, successively, his banker, his manager, his best friend, his mistress-wife, and his butler. The last piece drops into place, and Kane is summed up as a man who loved only himself, but demanded the love of the whole world as his birthright. His egoism destroys his marriages, alienates his friends, wrecks his political career, and brings him with iron inexorability to his death, a wretched, apoplectic old man alone in a dream castle crammed with meaningless possessions.

The portrait is beautifully done; if Kane were a private citizen, the film would be complete. But Kane is a publisher of enormous influence, an aspiring politician, a captain of industry, a friend of dictators; in short, what Mr. Roosevelt before his apostasy used to label a malefactor of great wealth. This, in real life, is his more important aspect; yet in the film it is given only occasional and casual mention. In two hours there is not one shot of Kane performing any significant political action. He makes love, he makes meaningless speeches; he goes to Europe and the opera; he rushes in and out of newspaper offices. We are told that he exerts great influence on the people of America. But we never see him doing it. True, there are references to his instigation of the Spanish-American War, his hob-nobbing with Hitler, his insincere pretense of speaking for the common man. But how does he instigate the war? what is behind his appearance with Hitler

Reprinted from *New Masses*, May 13, 1941.

on a balcony? how does he betray the common man? There is not even a hint. His only visible violation of journalistic ethics is an insistence upon favorable reviews of his blonde wife's appalling opera singing, and his only political activity seems to be getting caught in a love nest during a campaign. Not one glimpse of the actual content of his newspapers is afforded us. One or two advertised scenes of political relevance, indeed, appear to have been cut out of the picture. As a result the audience is left with a vast confusion as to what Kane really stands for in public life. This grotesque inadequacy in the midst of plenty keeps *Citizen Kane* from fulfilling its promises. In place of an analysis of Kane's true significance, the picture resorts to the trick of giving him a mysterious dying speech, supposed to be "the real clue to Kane," the sentimental explanation of which is coyly delayed until the fadeout.

Considered for its technique alone, however, *Citizen Kane* is worth a couple of visits. Sometimes splendid, sometimes merely showy, it is always interesting. The device of telling Kane's history no less than five times is ingeniously managed to supplement and intensify rather than to repeat. Welles has achieved the miracle of making photography "unphotographic"; instead of the usual unimaginative reproduction of scenes and faces, *Citizen Kane*'s camera seizes on a significant detail, emphasizes it in a flash, and swoops on to the next point. Like painting, it stresses the important; like poetry, it suggests far more than it says. Needless to say, this new technique is far from perfect. The staccato brevity of the earlier sequences is painfully confusing, and at times the story seems to be told entirely in a series of montages. There are far too many trick camera angles, too many fantastic combinations of light and shadow, indicating an incomplete translation of Welles' famous stage technique into screen terms. Frequently he lets his showmanship run away with him, preferring to astound rather than to convince. The construction of the film, otherwise magnificent, is weakened by the introduction of irrelevant suspense about the meaning of Kane's dying murmur, "Rosebud." Yet *Citizen Kane*, technically, may well serve to inspire a new school of film-making.

It is hardly necessary to add that the picture is brilliantly acted. Welles himself makes the overpowering and violent personality of Kane believable. The Mercury Actors are what Hollywood has needed for years; George Coulouris as the pompous banker, and Joseph Cotten as Leland, the honest friend who serves as a contrast to Kane, are superlative where all are good. And Welles' Hollywood discovery, Dorothy Comingore, is the most astonishing young actress since Garbo was a pup. To emotional power and versatility she unites an exquisite beauty as yet unremodeled by makeup artists. Bernard Herrmann's musical score is not the least of the film's distinctions, and Gregg Toland deserves as much praise as Welles for the camera work. The final word on *Citizen Kane*, in spite of its limitations, is that this reviewer is going to see it again—even if she has to pay to get in.

[*The Magnificent Ambersons*]

ANONYMOUS ["T. M. P."]

W ITH ONLY two pictures to his credit, last year's extraordinary "Citizen Kane" and now Booth Tarkington's "The Magnificent Ambersons," Orson Welles has demonstrated beyond doubt that the screen is his medium. He has an eloquent, if at times grandiose, flair for the dramatic which only the camera can fully capture and he has a truly wondrous knack for making his actors, even the passing bit player, behave like genuine human beings. And yet, with all his remarkable talent, Mr. Welles still apparently refuses to make concessions to popular appeal. The Capitol's new film, however magnificently executed, is a relentlessly somber drama on a barren theme.

In a world brimful of momentous drama beggaring serious screen treatment, it does seem that Mr. Welles is imposing when he asks moviegoers to become emotionally disturbed over the decline of such minor league American aristocracy as the Ambersons represented in the late Eighteen Seventies. While one may question Welles' choice of theme, as well as his conception of the Tarkington novel, it must be admitted that he has accomplished with marked success what he set out to do. For "The Magnificent Ambersons" is a dignified, resourceful character study of a family group, which incidentally reflects the passing of an era.

This time Welles does not participate as actor, but he does lend his impressive voice as an off-screen narrator, setting the scene and introducing the characters in much the same manner as he used to do on the radio. As the film opens, town gossipers are busily passing around word that beauteous Isabel Amberson is giving up fun-loving Eugene Morgan, because he imbibed too much and crashed through a bass fiddle, to marry the stuffy but more socially acceptable Wilbur Minafer.

Their marriage produces one son, George Amberson Minafer, a devilish, spoiled brat for all his beautiful golden curls, who imbues the elder townspeople with one burning desire—to witness the day that George gets his "come-upance." With the collapse of his grandfather's fortune George gets his "come-upance" with a vengeance in young manhood. But before fate delivers its humbling blows, the vain, arrogant youth cruelly wrecks the tender bitter-sweet romance that has been renewed between his now widowed mother and her old suitor, himself a widower and father of the girl whom George loves.

Tim Holt draws out all of the meanness in George's character, which is precisely what the part demands. As the mother, Dolores Costello proves that she is too beautiful and capable an actress to remain inactive for such long periods. Agnes Moorehead, playing the role of a romantically frustrated aunt, is splendid. Other fine performances are contributed by Ray Collins, Anne Baxter and the veteran Richard Bennett as the grandfather. Joseph Cotten, who has shown fine promise, gives an adequate though not distinguished performance as Eugene Morgan, a role which is not too well written.

All in all. "The Magnificent Ambersons" is an exceptionally well-made film, dealing with a subject scarcely worth the attention which has been lavished upon it.

[*The Stranger*]

JAMES AGEE

ORSON WELLES'S new movie, *The Stranger*, is a tidy, engaging thriller about a Nazi arch-criminal (Mr. Welles) who hides out as a teacher in a New England boys' prep school. It seems to have raised the question, in the minds of some people, whether Welles has any right to make movies at all. I think I understand why it raises such a question. For years Welles was fatuously overrated as a "genius," boy and otherwise; possibly, for that matter, he overrated himself. In any case, many people who overrated him and many others still who, knowing better and annoyed by all the talk, stupidly blamed Welles for it and underrated him—as I did for a while—are now so eager to think ill of him that they will hardly bother to look at what is before them. I am perfectly willing to agree with anyone who points out that this is "only human" if such people are equally willing to accept my synonyms for that, which are that it is also contemptible and, in its genteel way, criminal. So far as I can make out, Welles never was and never will be a genius, but he is just as gifted as he ever was. In this film he is not using the most adventurous, not to say florid, of his gifts, but neither is he indulging any of his weaknesses. There is nothing about the picture that even appears to be "important" or "new," but there is nothing pretentious or arty either, and although I have occasionally seen atmospheres used in films in far grander poetic context, I don't think I have seen them more pleasantly and expertly appreciated. In a quite modest way the picture is, merely, much more graceful, intelligent, and enjoyable than most other movies; and I think that anyone capable of looking at it without bias will find plenty of reason to be glad that Welles is back at work.

From James Agee, *Agee on Film*. New York: Grosset & Dunlap, 1967. Reprinted by permission of The James Agee Trust.

[*Othello*]

ERIC BENTLEY

To MENTION Orson Welles in any company, literary or theatrical, is to call forth tired jokes about his failure. Yet, to my mind, this man who bids fair to be only another of the disasters of the American theatre, could have been one of its chief glories. At a time when indignation about social evils and fascination with mental abnormality have been accepted as substitutes for the dramatic sense, Orson Welles has that rare gift—a specifically theatrical imagination. Someone has said that the actor's task is not to live on stage but to make the stage live, and none has known this better than Orson Welles, or known better what, as stage director, to do about it. By consequence, his best work stands out not merely as meritorious, but as potentially epoch-making—as work that might have given the whole history of theatre a different turn. "But yet the pity of it, Iago, oh Iago, the pity of it, Iago." Here is only, it would seem, yet another American story of self-destruction; Orson Welles seems as thoroughly lost as any member of the lost generation. From the Boy Wonder, the wonder has gone, if not the boyhood.

And so we get these pathetically puerile entertainments: the movie *Macbeth* with Scotch accents affected by assorted amateurs from Utah, the Paris production of Marlowe's *Faustus* with excruciating interpolations by the Boy Wonder, only accepted because the audience didn't understand English. And now *Othello*, a film bad from every point of view and for every public. It is, technically, gauche, the dialogue being all too obviously dubbed. It lacks popular appeal, as the story is neither simply nor skilfully told. To connoisseurs of Shakespeare, it can only be torture. And to the dwindling number of Welles admirers, the unhappy few among whom I count myself, it is one more disappointment. One is tempted to say that, while Shakespeare turned a sensational tale into high tragedy, Orson Welles has turned the tragedy back into a sensational tale. But this is to flatter Mr. Welles, who shows no sense of narrative, that is, of the procession of incidents, but only an interest in the incidents themselves—no, not even that, but only an interest in separate moments within the incidents, and this just for the opportunity they offer for effects, visual and auditory. Many of these effects are superb. Who but Welles would have given the curtain rings such a strident sound? Who but he would have set the opening of the temptation scene (Act 3, scene 3) to the clump of the actors'

From *The New Republic*, October 3, 1955. Reprinted by permission of *The New Republic* © 1955, The New Republic, Inc.

shoes on stone? If there were a real mind in charge of the production as a whole, Orson Welles would be the greatest assistant director of all time.

Yet if his failure as director is partial, as actor it is complete. Is Othello fat? Does he look as if he had a hangover? I am sure there are fat actors who could play the part. And Kean himself used to fortify his performances with brandy. But must not the fat actor seem to lose his fatness? And, as to alcohol, for all I know Mr. Welles was dead sober when the shots were taken. An actor has to look sober when he is drunk; if Mr. Welles looks drunk when he is sober, he is all the less an actor. At any rate, the Othello we meet at the outset should be soldierly, not to say heroic, and happy, not to say romantically ecstatic, whereas Orson Welles, on the screen, looks pudgy, sleepy, self-indulged, and miserable. On top of which, he never acts, he is photographed—from near, from far, from above, from below, right side up, upside down, against battlements, through gratings, and the difference of angle and background only emphasizes the flatness of that profile, the rigidity of those lips, the dullness of those eyes, the utter inexpressiveness and anti-theatricality of a man who, God save the mark! was born a theatrical genius. *The Daily Worker* has missed a trick if it hasn't held up Mr. Welles as a prize example of individualistic, bourgeois culture in decay. To which I suggest they add that the whole film is a precise example of formalistic decadence. Very much an Art Film, *Othello* is a rag-bag of the ideas of yesterday's avant-garde. In 1955 Orson Welles has caught up with the Cocteau of 1920—or perhaps one should say with the Gordon Craig of 1910—or even the Henry Irving of 1880, for the musical processionals with which the film opens and closes are very old-fashioned compared with the Hollywood *Julius Caesar* of two years ago. Even a Wellesite like myself, interested in each image as it impinges on the retina, sadly realizes at the close that the images add up to nothing.

Confidential Report [Mr. Arkadin]

FRANÇOIS TRUFFAUT

HERE IS Orson Welles back with another film of uncertain nationality. The director is American, the chief cameraman French, and the actors English, American, Turkish, Russian, German, Italian, French, and Spanish. The locations are equally varied: Barcelona, Munich, Paris, Mexico. And the backers are Swiss.

Confidential Report is an admirable film. It begins badly, really quite badly, a bit like a cheap thriller. Everything looks seedy and squalid—the sets, the costumes, the grayish image; and at the outset we even dislike the young romantic lead (Robert Arden). Welles himself, so long awaited, arrives on the screen, and even he is disappointing. Ordinarily so adroit at standing aloof while he creates his character, here he seems even to have messed up his makeup. How are we supposed to find this Gregory Arkadin marvelous when his wig is coming unglued, when he looks like Santa Claus, or even more like Neptune? (Welles was so conscious of this resemblance—whether he intended it in the beginning or not—to the underwater god that one of the characters in this intrigue actually compares Arkadin to Neptune in the dialogue.)

But then the spell begins to work; we accept the film's seediness and are drawn into the action. Gregory Arkadin, as arrogant as Charles Foster Kane, as cynical as the "Third Man," as proud as George Minafer Amberson, is very much a Wellesian character. The road that led to his fortune is strewn with still-warm corpses. But Arkadin has a daughter, Raina, whom he cherishes, and he suffers terribly as he watches her being wooed by questionable characters. The latest, Van Stratten (Arden), is a young con man, a sometime blackmailer. Arkadin has made inquiries and has found out that Van Stratten is only courting his daughter to uncover something about Arkadin himself for the purpose of blackmail. Arkadin pretends to have lost all memory of his distant past and hires Van Stratten to investigate it, retracing all his far-flung travels. The old millionaire takes advantage of this circuitous operation to assassinate his old accomplices and any witnesses to his tumultuous past, as Van Stratten proceeds to uncover it. When there is nobody left to get rid of except Van Stratten, his intended victim provokes Arkadin into killing himself by convincing him that he's going to tell his daughter the truth about her father's life. Van

From François Truffaut, *The Films in My Life*, transl. Leonard Mayhew (New York: Simon and Schuster), pp. 285–87. Copyright 1956 by François Truffaut, renewed 1984 by François Truffaut.

Stratten gains nothing except his own life, for Raina, who already mistrusts him and doesn't want anything more to do with him, runs off with a young English aristocrat who's been standing in the wings.

Throughout the film we follow Van Stratten, whose investigation takes him all over the world—Mexico, Munich, Vienna, Paris, Madrid. The actors are plastered against the walls of real apartments, and Welles's camera, usually so mobile, has to calm its feverish activity and catch them in tilted shots compressed beneath the inevitable ceilings of the rooms. A Spanish fete where the guests hide their faces behind Goya masks makes us long for a time that will never return, when the all-powerful RKO gave an absolutely free hand to a young man of twenty-five to make his first film, *Citizen Kane*, exactly as he wished. That freedom was brutally lost, then patiently recovered by force of will—but today's methods are not even those of low-budget Hollywood Westerns. Even Welles is forced into making a film using the worst kind of stage tricks. But in the long run what difference does the workmanship make, if the ideas are superbly expressed? And we do admire the ideas, for they are truly excellent. All his life, Orson Welles will be influenced by Shakespeare, whose lines he recited throughout his youth. He has, more than anyone, the gift of going beyond the particular action and situation and writing about the transcendence of the great, sophisticated philosophic and moral dialogues in which each sentence has a universal pertinence that rises above time and place.

Orson Welles is the only celebrity whose travels are not publicized; what you hear instead is "Welles was in New York the day before yesterday; last night, I had dinner with him in Venice; oh, I have a meeting with him in Lisbon the day after tomorrow."

At a certain moment, on the terrace of a Mexican hotel, Van Stratten is talking on the phone to Arkadin, whom he believes to be in Europe. The conversation ends with a roar of laughter from Arkadin, but Van Stratten hangs up and the roar continues. Arkadin is right there in Mexico, in the same hotel as Van Stratten. It used to be that Welles was a filmmaker of ambiguity. Now he's one of ubiquity.

One should really compare the filmmakers who stay put in one place to those who wander the world. The first make story movies—and only with great difficulty, usually at the end of their careers, do they succeed in moving from the particular to the universal. The latter gradually succeed in filming the whole world. Because their social situation keeps them sedentary, critics are as a whole unaware of the powerful beauty of the films of Renoir, Rossellini, Hitchcock, and Welles because these films are the conceptions of wanderers, emigrants, international observers. In the best of today's films, there's always an airport scene, and the best yet is in *Confidential Report* when Arkadin finds the plane full and shouts out that he will offer $10,000 to any passenger who will give him his seat. It is a marvelous variation on Richard III's cry, "My kingdom for a horse," in terms of the atomic age. It is indeed a Shakespearean inspiration that informs even the most minor sequences of the work of this astounding man whom André Bazin called, "a Renaissance man of the twentieth century." Welles's best friends lent their services more or less for nothing. They made no mistake. Never have Michael Redgrave, Akim Tamiroff, Suzanne Flon, Katina Paxinou, Mischa Auer, Peter van Eyck and Patricia Medina been better than in these brief, vivid profiles drawn from them by this inspired filmmaker, profiles of frightened people hunted down by adventurers, people who have a rendezvous with death within the hour.

In this gorgeous film, once again we find Welles's inspiration behind every image, that touch of madness and of genius, his power, his brilliant heartiness, his gnarled poetry.

There isn't a single scene which isn't based on a new or unusual idea. The film will undoubtedly be thought confusing, but certainly at the same time exciting, stimulating, enriching, a movie one could discuss for hours because it is filled with what we want most to find in any movie—lyricism and creativity.

[*Touch of Evil*]

HOWARD THOMPSON

Thanks to Orson Welles, nobody, and we mean nobody, will nap during "Touch of Evil," which opened yesterday at R. K. O. theatres. Just try.

The credits come on, for instance, to a sleepy, steady rumba rhythm as a convertible quietly plies the main street of a Mexican border town. The car is rigged with dynamite. And so, as a yarn-spinning director, is the extremely corpulent Mr. Welles, who co-stars with Charlton Heston and Janet Leigh in this Universal release.

Mr. Welles also adapted the novel by Whit Masterson called "Badge of Evil" (which would have been more like it), helping himself to the juicy role of a fanatical Texas cop who frames a Mexican youth for murder, and clashes with an indignant Mexican sleuth, Mr. Heston. In addition to battling Mr. Welles, a psychopath who runs the town, Mr. Heston has to fend off a vengeful narcotics gang menacing his young bride, Miss Leigh.

Any other competent director might have culled a pretty good, well-acted melodrama from such material, with the suspense dwindling as justice begins to triumph (as happens here). Mr. Welles' is an obvious but brilliant bag of tricks. Using a superlative camera (manned by Russell Metty) like a black-snake whip, he lashes the action right into the spectator's eye.

The careful groupings of the cast, the overlapping of the speeches and other stylized trade-marks of the director's Mercury Players unit are here. But the tempo, at least in the first half, is plain mercurial, as befits a thriller.

Where Mr. Welles soundly succeeds is in generating enough sinister electricity for three such yarns and in generally staging it like a wild, murky nightmare. Miss Leigh has the most blood-curdling time of all in two sequences, one involving a strangulation in a hotel room. The other—her siege by some young punks in an isolated motel—should make any viewer leery of border accommodations for a long time to come.

However, while good versus evil remains the text, the lasting impression of this film is effect rather than substance, hence its real worth. The cunningly designed climax, for instance, barely alludes to the framed youth at the outset (in a fine, ironic twist, by the way). The entire unsavory supporting cast is excellent, including such people as Joseph Calleia, Akim Tamiroff and Ray Collins. Marlene Dietrich, as an incidental "guest star," wisely advises Mr. Welles to "lay off the candy bars."

Two questions—the first to Mr. Welles, who obviously savors his dominant, colorful role. Why would a villainous cop, having hoodwinked the taxpayers for some thirty years, suddenly buckle when a tourist calls his bluff? And why, Mr. Heston, pick the toughest little town in North America for a honeymoon with a nice morsel like Miss Leigh?

All's Welles [*The Trial*]

ANONYMOUS

T HERE IS nothing very confusing about *The Trial*. This century has provided a continual exegesis of Franz Kafka's great work, and the
world has behaved as mindlessly, as madly as anything he ever dreamed
of. To the theme and spirit of the novel, to its atmosphere of frustration
and its absurd complexity, Orson Welles' film version is entirely wonderfully faithful.

In the past, Cocteau, Buñuel, Fellini, and Welles himself have all presented moments of weird and terrible beauty that were unmistakably
Kafkaesque. Now, in pure Kafka, Welles has the motherlode, and he mines
it manfully. It is amazing to see on the screen the most bizarrely cinematic
scenes and experience the shock of recognition—for the details are taken
straight from the book. The serried shelves of bundled reports, improba-
bly bedecked with drying laundry, in the oppressive, alternately cavernous
and crannied palace of injustice, the apartment of the advocate, blazing
with a forest of dripping candles and awash in legal briefs; the endless
array of desks stretching through Joseph K's office; the horrible hopeless-
ness of the raw buildings where K makes his home—all burn themselves
into the brain as by an etcher's acid.

OK, POOR K:
Anthony Perkins is K, the man who is accused of nothing in particular and
therefore of everything in the world. Perkins, whose great talent lies in his
ability to suggest the nut next door, is twitchy enough in his movements
and, at the same time, normal enough in his looks to be the perfect Kafka
hero. The guards come into his bedroom to announce that he is arrested,
and he responds with both indulgence and rage. He maintains this precari-
ous mixture through his endlessly desperate peregrinations among the
passionate cleaning women, the closeted clients, the abject accused, and
the fantastical functionaries who mark the random turnings of his unspeci-
fied "case."

Welles, who wrote and directed the film, also takes the part of K's advocate. Like a Tennessee Williams heroine, he lies in a huge bed piled high
with coverlets, and there he blandly observes the self-abasement of his
clients. With his hair cut rather short, he affects a scrubbed, boyish look
which is even more sinister for its apparent openness.

Welles has shifted various incidents from the order in which they appear in Kafka's novel. The result is that the inherent cinematographic values of the book become even more vivid. For instance, the encounter with Titorelli—the shabby painter who is supposed to have some influence with some of the minor judges—is postponed until almost the end so that Perkins can run through the open-slat corridor of Titorelli's grotesque studio pursued by the swarm of debauched little girls, then directly into the cathedral.

BLACK BEAUTY:
Jeanne Moreau, Romy Schneider, Elsa Martinelli, and Suzanne Flon provide the characteristically Kafkaesque note of sexual scintillation to the otherwise unrelieved and all but unendurably dismal business. Welles uses them in the way that he uses breathtaking shots of girders, pulleys, corridors, or benches—as the bright pigments he blends to make deep black.

The inevitable comparison is between "The Trial" and Welles' early masterwork "Citizen Kane." In that early picture, the *Wunderkind* of the film displayed a stylistic virtuosity that was dazzling. The virtuosity is diminished not a whit in "The Trial," but it is better used, and more intimately wedded to the substance of the work, showing the ghastly textures of a world gone mad. Here, at last, is the full flowering of the talent of which the famous "Rosebud" gave fair promise.

The World on Film [*F for Fake*]

JACK KROLL

MOVIES, BOTH the realest and most illusory of the arts, now seem to lead the arts in their distrust of official truth. "Illusion and Reality Around the World" might be the title of the thirteenth annual New York Film Festival. Beyond the merits of individual films—21 in all from nine countries—the festival at Lincoln Center comes across as an international concord of iconoclasm. From Switzerland to Senegal, from West Germany to South America, filmmakers, whatever their politics, whether they work with jackhammer montage or the ten-minute take, are subjecting the myths of their own societies and of man in general to a merciless dissection.

Two remarkable American films are right at the center of the festival's inadvertent theme of the real and the unreal. In fact, the symbolically presiding presence is the black-clad figure of Orson Welles, that Cagliostro of the cinema, in his first film in five years. *F for Fake* is a tour de force of prestidigitation, a Paganini rhapsody on the theme of art as trickery. Its very genesis is a shifty business: apparently Welles took over footage shot by French documentary filmmaker François Reichenbach on the island of Ibiza about Howard Hughes hoaxer Clifford Irving and Elmyr de Hory, the legendary art forger. To this Welles added more material, pulled it all together with his own screenplay, and above all orchestrated it into one of the most dazzling, equivocal and personal films ever made.

GENIUS:
F for Fake is a kind of oblique apologia for Welles himself, the artist-conjuror. Like a 60-year-old Puck, Welles glides through the film in magical ubiquity, eating oysters in Ibiza, making a girl disappear in a Paris railway station, pondering the mystery of Hughes in Las Vegas, evoking his "hoax," the "War of the Worlds" broadcast, meditating on the cathedral at Chartres. Finally he constructs an instant narrative involving an even greater art forger than Elmyr, his stupefyingly beautiful granddaughter and Pablo Picasso. Welles's philosophy of modern art as a con game (he quotes Picasso who said: "I can paint false Picassos as well as anyone") is both another con job on the audience and also contains the pathos of a genius who can't resist making himself disappear. But the genius is rampant in *F for Fake*, which confirms that Welles can use film as Picasso used paint— to fracture and refashion reality into a new reality that shocks the viewer's mind into a new life.

INTERVIEWS

Orson Welles

JUAN COBOS, MIGUEL RUBIO, AND JOSÉ ANTONIO PRUNEDA

QUESTION—*In* The Trial, *it seems that you were making a severe criticism of the abuse of power; unless it concerns something more profound. Perkins appeared as a sort of Prometheus . . .*

WELLES—He is also a little bureaucrat. I consider him guilty.

Q.—*Why do you say he is guilty?*

WELLES—Who knows? He belongs to something that represents evil and that, at the same time, is part of him. He is not guilty as accused, but he is guilty all the same. He belongs to a guilty society, he collaborates with it. In any case, I am not a Kafka analyst.

Q.—*A version of the scenario exists with a different ending. The executioners stab K to death.*

WELLES—That ending didn't please me. I believe that in that case it is a question of a "ballet" written by a pre-Hitler Jewish intellectual. After the death of six million Jews, Kafka would not have written that. It seemed to me to be pre-Auschwitz. I don't want to say that my ending was good, but it was the only solution. I had to move into high gear, even if it was only for several instants.

Q.—*One of the constants of your work is the struggle for liberty and the defense of the individual.*

WELLES—A struggle for dignity. I absolutely disagree with those works of art, those novels, those films that, these days, speak about despair. I do not think that an artist may take total despair as a subject: we are too close to it in daily life. This genre of subject can be utilized only when life is less dangerous and more clearly affirmative.

Q.—*In the transposition of* The Trial *to the cinema, there is a fundamental change; in Kafka's book, K's character is more passive than in the film.*

WELLES—I made him more active, properly speaking. I do not believe that passive characters are appropriate to drama. I have nothing against Antonioni, for example, but, in order to interest me, the characters must do something, from a dramatic point of view, you understand.

Transl. Rose Kaplin. Reprinted from *Interviews with Film Directors*, ed. Andrew Sarris (New York: Avon, 1969), pp. 528–57. Originally published in *Cahiers du Cinéma* 165 (April 1965).

Q.—*Was* The Trial *an old project?*

WELLES—I once said that a good film could be drawn from the novel, but I myself didn't think of doing it. A man came to see me and told me he believed he could find money so that I could make a film in France. He gave me a list of films and asked that I choose. And from that list of fifteen films I chose the one that, I believe, was the best: *The Trial*. Since I couldn't do a film written by myself, I chose Kafka.

Q.—*What films do you really want to do?*

WELLES—Mine. I have drawers full of scenarios written by me.

Q.—*In* The Trial, *was the long travelling shot of Katina Paxinou* [Ed.: actually Suzanne Flon] *dragging the trunk while Anthony Perkins talks to her an homage to Brecht?*

WELLES—I did not see it that way. There was a long scene with her that lasted ten minutes and that, moreover, I cut on the eve of the Paris premiere. I did not see the film as a whole except for one time. We were still in the process of doing the mixing, and here the premiere fell on us. At the last moment I abridged the ten minute scene. It should have been the best scene in the film and it wasn't. Something went wrong, I guess. I don't know why, but it didn't succeed. The subject of that scene was free will. It was stained with *comedie noire*; that was a fad with me. As you know, it is always directed against the machine and favorable to liberty.

Q.—*When Joseph K sees the shadow show at the end, with the story of the guard, the door, etc., does this concern your own reflections on the cinema?*

WELLES—It concerns a technical problem posed by the story to be told. If it were told at that precise moment, the public would go to sleep; that is why I tell it at the beginning and only recall it at the end. The effect then is equivalent to telling the story at that moment and I was able in this way to tell it in a few seconds. But, in any case, I am not the judge.

Q.—*A critic who admires your work very much said that, in* The Trial, *you were repeating yourself . . .*

WELLES—Exactly, I repeated myself. I believe we do it all the time. We always take up certain elements again. How can it be avoided? An actor's voice always has the same timbre and, consequently, he repeats himself. It is the same for a singer, a painter . . . There are always certain things that come back, for they are part of one's personality, of one's style. If these things didn't come into play, a personality would be so complex that it would become impossible to identify it.

It is not my intention to repeat myself but in my work there should certainly be references to what I have done in the past. Say what you will, but *The Trial* is the best film I have ever made. One repeats oneself only when one is fatigued. Well, I wasn't fatigued. I have never been so happy as when I made this film.

Q.—*How did you shoot Anthony Perkins' long running scene?*

WELLES—We built a very long platform and the camera was placed on a rolling chair.

Q.—*But it's enormously fast!*

WELLES—Yes, but I had a Yugoslavian runner to push my camera.

Q.—*What is astonishing in your work is this continual effort to bring solutions to the problems posed by directing . . .*

WELLES—The cinema is still very young and it would be completely ridiculous to not succeed in finding new things for it. If only I could make more films! Do you know what happened with *The Trial?* Two weeks before our departure from Paris for Yugoslavia, we were told that there would be no possibility of having a single set built there because the producer had already made another film in Yugoslavia and hadn't paid his debts. That's why it was necessary to utilize that abandoned station. I had planned a completely different film.

Everything was invented at the last minute because physically my film had an entirely different conception. It was based on an absence of sets. And this gigantism I have been reproached for is, in part, due to the fact that the only set I possessed was that old abandoned station. An empty railroad station is immense! The production, as I had sketched it, comprised sets that gradually disappeared. The number of realistic elements were to become fewer and fewer and the public would become aware of it, to the point where the scene would be reduced to free space as if everything had dissolved.

Q.—*The movement of the actors and the camera in relation to each other in your films is very beautiful.*

WELLES—That is a visual obsession. I believe, thinking about my films, that they are based not so much on pursuit as on a search. If we are looking for something, the labyrinth is the most favorable location for the search. I do not know why, but my films are all for the most part a physical search.

Q.—*You reflect about your work a great deal . . .*

WELLES—Never *a posteriori*. I think about each of my films when I am preparing for them. I do an enormous sketch when starting. What is marvelous about the cinema, what makes it superior to the theatre, is that it has many elements that may conquer us but may also enrich us, offer us a life impossible anywhere else. The cinema should always be the discovery of something. I believe that the cinema should be essentially poetic; that is why, during the shooting and not during the preparation, I try to plunge myself into a poetic development, which differs from narrative development and dramatic development. But, in reality, I am a man of ideas; yes, above all else—I am even more a man of ideas than a moralist, I suppose.

Q.—*Do you believe it is possible to have a form of tragedy without melodrama?*

WELLES—Yes, but that is very difficult. For any *auteur* who comes out of the Anglo-Saxon tradition, it is very difficult. Shakespeare never arrived at it. It is possible, but up to the present no one has succeeded. In my cultural tradition, tragedy cannot escape from melodrama. We may always draw from tragic elements and perhaps even the grandeur of tragedy but melodrama is always inherent to the Anglo-Saxon cultural universe. There's no doubt about it.

Q.—*Is it correct that your films never correspond to what you were thinking of doing before starting them? Because of producers, etc.*

WELLES—No, in reality, in what concerns me, creation, I must say that I am constantly changing. At the beginning, I have a basic notion of what the final aspect of the film will be, more or less. But each day, at every moment, one deviates or modifies because of the expression in an actress's eyes or the position of the sun. I am not in the habit of preparing a film and then setting myself to make it. I prepare a film but I have no intention of making *this* film. The preparation serves to liberate me, so that I may work in my fashion; thinking of bits of film and of the result they will give; and there are parts that deceive me because I haven't conceived them in a complete enough way. I do not know what word to use, because I am afraid of pompous words when I talk about making a film. The degree of concentration I utilize in a world that I create, whether this be for thirty seconds or for two hours, is very high; that is why, when I am shooting, I have a lot of trouble sleeping. This is not because I am pre-occupied but because, for me, this world has so much reality that closing my eyes is not sufficient to make it disappear. It represents a terrible intensity of feeling. If I shoot in a royal location I sense and I see this site in so violent a way that, now, when I see these places again, they are similar to tombs, completely dead. There are spots in the world that are, to my eyes, cadavers; that is because I have already shot there—for me, they are completely finished. Jean Renoir said something that seems to be related to that: "We should remind people that a field of wheat painted by Van Gogh can arouse a stronger emotion than a field of wheat in nature." It is important to recall that art surpasses reality. Film becomes another reality. Apropos, I admire Renoir's work very much even though mine doesn't please him at all. We are good friends and, truthfully, one of the things I regret is that he doesn't like his films for the same reason I do. His films appear marvelous to me because what I admire most in an *auteur* is authentic sensitivity. I attach no importance to whether or not a film is a technical *SUCCESS*: moreover, films that lack this genre of sensitivity may not be judged on the same level with technical or aesthetic knowingness. But the cinema, the true cinema, is a poetic expression and Renoir is one of the rare poets. Like Ford, it is in his style. Ford is a poet. A comedian. Not for women, of course, but for men.

Q.—*Apart from Ford and Renoir, who are the* cineastes *you admire?*

WELLES—Always the same ones; I believe that on this point I am not very original. The one who pleases me most of all is Griffith. I think he is the best director in the history of the cinema. The best, much better than Eisenstein. And, for all that, I admire Eisenstein very much.

Q.—*What about that letter Eisenstein sent you when you had not yet started in the cinema?*

WELLES—It was apropos *Ivan the Terrible.*

Q.—*It appears that you said his film was something by Michael Curtiz . . .*

WELLES—No. What happened is that I wrote a criticism of *Ivan the Terrible* for a newspaper and, one day, I received a letter from Eisenstein, a letter that came from Russia and ran to forty pages. Well, I answered him and in this fashion an exchange began that made us friends by correspondence. But I said nothing that could be seen as drawing a parallel between him and Curtiz. That would not be just. *Ivan the Terrible* is the worst film of a great *cineaste.*

It's that I judged Eisenstein on his own level and not in a way that would be appropriate to a minor *cineaste*. His drama was, before all else, political. It had nothing to do with his having to tell a story that he didn't want to tell. It was because, in my opinion, he was not suited to make period films. I think the Russians have a tendency to be more academic when they treat another period. They become rhetoricians, and academicians, in the worst sense of the word.

Q.—*In your films, one has the sensation that real space is never respected: it seems not to interest you . . .*

WELLES—The fact that I make no use of it doesn't in the least signify that it doesn't please me. In other terms, there are many elements of the cinematographic language that I do not utilize, but that is not because I have something against them. It seems to me that the field of action in which I have my experiences is one that is least known, and my duty is to explore it. But that does not mean to say that it is, for me, the best and only—or that I deviate from a normal conception of space, in relation to the camera. I believe that the artist should explore his means of expression.

In reality, the cinema, with the exception of a few little tricks that don't go very far, has not advanced for more than thirty years. The only changes are with respect to the subject of films. I see that there are directors, full of future, sensitive, who explore new themes, but I see no one who attacks form, the manner of saying things. That seems to interest no one. They resemble each other very much in terms of style.

Q.—*You must work very quickly. In twenty-five years of cinema, you have made ten films, you have acted in thirty, you have made a series of very long programs for television, you have acted and directed in the theatre, you have done narrations for other films and, in addition, you have written thirty scenarios. Each of them must have taken you more than six months.*

WELLES—Several of them even longer. There are those that took me two years but that is because I set them aside from time to time in order to do something else and picked them up again afterwards. But it is also true that I write very rapidly.

Q.—*You write them completely, with dialogue?*

WELLES—I always begin with the dialogue. And I do not understand how one dares to write action before dialogue. It's a very strange conception. I know that in theory the word is secondary in cinema but the secret of my work is that everything is based on the word. I do not make silent films. I must begin with what the characters say. I must know what they say before seeing them do what they do.

Q.—*However, in your films the visual part is essential.*

WELLES—Yes, but I couldn't arrive at it without the solidity of the word taken as a basis for constructing the images. What happens is that when the visual components are shot the words are obscured. The most classical example is *Lady From Shanghai*. The scene in the aquarium was so gripping visually that no one heard what was being said. And what was said was, for all that, the marrow of the film. The subject was so tedious that I said to myself, "This calls for something beautiful to look at." Assuredly, the scene was very beautiful. The first ten minutes of the film did not please me at all. When I think of them I have the impression it wasn't me that made them. They resemble any Hollywood film.

I believe you know the story of *Lady From Shanghai*. I was working on that spectacular theatre idea "Around the World in 80 Days," which was originally to be produced by Mike Todd. But, overnight, he went bankrupt and I found myself in Boston on the day of the premiere, unable to take my costumes from the station because 50,000 dollars was due. Without that money we couldn't open. At that time I was already separated from Rita; we were no longer even speaking. I did not intend to do a film with her. From Boston I got in touch with Harry Cohn, then director of Columbia, who was in Hollywood, and I said to him, "I have an extraordinary story for you if you send me 50,000 dollars, by telegram in one hour, on account, and I will sign a contract to make it." Cohn asked, "What story?" I was telephoning from the theatre box office; beside it was a pocket books display and I gave him the title of one of them: *Lady From Shanghai*. I said to him, "Buy the novel and I'll make the film." An hour later we received the money. Later I read the book and it was horrible so I set myself, top speed, to write a story. I arrived in Hollywood to make the film with a very small budget and in six weeks of shooting. But I wanted more money for my theatre. Cohn asked me why I didn't use Rita. She said she would be very pleased. I gave her to understand that the character was not a sympathetic one, that she was a woman who killed and this might hurt her image as a star in the public eye. Rita was set on making this film, and instead of costing 350,000 dollars, it became a two million dollar film. Rita was very coopera- tive. The one who was horrified on seeing the film was Cohn.

Q.—*How do you work with actors?*

WELLES—I give them a great deal of freedom and, at the same time, the feeling of precision. It's a strange combination. In other words, physically, and in the way they develop, I demand the pre- cision of ballet. But their way of acting comes directly from their own ideas as much as from mine. When the camera begins to roll, I do not improvise visually. In this realm, everything is prepared. But I work very freely with the actors. I try to make their life pleas- ant.

Q.—*Your cinema is essentially dynamic . . .*

WELLES—I believe that the cinema should be dynamic although I suppose any artist will defend his own style. For me, the cinema is a slice of life in movement that is projected on a screen; it is not a frame. I do not believe in the cinema unless there is movement on the screen. This is why I am not in agreement with certain direc- tors, whom, however, I admire, who content themselves with a static cinema. For me, these are dead images. I hear the noise of the projector behind me, and when I see these long, long walks along streets, I am always waiting to hear the director's voice say- ing, "Cut!"

The only director who does not move either his camera or his actors very much, and in whom I believe, is John Ford. He suc- ceeds in making me believe in his films even though there is little movement in them. But with the others I always have the impression that they are desperately trying to make Art. However, they should be making drama and drama should be full of life. The cinema, for me, is essentially a dramatic medium, not a literary one.

Q.—*That is why your mise-en-scène is lively: it is the meeting of two movements, that of the actors and that of the camera. Out of this flows an anguish that reflects modern life very well* . . .

WELLES—I believe that that corresponds to my vision of the world; it reflects that sort of vertigo, uncertainty, lack of stability, that *melange* of movement and tension that is our universe. And the cinema should express that. Since cinema has the pretension of being an art, it should be, above all, film, and not the sequel to another, more literary, medium of expression.

Q.—*Herman G. Weinberg said, while speaking of* Mr. Arkadin, *"In Orson Welles' films, the spectator may not sit back in his seat and relax, on the contrary he must meet the film at least halfway in order to decipher what is happening, practically every second; if not, everything is* lost."

WELLES—All my films are like that. There are certain *cineastes*, excellent ones, who present everything so explicitly, so clearly, that in site of the great visual power contained in their films one follows them effortlessly—I refer only to the narrative thread. I am fully aware that, in my films, I demand a very specific interest on the part of the public. Without that attention, it is lost.

Q.—Lady From Shanghai *is a story that, filmed by another director, would more likely have been based on sexual questions* . . .

WELLES—You mean that another director would have made it more obvious. I do not like to show sex on the screen crudely. Not because of morality or puritanism; my objection is of a purely aesthetic order. In my opinion, there are two things that can absolutely not be carried to the screen: the realistic presentation of the sexual act and praying to God. I never believe an actor or actress who pretends to be completely involved in the sexual act if it is too literal, just as I can never believe an actor who wants to make me believe he is praying. These are two things that, for me, immediately evoke the presence of a projector and a white screen, the existence of a series of technicians and a director who is saying, "Good. Cut." And I imagine them in the process of preparing for the next shot. As for those who adopt a mystical stance and look fervently at the spotlights . . .

For all that, my illusion almost never ends when I see a film. While filming, I think of someone like myself: I utilize all of my knowledge in order to force this person to want to see the film with the greatest interest, I want him to believe what is there on the screen; this means that one should create a real world there. I place my dramatic vision of a character in the world . . . if not, the film is something dead. What there is on the screen is nothing but shadows. Something even more dead than words.

Q.—*Do you like comedy?*

WELLES—I have written at least five scenarios for comedy and in the theatre I have done more comedies than dramas. Comedy fills me with enthusiasm but I have never succeeded in getting a film producer to let me make one. One of the best things I did for television was a program in the genre of comedy. For example, I like Hawks' comedies very much. I even wrote about twenty-five minutes of one of them. It was called, *I Was a Male War Bride*. The scenarist fell ill and I wrote almost a third of the film.

Q.—*Have you written scenarios of comedies with the intentions of making them?*

WELLES—I believe the best of my comedies is "Operation Cinderella." It tells of the occupation of a small Italian town (which was previously occupied by the Saracens, the Moors, the Normans and, during the last war, by the English and, finally, the Americans) by a Hollywood film company . . . and this new occupation unfolds exactly like a military operation. The lives of all the inhabitants of the town are changed during the shooting of the film. It's a gross farce. I want very much to do a comedy for the cinema.

In a certain sense, *Quixote* is a comedy, and I put a lot of comedy in all of my films but it is a genre of comedy that—and I regret to tell you this because it is a weakness—is understood only by Americans, to the exclusion of spectators in other countries, whatever they may be. There are scenes that, seen in other countries, awake not the slightest smile and that, seen by Americans, immediately appear in a comic vein. *The Trial* is full of humor, but the Americans are the only ones to understand its amusing side. This is where my nationality comes through: my farces are not universal enough. Many are the arguments I've had with actors due to the fact that scenes are posed in absolute forms of comedy and only at the last five minutes do I change them into drama. This is my method of working: showing the amusing side of things and not showing the sad side until the last possible second.

Q.—*What happened when you sold the subject of* Monsieur Verdoux *to Chaplin?*

WELLES—I never argued with Chaplin because of *Monsieur Verdoux*. What annoys me is that now he pretends that he did not buy this subject from me. As an actor, Chaplin is very good, sensational. But in the comic cinema I prefer Buster Keaton to him. There is a man of the cinema who is not only an excellent actor but an excellent director, which Chaplin is not. And Keaton always has fabulous ideas. In *Limelight*, there was a scene between the two of them that was ten minutes long. Chaplin was excellent and Keaton sensational. It was the most successful thing he had done in the course of his career. Chaplin cut almost the entire scene, because he understood who, of the two, had completely dominated it.

Q.—*There is a kinship between your work and the works of certain authors of the modern theatre, like Beckett, Ionesco and others . . . what is called the theatre of the absurd.*

WELLES—Perhaps, but I would eliminate Ionesco because I do not admire him. When I directed *Rhinoceros* in London, with Laurence Olivier in the principal role, as we repeated the work from day to day it pleased me less. I believe that there is nothing inside it. Nothing at all. This kind of theatre comes out of all types of expression, all types of art of a certain epoch, is thus forged by the same world as my films. The things this theatre is composed of are the same composed in my films, without this theatre's being in my cinema or without my cinema's being in this theatre. It is a trait of our times. There is where the coincidence comes from.

Q.—*There are two types of artists: for example, Velasquez and Goya; one disappears from the picture, the other is present in it; on the other hand you have Van Gogh and Cezanne . . .*

WELLES—I see what you mean. It's very clear.

Q.—*It seems to me that you are on the Goya side.*

WELLES—Doubtless. But I very much prefer Velasquez. There's no comparison between one and the other, as far as being artists is concerned. As I prefer Cezanne to Van Gogh.

Q.—*And between Tolstoy and Dostoievsky?*

WELLES—I prefer Tolstoy.

Q.—*But as an artist . . .*

WELLES—Yes, as an artist. But I deny that, for I do not correspond to my tastes. I know what I'm doing and when I recognize it in other works my interest is diminished. The things that resemble me the least are the things that interest me the most. For me Velasquez is the Shakespeare of painters and, for all that, he has nothing in common with my way of working.

Q.—*What do you think of what is called modern cinema?*

WELLES—I like certain young French *cineastes*, much more than the Italians.

Q.—*Did you like* L'Année dernière à Marienbad?

WELLES—No. I know that this film pleased you; not me. I held on up to the fourth reel and after that I left at a run. It reminded me too much of *Vogue* magazine.

Q.—*How do you see the development of the cinema?*

WELLES—I don't see it. I rarely go to the movies. There are two kinds of writers, the writer who reads everything of interest that is published, exchanges letters with other writers, and others who absolutely do not read their contemporaries. I am among the latter. I go to the movies very rarely and this is not because I don't like it, it is because it procures me no enjoyment at all. I do not think I am very intelligent about films. There are works that I know to be good but which I cannot stand.

Q.—*It was said that you were going to make "Crime and Punishment"; what became of this project?*

WELLES—Someone wanted me to do it. I thought about it, but I like the book too much. In the end, I decided that I could do nothing and the idea of being content to illustrate it did not please me at all. I don't mean to say by that that the subject was beneath me, what I mean is that I could bring nothing to it. I could only give it actors and images and, when I can only do that, the cinema does not interest me. I believe you must say something new about a book, otherwise it is better not to touch it.

Aside from that, I consider it to be a very difficult work, because, in my opinion, it is not completely comprehensible outside of its own time and country. The psychology of this man and this constable are so Russian, so nineteenth century Russian, that one could never find them elsewhere; I believe that the public would not be able to follow it all the way.

Q.—*There is, in Dostoievsky, an analysis of justice, of the world, that is very close to yours.*

WELLES—Perhaps too close. My contribution would most likely be limited. The only thing I could do is to direct. I like to make films in which I can express myself as *auteur* sooner than as interpreter. I do not share Kafka's point of view in *The Trial*. I believe that he is a good writer, but Kafka is not the extraordinary genius that people today see him as. That is why I was not concerned about excessive fidelity and could make a film by Welles. If I could make four films a year, I would surely do "Crime and Punishment." But as it costs me a great deal to convince producers I try to choose what I film very carefully.

Q.—*With you, one seems to find, at the same time, the Brechtian tendency and the Stanislavski tendency.*

WELLES—All I can say is that I did my apprenticeship in Stanislavski's orbit; I worked with his actors and found them very easy to direct. I do not allude to "Method" actors; that's something else altogether. But Stanislavski was marvelous. As for Brecht, he was a great friend to me. We worked together on "Galileo Galilei." In reality he wrote it for me. Not for me to act in, but in order for me to direct it.

Q.—*How was Brecht?*

WELLES—Terribly nice. He had an extraordinary brain. One could see very well that he had been educated by the Jesuits. He had the type of disciplined brain characterized by Jesuit education. Instinctively, he was more of an anarchist than a Marxist, but he believed himself a perfect Marxist. When I said to him one day, while we were talking about "Galileo," that he had written a perfectly anti-communist work, he became nearly aggressive. I answered him, "But this Church you describe has to be Stalin and not the Pope, at this time. You have made something resolutely anti-Soviet!"

Q.—*What relationship do you see between your work as a film director and as a theatre director?*

WELLES—My relationships with these two *milieux* are very different. I believe that they are not in intimate rapport, one with the other. Perhaps in me, as a man, that relationship exists, but technical solutions are so different for each of them that, in my spirit, I establish absolutely no relationship between these two mediums.

In the theatre, I do not belong to what has succeeded in becoming the Brechtian idea of theatre; that particularly withdrawn form has never been appropriate to my character. But I have always made a terrible effort to recall to the public, at each instant, that it is in a theatre. I have never tried to bring it into the scene, I have rather tried to bring the scene to it. And that is the opposite of the cinema.

Q.—*Perhaps there is a relationship in the way the actors are handled.*

WELLES—In the theatre there are 1,500 cameras rolling at the same time—in the cinema there is only one. That changes the whole aesthetic for the director.

Q.—*Did Huston's* Moby Dick, *on which you worked, please you?*

WELLES—The novel pleases me very much, but it doesn't please me as a novel so much as a drama. There are two very different things in the novel: that sort of pseudo-biblical element that is not very good, and also that curious nineteenth century American element, of the apocalyptical genre, that can be rendered very well in the cinema.

Q.—*In the scene you acted in the film—did you make any suggestions as to the way of handling it?*

WELLES—All we did was discuss the way in which it would be shot. You know that my discourse is very long. It goes on throughout a full reel, and we never repeated it. I arrived on the set already made-up and dressed. I got up on the platform and we shot it in one take. We did it using only one camera angle. And that is one of Huston's merits, because another director would have said, "Let's do it from another angle and see what we get." He said, "Good," and my role in the film ended right there!

Q.—*You are in the process of preparing for a film on bullfighting.*

WELLES—Yes, but a film about the amateurs of bullfighting, the following . . . I think that the true event in the *corrida* is the arena itself—but one cannot do a film about it. From the cinematographic point of view the most exciting thing about it is the atmosphere. The *corrida* is something that already possesses a well defined personality. The cinema can do nothing to render it dramatic. All one may do is photograph it. Actually, my biggest preoccupation is knowing that Rosi is already in the process of shooting while I have put in four years, off and on, writing my scenario. Because of him, finding the necessary money will be more difficult: they'll say to me, "We already have a film about bullfighting, made by a serious *cineaste*; who wants one more?" However, I hope I will succeed in making this film, but I still don't know how I'm going to find the money. Rosi shot something last year at Pamplona, in 16 mm. He showed it to Rizzoli, and said, "Look at this beautiful thing," and Rizzoli gave him carte blanche. Now it's only a matter of knowing whether it will be a good film or a bad film. It is better for me that the film be good. If it fails, I will have even more trouble raising the funds.

Q.—*There is talk from time to time of your first sojourn in Spain, before the Civil War.*

WELLES—When I arrived in Spain, for the first time, I was seventeen years old and had already worked in Ireland as an actor. I only stayed in the south, in Andalusia. In Seville, I lived in the Triana section. I was writing detective stories: I spent only two days a week on this and it brought in three hundred dollars. With this money I was a *grand seigneur* in Seville. There were so many people thrilled by the *corrida* and I caught the virus myself. I paid the novice fee at several *corridas* and thus was able to *debut*—on the posters I was called "The American." My greatest thrill was being able to practice the *metier* of *torero* three or four times without having to pay. I came to the realization that I was not good as a *torero* and decided to apply myself to writing. At that time I hardly thought of the theatre and still less of the cinema.

Q.—*You said one day that you have had a great deal of difficulty finding the money to make your films, that you have spent more time struggling to get this money than working as an artist. How is this battle at this time?*

WELLES—More bitter than ever. Worse than ever. Very difficult. I have already said that I do not work enough. I am frustrated, do you understand? And I believe that my work shows that I do not do enough filming. My cinema is perhaps too explosive, because I wait too long before I speak. It's terrible. I have bought little cameras in order to make a film if I can find the money. I will shoot it in 16 mm. The cinema is a *metier* . . . nothing can compare to the cinema. The cinema belongs to our times. It is "the thing" to do. During the shooting of *The Trial*, I spent marvelous days. It was an amusement, happiness. You cannot imagine what I felt.

When I make a film or at the time of my theatrical premieres, the critics habitually say, "This work is not as good as the one of three years ago." And if I look for the criticism of that one, three years back, I find an unfavorable review that says that that isn't as good as what I did three years earlier. And so it goes. I admit that experiences can be false but I believe that it is also false to want to be fashionable. If one is fashionable for the greatest part of one's career, one will produce second-class work. Perhaps by chance one will arrive at being a success but this means that one is a follower and not an innovator. An artist should lead, blaze trails.

What is serious is that in countries where English is spoken, the role played by criticism concerning serious works of cinema is very important. Given the fact that one cannot make films in competition with Doris Day, what is said by reviews such as *Sight and Sound* is the only reference.

Things are going particularly badly in my own country. *Touch of Evil* never had a first-run, never had the usual presentation to the press and was not the object of any critical writing in either the weeklies, the reviews or the daily papers. It was considered to be too bad. When the representative from Universal wanted to exhibit it at the Brussels Fair in 1958, he was told that it wasn't a good enough film for a festival. He answered that, in any case, it must be put on the program. It went unnoticed and was sent back. The film took the *grand prix*, but it was no less sent back.

Q.—*Do you consider yourself a moralist?*

WELLES—Yes, but against morality. Most of the time that may appear paradoxical, but the things I love in painting, in music, in literature, represent only my penchant for what is my opposite. And moralists bore me very much. However, I'm afraid I am one of them!

Q.—*In what concerns you, it is not so much a question of a moralist's attitude but rather an ethic that you adopt in the face of the world.*

WELLES—My two Shakespearean films are made from an ethical point of view. I believe I have never made a film without having a solid ethical point of view about its story. Morally speaking, there is no ambiguity in what I do.

Q.—*But an ambiguous point of view is necessary. These days, the world is made that way.*

WELLES—But that is the way the world appears to us. It is not a true ambiguity: it's like a larger screen. A kind of a moral cinemascope. I believe it is necessary to give all the characters their best arguments, in order that they may defend themselves, including those I disagree with. To them as well, I give the best defensive arguments I can imagine. I offer them the same possibility for expression as I would a sympathetic character.

That's what gives this impression of ambiguity: my being chivalrous to people whose behavior I do not approve of. The characters are ambiguous but the significance of the work is not. I do not want to resemble the majority of Americans, who are demagogs and rhetoricians. This is one of America's great weaknesses, and rhetoric is one of the greatest weaknesses of American artists; above all, those of my generation. Miller, for example, is terribly rhetorical.

Q.—*What is the problem in America?*

WELLES—If I speak to you of the things that are wrong it won't be the obvious ones; those are similar to what is wrong in France, in Italy or in Spain; we know them all. In American art the problem, or better, one of the problems, is the betrayal of the Left by the Left, self-betrayal. In one sense, by stupidity, by orthodoxy and because of slogans; in another, by simple betrayal. We are very few in our generation who have not betrayed our position, who have not given other people's names . . .

That is terrible. It can never be undone. I don't know how one starts over after a similar betrayal that, however, differs enormously from this, for example: a Frenchman who collaborated with the gestapo in order to save his wife's life—that is another genre of collaboration. What is so bad about the American Left is that it betrayed in order to save its swimming pools. There was no American Right in my generation. Intellectually it didn't exist. There were only Leftists and they mutually betrayed each other. The Left was not destroyed by McCarthy: it demolished itself, ceding to a new generation of Nihilists. That's what happened.

You can't call it "Fascism." I believe that the term "Fascism" should only be utilized in order to define a quite precise political attitude. It would be necessary to find a new word in order to define what is happening in America. Fascism must be born out of chaos. And America is not, as I know it, in chaos. The social structure is not in a state of dissolution. No, it doesn't correspond at all to the true definition of Fascism. I believe it is two simple, obvious things: the technological society is not accustomed to living with its own tools. That's what counts. We speak of them, we use them but we don't know how to live with them. The other thing is the prestige of the people responsible for the technological society. In this society the men who direct and the savants who represent technique do not leave room for the artist who favors the human being. In reality, they utilize him only for decoration.

Hemingway says, in *The Green Hills of Africa*, that America is a country of adventure and, if the adventure disappears there, any American who possesses this primitive spirit must go elsewhere to seek adventure: Africa, Europe, etc. . . . It is an intensely romantic point of view. There is some truth in it, but if it is so intensely romantic it is because there is still an enormous quantity of adventure in America. In the cinema, you cannot imagine all that one may do in it. All I need is a job in cinema, is for someone to give me a camera. There is nothing dishonorable about working in America. The country is full of possibilities for expressing what is happening all over the world. What really exists is an enormous compromise. The ideal American type is perfectly expressed by the Protestant, individualist, anti-conformist, and this is the type that is in the process of disappearing. In reality, a very few of him remain.

Q.—*What was your relationship with Hemingway?*

WELLES—My relationship with Hemingway has always been very droll. The first time we met was when I had been called to read the narration for a film that he and Joris Ivens had made about the war in Spain; it was called *Spanish Earth*. Arriving, I came upon Hemingway, who was in the process of drinking a bottle of whiskey; I had been handed a set of lines that were too long, dull, had nothing to do with his style, which is always so concise and so economical. There were lines as pompous and complicated as this: "Here are the faces of men who are close to death," and this was to be read at a moment when one saw faces on the screen that were so much more eloquent. I said to him, "Mr. Hemingway, it would be better if one saw the faces all alone, without commentary."

This didn't please him at all, and since I had, a short time before, just directed the Mercury Theatre, which was a sort of avant-garde theatre, he thought I was some kind of faggot and said, "You—effeminate boys of the theatre, what do you know about real war?"

Taking the bull by the horns, I began to make effeminate gestures and I said to him, "Mister Hemingway, how strong you are
and how big you are!" That enraged him and he picked up a
chair; I picked up another, and right there, in front of the images
of the Spanish Civil War as they marched across the screen, we
had a terrible scuffle. It was something marvelous: two guys like
us in front of these images representing people in the act of
struggling and dying . . . we ended by giving each other acco-
lades and drinking a bottle of whiskey. We have spent our lives
having long periods of friendship and others during which we
barely spoke. I have never been able to avoid gently making fun
of him, and this no one ever did—everyone treated him with the
greatest respect.

Q.—*As an artist and as a member of a certain generation, do
you feel isolated?*

WELLES—I have always felt isolated. I believe that any good artist
feels isolated. And I must think that I am a good artist, for otherwise I would not be able to work and I beg your pardon for taking
the liberty of believing this; if someone wants to direct a film, he
must think that he is good. A good artist should be isolated. If he
isn't isolated, something is wrong.

Q.—*These days, it would be impossible to present the Mercury
Theatre.*

WELLES—Completely impossible for financial reasons. The
Mercury Theatre was possible only because I was earning three
thousand dollars a week on the radio and spending two thousand
to sustain the theatre. At that time, it was still cheap to sustain a
theatre. Plus I had formidable actors. And what was most exciting
about this Mercury Theatre was that it was a theatre on Broadway,
not "off." Today, one might have a theatre off-Broadway, but that's
another thing.

What characterized the Mercury Theatre was that it was next door
to another where they were doing a musical comedy, near a commercial theatre, it was in the theatre center. Part of the neighboring bill of fare was the Group Theatre which was the official
theatre of the Left: we were in contact without having an official
relationship; we were of the same generation, although not on the
same path. The whole thing gave the New York of that time an
extraordinary vitality. The quality of actors and that of spectators is
no longer what it was in those marvelous years. The best theatre
should be in the center of everything.

Q.—*Does that explain your permanent battle to remain in the
milieu of the cinema and not outside of the industry?*

WELLES—I may be rejected, but as for me, I always want to be
right in the center. If I am isolated, it is because I am obliged to

be, for such is not my intention. I am always aiming for the center: I fail, but that is what I try to attain.

Q.—*Are you thinking of returning to Hollywood?*

WELLES—Not at the moment. But who knows what may change at the next instant? . . . I am dying to work there because of the technicians, who are marvelous. They truly represent a director's dream.

Q.—*A certain anti-Fascist attitude can be found in your films* . . .

WELLES—There is more than one French intellectual who believes that I am a Fascist . . . it's idiotic, but that's what they write. What happens with these French intellectuals is that they take my physical aspect as an actor for my idea as an *auteur*. As an actor I always play a certain type of role: Kings, great men, etc. This is not because I think them to be the only persons in the world who are worth the trouble. My physical aspect does not permit me to play other roles. No one would believe a defenseless, humble person played by me. But they take this to be a projection of my own personality. I hope that the great majority at least considers it obvious that I am anti-Fascist . . .

True Fascism is always confused with Futurism's early fascistic mystique. By this I make allusion to the first generation of Italian Fascism, which was a way of speaking that disappeared as soon as the true Fascism imposed itself, because it was an idiotic romanticism, like that of d'Annunzio and others. That is what disappeared. And that is what the French critics are talking about.

True Fascism is gangsterism of the low-born middle class, lamentably organized by . . . good, we all know what Fascism is. It is very clear. It is amusing to see how the Russians have been mistaken about the subject of *Touch of Evil*. They have attacked it pitilessly, as if it were a question of the veritable decadence of Western civilization. They were not content to attack what I showed: they attacked me too.

I believe that the Russians didn't understand the words, or some other thing. What is disastrous, in Russia, is that they are fully in the middle ages, the middle ages in its most rigid aspect. No one thinks for himself. It is very sad. This orthodoxy has something terrible about it. They live only by slogans they have inherited. No one any longer knows what these slogans signify.

Q.—*What will your* Falstaff *be like?*

WELLES—I don't know . . . I hope it will be good. All I can say is that from the visual point of view, it will be very modest and, I hope, at the same time satisfying and correct. But as I see it, it is essentially a human story and I hope that a good number of stupid cinema people will feel deceived. That is because, as I just said, I consider that this film should be very modest from the visual point of view. Which doesn't mean it will be visually non-existent but rather that it will not be loud on this level. It concerns a story about 3 or 4 people and these should, therefore, dominate completely. I believe I shall use more close-ups. This will really be a film completely in the service of the actors.

Q.—*You are often accused of being egocentric. When you appear as an actor in your films, it is said that the camera is, above all, in the service of your personal exhibition . . . For example, in* Touch of Evil *the shooting angle moves from a general shot to a close-up in order to catch your first appearance on getting out of the car.*

WELLES—Yes, but that is the story, the subject. I wouldn't act a role if it was not felt as dominating the whole story. I do not think it is just to say that I utilize the camera to my profit and not to the profit of the other actors. It's not true. Although they will say it even more about *Falstaff*: but it is precisely because in the film I am playing Falstaff, not Hotspur.

At this time I think and rethink, above all, of the world in which the story unfolds, of the appearance of the film. The number of sets I will be able to build will be so restrained that the film will have to be resolutely anti-Baroque. It will have to have numerous rather formal general shots, like what one may see at eye level, wall frescoes. It is a big problem creating a world in period costumes. In this genre, it is difficult to get a feeling of real life; few films arrive at it. I believe this is due to the fact that one has not concretized, in all its details, before starting to work, the universe presupposed by such a film.

Falstaff should be very plain on the visual level because above all it is a very real human story, very comprehensible and very adaptable to modern tragedy. And nothing should come between the story and the dialogue. The visual part of this story should exist as a background, as something secondary. Everything of importance in the film should be found on the faces; on these faces that whole universe I was speaking of should be found. I imagine that it will be "the" film of my life in terms of close-ups. Theoretically, I am against close-ups of all types, although I consider few theories as given and am for remaining very free. I am resolutely against close-ups, but I am convinced that this story requires them.

Q.—*Why this objection to close-ups?*

WELLES—I find it marvelous that the public may choose, with its eyes, what it wants to see of a shot. I don't like to force it, and the use of the close-up amounts to forcing it: you can see nothing else. In *Kane*, for example, you must have seen that there were very few close-ups, hardly any. There are perhaps six in the whole film. But a story like *Falstaff* demands them, because the moment we step back and separate ourselves from the faces, we see the people in period costumes and many actors in the foreground. The closer we are to the face the more universal it becomes; *Falstaff* is a somber comedy, the story of the betrayal of friendship.

What pleases me in *Falstaff* is that the project has interested me as an actor although I am rarely interested in something for the cinema in terms of being an actor. I am happy when I do not perform. And *Falstaff* is one of the rare things that I wish to achieve as an actor. There are only two stories I wish to do as an actor that I have written. In *The Trial* I absolutely did not want to perform and, if I did it, it is because of not having found an actor who could take the part. All those we asked refused.

Q.—*At the beginning you said you would play the part of the priest* . . .

WELLES—I shot it, but, as we hadn't found an actor for the role of the lawyer, I cut the sequences in which I appeared as a priest and started shooting again. *Falstaff* is an actor's film. Not only my role but all the others are favorable for showing a good actor's worth. My *Othello* is more successful in the theatre than on film. We shall see what happens with *Falstaff*, which is the best role that Shakespeare ever wrote. It is a character as great as Don Quixote. If Shakespeare had done nothing but that magnificent creation, it would suffice to make him immortal. I wrote the scenario under the inspiration of three works in which he appears, one other in which he is spoken of, and complete it with things found in still another. Thus, I worked with five of Shakespeare's works. But, naturally, I wrote a story about Falstaff, about his friendship with the prince and his repugnance when the prince becomes King. I have great hopes for this film.

Q.—*There is a line spoken by John Foster* [Sic. Actually Charles Foster Kane—Ed.] *to his banker, which we would like very much to hear you explain: "I could have been a great man, if I hadn't been so rich."*

WELLES—Good, the whole story is in that. Anything at all may destroy greatness: a woman, illness, riches. My hatred of richness in itself is not an obsession. I do not believe that richness is the only enemy of greatness. If he had been poor, Kane would not have been a great man but one thing is sure and that is that he would have been a successful man. He thinks that success brings greatness. As for that, it is the character that says it, not I. Kane arrives at having a certain class but never greatness.

It isn't because everything seems easy to him. That is an excuse he gives himself. But the film doesn't say that. Obviously, since he is the head of one of the biggest fortunes in the world, things become easier, but his greatest error was that of the American plutocrats of those years, who believed that money automatically conferred a certain stature to a man. Kane is a man who truly belongs to his time. This type of man hardly exists anymore. These were the plutocrats who believed they could be President of the United States, if they wanted to. They also believed they could buy anything. It wasn't even necessary to be intelligent to see that it isn't always like that.

Q.—*Are they more realistic?*

WELLES—It's not a question of realism. This type of plutocrat no longer exists. Things have changed a great deal, above all economic structures. Very few rich men today succeed in retaining absolute control of their own money: their money is controlled by others. It is, like many other things, a question of organization. They are prisoners of their money. And I don't say this from a sentimental point of view; there is no longer anything but boards of directors and the participation of diverse opinions . . . they are no longer free to commit the sort of follies that used to be possible. The moment has passed for this type of egocentric plutocrat, in the same way that this type of newspaper owner has disappeared.

What is very specific about Kane's personality is that he never earned money; he passed his life doing nothing but spending it. He did not belong to that category of rich men who made fortunes: he only spent it. Kane didn't even have the responsibility of the true capitalist.

Q.—*Did* Citizen Kane *bring in a lot of money?*

WELLES—No, it's not a question of that. The film went well. But my problems with Hollywood started before I got there. The real problem was that contract, which gave me, free and clear, carte blanche and which had been signed before I went out there. I had too much power. At that time I was faced with a machination from which I have never recovered, because I have never had an enormous box office success. If you have such success, from that instant on you are given everything!

I had luck as no one had; afterwards, I had the worst bad luck in the history of the cinema, but that is in the order of things: I had to pay for having had the best luck in the history of the cinema. Never has a man been given so much power in the Hollywood system. An absolute power. And artistic control.

Q.—*There are* cineastes, *in Europe, who possess this power*.

WELLES—But they don't possess the American technical arsenal, which is a grandiose thing. The man who pushes the camera, those who change the lights, the one who handles the crane—they have children at the University. You are side by side with men who don't feel themselves to be workers but who think of themselves as very capable and very well paid artisans. That makes an enormous difference; enormous.

I could never have done all that I did in *Touch of Evil* elsewhere. And it is not only a question of technique; it essentially concerns the human competence of the men with whom I worked. All this stems from the economic security they enjoy, from the fact that they are well paid, from the fact that they do not think of themselves as belonging to another class.

Throughout the entire European cinema industry, to a greater or lesser degree, one feels that there is a great barrier posed by educational differences. In all European countries one is called "Doctor," "Professor," etc., if one has gone to a university; the great advantage in America is that there, at times, you find directors who are less learned than the man who pushes the camera. There is no "professor." Classes do not exist in the American cinema world. The pleasure one experiences working with an American crew is something that has no equivalent on earth. But you pay a price for that. There are the producers, and that group is as bad as the technicians are good.

Q.—*How did you shoot that very long sequence in Marcia's living room during the interrogation of Sanchez?*

WELLES—In Europe, there are three cameramen as good as the American cameramen. The one who made *The Trial* with me is sensational. But what there isn't is someone capable of handling the crane. In America, this man has an enormous car; he is educated and he considers himself as important to the film as the cameraman himself. In that scene in Marcia's house there were about sixty chalk marks on the ground: that tells you how knowledgeable and intelligent the man who guides the camera must be in order to do well. At that moment, I am at his mercy, at the mercy of his precision. If he can't do it with assurance, the scene is impossible.

Q.—*Was it really Charlton Heston who proposed you as director of* Touch of Evil?

WELLES—What happened is even more amusing. The scenario was proposed to Charlton Heston who was told that it was by Orson Welles; at the other end of the line, Heston understood that I was to direct the film, in which case he was ready to shoot anything at all, no matter what, with me. Those at Universal did not clear up his misunderstanding; they hung up and automatically telephoned me and asked me to direct it. The truth is that Heston said, textually, this: "I will work in any film at all directed by Orson Welles." When they proposed that I direct the film I set only one condition: to write my own scenario! And I directed and wrote the film without getting a penny for it, since I was being paid as an actor.

Q.—*In relation to the original novel, you made many changes* . . .

WELLES—My God! I never read the novel; I only read Universal's scenario. Perhaps the novel made sense, but the scenario was ridiculous. It all took place in San Diego, not on the Mexican border, which completely changes the situation. I made Vargas a Mexican for political reasons. I wanted to show how Tijuana and the border towns are corrupted by all sorts of mish-mash—publicity more or less about American relations: that's the only reason.

Q.—*What do you think of the American Cinema, as seen from Europe?*

WELLES—I am surprised by the tendency of the serious critics to find elements of value only among the American directors of action films, while they find none in the American directors of historical films. Lubitsch, for example, is a giant. But he doesn't correspond to the taste of cinema aesthetes. Why? I know nothing about it. Besides, it doesn't interest me. But Lubitsch's talent and originality are stupefying.

Q.—*And Von Sternberg?*

WELLES—Admirable! He is the greatest exotic director of all time and one of the great lights.

Q.—*Let's talk about other directors. What do you think of Arthur Penn? Have you seen* The Left-Handed Gun?

WELLES—I saw it first on television and then as cinema. It was better on television, more brutal, and beyond that I believe that at that time Penn had more experience directing for television and so handled it better, but for cinema this experience went against him. I believe him to be a good theatre director, an admirable director of actresses—a very rare thing: very few *cineastes* possess that quality.

I have seen nothing by the most recent generation, except for a sampling of the avante-garde. Among those whom I would call "younger generation" Kubrick appears to me to be a giant.

Q.—*But, for example,* The Killing *was more or less a copy of* The Asphalt Jungle?

WELLES—Yes, but *The Killing* was better. The problem of imitation leaves me indifferent, above all if the imitator succeeds in surpassing the model. For me, Kubrick is a better director than Huston. I haven't seen *Lolita* but I believe that Kubrick can do everything. He is a great director who has not yet made his great film. What I see in him is a talent not possessed by the great directors of the generation immediately preceding his, I mean Ray, Aldrich, etc. Perhaps this is because his temperament comes closer to mine.

Q.—*And those of the older generation? Wyler, for example? and Hitchcock?*

WELLES—Hitchcock is an extraordinary director; William Wyler a brilliant producer.

Q.—*How do you make this distinction between two men who are both called directors?*

WELLES—A producer doesn't make anything. He chooses the story, works on it with the scenarist, has a say in the distribution and, in the old sense of the term American producer, even decides on the camera angles, what sequences will be used. What is more, he defines the final form of the film. In reality, he is a sort of director's boss.

Wyler is this man. Only he's his own boss. His work, however, is better as boss than as director, given the fact that in that role he spends his clearest moments waiting, with the camera, for something to happen. He says nothing. He waits, as the producer waits in his office. He looks at twenty impeccable shots, seeking the one that has something, and usually he knows how to choose the best one. As a director he is good but as a producer he is extraordinary.

Q.—*According to you, the role of director consists in making something happen?*

WELLES—I do not like to set up very strict rules, but in the Hollywood system, the director has one job. In other systems he has another job. I am against absolute rules because even in the case of America we find marvelous films achieved under the absolute tyranny of the production system. There are even films much respected by film societies that weren't made by directors but by producers and scenarists. . . . Under the American system, no one is capable of saying whether a film was or was not directed by a director.

Q.—*In an interview, John Houseman said that you got all of the credit for* Citizen Kane *and that this was unfair because it should have gone to Herman J. Mankiewicz, who wrote the scenario.*

WELLES—He wrote several important scenes. (Houseman is an old enemy of mine.) I was very lucky to work with Mankiewicz: everything concerning Rosebud belongs to him. As for me, sincerely, he doesn't please me very much; he functions, it is true, but I have never had complete confidence in him. He serves as a hyphen between all the elements. I had, in return, the good fortune to have Gregg Toland, who is the best director of photography that ever existed, and I also had the luck to hit upon actors who had never worked in films before; not a single one of them had ever found himself in front of a camera until then. They all came from my theatre. I could never have made *Citizen Kane* with actors who were old hands at cinema, because they would have said right off, "Just what do you think we're doing?" My being a newcomer would have put them on guard and, with the same blow, would have made a mess of the film. It was possible because I had my own family, so to speak.

Q.—*How did you arrive at* Citizen Kane*'s cinematic innovations?*

WELLES—I owe it to my ignorance. If this word seems inadequate to you, replace it with innocence. I said to myself: this is what the camera should be really capable of doing, in a normal fashion. When we were on the point of shooting the first sequence, I said, "Let's do that!" Gregg Toland answered that it was impossible. I came back with, "We can always try; we'll soon see. Why not?" We had to have special lenses made because at that time there weren't any like those that exist today.

Q.—*During the shooting, did you have the sensation of making such an important film?*

WELLES—I never doubted it for a single instant.

Q.—*What is happening with your* Don Quixote? *It was announced so long ago.*

WELLES—It's really finished; it only needs about three weeks' work, in order to shoot several little things. What makes me nervous is launching it: I know that this film will please no one. This will be an execrated film. I need a big success before putting it in circulation. If *The Trial* had been a complete critical success, then I would have had the courage to bring out my *Don Quixote*. Things being what they are I don't know what to do: everyone will be enraged by this film.

Q.—*How do you see the central character?*

WELLES—Exactly as Cervantes did, I believe. My film takes place in modern times but the characters of Don Quixote and Sancho are exactly as they were, at least, I repeat, to my way of thinking. This wasn't the case with Kafka; I utilize these two characters freely but I do it in the same spirit as Cervantes. They are not my characters, they are the Spanish writer's.

Q.—*Why did you choose to film* Don Quixote?

WELLES—I started by making a half hour television out of it; I had just enough money to do it. But I fell so completely in love with my subject that I gradually made it longer and continued to shoot depending on how much money I had. You might say that it grew as I made it. What happened to me is more or less what happened to Cervantes, who started to write a novella and ended up writing *Don Quixote*. It's a subject you can't let go of once you've started.

Q.—*Will the film have the same skepticism as the novel?*

WELLES—Certainly! I believe that what happened to the book will happen to my film. You know that Cervantes started out to write a satire on books of chivalry and he ended up creating the most beautiful apology for them that can be found in literature. However, touching on the defense of that idea of chivalry, the film will be more sincere than the novel, even though today it is more anachronistic than when Cervantes was writing.

I myself appear in the character of Orson Welles, but Sancho and Don Quixote say only the lines given them by Cervantes; I have put no words in their mouths.

I do not think the film is less skeptical because I believe that, if we push the analysis to the end, Cervantes' skepticism was in part an attitude. His skepticism was an intellectual attitude: I believe that, under the skepticism, there was a man who loved the knights as much as Don Quixote himself. Above all, he was Spanish.

It is truly a difficult film. I should also say that it is too long; what I am going to shoot will not serve to complete the footage—I could make three films out of the material that already exists. The film, in its first form, was too commercial; it was conceived for television and I had to change certain things in order to make it more substantial. The drollest thing about it is that it was shot with a crew of six people. My wife was script-girl; the chauffeur moved the lights around, I did the lighting and was second cameraman. It is only with the camera that one can have his eye on everything in such a way.

Heston on Welles

JAMES DELSON

INT.: How did the *Touch of Evil* project come to be produced?

HESTON: It was submitted to me in December of 1956 by Universal, for whom I had made a successful comedy called *The Private War of Major Benson*. Since its release I had finished *Ten Commandments*, done a play in New York, and I was loafing over the holiday when Universal sent the script.

"It's a good enough script," I said, "but police stories, like westerns and war stories, have been so overdone that it really depends on who's going to direct it." I told them I'd put it down and call them later.

They told me that although they didn't know who was going to direct it, Orson Welles was going to play the heavy. "You know, Orson Welles is a pretty good director," I said. "Did it ever occur to you to have him direct it?" At that time, Orson had not directed a picture in America since *Macbeth*. They were a bit nonplussed, but they got back to me in a couple of days and said "Yeah, well that's a very good idea. A startling idea."

INT.: At this time, was Welles considered a cult figure at all?

HESTON: About *Citizen Kane* he was. There was a rich preoccupation with the idea of Welles as a rebel, I guess, but they brought him in on the picture. He totally rewrote the script in about seventeen days, which I knew he would, and didn't object to.

INT.: He got a solo writing credit for it.

HESTON: Well he deserved it. He gives you your value. He has a reputation as being an extravagant director, but there are directors who have *wasted* more money on one film than Orson has spent on all the pictures he's directed in his career.

Nonetheless, people say "Oh, you can't hire Orson because he's extravagant." Mike Nichols went farther over budget on *Catch-22* than Orson has spent on all the films he has directed, put together. In my experience, in the one film I made for him, Orson is by no means an extravagant director. As I recall, we had something like a forty- or forty-two-day shooting schedule and a budget of slightly under a million dollars, and we went a couple of days and about seventy-five thousand dollars over the budget. Now that

Reprinted from *Take One* 3 (July/August 1971): 7–10.

really is not an outlandish, horrifying situation at all. The difference between that film *with* Welles and that film *without* Welles would be remarkable. His contribution as an actor, of course, was incredible. I would say the only major error that Orson made in the film was his conviction that he had to conceal something: the fact that his part was the best part in the film, as he had re-written the script. In fact, it was evident anyway—I knew it. *Touch of Evil* is about the decline and fall of Captain Quinlan. My part is a kind of witness to this. It would have . . .

INT.: I agree that he wrote the best part for himself, but you're one of the three or four actors who have worked with Welles without being dwarfed by him, physically in terms of screen persona, or dramatically in terms of just plain showmanship. In watching the film recently this is one of its aspects that I noted most carefully, knowing that this point would come up. I was looking to see how you would handle yourself when the famous Wellesian scene-stealing took place. In the scene where Joe Calleia "finds" the sticks of dynamite in the shoebox, Welles is playing it up, but you, through the opposite means, subduing every gesture and restraining yourself, manage to hold your own, which is a feat.

HESTON: Well, I am happy to subscribe to the thesis that I can stand on equal ground with Orson in a scene, but that doesn't change the fact that Orson is party to that part, and that the film is *about* Captain Quinlan, really. But that's the way it should be. That's the story. I play a man who's looking for his wife, really.

Actually, I have Orson to thank for the fact that the part is as interesting as it was, because it was his idea to make it a Mexican detective. I said "I can't play a Mexican detective!" He said "Sure you can! We'll dye your hair black, and put on some dark makeup and draw a black moustache, sure you can! We'll get a Mexican tailor to cut you a good Mexican suit." And they did, and it's plausible enough I suppose. I play a plausible Mexican. As a matter of fact it doesn't contribute to the stereotype of the sombrero Mexican lazing around in the shade.

INT.: Did Universal agree to let Welles act in the film so long as he directed it?

HESTON: They imposed on him, for budget reasons. They were willing to take a chance on him directing, but only on that budget.

INT.: Was casting begun immediately upon the signing of Welles?

HESTON: No. The first thing was his reworking of the script. He wanted it to be set on the Mexican border, and they wouldn't go for location work at that time. You must remember that this was sixteen years ago. Welles found an entirely acceptable substitute in Venice, California.

INT.: It was more than acceptable. Remind me not to visit Venice, California. Welles achieved a new low in ramshackle buildings, locations, and degeneracy, as played most ably by US-for-Mexico shooting. In searching for locations, and other pre-production work, did you play an active part?

HESTON: Not *nearly* the amount I do now. I was consulted about things, but did not really participate on a serious level. I helped in things like casting. I had approval.

INT.: Was there anybody cast who you were either exceedingly pleased or displeased over?

HESTON: I thought all of the casting was marvelous. There was some uncertainty over the casting of the girl, who was played by Janet Leigh.

INT.: I guess she was very big at that time.

HESTON: The studio wanted to use her very much. This casting was, in fact, almost imposed, and . . . as a matter of fact, it turned out better than I thought it would. I thought she was quite good. I don't think Orson was terribly upset about it. All the other casting I had approval on and, as far as I know, Orson made all the other castings. There were some fine performances, especially Joe Calleia. I think it's one of the very best pieces of work he did in his whole career.

INT.: I thought the cameos were a nice touch.

HESTON: Orson got his cronies to do them. Joe Cotten and Marlene Dietrich were fun, yeah.

INT.: Orson Welles as director. That's the dream of many fine actors. What is it that makes him special to work with?

HESTON: He's exciting. He makes it fun.

INT.: Then why is it that he can't get the money to make films? He makes films that are literate, and as close as one can get to pure cinema, both in terms of artistic achievement and entertainment. I'm sorry. That was a rhetorical outburst. We were talking about how Welles works.

HESTON: Film acting is not often very interesting. Even if you have a fascinating part with four or five major scenes, which is unusual, those scenes don't take up half the running time of the film, or the shooting time of the film, either. The bulk of your day is . . . well a good case in point is a scene from *Skyjacked*, where I came out of the flight deck and went into the john, where I saw the scrawled message saying that the plane was being skyjacked. I didn't say anything. I looked at Yvette (Mimieux), and in the course of that look, what they describe as a "charged look," I had to show "problems, what am I doing here, what are all these carryings on," and also "I'm involved in some kind of complicated relationship with this girl, and I'd really rather not be flying with her. All things considered, but on the other hand . . ." That's about all there is to the first shot. No lines . . . That was my first day's work on the picture. That's *all* there was to the first day. That's not all *they* did, but that's all *I* did. You understand the motivation, you've read the script, you know the importance of establishing the thing with the girl, but still it's really not the most marvelous day's work you've ever done. Orson has the capacity as a director to somehow persuade you that each time is *indeed* the most important day in the picture, and that's kind of marvelous, and I applaud it.

INT.: Is he this way with all the actors? Minor scenes as well, bit parts?

HESTON: I think so, yes.

INT.: Can we talk about the first shot? The famous first shot?

HESTON: This first shot in *Touch of Evil* is, as I said, technically one of the most brilliant shots I have ever seen in any film. Among film buffs it has become a classic shot.

INT.: It's in all of the books.

HESTON: Is it? Is it in some books? Well, for the record, it begins on a close-up insert of a bundle of sticks of dynamite, and it pans up just enough to apprehend an unidentifiable figure dashing out of the frame. As the pan continues, you see in the middle distance a couple coming out of the door of a bar, and going even deeper into the background, and turning around the back of the building and disappearing. Led by the couple's exit, the camera pans down the alley in the direction in which the figure holding the dynamite has fled, on the near side of the building, going in the same direction. You see the figure (and of course now you can't possibly identify him) dart behind the building. Following with the camera, but still too far away to tell who he is, he lifts the trunk of a car and puts what is obviously a bomb into the car, slams the lid and disappears into the shadows just as the camera, now lifting above the car, picks up the couple coming around the other side of the building and getting in the car. You establish him as a fat political type and she a floozy blond type. And they carry on—there's enough awareness of their dialogue to establish a kind of drunken nonchalance.

The camera booms up on a Chapmain boom as the car drives out of the parking lot and out into the street. The boom sinks down, picks up the car, and picks up me and Janet Leigh walking along and talking. The camera then moves ahead of both us and the car, the car's progress being to some degree impeded by foot traffic, so as to keep us more or less in the same context. But first you pick up the car and then us walking, and in the course of our movement you establish that we are just married and honeymooning. All the time, on the sound track you hear the ticking of the bomb.

By this time we get to the border station and have a little dialogue that established me as a government official. We go through the Mexican station, and then through the U.S. station, and the car does too, and there's a little carrying-on that makes it clear that this fellow is a guy with some political clout.

INT.: And the girl says, "My watch is awfully loud, I think I hear something ticking."

HESTON: No. "There's this ticking in my head" . . . she's drunk. The car zooms past us out of shot, we now being in the United States, and there's some dialogue to the effect that we've just been married and I haven't kissed her in an hour, and I pull her into my arms and kiss her and of course as our lips touch the car explodes off screen. That's quite a shot.

INT.: That is called Orson Welles.

HESTON: It took *all* one night to shoot, as indeed it might. And the spooky thing about night-shooting, night exteriors, is that when the sun comes up that's all, you've got to quit. And we were shooting in Venice and we . . . Oh, I don't know, laying the shot was incredibly complicated. The boom work with the Chapmain boom was the major creative contribution. The men who ran the boom had a *terribly* difficult job, but they finally were getting so it was working well enough to do takes on it, and we did two or three or four takes, and in each take the customs man, who had just one line, would flub his line.

INT.: Oh Christ.

HESTON: Cause he'd see this great complex of cars and lights and Chapmain booms bearing down on him from three blocks away, and they'd get closer and closer, and finally there they would all be, and he would blow his line. I will concede that Orson did not do a great deal to stimulate his . . . Orson said, "Look, I don't care what you say, just move your lips, we can dub it in later. Don't just put your face in your hands and say 'Oh my God, I'm sorry.'" And of course the fellow never did get the line. He finally managed to blow the line impassively. He just stood there moving his lips impotently.

INT.: At which point Welles gave him a medal and his walking papers. At this time, were you beginning to take a creative interest in the technical aspects of the films you were working on?

HESTON: Well, you begin to, if you have any brains, the first time you work on a film. This was the first film on which I was quite as aware of the enormous creative composition of the camera, which is not surprising since Russ Metty was the cameraman. It was also the first film on which I spent any time in the cutting room. I sat and watched Orson fiddle with sequences with his cutter, and it was a very learningful experience.

INT.: That's the kind of experience that most of us would give our shirts for.

HESTON: Yeah, it's valuable.

INT.: Is he a perfectionist?

HESTON: No.

INT.: In terms of just putting things right?

HESTON: I think that's the last thing Orson is. He probably has a larger measure of talent, whatever the hell that means, than anybody else I've ever met, but a perfectionist he is not. He can get an *incredible* idea about how to solve a scene, or a piece of casting, or a bit of writing, or an editing problem. But rather than polish it to perfection, he is likely to substitute still another idea that is nearly as good or maybe better. But, I would say, he is disinclined to sandpaper.

INT.: Does he get a lot of coverage? I know Sam Peckinpah sometimes uses eighteen or nineteen cover shots on one set-up.

HESTON: No. Now mind you, at the time I made *Touch of Evil* I wasn't as sophisticated an observer of the mechanics of filmmaking as I am now. But, nonetheless, in my memory . . . well, the first shot is . . . what I've said to you. There is no cutting to that. They just got the slate off it and that's the first three minutes of the film.

INT.: The studio likes that kind of thing. (both laugh)

Was Welles doing any rewriting when the film was being made? Or was he working straight through?

HESTON: Not once we started shooting. I think that's one of the reasons *Touch of Evil* could be said to have turned out better than *Major Dundee*. Sam had to attempt to undertake his rewrite while shooting the film. Orson undertook his and accomplished it before shooting.

INT.: How would you describe the working relationship you had with him during the film?

HESTON: Enchanted. Orson *seduces* you in a marvelous way. You know he's one of the most charming men in the world, if it's important to him to be charming. He is, at *minimum*, interesting—but if it's important to him to enlist your support and cooperation, he is as charming a man as I have ever seen.

INT.: And was he so with the rest of the crew as well would you say?

HESTON: Oh yes. See, that's an important thing. Orson elicits remarkable support from his companies, he asks a lot from them, his crews too, but he jokes with them and recognizes what they're doing, their contributions, and it works *marvelously*. They put out a great effort for him.

INT.: It shows in the fact that he got tiny performances, one-scene performances, that are memorable.

HESTON: Yeah, that's it. Sam, on the other hand, *requires* your commitment, and that's not quite the same thing as *eliciting* your support. Because you can choose not to deliver your commitment. Personally, in my own style of work, I prefer working as an individual film actor, in a somewhat more detached manner. I think you tend to get into a hothouse atmosphere. You're living in each other's laps anyway, and it's long days, and I frankly prefer a little more detached and cool relationship. But you've got to do it the way the director wants. In both the case of Sam, who demanded it and required it, and Orson, who elicits it, that's the way you go. But some people won't make that kind of commitment to Sam.

INT.: On individual scenes, when you'd be working with Welles—would he say do this and this and this and this—in a way some directors will—or is he a director who will let you create and then say "Well, maybe this and maybe this?"

HESTON: By and large, assuming the contribution of professional actors . . . in my experience on 40 films the complexities of the mechanics of filming and the creative problems they present tend to preoccupy a director to a large degree. A good actor is likely to have a fairly free hand in the shaping of his . . . certainly of his character, possibly of the scene as well. I'm not speaking of a Wyler or Stevens or Lean, but most directors, even directors like those I've mentioned, who work in *incredibly tiny detail* in altering facets of a performance, they often tend not to do so in acting terms, if you follow me. I think Wyler, for example, has an absolutely *infallible* taste for a performance. If he says it's right—it's *right*. There's just no question. But I don't think he's particularly emphatic with actors.

Orson probably taught me more about acting than any film director I've worked for. Which is not to say I necessarily did my best film performance for him, but he taught me a great deal about acting—the whole, acting generically. He's both specific in technical details, and in broad concepts about acting, and I found it an enormously stimulating experience.

INT.: The scenes you did with Welles—did you find those to be your most difficult scenes?

HESTON: The most difficult?

INT.: The most difficult, or the most draining, I would say. It's really the word I would use. Draining would also mean that when you were finished with them you probably felt the most satisfied.

HESTON: I recall performing in the whole picture, doing the whole picture, as being as satisfying creatively as anything I've ever done. I don't recall it as being—the part was not an enormously difficult part. There was never a scene that you look on as a major jump— you know, a barrier that somehow you have to clear. Like the dagger speech in *Macbeth*. Or Antony's suicide. They were scenes that you did with as much creative juice as you could call on at that time. Orson helps you quite a lot.

INT.: The sequence with the shoebox is a brilliant scene. It's also brilliantly directed and photographed, again because the camera is constantly moving in that scene.

HESTON: That's about thirteen pages. That was the first day's work on the picture. And Orson deceived the studio, and he conned them, because the scene was scheduled for three days of shooting, which is about reasonable, which would be a little over four pages a day—which is a respectable day's work in an "A" picture. He, in fact, had rehearsed the scene in his home with the actors over a Sunday or two. He proceeded to lay out the scene in terms of *one* shot with a crab dolly, that encompassed all the eight or nine performers who had lines in the scene. The action ranged through two rooms, a closet and a bathroom, and, as I said, thirteen pages of dialogue. It was quite a complex shot, with doors having to be pulled, walls having to be pulled aside—very intricate markings, inserts on the shoebox, and things like that. All of which were in one shot.

When you're shooting, the production office is informed when the camera turns over the first time, when the first print is made, and so on. And of course we never turned a camera until way . . . Lunch went by, and uneasy little groups of executives began to huddle about in the shadows, not quite willing to approach Orson but increasingly convinced that they were on the brink of disaster, cause we hadn't turned a camera and it was, by now, three or four o'clock in the afternoon. Finally, at about 4:30, we turned. And of course it was tricky. We did several takes—seven or eight takes. Finally we got a print, just before six o'clock. And Orson said, "OK, that's a print. Wrap." He said, "We're two days ahead of schedule. We go to the other set tomorrow."

INT.: The executives must have been down on their knees.

HESTON: Everybody thought it was marvelous. Of course he never did that again, you see, but they always thought he *might*.

INT.: It's a brilliant idea.

HESTON: Just great. They never gave him any trouble again after that. They thought, "My God, he did three day's work in one shot!"

INT.: The little touches that he adds from scene to scene. Were they all in the script? The things like Akim Tamiroff's hairpiece which was a running gag throughout the whole film.

HESTON: That was not in the script, no. And of course, I wasn't in those scenes, so I don't know how they were created, but I know they weren't—it wasn't in the script. The scenes are put together in a very loose atmosphere that makes for that kind of creativity.

INT.: Was there any ad libbing in terms of dialogue?

HESTON: Orson has a marvelous ear for the way people talk. One of the many things I learned from him was the degree to which people in real life overlap one another when they're talking. In the middle of somebody's sentence you will, in fact, apprehend what he's talking about and you will often start to reply through his closing phrase. People do that all the time. Orson directs scenes that way—to a larger degree than most directors do.

There's a marvelously counterpointed scene in *Lady from Shanghai* in which the people sit in the dark—obviously he doesn't want a visual image to intrude—and you hear two conversations interwoven. He likes that, and I do too. I think it's very valuable, and I've tried to use it in scenes myself since. He not only changes dialogue, as . . . dialogue is changed all the time on film. It's some of the most creative work in putting a scene together.

INT.: All of Hawks.

HESTON: Pardon?

INT.: All of Hawks had to be written on a daily basis.

HESTON: It goes on all the time. Sure. Orson is, as I said, a very instinctive, intuitive creator, and he would restage whole scenes. I mean put them in different places. We were shooting in this crummy hotel in Venice, and at three o'clock in the morning—in the middle of night shooting—we were down in the basement of this old hotel, peeing in a drain in the corner of this old basement, and he said, "Gee, these pipes and this boiler. That's marvelous. You know this—we should do the scene with Joe Calleia here—where he shows you the cane."

He zipped up his fly and said to the first assistant, "Get Joe Calleia down here." They said, "Jesus, Orson, we were gonna do that scene on Friday, they've got it set up at the studio." He said, "That's terrible. That's no place. We're going to do it down here. We'll do it right now." And they said, "Well, we've got to finish this scene." He said, "I can finish this scene in one shot. It'll take you an hour to get Calleia out of bed. Get him down here and I'll have this scene finished by then." And he did.

INT.: That's beautiful.

HESTON: And it is better there.

INT.: Cause that is the turning point of the film.

HESTON: It's a great scene. And part of the reason it's good is he . . . Here's Joe Calleia getting up out of bed in the middle of the night, and staggering down to Venice. They take him down in this stinking basement and they give him the cane, and they say "Joe, now do it." And he says, "What—what—what???" "The scene." "Where?" You know, and it's marvelous.

ESSAYS

Orson Welles: Of Time and Loss

WILLIAM JOHNSON

J UDGED BY first—even second or third—impressions, Welles's films are a triumph of show over substance. His most memorable images seem like elephantine labors to bring forth mouse-size ideas.

His films bulge with preposterously vast spaces: the echoing halls of Kane's Xanadu; the rambling castles of Macbeth, Othello, and Arkadin; the vertiginous offices of *The Trial*; the cathedral-like palace and tavern of *Falstaff*.

His camera moves with a swagger, craning down through the skylight of El Rancho in *Kane* and up over the bomb-carrying car in *Touch of Evil*. When the camera is still, the composition may cry out for attention with anything from multiple reflections (the hall of mirrors in *Lady from Shanghai*) to a flurry of silhouettes (the battle in *Falstaff*).

The action often runs along the edge of violence, and sometimes topples over with a spectacular splash: Kane destroying Susan's room after she leaves him; Mike's brawl in the judge's office in *Lady from Shanghai*; Macbeth overturning the huge banquet table after Banquo's ghost appears; Vargas running amuck in the bar in *Touch of Evil*. At other times Welles expresses his love of spectacle in a show-within-a-show: the dancing girls at Kane's newspaper party and the opera in which Susan stars; the magician's act in *Journey into Fear*;[1] the Chinese theater in *Lady from Shanghai*; the flea circus in *Arkadin*; the slide show that begins and ends *The Trial*.

What makes all these Barnum qualities really seem to stick on Welles the director is the style and appearance of Welles the actor. With the sole exception of *Magnificent Ambersons*, the bravura manner of Welles's films centers around characters that he himself plays. It is Welles whose voice booms across the cavernous drawing room of Xanadu, it is Welles who overturns the banquet table at Glamis castle, it is Welles who conducts the slide show in *The Trial*. And the Barnum image is reinforced by his roles in other people's films, from the tongue-in-cheek sophistries of Harry Lime in *The Third Man* to the flamboyant magic of Le Chiffre in *Casino Royale*.

Of course, showmanship can be sublime, and even the harshest critics of Welles's films have some kind words for *Citizen Kane*. Judged simply by its style, the film must be accounted an impressive achievement for any director, let alone a 25-year-old newcomer to the movie medium. Many of

© 1967 by the Regents of the University of California. Reprinted from *Film Quarterly* Vol. 21 No. 1 (Fall 1967), pp. 13–24, by permission.

the stylistic effects that Welles used with such apparent ease in *Kane* have become common screen currency only during the last ten years—wide-angle perspective, unusually long takes, abrupt cuts, intricate leaps in time, terse vignettes, heightened natural sound, and so on. Though precedents can be found for each of these devices, Welles was the first director to develop them into a full-blown style. With the exception of some typical forties process shots, the whole of *Kane* looks and sounds almost as modern today as it did in 1941—a good deal more modern, in fact, than many films of 1967.

Moreover, Welles's protean style clearly reflects the character of Kane—himself a kind of Barnum who conceals his private self behind a dazzling set of public images. It's possible for a critic to see no deeper into *Kane* than this and still give the film high marks for matching style and content.

Judged by these standards, Welles's other films are inferior. Neither their stylistic inventiveness nor their matching of style and content stands out so obviously as *Kane*'s. After a brilliant start, Welles's directing career seems to decline into potboilers (*Stranger, Lady from Shanghai, Touch of Evil*), distortions of literary originals (the Shakespeare films and *Trial*) and a rehash of *Kane—Arkadin*—which demonstrates only too clearly the coarsening of his showmanship.

The foregoing view of Welles is, I believe utterly wrong, and yet it has plausibility because it rests on a few points of truth. *Arkadin*, for example, *is* an inferior rehash of *Kane*, with grotesques instead of characters and with episodes loosely strung together instead of interlocking. *Macbeth*, with or without due allowance for the conditions under which it was made, *is* often ludicrous. There are other examples which I will come to later.

But it's difficult to maintain a balanced view of Welles's strengths and weaknesses. While his detractors see little but empty showiness, anyone who likes most of his work runs the risk of slipping to the opposite extreme. With a film-maker as vigorous and idiosyncratic as Welles, it's temptingly easy to find some justification for nearly everything he does. *Arkadin* is based on an exciting and fruitful idea; some of the sequences in the film are excellent; many others are exciting or fascinating—and so I could go on, justifying the film piece by piece to the conclusion that it is all good. But here I'd be falling into the same trap as those who deny the originality of *Kane* because (for example) Renoir had previously used deep focus. It's the total effect that counts, and just as the total effect of Welles's deep focus is quite different from Renoir's, and much more far-reaching, so the total effect of *Arkadin* falls far short of its piecemeal felicities.

Similarly, Welles's films *are* showy, but this is only one side of them. The other, quieter side gives a far better clue to what his films are all about.

One of the finest scenes in *Kane* features no craning or dollying, no dramatic chiaroscuro, no optical distortions, no unusual sound effects, no jump cuts or, for that matter, cuts of any kind whatsoever. The reporter visits Kane's former lawyer, Bernstein, to see if he can explain "Rosebud." Bernstein suggests that it may have referred to some very fleeting experience in Kane's past, and cites as an example his own memory of a girl dressed in white whom he glimpsed forty years earlier. "I only saw her for a second," says Bernstein, "and she didn't see me at all, but I bet a month hasn't gone by that I haven't thought about her." Throughout the scene the camera remains absolutely still: all one sees is the back of the reporter's head, Bernstein at his desk and rain falling outside the window. This unexpected plumbing of the depths of the cheery Bernstein is made all the more moving by the sudden stillness with which Welles films it.

One of Welles's films—*Magnificent Ambersons*—is nearly all stillness, or only the most leisurely of movements. Its tempo is set by the horse and buggy typical of the age that is ending when the film's action takes place. There is indeed an extremely long, gentle dolly shot that follows George and Lucy as they ride a buggy together through the town. But the basic tempo extends even to Gene Morgan (Joseph Cotten), the man who is hastening the death of the horse-and-buggy age by designing automobiles: he walks with an easy-going gait, and he talks with measured reasonableness even under verbal attack from the arrogant George.

The elegiac mood of *Ambersons* sets it apart from the rest of Welles's films, but its theme recurs in all of them, sometimes burrowing deep beneath the surface, sometimes coming out into the open as in the Bernstein reminiscence. This theme can be summed up as loss of innocence.

Bernstein's regret for a bright moment of his youth is a minor variation of the theme. It is Kane himself who provides the first and most sustained example of lost innocence—though it is one that may easily be misunderstood. Because Freudian symbolism was just creeping into Hollywood films when *Kane* appeared, the sled named Rosebud was widely seized upon as a psychoanalytic key to Kane's character. It is a simpler and more lyrical symbol—of Kane's childhood innocence that cannot be recovered.

Welles does not, of course, thrust a symbol at us and leave it at that. He has designed the whole film so as to bring Kane's predicament to life before our eyes; and he does this largely by giving an almost tangible presence to the passing of time. This might be called a 3-D film, with time instead of spatial depth as the salient third dimension. Nearly everything in the film contributes to this effect: the juxtaposition of scenes showing the different ages not only of Kane but also of those who know him, notably Jed Leland alternating between handsome youth and garrulous senility, Susan between wispy naiveté and sufficient toughness to leave Kane; the use of a different quality of image and sound in the newsreel of

Kane's life, adding distance to the events featured in it and, by contrast, adding immediacy to the events filmed straight; and even such normally gimmicky devices as the dissolves from a still photograph to its subject in motion. Above all it is the structure of the film that brings Welles's theme to life. Two strands are intertwined throughout. In the film's present tense, there is the reporter's vain search for the meaning of Rosebud, which mirrors the aged Kane's own yearning for his lost innocence. Concurrently, the flashbacks into Kane's past follow him step by step as he loses that innocence. These alternating images of past and present fuse together stereoscopically into a powerful, poignant vision of Kane's loss.

Welles's other films present variations of this basic theme. Whereas *Kane* states it comprehensively, spanning almost a lifetime of change, several of the other films focus on particular stages: on the initial innocence of Mike in *Lady from Shanghai* and of Joseph K in *The Trial*; on the moment of loss for Macbeth and Othello; on a time long after the loss for Arkadin and for Hank Quinlan in *Touch of Evil*. In the other three films the theme is not tied so closely to a single character: in *The Stranger*, Nazi-in-hiding Franz Kindler threatens the innocent coziness of a New England village; in *Falstaff*, as in *Ambersons*, the loss of innocence lies in the transition between two historical ages.

Far from clashing with this lyrical theme, Welles's bravura qualities enrich it. Kane's onslaught on Susan's room comes to a halt when he sees the snow-scene paperweight: the sudden stillness, the whiteness of the paperweight as he cradles it in his hand, his whisper of "Rosebud" are all the more moving because of the lengthy destruction that went before. Similarly, in *Touch of Evil*—the most agitated of all Welles's films—the calm of Tanya's place draws a charge of lyrical power from the surrounding frenzy. The odd parlor, where a TV set is perched on top of a player piano, is like a time machine that whisks Quinlan away to confront him with his distant, innocent past.

In all of his films Welles uses this contrast between movement and stillness to embody the the fragility of life, to compress the change of a lifetime or even of an age into a few vivid moments. Sometimes he reverses his usual method of injecting stillness into movement. The calm flow of events in *Ambersons*, for example, is broken by the lively sleigh-riding sequence, its liveliness sharpened by the brightness of the snow and the airy rapidity of Bernard Herrmann's music. The sudden release of movement gives a physical reality to the passing of time.

Falstaff is one gigantic contrast of this kind. Its opening and closing scenes form a reflective prologue and epilogue that stand apart from the main action. The epilogue is straightforward: it shows Falstaff's bulky coffin being trundled slowly off into the distance. The prologue is more unusual. To create it, Welles has sliced half a dozen lines out of the middle of the scene in which Shallow summons potential recruits for Falstaff

(*Henry IV*, Part II, Act III, scene ii). In these few lines Falstaff and Shallow reminisce about their youth. "We have heard the chimes at midnight, Master Shallow." "That we have, that we have. . . . Jesus, the days that we have seen!" Singled out in this way, the brief exchange carries a more powerful charge of nostalgia than in the scene as Shakespeare wrote it; and since the main action of the film is appended to the prologue like a huge flashback, this nostalgia affects everything that follows. Indeed, Welles has left the time and place of the prologue so vague that one may end up linking it with the epilogue, as if Falstaff and Shallow are viewing the past from some limbo outside time.

Seen in this context, such excesses of agitation as the battle scenes are only minor flaws. They do not in any way undermine the total effect of the film, of action embedded in reflection. As to other apparent excesses, they turn out to be no excesses at all. The vastness of the film's spaces serve to deepen the sense of nostalgia. The tavern, for example, is enlarged beyond probability in much the same way that a childhood haunt is enlarged in one's memory: this is how Falstaff, the perpetual child, would remember it. Similarly, the wide horizons of the film's outdoor scenes (actually shot in Spain) evoke the spacious, innocent Olde Englande that Falstaff imagined he lived in. Naturalistic settings would have called attention to the costumes, the archaic language, the theatrical structure of the scenes, everything except what's really important—the characters and their changing world. Welles's exaggerations give the film its human perspective.

Though nostalgia for lost innocence recurs in all the films, in none except *Arkadin* is there any sense of Welles repeating himself. Endless variations on his basic theme are possible, and Welles remains receptive to any or all of them. This is where his other Barnum characteristics—from swaggering camera to tongue-in-cheek humor—come into play. They are usually a sign of the unexpected.

In *Kane*, for example, when Susan makes her operatic debut, the camera suddenly takes off into the flies until it comes to rest on two stagehands, one of whom expressively grasps his nose with thumb and forefinger. The scene is very funny, all the more so because Welles builds it up with the same kind of camerawork he uses elsewhere for serious purposes: the long upward movement apes Kane's inordinate efforts to launch Susan's feeble talent. An even briefer example of this double-edged humor occurs in *Falstaff* when Sir John is lying supine on the tavern floor and Doll Tearsheet, coming to comfort him, climbs over his belly to reach his face. In one stroke Welles translates a Shakespearian metaphor into literal terms ("a mountain of flesh") and draws both humor and poignancy out of this new slant on Falstaff's fatness.

Welles's ability to bring out the unexpected in things usually taken for granted is at work throughout his best films. The most obvious example is found in the opposition between old and new in *Ambersons*. George, who stands for the innocent age that is dying, is the film's most objectionable character; Gene Morgan, who is helping create the age of noise and crowds and air pollution, is its most likable.

Characters like Kane and Quinlan gain depth from similar contradictions. Here, though, Welles avoids not only the obvious cliché of making them out-and-out monsters but the less obvious cliché of making them sympathetic monsters. They do not arouse any set pattern of responses.

One's feelings about Kane, for example, change continually from repulsion to pity, indignation to amusement. At the point where Kane is running for governor and Boss Gettys summons Kane's wife to Susan's apartment with intent to blackmail, one is generally sympathetic to Kane. But in this scene, unexpectedly, it is Gettys who behaves with dignity, and one's sympathies switch from Kane to him. Welles accomplishes the switch without trickery: Kane behaves completely in character, and there is no suggestion that Gettys is a decent politician or has a heart of gold.

The cross-currents in *Touch of Evil* are even more complex, though at first sight they do not seem so: Vargas is likable and right, Quinlan is repulsive and wrong. But it so happens that Quinlan is right about Sanchez's guilt (as he was no doubt right about many he framed in the past), which means that the moral issue between him and Vargas is not at all neat and abstract—it pivots on the possibility that a callous murderer may not only get away with his crime but his victim's daughter and wealth, too. Moreover, despite Vargas's moral stand, he is teetering on the same brink that Quinlan stepped over decades before, when his wife's murderer escaped punishment for lack of evidence. As soon as Vargas learns that his own wife has been abducted he too takes the law into his own hands. "I'm not a police officer, I'm a husband!" he shouts in the bar where Grandi's gang hangs out, and when they refuse to tell him anything he tries to beat the information out of them. It is only a touch of evil indeed that separates his destiny from Quinlan's.[*]

Welles's gift for making a vivid point with some unexpected development is at work even in the minor characters of *Touch of Evil*. Two of these, in particular, are involved in the moral issue—or rather, represent the kind of bystanders who try to avoid getting involved. The night man at the motel where Susan Vargas is being held prisoner is a weak, neurotic creature, so outraged at the slightest infringement on what he considers to be his rights that he has no thought to spare for anyone else's rights. In most films he would merely be contemptible; Welles makes him hilarious and unforgettable. Then there is the blind woman in the store where Vargas phones his wife. As he talks, the woman stands utterly still beside a

---

[*]In the novel from which Welles adapted the film, *Badge of Evil* by Whit Masterson, the framed man is innocent and there is nothing to explain why the police officer ever started framing suspects. These touches are Welles's own.

sign that reads: "If you are mean enough to steal from the blind, go ahead." The scene arouses no sympathy for the woman but a sense of unease. The impression is that she is trading on her helplessness, refusing to take the slightest responsibility for what other people may do.

Perhaps the most subtly unexpected relationships in any of Welles's films are found in *Falstaff*. As portrayed by Shakespeare, Falstaff is not only lazy, gluttonous, cowardly, lecherous, dishonest and the rest but also a great innocent. He is devoid of malice or calculation; no matter what is done to him, he remains open and trusting. He lives in a dream world where there are no politicians or policemen or pedagogues; and when Hal destroys that world by rejecting him, he does not adjust to reality but dies.

Welles magnifies this innocence both by uniting the Falstaff scenes from several plays and by establishing the strong mood of nostalgia discussed earlier. But—and this is the unexpected stroke—he does not do this at Hal's expense. Even in the two parts of *Henry IV* as Shakespeare wrote them—and as they are usually produced on stage—it is hard not to take a dislike to Hal for his callousness and calculation. But Welles makes it as difficult as he can for the audience to take sides between Hal and Falstaff—or rather, to take one side and stick to it throughout.

In the film, Hal is at his least likeable right at the beginning, even before the asides in which he talks of one day renouncing Falstaff's companionship. Welles presents him as an insecure, somewhat unstable, somewhat untrust-worthy-looking youth, combining the flaws of immaturity with the shifty traits of his father.* Then, little by little, he acquires firmness and stature. The turning point comes on the battlefield at Shrewsbury. While King Henry is parleying with the rebel Worcester, Hal and Falstaff stand listening side by side. But their reactions are very different: Falstaff tosses out a frivolous remark; Hal silences him with a quiet "Peace, chewet, peace!" and walks over to join his father. During the battle itself, Hal emerges suddenly in close-up from a cloud of dust and is seen for the first time wearing his Prince of Wales coat of arms. From now on he is more and more the political-minded Prince Henry, less and less the irresponsible Hal. But because Welles has made him develop into a more likable human being at the same time that he has assumed his impersonal role, the prince manages to appear reasonable and humane even in the final confrontation with Falstaff: "I know thee not, old man. Fall to thy prayers. How ill white hairs become a fool and jester!"

Like Gene Morgan in *Ambersons*, Hal is changing the world for both better and worse. His political techniques, which Shakespeare depicts

---

*According to Shakespeare, Henry IV acquired the crown by force and duplicity. The subtlety of Hal's characterization—interpreted superbly by Keith Baxter—is obscured a little by John Gielgud's misreading of Henry. While the king has mellowed and weakened with age, he would never suggest—as Gielgud's plaintive declamation does—that the crown was thrust on him.

more fully in *Henry V*, will lead to Maoism and McCarthyism, but they will also lead to honest and efficient government. While the mood of the film is in sympathy with Falstaff, Welles makes it clear that there can be no final choice between Falstaff's anarchic freedom and Hal's well-ordered conformity.

The struggle between tradition and progress, old and new, order and disorder is one of the most powerful forces behind Welles's work. It is reflected in his American background and his love of Europe, and in his film-making that embraces both Shakespeare and modern American thrillers.

This drive to reconcile the irreconcilable goes beyond the subjects and themes of his films. In his European-made films it is at work even in the casting, which almost seems to be done on the assumption that Europe is a single country. The entire shaping of each film from *Kane* through *Falstaff* shows a desire to burst out of commonly accepted limitations. Welles is not content with a single viewpoint—in *Kane* there are at least seven different ones (the reminiscences of the five people interviewed by the reporter, the newsreel, and the God's-eye-view opening and closing scenes), while in all his films he alternates between the detachment of stationary long shots and the involvement of wide-angle close-ups or of dolly shots that stalk the action like a hungry leopard. He is not content with the straightforward flow of time—four of his films (*Kane, Othello, Arkadin, Falstaff*) begin with the end of the action before leaping to the beginning, and *Kane* continues leaping throughout; *Ambersons* frequently skips across the years with the most laconic of vignettes. In *Touch of Evil* and *The Trial* the leaps are not so much in time as in space.

The same drive makes itself felt in almost every aspect of Welles's style. It is found not only in the contrast between successive scenes—from stillness to movement, as described earlier, or from silence to noise, darkness to light, and so on—but also within individual scenes, many of which contain visual extremes or discords that threaten to burst the frame. Welles is continually using a wide-angle lens to throw a gulf between foreground and background, making figures near the camera loom preternaturally large over those further away. There are more unusual optical devices: the paperweight that falls from Kane's dying hand, covering and distorting half of the image; the hall of mirrors in *Lady from Shanghai*, splintering the screen into a dozen images; the magnifying glass that enlarges the flea trainer's eye in *Arkadin*. In other scenes the splintering is done by highlight and shadow: the reporter gesturing in the projector beam in *Kane*; Macbeth's breastplate highlighted, the rest of him in deep shadow after his "Tomorrow, and tomorrow, and tomorrow" soliloquy; the silhouetted funeral procession in *Othello*; the zebra stripes of light and dark that fall on Joseph K as he runs out of Titorelli's studio.

Welles's persistent attempts to harness opposites and contradictions generate a tremendous potential energy in his films. Usually this energy is released little by little, like a controlled nuclear reaction, maintaining a steady urgency that compels attention. But even his most controlled films are often on the verge of exploding. The three Shakespeare films, for example, suffer in varying degrees from inconsistency of acting styles and accents. The French accents of Jeanne Moreau as Doll Tearsheet and Marina Vlady as Lady Percy in *Falstaff* are the most egregious, but the roles are not central. More damage is done by Margaret Rutherford's assumed Irish accent as Mistress Quickly, since it reduces her description of Falstaff's death to a flat, self-conscious recitation; but Welles immediately repairs the damage in the touching epilogue of Falstaff's coffin.

The two biggest casualties of Welles's explosive pressure are *Arkadin* and *The Trial*. *Arkadin* is like a grenade that flies apart chiefly along its groovings: each episode holds together fairly well, but fails to connect with the others. *The Trial* is more like the nuclear explosion with which it ends: nearly everything in it disintegrates.

All the centripetal elements of Welles are present in force in *The Trial*. The repeated use of an extreme wide-angle lens exaggerates the depth of each scene, which is further splintered by the application of chiaroscuro to complex settings (the halls and catwalks of the law offices; Hastler's candle-dotted apartment; the cathedral). There are abrupt leaps in space and time not only from episode to episode but frequently from scene to scene. Both the cast and the locations are multi-national.

Even the style and mood of the film come in fragments. Much of the decor derives from German expressionism of the 1920s, as do the *Metropolis*-like scenes in the vast office where Joseph K works and the rows of bare-chested accused waiting outside the law courts. The opening scenes in Joseph K's room are more like Hitchcock of the *Rope* period. The scene with Leni and Block in Hastler's kitchen (filmed partly with a long-focus lens) have a quiet hallucinatory quality reminiscent of *Last Year at Marienbad*.

The idea of continually changing the settings and mood of the film sounds as if it might have created an apt sense of unease, keeping the audience in the same off-balance frame of mind as Joseph K. Occasionally it does work like that. There is one superb example when K first visits the law courts and walks from a deserted corridor into a jam-packed courtroom. Welles intensifies the transition by having everyone rise to their feet as K enters, and the noise of their movement bursts into the silence like a menacing roar. (This is Welles's own addition—in Kafka's book no one in the courtroom takes any notice of K.)

Most of the transitions, however, break the tension instead of heightening it. The varied settings do not fuse together into an eerie world of their own but remain obstinately separate. Thus when K walks from the huge office into the storeroom where the policemen are being punished, the agoraphobic size of the former and the claustrophobic darkness of the latter tend not to reinforce but to neutralize each other. Time and time again in the film the nightmare is short circuited.

To explain the failure of *The Trial* it's easy to fall back on the accusation of size and showiness. It's easy to argue that Welles's style is too florid for Kafka, who relied on restraint to convey the bizarre misadventures of Joseph K. But these criticisms are irrelevant because they can be leveled at Welles's other films which do not fall to pieces.

Consider *Othello*, which has just as many reasons as *The Trial* for disintegrating. Much of the film leaps from place to place with no regard for topographical continuity: any attempt to visualize the interior layout of Othello's castle is quite pointless. As with *The Trial*, Welles in adapting the original shifts some scenes and alters others (such as the extended bath-house scene where Iago kills Roderigo). He breaks up the rhythms of Shakespeare's play, sometimes accelerating, sometimes almost halting the action. The settings and the cast are multi-national. Most disruptive of all, his work on the film continued on and off for a period of three years.

Yet the film translates Shakespeare into screen terms with a superb coherence. Welles sets the whole tragedy in perspective with an opening sequence that interweaves the funeral corteges of Othello and Desdemona and the dragging of Iago to his punishment. In contrast to the sweeping flow of these scenes, the beginning of the action has a staccato rhythm as Iago and Roderigo follow Othello and Desdemona to their wedding and then rouse Brabantio. Calm is restored when Othello comes to justify his marrying Desdemona. But from this point on the staccato rhythm associated with Iago gradually imposes itself on Othello's stately rhythm, and the increasing complexity of the film's movements suggests the increasing turmoil of doubt in Othello's mind. In the death scene, when Othello has finally decided there *is* no doubt of Desdemona's infidelity, the stately rhythm reasserts itself. Then there is a brief flurry of movement as Iago's duplicity is exposed and Othello kills himself, followed by a reprise of the grave calm of the opening scene.

There is only one moment, near the end of the film, where the disintegrating forces win out. Welles has Othello stab himself before instead of after the long speech in which he refers to himself as "one whose hand, / Like the base Indian, threw a pearl away / Richer than all his tribe." During part of the speech Othello strides across the hall toward Desdemona's body, and this rather improbable movement is intercut with a jarring close-up in which Welles has a Harry-Lime-like smile on his face. This one lapse cannot spoil the film: it does, however, make one realize just how cohesive the rest of the film has been.

The binding force in *Othello* and in most of Welles's other films is his use of symbolism. Even the most explicit of Welles's symbols do not exist in isolation: they are rooted deep in the action of the film and share the same degree of reality.

Rosebud, for example, appears at first to be a pat and superficial symbol. As with all mysteries, its revelation is something of a letdown: the sled is "only" a symbol of Kane's childhood. But the symbolism is not confined to the object itself. In fact, the adult Kane is never seen looking at it—the word Rosebud is triggered by the sight of Susan's paperweight. But here again the symbolism goes beyond the object. The paperweight is not merely an artificial snow scene recalling a real one but a snow scene encapsulated and unattainable, like Kane's lost innocence. Moreover, when the paperweight appears in close-up Welles highlights it so that it takes on a glowing halation—very much like the glare of the stage lights when Susan makes her operatic debut. Kane drives Susan to her vocal disaster not just to show his power but because, his own desire being unattainable, he wants hers to come true. Susan fails—the ironic floodlight flickers out as her voice trails away—and she is able to come to terms with reality. But the glow of Kane's desire continues to the end: the paperweight falls and smashes only after his death.

There are further ramifications to this symbolism. When the paperweight is shaken, its artificial snow settles again with preternatural slowness, prolonging and intensifying the matter-of-fact snowfall that covers the sled after young Kane leaves home. This slow settling, which is paralleled in the lingering dissolves between the reporter's interviews and his interviewees' reminiscences, suggests not only the loss of Kane's childhood innocence but the loss of all things with the relentless flow of time. At the end of the film Welles brings out this wider implication still more powerfully by accelerating the time effect. The whole of Kane's life is compressed symbolically into a few seconds as the sled—his childhood reality and manhood dream—burns and dissolves into smoke.

I'm not implying that Welles consciously planned all these interrelationships. But I do believe that he chose the particular objects, incidents, and techniques in these scenes because they felt right to him—and they felt right because they connected with the underlying symbolism. Anyone who thinks my analysis is farfetched should try to explain why the burning of Rosebud is such a powerful scene—even more powerful than the book-burning scenes in *Fahrenheit 451*. After all, a sled lacks the ready-made associations that books have; and Rosebud is not even a new and handsome object like Dali's *Secret Life*, over whose destruction Truffaut lingers for the longest time. It is the interlinking of symbols beneath the surface of *Kane* that accumulates the power of the final scenes.

This symbolism underlying conspicuous symbols can be found in nearly all of Welles's films. Anyone who's seen *The Lady from Shanghai* will remember the squid that pulses up and down in the aquarium as Mike and Elsa kiss. In isolation this might be an overemphatic comment on Elsa's predatory nature, but it works because Welles has imbued the whole film with visual and verbal imagery of the sea. The Lady herself comes from one seaport and has settled in another (San Francisco), and many scenes take place on or by the water. The squid is one of several images involving dangers that lurk beneath the surface, just as they lurk behind Elsa's alluring exterior: there are shots of a water snake and an alligator, and Mike relates a parable about sharks that destroy one another. Even the hall of mirrors connects with the pelagic imagery: the multiple reflections are like waves receding row after row, and when the mirrors are smashed Mike can finally step out onto terra firma, ignoring Elsa's last siren call. It is this cumulative imagery that helps place *The Lady from Shanghai* above other superior thrillers, which owe their success either to a series of disparate effects (like *The Wages of Fear*) or to sheer verve (like *The Big Sleep*).

The binding symbolism of *Othello* is also based on a sea-to-dry-land progression, but Welles develops it far more subtly than in *The Lady from Shanghai* and with a totally different meaning. Othello is a naval general and water is his element. At the beginning of the film, when he is strong and self-assured, he glides with Desdemona in a gondola, he commands a warship on the billowy sea, he strides beneath pennants that flutter in a stiff sea breeze. Then, as doubts about Desdemona grow in his mind, he begins to flounder out of his element. The one really spectacular scene in the film shows this transition with extraordinary vividness. When Iago says that Cassio has talked of having slept with Desdemona, Othello staggers away (Shakespeare's stage direction reads that he "falls in a trance") and finds himself lying on the waterfront beneath a parapet from which a row of people stare down at him. Welles uses a wide-angle lens and places Othello's bemused face in close-up so that it completely dwarfs the figures above: it is as if Othello were a beached whale. In more and more of the later scenes Welles draws the action away from the sea and the open air to keep Othello stranded. And in these interior scenes he leaves the walls and floors as bare as possible, criss-crossing them with spikes of shadow, in order to accentuate their dryness and airlessness.

In films with fewer centrifugal pressures than *Othello* or *Kane* the underlying symbolism plays a less important role. Indeed, it may merge indistinguishably into style: the leisurely movement of *Ambersons* and the vast spaces of *Falstaff* might be described as both medium and message.

Elsewhere the symbolism may be too rigid for the theme, or the theme too weak for the symbolism. *Macbeth* is conceived in terms of darkness, which is appropriate enough, but the darkness hardly varies: the film consists of one low-key scene after another. There is no vivid impression of Macbeth sinking from innocence into evil and despair as there is of Othello sinking from innocence into anguish. In *The Stranger* Welles does oppose darkness with light, as the film alternates between the shadowy belfry where Franz Kindler tinkers with the church clock and the whiteness of the New England colonial buildings. But here the situation is too static: the Nazi war criminal pretending to be a good small-town citizen is unchangingly evil all along.

Arkadin fails because its symbolism doesn't counteract but reinforces the centrifugal pressures. In order to suggest the multiple layers of Arkadin's personality, Welles locates the film in different elements—land, sea, air—and in different climates, from the sunny Mediterranean to wintry Germany. But the symbolism lacks a second layer of its own that would bind this geographic diversity together.

As to *The Trial*, it has no underlying symbolism whatsoever—all its symbolism is on the surface. The trouble is not so much that Welles departs from the book but that he does not depart far enough. In the book, Kafka grafts bizarre scenes onto the everyday settings of Prague, binding them together with a matter-of-fact style of writing. But it is impossible to film the scenes as Kafka describes them and at the same time remain matter-of-fact. For example, Kafka can casually write that "the size of the Cathedral struck him as bordering on the limit of what human beings could bear," but this scene cannot be filmed with anything approaching casualness. In adapting the book for the screen Welles had two choices: to tone down Kafka's incidents until they could plausibly fit the everyday settings of a real city, or to amplify Kafka's settings until they fitted the bizarre incidents. The latter choice, arguably the more faithful, was the one Welles made; and he amplifies the style along with the settings.

In making this choice, however, Welles cut himself off from a prime source of strength. *The Trial* is the only one of his films that is not rooted in reality. The best films are worlds of their own that touch common experience at enough points to be accepted as reflections of the real world. It is this basis of reality that sustains Welles's underlying symbolism, which is nearly always elemental in nature—images of air, water, snow, fire, light, darkness.

The Trial is not one world but a succession of different worlds. Many of the scenes are so dissimilar in location, tempo, and atmosphere that it is hardly possible to imagine them co-existing on any plane of reality. Weather, the progression of night and day, natural processes of all kinds are almost completely eliminated. There is nothing for any elemental symbolism to get a grip on.

It may be argued that *The Trial* is not meant to be coherent like Welles's other films for the simple reason that it is portraying an incoherent world—that by basing the style of this film on loose ends and non-sequiturs, Welles conveys the sharpest possible sense of the menacing absurdity of modern life. This is all very plausible and could lead to long and inconclusive discussion about the merits of portraying incoherence incoherently, boredom boringly and so on. Luckily Welles has provided his own standard of comparison in *Touch of Evil*, which portrays the incoherence of modern life with a remarkable coherence of style and symbolism.

This is a film of darkness. It begins and ends in the night, and there are many other nocturnal or twilit scenes in between. But it is not a monotonously dark film like *Macbeth*. The night is punctuated throughout with lights that make the darkness more menacing, from the glare of the exploding car to the pulsing of neon signs.

It is in this mechanical pulsing rather than in the light and darkness themselves that the underlying symbolism is to be found. *Touch of Evil* is geared to the automatic machinery of our time. The film opens with a close-up of the time bomb as it is set to tick its way to destruction. The film ends with Quinlan unwittingly confessing to a tape recorder. The two machines are uncannily similar in appearance—and also in effect, since the recorder in its own way destroys Quinlan as thoroughly as any bomb.

In between these two mechanical destroyers, other machines dominate the action. In the famous three-minute opening scene the camera follows the car but never allows a clear glimpse of the man and woman riding in it. When Susan Vargas stands on the hotel fire escape calling for help, the engine of Vargas's car drowns out her voice and he speeds unknowingly past her. Quinlan's car is his alter ego: it is big and fat (and Welles exaggerates its fatness with the wide-angle lens), and when it lurches across the quarrying site where the dynamite was stolen it translates Quinlan's lazy ruthlessness into action. In a way, Quinlan himself is a machine—he has lost nearly all of his human flexibility in order to become an efficient manufacturer of convicted criminals. In the final scene his voice is heard alternately from the radio pick-up and direct from his mouth, as if there were little difference between the two sources; while all around him the oil wells pump on and on in a monstrous parody of his obsession.

Though Quinlan is the only character who has succumbed to the temptation of being a machine, nearly everyone in the film is under pressure to do so. Action, dialogue, camera movement, and editing conspire to keep the film rolling onward with machine-like relentlessness. Characters are caught up in this tremendous momentum in much the same way that Joseph K is caught up in the legal labyrinth of *The Trial*: the important difference is that the momentum of *Touch of Evil* is not conveyed indirectly through fantasy but as a direct, tangible force.

A few of the characters avoid being caught up in the momentum—at a price. Tanya and the blind store woman choose to be bystanders in life. The night clerk at the motel is outraged to find himself in a situation that requires positive action. The scenes involving each of these three have an unexpected spaciousness that heightens the ruthless urgency of the rest of the film.

It is the character who accepts the greatest responsibility, Vargas, who runs the greatest risk of succumbing to the machines. The time bomb at the beginning of the film is in the hands of a murderer; the recorder at the end is in Vargas's hands. There is no doubt that Vargas is right to destroy Quinlan; but the film leaves the audience to wonder whether in so doing Vargas has begun to destroy himself.

I don't want to overpraise *Touch of Evil*. For all its richness it remains a thriller with a Hollywood hero.* But it does succeed superbly where *The Trial* fails—in revealing a nightmare world behind everyday reality.

Moreover, in *Touch of Evil* Welles is once again several years ahead of his time. It is only in the sixties that film-makers have really assimilated the effects of post-World War II technological development on everyday life. Before then technology was usually featured either as mere decor or (in its noisier and uglier manifestations) as the antithesis to a quiet upper-income semi-rural existence. Welles makes it an integral part of life, and though he also uses it to symbolize the temptation of evil he certainly does not present it as the cause. In this, *Touch of Evil* anticipates Truffaut's approach to gadgetry in *The Soft Skin* and, more indirectly Godard's in *The Married Woman*. It's also worth noting that a 1967 film like Furie's *The Naked Runner*, which links modern gadgetry to the amoral expedients of espionage, says nothing that *Touch of Evil* didn't say far better and far less pretentiously ten years before.

It may seem a measure of Welles's limitations that his Hollywood-made *Touch of Evil* is better than his independently made *Trial*. But his work resists easy generalizations. Each of his really outstanding films—*Kane, Ambersons, Othello*, and *Touch of Evil*, with *Falstaff* as a close runner-up—was made under very different conditions. If his most independent film is a failure, it may well be because he seized the opportunity to take bigger risks.

In every one of his films Welles has taken some kind of risk. He has always been willing to pit his recurring theme of lost innocence and his elemental symbolism against the explosive diversity of his other resources. His films depend for their success on a fine balance of all kinds of opposites—sophistication and simplicity, realism and expressionism; introversion and extroversion, clarity and confusion. And yet, with each film, he has rejected the cautiousness and calculation that could assure him of balance at the expense of richness and resonance. He himself has never lost all of the innocence with which he first tackled *Kane*.

Note

1. Welles's hand in *Journey*, officially directed by Norman Foster, is uncertain, and I have avoided citing any further examples from this film.

* Even though Charlton Heston plays Vargas well, the mere fact that he is a star suggests that Vargas is unequivocally in the right.

Citizen Kane

DAVID BORDWELL

T HE BEST way to understand *Citizen Kane* is to stop worshiping it as a triumph of technique. Too many people have pretended that Orson Welles was the first to use deep-focus, long takes, films-within-films, sound montage, and even ceilings on sets when these techniques were child's play for Griffith, Murnau, Renoir, Berkeley, Keaton, Hitchcock, Lang, and Clair. To locate *Kane*'s essential originality in its gimmicks cheapens it; once we know how the magician does his tricks, the show becomes a charade. *Kane* is a masterpiece not because of its tours de force, brilliant as they are, but because of the way those tours de force are controlled for large artistic ends. The glitter of the film's style reflects a dark and serious theme; *Kane*'s vision is as rich as its virtuosity.

The breadth of that vision remains as impressive today as thirty years ago. *Citizen Kane* straddles great opposites. It is at once a triumph of social comment and a landmark in cinematic surrealism. It treats subjects like love, power, class, money, friendship, and honesty with the seriousness of a European film; yet it never topples into pretentiousness, is at every instant as zestful, intelligent, and entertaining as the finest Hollywood pictures. It is both a pointed comedy of manners and a tragedy on a Renaissance scale. It has a Flaubertian finesse of detail and an Elizabethan grandeur of design. Extroverted and introspective, exuberant and solemn, *Kane* has become an archetypal film as boldly as Kane's career makes him an archetypal figure. "I am, always have been, and always will be only one thing—an American," he declares, and the contradictions in *Citizen Kane* echo those of an entire country. No wonder the film's original title was *American*: like the nation, the film and its protagonist hold contraries in fluid, fascinating suspension.

To unify such opposites, *Kane* draws together the two main strands of cinematic tradition. As both a mechanical recorder of events and a biased interpreter of the same events, cinema oscillates between the poles of objective realism and subjective vision. This tension, implicit in every film (and, as Pasolini points out, in every image), is at the heart of *Citizen Kane*. Faithful to the integrity of the external world, the film is simultaneously expressive of the processes of the imagination. As the ancestor of the works of Godard, Bergman, Fellini, Bresson, and Antonioni, *Kane* is a monument in the modern cinema, the cinema of consciousness.

Reprinted from *Film Comment* 7 (Summer 1971): 38–47.

Since Lumière, motion pictures have been attracted to the detailed reproduction of external reality. Still photography, the literary school of Naturalism, and the elaborate theatrical apparatus of the nineteenth century gave impetus to the documentary side of film. Thus most of the films made before 1940 reflect this sort of objective realism in their mise-en-scène. But running parallel to this documentary trend is a subjectivity that uses film to transform reality to suit the creator's imagination. From Méliès' theatrical stylization and cinematic sleight-of-hand come the distorted décor of *Caligari* and the camera experimentation of the European avant-garde.

This tandem line of development highlights the significance of Eisenstein in film aesthetics. He demonstrated that montage could assemble the raw data of the Lumière method in patterns which expressed the poetic imagination. Dialectical montage was an admission of the presence of artistic consciousness in a way that Griffith's "invisible" cutting was not. The audience was made aware of a creator's sensibility juxtaposing images to make a specific emotional or intellectual point. Eisenstein claimed to control montage of attractions "scientifically" (sometimes to the point of reducing metaphor to rebus), but after Eisenstein, a less didactic, more associational montage became a dominant poetic style of the avant-garde.

In its own way, *Citizen Kane* also recapitulates and extends film tradition. On a primary level, it makes sophisticated allusions to several genres: the detective thriller, the romance, the musical, the horror fantasy, the hard-boiled newspaper film, the big-business story, the newsreel, and the social-comment film. But *Kane* is more than an anthology. Testing the Lumière-Méliès tension, Welles, like Eisenstein, gives the cinema a new contemplative density by structuring his material on the nature of consciousness. What Eisenstein does between individual shots, Welles does in the film's total organization. *Kane*'s great achievement, then, is not its stylistic heel-clicking, but its rich fusion of an objective realism of texture with a subjective realism of structure. Welles opens a new area to the cinema because, like Eisenstein, he not only shows what we see, but he symbolizes the way we see it.

Kane explores the nature of consciousness chiefly by presenting various points of view on a shifting, multiplaned world. We enter Kane's consciousness as he dies, before we have even met him; he is less a character than a stylized image. Immediately, we view him as a public figure—fascinating but remote. Next we scrutinize him as a man, seen through the eyes of his wife and his associates, as a reporter traces his life story. Finally, these various perspectives are capped by a detached, omniscient one. In all, Kane emerges as a man—pathetic, grand, contradictory, ultimately enigmatic. The film expresses an ambiguous reality through formal devices that stress both the objectivity of fact and the subjectivity of point of view. It is because the best contemporary cinema has turned to the exploration of such a reality that *Kane* is, in a sense, the first modern American film.

The opening twelve minutes of *Citizen Kane* capsulize its approach and scope. At the very start, Welles uses a basic property of film to establish *Kane*'s method and pays homage to the two founts of cinema—the fantasy of Méliès and the reportage of Lumière.

The camera glides slowly up a fence. NO TRESPASSING, warns a sign. Immediately, the camera proceeds to trespass. It is a tingling moment, because the driving force of cinema is to trespass, to relentlessly investigate, to peel back what conceals and confront what reveals. "The camera," writes Pudovkin, "as it were, forces itself, ever striving, into the profoundest deeps of life; it strives thither to penetrate, whither the average spectator never reaches as he glances casually around him. The camera goes deeper." Cinema is a perfecting of vision because the eye of the camera, unlike that of the spectator, cannot be held back by fences or walls or signs; if anything interferes with the steady progress into the heart of a scene, we know it is an artificial and temporary obstacle. Thus it is this forward-cleaving movement, begun in *Kane*'s first scene, that is completed at the climactic track-in to the Rosebud sled.

Immediately, the imagery becomes dreamlike: a castle, a light snapped out and mysteriously glowing back to life, a man's lips, eerily sifting snow, a shattered crystal, a tiny cottage. Dissolves languidly link huge close-ups; space is obliterated; the paperweight smashes but makes no sound; a nurse enters, distorted in the reflection. We then see the deathbed dark against an arched window, and the shot fades out. The sequence is a reprise of the dream-structure of the European avant-garde films, especially *Caligari, Un Chien Andalou*, and *Blood of a Poet*. Welles celebrates the magic of Méliès and stresses, in both the content and the juxtaposition of the images, the subjective side of cinema.

But suddenly, in one of the most brilliant strokes in film, the "News on the March" sequence bursts on our eyes, history fills the screen, and we are confronted with the Lumière side of cinema, reality apparently unmanipulated. The stentorian announcer, the corny sensationalism, the *Time* style, and the histrionic music announce the newsreel's affinity with the popular *March of Time* shorts. (It is still the funniest parody of mass-media vulgarity ever filmed.) Furthermore, since each shot looks like period footage, "News on the March" virtually recapitulates the technical development of cinema from 1890 to 1941. Scratches on the emulsion, jerky movement, jump cuts, overexposures, handheld camerawork, insertion of authentic newsreel clips, the use of different filmstocks and cameras—each frame is historically persuasive. Glimpses of Chamberlain, Teddy Roosevelt, and Hitler are immediately and indelibly convincing. Thus as the first sequence had given us a private, poetic image of Kane, so this sequence supplies the public, documentary side of him. In clashing the two together, Welles immediately establishes the basic tension of *Kane* (and cinema itself): objective fact versus subjective vision, clearness and superficiality versus obscurity and profundity, newsreel versus dream. By making us question the very nature of experience, this clash of forms and styles produces the tension between reality and imagination that is the film's theme.

"News on the March" does more, though. Jumping, skittery, grainy, the sequence is the narrative hub of the film, the argument of the story, simultaneously running through Kane's life and outlining the story we are about to see. It builds our curiosity, plants a handful of clues, establishes the film's leaping, elliptical form, and, anticipating a major tendency of contemporary films, reminds the audience *à la* Brecht's "A-effect" that it is an audience and that it is watching a film.

Structurally, "News on the March" is the whole of *Citizen Kane* in miniature, a subliminal preparation for the narrative to come. It opens, as does the film proper, with shots of Xanadu—this time giving us detailed background information. Abruptly, Kane's death is referred to in the shots of pallbearers, and a montage swiftly reviewing Kane's wealth suggests the summarizing function that the newsreel itself serves in the entire film. Then we are shown two faded photographs, one of Kane beside his mother (hinting at the importance of their relationship) and another of Mrs. Kane's boarding house: these parallel the moment in Kane's childhood when his parents sent him away with Thatcher. That man himself is seen immediately, condemning Kane as "nothing more nor less than a Communist," suggesting his distrust of Kane, which is explored later in the film.

Instantly we are shuttled to Union Square, where a demagogue denounces Kane as a Fascist; and immediately Kane himself asserts that he is only an American. The quick linkage of these various opinions of Kane establishes the method of the film—a comparison of colliding viewpoints, the conflicting judgments that portray Kane and his life. Bernstein's story, primarily centering on Kane's journalistic career, is paralleled by the section, "1895 to 1941—All of these he covered, many of these he was." We see Kane's support of the Spanish-American war and Roosevelt's campaign, corresponding to the era presented in Bernstein's story.

The newsreel goes on to cover the material in Leland's narrative: Kane's marriage to Emily, his affair with Susan, and his political career. Then we see the 1929 closure of several Kane papers and Kane's trip abroad in 1935; these shots plug the gap between Leland's narrative and the final stage of Kane's life. Shots of Xanadu return and suggest Susan's narrative. Finally, glimpses of the old hermit on the grounds of his estate evoke the years of decay and loneliness which Raymond's story will verify later. The newsreel closes with the Times Square marquee: "Latest News—Charles Foster Kane is dead."

Thus in eight-and-a-half minutes and 121 shots, the entire progress of the ensuing film is mapped out and an enormous amount of information is given—about Kane, about the climate of the country, about the method of the film. Interestingly, this extraordinary device is prefigured in the "War of the Worlds" radio play, in which Welles and writer Howard Koch molded their narrative to the specific shape of the radio medium. At the beginning, a conventional music program is interrupted by a bulletin announcing a meteorite's landing; the music show resumes, to be cut off again by an on-the-scene-report, and so on. This device made the fantastic plot plausible enough to jam highways with fleeing listeners. Just as "The War of the Worlds" mimicked the form of radio broadcasting to persuade its audience of a Martian invasion, "News on the March" imitates the uniquely cinematic form of the newsreel to corroborate the existence of Charles Foster Kane.

We accept the newsreel's argument too quickly, though. Welles immediately points out that the Kane of "News on the March" is literally only an image. The newsreel's final fanfare is abruptly cut off, the screen goes blank, and we are yanked into the screening room, where we are privy to the shadowy manipulations of 1940 media-men. Their talk dispells the hypnotic authority of the newsreel, reminding us that facts are not the truth, that data can be shuffled in any order. One side of us shares the boss's demand for a key that will impose a pattern on life; the other side suspects that life will not submit to tidy arrangement. Objective fact invites subjective interpretation, and several such interpretations will be supplied in the rest of the film.

Henry James described the structure of *The Awkward Age* as "a circle consisting of a number of small rounds disposed at equal distance around a central object. The central object was my situation . . . and the small rounds represented so many distinct lamps . . . the function of each of which would be to light with due intensity one of its aspects . . ." If we substitute "character" for "situation," we have a good description of the structure of *Citizen Kane*. The film is like one of Susan's jigsaw puzzles; each piece contributes something essential, but some pieces are missing.

Two parts of *Kane*'s structure act as summations. The first, the "News on the March" sequence, maps out the course the film will take. But by the end of the film, the personality depicted in the newsreel has been reduced to mere objects. The second summation, the final scene in Xanadu, balances "News on the March." We already know Kane's life story, but Welles gives us a reprise—the piano Susan played, the "Welcome Home" loving cup, the statuary, the bed from the *Inquirer* office, the stove in Mrs. Kane's boarding house. The camera tracks ominously over these from the most recent to the most remote, backwards through Kane's life, to settle on the symbol of his childhood: the Rosebud sled. The uninterrupted flow of this extravagant sequence reassembles the life that has been presented in so fragmented a fashion.

Between these two summations the film rests. Told from the viewpoints of five different people, the movie uses the thread of the reporter Thompson's search for the meaning of Rosebud to stitch the stories together. The sections are for the most part chronological and overlapping; with the exception of Thatcher, each narrator begins his story a little before his predecessor ended and carries it past the point from which the next narrator will begin. Some events, then—such as Susan's rise and fall as an opera singer—are shown twice, but from different perspectives.

Kane's multiple-viewpoint form has a simpler but startling antecedent in William K. Howard's *The Power and the Glory* (1933). In that film, after the burial of Thomas Garner, a railroad tycoon, his story is told by Henry, his best friend—but not in chronological order. When Henry's wife makes an accusation against Garner, he counters with a remembered incident in Garner's defense. As a result, chronology is violated—a scene of Garner ruling his board of directors precedes a scene of young, illiterate Garner working as a track layer—and we are shown the play of conflicting opinion surrounding a famous man's career. Like Kane, Garner is a grand figure, both loved and hated, and Henry is qualified to reveal the private side of a public man. Scripted by Preston Sturges from an original idea, *The Power and the Glory* remains a daring experiment in the narrative method Welles and Herman Mankiewicz would refine.

But Welles brought to *Kane* his own special interest in point of view. His first, never-realized project for RKO was to be Conrad's *Heart of Darkness*, in which the narrator Marlow was not seen on screen. It may not be too much to see in this the genesis of the moral complexity Welles infuses into *Kane*'s subjective points of view. "I believe it is necessary to give all the characters their best arguments," he has remarked, ". . . including those I disagree with."

But *Kane* should not be seen as a *Rashomon*-like exploration of the relativity of fact. At no point does Welles suggest that Kane's story is being distorted, wilfully or unconsciously, by any narrator. In fact, we are sometimes made to feel quite differently from the narrator (as in Thatcher's and Leland's narratives) and the narrator's presence is so little stressed during each segment that sometimes scenes are included which the narrators were not present to witness. There is thus no doubt about the *facts* which are revealed.

The film's complexity arises from the narrator's conflicting *judgments*, their summing-ups of Kane. Each one sees a different side of him at a different stage of his life, yet each takes his estimate of Kane as definitive. To Thatcher, Kane is an arrogant smart aleck who became "nothing more nor less than a Communist." Bernstein's Kane is a man of high principles, with a sharp business sense and a love of the common man. Leland's Kane, only "in love with himself," is a man of no convictions, a betrayer of the masses. Susan sees Kane (in imagery that recalls Caligari and Svengali) as a selfish but piteous old man. And Raymond's story of Kane as a lonely hermit betrays the cold detachment of his own nature. Each narrator judges Kane differently, and each judgment leaves out something essential. As T. S. Eliot puts it in *The Confidential Clerk*: "There's always something one's ignorant of about anyone, however well one knows him: And that may be something of the greatest importance."

The effect of seeing so many conflicting assessments is to restrain us from forming any opinions of Kane we might take as definitive. As each character tells his story, the reporter's search for an accurate judgment is taken up by the audience as well. Thompson, whose face we never see, is a surrogate for us; his job—voyeuristic and prying, yet ultimately disinterested and detached—is the perfect vehicle for the curiosity without consequences that film uniquely gratifies. The more we see of Kane, the harder it becomes to judge him; understanding passes beyond praise or condemnation. This complex frame of mind in the audience is central to much of contemporary cinema, from *Vertigo* to *La Chinoise*, and is a major source of *Kane*'s originality. Its multiple-narration structure warns us not to look for conventional signals of recognition and resolution. A film that opens and closes with NO TRESPASSING and that completes its dialogue with "I don't think that any word can explain a man's life" suggests that the authors mean no simple judgment can be final. The portrait of Kane that has emerged is contradictory and ambiguous. "The point of the picture," Welles has remarked, "is not so much the solution of the problem as its presentation."

The problem may have no solution but it does have a meaning. The structure of the film, while discouraging easy judgments, leads us down a path of widening insight. The newsreel surveys Kane's public career but does not penetrate to his soul. Thatcher's narrative offers us our first clue, hinting at matters of love, childhood, and innocence. Bernstein's story renders Kane sympathetically, suggesting that Rosebud may be "something he lost." Leland's narrative prickles with his urge to puncture Kane's reputation, but his invective doesn't obscure a further clue: "All he ever wanted was love." Finally, Susan's narrative demonstrates that Kane bought love from others because he had no love of his own to give. Thus we are led, step by step, to confront an ego bent on domination; like Elizabethan tragedy, the film proposes that action becomes an egotistical drive for power when not informed by love.

Love is the key to *Kane* and Kane. Sent from home as a child, raised by the cold Thatcher, Kane lost forever the love symbolized by the Rosebud sled and the snowstorm paperweight containing that little cottage that resembles his mother's boarding house. The sled isn't really the cheap

Freud some (including Welles) have claimed; although it stands for the affection Kane lost when he was wrenched into Thatcher's world, the sled is clearly not to be taken as the "solution" of the film. It is only one piece of the jigsaw puzzle, "something he couldn't get or something he lost." The Rosebud sled solves the problem that Thompson was set—"A dying man's last words should explain his life"—but by the end Thompson realizes that the problem was a false one: "I don't think that any word can explain a man's life." The appearance of the sled presents another perspective on Kane, but it doesn't "explain" him. His inner self remains inviolate (NO TRESPASSING) and enigmatic. The last shots of the sign and of Xanadu restore a grandeur to Kane's life, a dignity born of the essential impenetrability of human character.

Part of Kane's love problem is bound up with his mother. Hinted at throughout, this is made explicit in the scene in which Kane, having just met Susan, talks with her in her room. Here, for the first time in a character's narrative, the snowstorm paperweight is seen—on Susan's dressing table, among faded childhood snapshots. Kane tells her he had been on his way to a warehouse "in search of my youth," intending to go through his dead mother's belongings: "You know, sort of a sentimental journey." But now, with Susan's reflection behind the paperweight, he decides to remain here; all the elements are present for a symbolic transfer of Kane's love to this new mother figure. And when Susan tells him that her desire to sing was really her mother's idea, the transfer is complete. Kane quietly agrees that he knows how mothers are.

Kane seeks love from anyone—Leland, Bernstein, Emily, Susan, "the people of this state"—but the film traces a growing-apart, through imagery of separation, as Kane's life, from the moment he leaves home, becomes haunted by lovelessness. His relations with his wives typify this: the intimacy of the honeymoon supper yields to the distance of the long breakfast table and, eventually, to husband and wife shouting across the halls of Xanadu. The movement is from crowdedness (the busy *Inquirer* office) to emptiness (the hollow vaults of Xanadu); from cheerfulness (Kane as a young editor) to despair (after Susan has left); from true friendship (Bernstein and Leland) through gradually materialistic relationships (Emily and Susan) to sheerly mercenary companionship (Raymond); from a quick tempo (the liveliness of the *Inquirer*'s crusades) to a funereal one (the picnic cortege and Kane's final, deadened walk); from self-sacrifice to selfishness; from the brash openness of youth to the cancerous privacy of NO TRESPASSING, from intimate joking with Leland to shouts in a mausoleum and long silences before a huge fireplace. Kane's degeneration parallels these shifts in relationships: his contacts with people slough off in proportion to the accumulation of his material goods until, solitary and friendless, only cherishing a cheap snowstorm paperweight, he is engulfed by infinite extensions of his ego.

In the central portion of *Citizen Kane*, then, the various points of view balance the stream of consciousness of the opening and the detachment of "News on the March." Charles Foster Kane is observed from various angles, making the film more kaleidoscopic portrait than straightforward plot. But the matter is complicated because Kane's character changes with time, as does that of each narrator. Thus the clash of fact and bias, objectivity and prejudice, interweaving through the history of a personality, creates a world that is nearly as complex as reality and yet as unified as great art.

That complexity and unity are achieved in large part by the use of symbolic motifs, which both reinforce the realism of the milieu and accent the subjective flow of the narrative.

Whiteness, for instance, takes on strong symbolic associations. From the beginning, the white window of Kane's castle is a focal point toward which our eye is relentlessly drawn. The white of the window dissolves to the snow in the paperweight. Later, the white of Thatcher's manuscript dissolves to the whiteness of Kane's winter childhood days. The beloved sled is covered slowly by snow at the end of that winter scene; cut to the whiteness of a package wrapping as Charles receives a new sled from Thatcher. Bernstein tells his story of a girl dressed in white, with a white parasol: "Do you know, I bet there hasn't been a single month when I haven't thought of that girl." White suggests a lost love and innocence—"something he couldn't get or something he lost"—but it is also the color of death. The cold whiteness of the marble and alabaster of Xanadu contrasts ironically with the nostalgic warmth of the whiteness of Kane's childhood, and the women in his life—Emily and the blonde Susan, both of whom are first seen dressed in white—have given way to the professional nurse in her white uniform.

Accompanying the whiteness motif is that of the snowstorm paperweight, first seen as it falls from the hand of the dead Kane and smashes on the floor. The paperweight enters Kane's life in that crucial scene in Susan's apartment on the night he first meets her. Later, on the morning after Susan's premiere, the paperweight can be glimpsed on the mantelpiece, but no attention is called to it. We see it for the last time when Kane, after wrecking Susan's room, stumbles up to it, clutches it, and mutters, "Rosebud." Thus the paperweight links three crucial scenes in the Kane-Susan-relationship, in the meantime becoming a symbol of Kane's lost childhood. Kane's treasuring of the paperweight suggests that it recalls both the night he first met Susan and the day he lost his innocence.

In making a film about a man possessed by an overriding egotism, Welles uses acting and dialogue to suggest the legend that the character fabricates around himself. But he also embodies Kane's myth in arresting visual symbols. Xanadu is the primary one: decaying, uncompleted, hollow, filled with objects and empty of love, it embodies the grandeur and tragic shortsightedness of Kane's vision. Its name suggests he is "Kubla-

Kane"; Xanadu is indeed "a sunny pleasure dome with caves of ice." *Kubla Khan* and *Citizen Kane* are both about the recreation of reality by the Imagination; like Coleridge's narrator, Kane tries to incarnate his vision of "a damsel with a dulcimer." The process works for Coleridge and Welles, and the result is "a miracle of rare device"; it fails for Kane, and "the pool becomes a mirror."

Thus the vault of mirrors that encases the aged Kane at the end of the film is the culmination of the K-images which enclose him throughout. A K surmounts the gates of Xanadu, and is carved in ice at the *Inquirer* party, wrought in metal as a stickpin, sewn in gilt monogram on a bathrobe, and stitched into campaign ribbons. Even Kane's son is seen only as a miniature version of his father. The name, in itself harsh, crisp, and powerful, is constantly pounding at the spectator, from the first sight of the screen-filling title to the final shot of Xanadu with the K gate looming in the foreground. Welles utilizes every chance to flood the screen with a picture of a man filled with his own importance.

Welles also uses musical allusions and motifs to make thematic points. For example, Susan's singing "Una voce poco fa" from *The Barber of Seville* economically evokes the play's themes of youth imprisoned by age and of the abuse of personal authority. Another example is the recurring tune, "It Can't Be Love." Sung at Kane's Everglades picnic, its melody is heard earlier as a mournful piano version in the two scenes with Susan at the nightclub. The repetition ironically links three bleak scenes.

One could trace other motifs: Bernstein in front of a small fireplace over which hangs a portrait of Kane—Kane in front of a larger fireplace on the morning after Susan's premiere—Kane in front of the colossal fireplace at Xanadu; the repeated associations of Susan and rain; the waltz music accompanying Kane's return from Europe which is heard again, mockingly, in the breakfast-table sequence; the movement from the chilliness of the opening to the blazing furnace of the finale. Each detail, entirely realistic in itself, gathers meaning and force as a symbol.

By now it should be clear that *Kane*'s stylistic pyrotechnics are not just meaningless virtuosity, but rather aural and pictorial expressions of the tension between reality and imagination at the heart of the film. Objectively, the wide-angle lens renders every plane of a shot, from the nearest to the most distant, in sharp focus. Thus there is no stressing of one image by throwing its context out of focus; ambiguity increases when all characters and objects are equal in definition. As André Bazin puts it, "The uncertainty in which we find ourselves as to the spiritual key or interpretation we should put on the film is built into the very design of the image." There are scarcely a dozen true closeups in the film, and most appear at the very beginning, as an abstract procession of images which contrasts with the spatial authenticity of the rest of the film. Montage, which stresses the juxtaposition of images more than the images themselves, always implies the shaping hand of a creator, but the compression of multiple meanings into one shot can seem to efface the director, giving the illusion of unarranged reality. Thus the compositional detachment of each shot corroborates the film's pull toward realism.

Keeping all the action in the frame may suggest a kind of objectivity, but camera angle belies the detachment by expressing attitudes toward the action. For instance, when Kane is a child, the viewpoint is usually that of the adult looking down. But as Kane's career progresses, he is often shot from an increasingly low angle, not only to indicate his growing power but also to isolate him against his background as he becomes more and more lonely. In Xanadu, though, Kane is again seen from a high angle which points out his smallness within the cavernous crypt he has erected. Within the objectivity of the single frame, Welles' angles (unlike, say, Hawks') suggest subjective bias and point of view.

Welles' *mise-en-scène* modulates the drama's flow with great subtlety, using angle to indicate patterns of domination. Recall the climactic scene when Kane confronts Boss Jim Gettys in Susan's apartment. Gettys' entrance is as thunderous as a kettledrum roll: Kane, Emily, and Susan are on the staircase, light is pouring out of the doorway, and quietly Gettys' silhouette steps into the shot; for once someone has the upper hand over Kane; Nemesis has caught up with the hero. (In Welles' *Macbeth*, Macduff storms out of a smoking beam of light on a similar mission.) Inside Susan's bedroom, the angles crisply build the tension. First, a shot frames Emily in the foreground, Susan in the middle ground, and Gettys and Kane facing each other deep in the shot. But as Gettys explains the power he has over Kane, he advances to the foreground, dwarfing his rival; Emily says that apparently Kane's decision has been made for him; Kane, in the distance, seems overpowered by circumstance. But when Kane decides to assert his will, the shot cuts to an opposite angle: he dominates the foreground, and Gettys, Susan, and Emily taper off into the background. Then, a head-on shot, with Kane in the center, Susan on the left, and Gettys on the right, capsulizes his choice: he can save his mistress or fight his opponent. Welles' arrangement of actors in the frame and his timing of the cuts brilliantly articulate the drama of the scene. The material seems to be objectively observed (no close-ups or first-person points of view), but the structure of each shot and the pacing of the editing inject subjective attitudes.

Welles can also use the moving camera to efface the director's controlling hand by choreographing the material in fluid, unobtrusive patterns. Take, for instance, the scene in which the boy Charles is sent from home. (1) In long-shot we see the boy playing in the snow. (2) A snowball hits the sign over the porch. (3) The camera travels back from the boy in the snow through the window as his mother closes it, and back from her, Thatcher, and Mr. Kane as they advance to the desk, where the papers are read and signed; the camera then follows them back to the window. (4)

We are now outside the window, and after the camera travels back to the snowman and Charles, the scuffle between the boy and Thatcher takes place in the same shot. (5) A close-up of Charles and his mother closes the scene. In a sequence of several minutes, we have five shots, two of negligible length. Yet the shots seem realistically observed because Welles has intricately moved his actors and his camera; despite the complexity of the set-ups, we gain a sense of a reality—actual, unmanipulated, all of a piece.

Yet the moving camera can suggest the drift of subjective interest too, because it is also a tool of discovery. Again and again the camera probes like an inquisitive reporter, nosing relentlessly to the center of a scene, gradually stripping away extraneous dramatic matter. Welles' tracking shots imitate the process of investigation itself—a gradual narrowing of the field of inquiry—so that the progress *inward*, toward the heart of a mystery, becomes the characteristic camera movement. The opening dissolves which draw us deeper into Xanadu; the slow dolly up to the flashing "El Rancho" roof sign and then between the letters to the skylight; the imperceptible closing in on Bernstein as he begins his narrative; the diagonal descent to Susan and Kane meeting on the street; the sudden, curious rush to Susan's door when Kane shuts it; the traveling shot over the heads of the audience at Kane's speech; the implacable track to Kane and Emily standing at the door of Susan's house—all these are preparations for the portentous tracking shots through the costly rubbish of Xanadu, coasting slowly over Kane's belongings to settle on the Rosebud sled—the answer to the quest.

Welles' use of sound is indebted, intentionally or not, to Lang's *M* and Clair's *A Nous La Liberté*. In the latter film, a policeman outdoors saying, "We must all—" cuts to a teacher in a classroom saying, "—work." Welles called these "lightning mixes," in which the sound continues (although from a different source) while the scene cuts or dissolves to a new locale and time. A shot of Susan at the piano in her shabby rooming house dissolves to a shot of her, much better-dressed, at a finer piano in a more elegant house, while she continues to play the same piece. Kane's applause immediately dissolves to a crowd's applause of Leland's harangue. Thatcher says to the child Kane, "Merry Christmas, Charles," the boy answers, "Merry Christmas—" and the story leaps ahead seventeen years to Thatcher saying, "And a Happy New Year." Leland's promise to a street crowd that "Charles Foster Kane . . . entered upon this campaign—" cuts to Kane himself in a huge auditorium bellowing, "—with one purpose only . . ." Scenes Eisenstein would have linked by visual metaphor Welles links by the soundtrack. Eisenstein would have announced the presence of a manipulating directorial intelligence, while Welles suggests the interlocked imagery of mental-association processes.

We should not overlook Welles' celebrated *tours de force*, those moments of sheer cinematic pluck that everyone cherishes in *Kane*. When

Kane, Leland, and Bernstein peer in the *Chronicle* window, the camera moves up to the picture of the *Chronicle* staff until it fills the screen; Kane's voice says, "Six years ago I looked at a picture of the world's greatest newspaper staff . . ." and he strides out in front of the same men, posed for an identical picture, a flashbulb explodes, and we are at the *Inquirer* party. Another famous setpiece is the breakfast-table sequence, in which the deterioration of Kane's marriage is traced in a number of brief scenes linked by a whirling effect (swish pans over the windows of the *Inquirer* building). The music pulsates in the background, rising in tension, and the mounting pace of the cutting gives impetus to the final surprises: Mrs. Kane reading the *Chronicle* and the length of the breakfast table.

These, then, are the techniques Welles drew on in *Kane*. Exciting in themselves, they coalesce into a unified style by expressing the film's juxtaposition of reality and imagination. The spatial and temporal unity of the deep focus, the simultaneous dialogue, the reflections and chiaroscuro, the detached use of the moving camera, the intrusion of sounds from outside the frame—all increase the objectively realistic effect. These are correlatives for the way we seem to see and hear in life. The inquisitive camera movements, the angled compositions, the "lightning mixes" of sound and image—these suggest subjective attitudes and the workings of narrators' memories. They are stylistic equivalents for the way we seem to channel our thoughts in life. The cinematic traditions of Lumière and Méliès become surrogates for an epistemological tension. Here are the facts; here are subjective interpretations. Alone, neither has value. Can we then ever know "the" truth? Thompson's final remark "I don't think any word can explain a man's life," the enigma of the Rosebud sled, NO TRESPASSING, the black smoke drifting into a gray sky—these, finally, unmistakably, convey the film's answer.

At bottom, the film's reality/imagination tension radiates from the hero's own nature. *Citizen Kane* is a tragedy on Marlovian lines, the story of the rise and fall of an overreacher. Like Tamburlaine and Faustus, Kane dares to test the limits of mortal power; like them, he fabricates endless *personae* which he takes as identical with his true self; and, like them, he is a victim of the egotism of his own imagination.

Up to a point, Kane's career rises steadily. He is a rich, successful publisher, he has married well, he has a chance to become governor. But his flaw is that he sees love solely in terms of power. His friends, Leland and Bernstein, are also his employees; his wife Emily is the President's niece. He expands his idea of love to include "the people," his aspiration to public office is a confirmation of his confusion of love with power. Thus his liaison with Susan (whom he calls "a cross-section of the American public") represents the pathetic side of his desire, the need for affection which his mother aroused and which Emily could not gratify. Ironically, it is this weakness which undoes him, for in the end, Kane's immense vision of love as power falls tragically short of basic humanity.

The turning point of Kane's life is the confrontation with Gettys in Susan's room. It is the climax of his personal life (Emily or Susan, which will he choose?) and of his political career (the love of "the people" or the love of his family and mistress?). Surprisingly, Gettys turns out to be more sensitive and humane than Kane. He was led to blackmail Kane by the newspaper cartoons Kane printed of him, which humiliated him before his children and, significantly, his mother. Unlike Kane, Gettys distinguishes between attacking a man personally and attacking him politically; thus he gives Kane a chance ("more of a chance than he'd give me") to avoid personal embarrassment. Gettys assumes that Kane places the same value on personal relations that he does.

He is wrong. Up till now Kane has always defined himself by telling others what to do, by bossing Mr. Carter, Leland, Bernstein, Emily, and Susan. Now morality demands that Kane give in and for once define himself by placing others' welfare above his own. But Kane cannot relinquish the role of an autonomous power: "There's only one person who's going to decide what I'm going to do, and that's me." It is the voice of the bully, but also that of the tragic hero. By sacrificing others to his delusion of moral omnipotence, Kane commits his energy to an idea of himself that has become divorced from human values. How can he accept "the love of the people of this state" when he will not show love for his family and mistress? This refusal of imagination to recognize reality constitutes tragic recklessness, but Kane's punishment brings no recognition. Gettys is prophetic: "You're gonna need more than one lesson, and you're gonna get more than one lesson."

After his defeat at the polls, Kane's career declines. His image shattered, he constructs a new one: Susan's singing career. He announces, "*We're* going to be a great opera star"; as his alter ego, she may find the public acclaim in art that he couldn't find in politics. At the opera, Kane in the balcony dwarfs the tiny Susan onstage like a harsh god overseeing his creation. From singing lesson to opera rehearsal, Susan is not an identity in her own right, only an extension of himself. But again Kane fails to win the love of "the people"; the public's response to Susan's premiere is symbolized by the judicious grimace of the stagehand high in the flies. So, when Susan attempts suicide, Kane must change his *persona* again.

The next image Kane constructs is on a mammoth scale. He builds Xanadu, a miniature world, which he stocks with every kind of animal. This parody of God's act of creation gives a blasphemous dimension to Faustus-Kane's galactic vision of power. Yet in the end this god is swallowed up by his own universe. Since he can breathe no life into his creations, he gradually becomes an object like them. Appropriately, the last time we see Kane is as an *image*: a zombie moving stiffly against an end-lessly receding tunnel of mirrors, mocking duplications of his own self-absorption. Dying, he can only clutch the icon of love and innocence: his last moment becomes a final assertion of imagination in the face of the ultimate reality of death.

Kane may not be able to reconcile the tragic discord between his inner vision and the outer world, but Welles' creative imagination is larger than Kane's sterile one. The conflicts we noted at the start—between social realism and surrealism, tragic seriousness and comic high spirits, rich detail and complex superstructure—are contained by Welles' broad vision of aspiration and waste.

To my way of thinking, that vision was not permitted utmost scope again until 1965, when Welles completed *Chimes at Midnight*. He has called Falstaff "the most completely good man in all drama," but the film's hero is far from the sentimentalized sack of guts of a (happily, dying) criti-cal tradition. Like Kane, Falstaff is admirable because of his appetite and his imagination, but his fall is observed with no less objectivity. Welles (and Shakespeare) have it both ways: Falstaff is both the Pan of mythology and the Vice of the morality plays, and Prince Hal may love him but he must reject him.

Chimes at Midnight is as morally complex as *Citizen Kane*, but here cinematic traditions are not analogues for epistemological modes. *Chimes'* style and form are translucent, like *The Immortal Story*'s, but without that later effort's crude parody of the reality/imagination theme. In *Chimes at Midnight*, Welles concentrates straightforwardly on a set of characters sym-bolizing the alternatives surrounding the problem that obsessed Kane: the connection between personal and political power.

Prince Hal must choose among three ways of life—that of king, warrior, and roisterer—as represented by his father King Henry IV, his distorted mirror-image Hotspur, and his adopted father Falstaff. Henry, though regal and commanding, struck in a chilly shaft of light that suggests divine authority, is nonetheless aloof and solitary, entombed in cold gray stone. Hotspur is vigorous and manly, but also crude, hotheaded, and notably solitary. Falstaff is a vulgar buffoon, but he inhabits a glowing world of comradely merrymaking. The three worlds rotate on the same axis: Falstaff lives by robbing, Henry has usurped the throne, and Hotspur seeks to steal the crown from Henry. By a music motif (Henry summons musicians to salve his illness, Hotspur's trumpeters blast pompously and phallically while he ignores the blandishments of his lovely wife, and Falstaff calls for music to ease his melancholy), Welles suggests that each way of life has become sterile. The whole of medieval England—king, fighter, and déclassé—is sick, barren, dying.

Hal, man of the Renaissance, becomes almost cynically adept in all three worlds. He bests Falstaff at thieving and lying; he wins his father's respect by stately eloquence; and he vanquishes Hotspur in battle. Supreme in all three arenas, Hal becomes their synthesis. Like the sun he compares himself to, he is a source of the power that will revivify England.

Still, he cannot live permanently divided. He must choose among the court, the battlefield, and the tavern. Since possessing the crown permits him to legislate his wisdom in the other areas, he must sooner or later renounce his dissolute life, which comes down to renouncing Falstaff. Hal's "I know you all" speech is a soliloquy in the original play, but Welles makes it Hal's direct warning to Falstaff. Henceforth, fat Jack should expect to be abandoned. And when, in the comic crowning scene at the Boar's Head, Falstaff begs not to be forgotten—"Banish plump Jack and banish all the world"—Prince Hal reminds him of his fate in a reply that reverberates like a thunderclap: "I do, I will."

Since *Chimes at Midnight*, like *Kane*, is about personal and political authority, Welles again creates the drama of power within the shot by means of camera angle. When, at Justice Shallow's house, Falstaff has been meditating on his death, a deep shot shows Falstaff sitting stonily in the distance, for once positively miniscule. Pistol bursts in to announce Henry's death, and suddenly Falstaff lumbers into the foreground, filling the frame, towering like a colossus as he gasps, "What? . . . Is the old king—*dead*?" The shot depicts his vision of the power he has dreamed of. But after the coronation and Hal's repudiation of him, in which angle shots have expressed the new king's sovereignty over his former companion, Falstaff leaves Shallow, walking off into a distant corridor—like Kane, dwarfed by real forces his imagination could not control.

Welles' imagination, though, is large enough to make great art of his heroes' defeats. Joseph McBride has argued that Hal's rejection of Falstaff and his declaration of war with France label him a villain and Falstaff a victim. This underestimates Welles' irony. Hal is a practical politician. Like Kane, he must eventually choose between political and personal virtue, but (more sensitively than Kane), Hal struggles to keep them distinct, publicly humiliating Falstaff only to aid him privately later. Hal will mock him with Poins, but he will hide him when the king's men come. He will burlesque him before the tavern crowd, but he will give him a post in his army. And even after the rebuff at the coronation, Hal privately (in an inserted text from *Henry V* that originally did not refer to Falstaff) orders his counselors to "enlarge" (!) Falstaff: "If little faults, proceeding on distemper / Shall not be winked at, how shall we stretch our eye / When capital crimes, chewed, swallowed, and digested / Appear before us?" He tempers the inevitable wickedness of his repudiation with a measure of regal mercy. Welles sees public ethical problems as private ones writ large, yet between the two is an irreconcilable tragic tension. Nym summarizes the complexity of the problem as Falstaff lies dying: "The King is a good King. But it must be as it may."

Thus the final words from Holinshed, ". . . and so human withal that he left no offence unpunished, nor friendship unrewarded," reverberating over the shot of Falstaff's coffin, constitute not a sarcastic dig but a sublime irony. *Chimes at Midnight*, like *Citizen Kane*, shows both sides—public good and private misery, heroic ambition and tragic necessity, pragmatic reality and alluring imagination—sympathizing with each but, finally, presenting both honestly. The irony is the richest and most basic one of man's experience, so vast that usually we must split it into tragedy and comedy. That Welles art is able to serenely contain and transcend both might be the final estimate of his genius.

Orson Welles's Use of Sound

PHYLLIS GOLDFARB

SOUND AND space are immutably related, whether they complement one another or, as is often the case in the movies of Orson Welles, they conflict. Welles's early films, especially *Citizen Kane*, were remarkable for the way in which sound was used to elongate space. The screen was forced to give up part of the flatness of its nature. In later films, sound is put to a variety of uses, not the least of which is a negation of reality. What we hear no longer works in conjunction with what we see. Eisenstein might have called it harmonized counterpoint. The sound is temporally synchronized with its source, but at the same time mismatched—not in terms of direction (since, in most theaters, there is a single loudspeaker), but of distance and surroundings. As a result, there is a tension created between the space and the sound, between our aural and visual perceptions. If this tension remains unresolved, a partial fragmenting of our senses takes place. Sound becomes disembodied and takes on a force and presence of its own.

Every time a movie is projected on a screen in front of us, we relinquish part of the power we have over our psyches. The narrative film invites us to participate in a fantasy, and to a certain extent we always do. The creative artist is able to take advantage of the vulnerable position in which the moving picture medium places its audience, in order to present a previously unavailable experience. Orson Welles is such an artist. He gains control over our ability to organize the barrage of stimuli that is constantly assaulting us. A careful study of *Citizen Kane*, *The Magnificent Ambersons*, *Lady from Shanghai* and *Touch of Evil* reveals a progression toward manipulation of the viewer's powers of concentration, his visual and aural perception, and disorientation of his spacial and temporal organization.

If there is a progression toward fragmentation and disorientation in these four films of Welles, it is not to be found within the narratives; in these four movies the narratives move away from fragmentation, toward consolidation in terms of time, place and structure. *Kane* moves forward and backward through time and space; it covers perhaps three generations. While *The Magnificent Ambersons* is composed of a number of moments just before and during Georgie Amberson's life, with an extended examination of one experience (his reaction to the Morgans), the narrative is limited to forward movement in time, and the action takes place within the perimeters of one city. The geographic area covered in *Lady*

From *Take One* 3 (July/August 1971): 10–14.

from Shanghai is quite extensive, but in a dramatic sense the narrative movement is more limited than it would be if it took place within the confines of a small town. The drama's settings are forced upon the hero—first as an employee, then as a prisoner. He doesn't have the freedom that Georgie and Kane are allowed. In addition, temporal and structural elements are incontestably consolidated. There is a beginning, a middle, an end, a climax and a denouement—all of which take place within one year. Finally, *Touch of Evil* is the most compact of all. Its narrative is so tightly interconnected it unravels rather than unfolds. It is wholly contained within a 24-hour period, and all the action takes place around one point on the Mexican-American border.

Disorientation is accomplished not within the narrative structures of the films, but by fragmentation of our perceptions and manipulation of our responses. In order to understand how this comes about, it is necessary to have a clear conception of the role that sound plays in film, and of the processes of aural perception.

There are three basic classes (or "uses") of cinematic sound: spacial sound, ideational sound, and music. Everything we hear falls into one of these categories—or is a combination of two or three.

Spacial sounds obey the laws of real sound. Our ears place the source of the sound within space. We're not limited, aurally, as we are visually by the flat screen. If the soundtrack of a movie accurately conforms to the behavior of natural sound in space, we receive aural cues with which we can determine the surroundings, direction and distance of the sound source. This results in a definition of space.

Surroundings are determined by volume and quality of sound. For example, a sound made and heard in a closet full of clothing will be appreciably different in quality from the identical sound made in a cave. Compare the quality of Kane's voice in the halls of Xanadu to that of his voice in the car on the way to the picnic. The reason for this is that various objects absorb and reflect different amounts and frequencies of sound. It follows, then, that sound heard from inside a room won't register exactly like the same sound heard from the other side of a glass partition, or a closed door—a variation Welles carefully manipulates when Quinlan enters the hotel room to strangle Joe Grandi in *Touch of Evil*.

The reason I have concerned myself with something that seems so obvious is that when this factor is ignored, or purposely used to distort the duplication of real sound, the mismatch makes us vaguely uncomfortable, slightly dislocated, usually without knowing why. The reaction is very subtle. A sort of floating tension is created which can be used, by the filmmaker, in directing audience response. Welles uses this device, in *Lady from Shanghai* and *Touch of Evil*, but leaves the tension unresolved. The voices in the post-explosion confusion in *Touch of Evil*, for example, sound as if they were being emitted within a confined area, but the scene takes place in the open air. The disembodied quality of the voices sets a pattern that is reinforced throughout the movie. It has the effect of partially disorganizing our perceptions: the visuals and aurals don't fit.

Direction is understood biaurally. Our ears are incredibly sensitive: we can detect a time difference between the two ears, if the onset of the sound is sharp, of 0.65 milliseconds. This, coupled with the minute difference in volume due to the sound shadow the head casts, and one ear catching the sound wave at a different point in its compression-rarefaction phases, accounts for the accuracy with which we can determine direction. Unfortunately, the closest we can come to experiencing it in the cinema (a monaural medium) is by interpreting visual cues. We know where a voice is coming from because we see the speaker's lips moving. If the source of sound is outside our visual field, we follow the gaze or reaction of a character on the screen.

Distancing is the one aural space-defining factor that all filmmakers are aware of. Amplitude (or loudness) increases as the source of sound moves toward us, but because there are so many variables in sound production, and because of our poor aural storage and/or retrieval systems, we aren't able to make more than a crude approximation of absolute distance. That's why movies, which have dialogue varying from close-up to medium shot, don't expend much effort modulating the volume as the camera, or characters, move.

Sound, then, opens up and makes us aware of space. The accurate and creative use of volume alone has the effect of giving depth to the flat screen image. Using sound in this way is one of the most impressive innovations of *Citizen Kane* and is also prominent in *Magnificent Ambersons*. There may be no scene in the history of film that is more two-dimensional than the good-bye at the train station between Georgie Amberson and his uncle. Visually, we perceive depth on a flat surface by certain cues—such as lines diminishing to a vanishing point, objects in the distance getting smaller, objects cut off by others in front of them, etc. In this scene, with the two men surrounded by mist, there are no visual cues—so there is really no feeling for depth until the older man turns and walks diagonally across the screen. Even then, it is only the sound of his receding footsteps that gives us a sense of space.

Welles wasn't satisfied with merely defining space. In *Lady from Shanghai* and *Touch of Evil* he deliberately undermines space perception by mismatching the sound and its source. The roar of the jalopies is heard in close-up long before they approach the motel in *Touch of Evil*. In the middle of an intimate scene between Mike and Elsa in *Lady from Shanghai*, Grisby's voice intrudes in close-up while the sound of the launch he's in is distanced correctly. Grisby is nowhere near the couple. In fact, his voice always seems a little too loud, a little too close. The sound takes on a presence of its own.

Welles goes beyond undermining aural reality. By substituting and confusing sound with its reproduction, and objects with their reflections, silhouettes and shadows, Welles manages to separate sound from its source, and from space. By the end of *Lady from Shanghai* we have no idea from what direction the sound is coming. By the end of *Touch of Evil* we have not only lost all sense of distance and direction, we are also confused about the source itself. Quinlan and Menzes' voices physically separate from their bodies, as the soundtrack is taken, in part, from a small radio receiver/tape recorder which is picking up transmissions from a concealed microphone carried by Menzes. We hear the voices in tinny close-up, off the radio receiver, at the same time as we see the two men moving in the distance.

At one point, as they are crossing the bridge into Mexico, sound becomes directly involved in its own disassociation: Quinlan hears his voice coming from the receiver—a sound which is twice removed from the filmic reality, but which has a central place within the narrative. It leads directly to Menzes' death. We don't see the actual shooting—we only experience it second-hand, through sound: we see a close-up of the tape as it records the events that are going on above, on the bridge. Moments later, we hear the playback—with the camera again focused on the recorder. This repeat is no different from our first experience, and no more closely related to real filmic space, time or character.

The fragmentation of the relationship between a sound and its source is such a dominating feature throughout *Touch of Evil* that we don't even notice all sorts of anomalies in sound, space and narrative. We don't find it peculiar for Vargas to turn his back on the blind lady so she won't hear him telephoning his wife, nor are we disturbed by the fact that he doesn't hear Suzy's shouts from the hotel fire escape, even though we hear her voice booming across the crowd that has gathered below her, and through which he drives in search of her. His visual and aural dislocations aren't questioned, because our own are so pronounced.

Most of the time the kinds of sounds that define space are sound effects and background noise. Straight dialogue usually draws and holds our attention away from the spatial dimension: we are more concerned with what is being said than the relationship between the source and space. Dialogue has the effect of taking us out of space and placing us in the realm of ideas. The transition is completed by the sound editor's toning down of background noise. Normally, we have the ability to disregard distracting stimuli and focus our attention on whatever we choose. Cinema usurps that power. It may be the speed at which images are presented, or the rapidity with which we are shifted about in time and space, but whatever the cause there is a pronounced impairment of our ability to tune out surrounding stimuli and the sound editor has to do it for us. Reintroducing, or increasing the level of, these effects takes us back to the spatial dimension. Our attention is caught by the aural change and the switch is made.

This gives us a whole new perspective for appreciating the courtroom sequence in *Lady from Shanghai*. Welles has no intention of allowing us to focus on the trial proceedings. Thus, he makes escape to the ideational difficult by constantly reintroducing spatial elements. Coughing and whispering in the jury box are typical of this effort, as are the cutaways to audience reactions. There's something particularly interesting about these. The first few times Welles cuts away, he synchronizes it with sound. The later cutaways have no track; but they have a noisy effect. We can almost hear the rustling. When Elsa finally admits to having kissed O'Hara in the aquarium, the camera doesn't cut away, but we hear the silence and feel the weight of the courtroom bearing down on her.

To say that conversation removes us from the spatial and places us in the ideational is not to say that it can't be used to define space. Speech works on both levels. Mrs. Kane closes the window on little Charlie, playing outside, when she gets ready to discuss her decision to send him away. It's not as if she does this just because she is concerned about his overhearing. Welles is making sure that we don't miss these important details of Kane's life, since distance and its concomitant definition of space tends to distract us from what is being said.

If conversation takes us out of space, what is the effect of narration? The narrator is twice removed from spatial reality. Not only are his words ideational, and consequently flattening to the screen image, but his intrusion upon the story reminds us of the unreality of the whole filmic experience. The result is a reflexivity that is increased in Welles by his deliberate flouting of narrative convention. The narrator is supposed to set the scene, and perhaps fill in some background, but it is clearly against the "rules" for his words to be synchronized to the character's lips. "'Fine weather we're having,' I said to break the ice," says O'Hara, as *narrator*, over a medium close-up of O'Hara walking and talking beside Elsa's carriage. Convention dictates that we already be within the scene. The character can, and should, speak his own lines. Anything that goes against a convention (and our expectation) calls attention to itself, and reflects on the medium that has promulgated that convention. We end up, momentarily, conscious of the film as a vehicle of fantasy.

There are a number of forms narration can take. Welles apparently prefers to fade the narrator out during the first quarter of the film, and then in again toward the end. He uses this method in both *Magnificent Ambersons* and *Lady from Shanghai*. This would ordinarily leave a large center portion virtually without moments of reflexivity. Welles lets this happen in *Ambersons*, but in *Shanghai* and *Evil* where there is no narrator at all, Welles forces us to become aware of film as a medium by manipulating our expectations of musical convention.

Background music in a Hollywood movie sometimes has its source within the ongoing scene; usually it is just mood music added in the sound mix. It is never supposed to compete for our attention. Such is not the case in *Shanghai* or *Evil*. Typically, the music and visual start out simultaneously, with the music in the background. All of a sudden we are made to realize that the music is real music within the film's narrative. It eventually slips back into the background. The first shot after Elsa's singing scene in *Shanghai* is of Elsa sunning herself on the ship's deck. O'Hara is at the wheel. On the soundtrack is brassy popular music of the forties. It is brought to our attention because it is so loud, and so incongruous with the rather idyllic visual. Suddenly the music stops, and a disc jockey starts to talk. It is only Elsa's radio. The disc jockey goes off, and soft music comes on. This becomes background music which is toned down when Elsa and O'Hara begin to talk.

In an earlier scene in the same film, a juke box and its music is brought to our attention when the record ends. Goldy turns to a waiter and says, "Would you put these in crank number four? That's all we want to listen to." After this, the music returns to its place in the background until it is again referred to in the conversation. By constantly surprising us with new methods of presenting this pattern—from background to foreground—the effect remains fresh. The music has been brought to our attention, and has served the movie reflexively.

In *Evil* our awareness of music is so intense that it takes on an ideational quality. We respond to it directly, rather than to a mood it creates. The volume and persistence of the irritating music in the motel scenes invades our consciousness much as it does Suzy's. It is a pervasive force in her presence, and seeps into Vargas' as well by way of his car radio, but it belongs by association to the teenage hoodlums. This isn't the only association of character and music that exists in the film. Mexican nightclub music belongs to Joe Grandi and player-piano to Tanya, the Marlene Dietrich character. Most of the time, although not always, these sounds also conform to spatial limitations. There are times when what had been real music swells to reinforce a climax in the narrative, and other times, especially with the player-piano music; when the sound is toned down under conversation that is put into aural foreground.

Music, dialogue, effects, any type of aural signal can also be used ideationally, as a transitional element when the narrative is moving through time and/or space. When Elsa leaves the nightclub in Acapulco, the orchestra music follows her and continues, reduced to a single guitar, when she meets O'Hara. In *Kane* Susan's singing in the parlor is heard, without a lapse, over the dissolve which moves us to the parlor at a later date. Then Kane's applause turns into light clapping heard behind Leland's campaign speech. Leland's voice, in turn, becomes Kane's heard over the microphone in a large auditorium.

The transitions between scenes become tighter through the four movies. In *Evil* almost every scene has some element to bridge the gap to the next. Grandi's son decides to call his father for instructions, and we cut away from him at the phone to Quinlan and Grandi in a bar. A few seconds later the telephone in the background rings. We leave these two men when Grandi puts a coin in the juke box, whose music is associated with the Grandi boys, who are at the motel, where rock and roll is being piped into Suzy's room. That's where we end up.

The transitions in *Shanghai* aren't as tight as they are in *Evil*, and in *Ambersons* they are rarely anything but straight cuts. In *Citizen Kane* the aural equivalents of match dissolves are used in conjunction with visual dissolves to move us across spatial-temporal coordinates, but the process is different in the later films. In *Kane* the sound is a technical device used to make the transition smoothly. In *Evil* an element integral to one scene is present in, and brings us to, the next.

Spatial definition is one of two perceptual contributions to the aural experience. The other is an attention-focusing mechanism. We are perpetually surrounded by noise, but we're only aware of part of it. The rest is toned down by our mental processes and remains on a lower level of consciousness. Generally, our attention is drawn to an object that is producing sound, especially if it is moving, or given visual prominence in some other way. There's an interesting maneuver in *Shanghai* that manipulates and moves our attention by changing only what we hear. As Elsa enters the courtroom, we follow her movement down the aisle. On the soundtrack we hear the noise that surrounds her. The camera stops as she finds a row with a seat, but the sound continues forward, carrying our attention with it, away from Elsa to the courtroom proceedings at the far end of the room. These are sounds that were previously unheard.

Loud or unremitting sounds force themselves on our attention, as in the mote scenes in *Evil*. Any change in volume or quality also attracts our attention, so we could be diverted by a new sound, especially if it was coming from outside our visual field. This probably stems from a survival instinct: anything that makes a noise within hearing distance is a possible threat, especially if we were previously unaware of its presence, and we respond involuntarily to such a stimulus. This reaction is used in *Ambersons* as a means of splitting our attention. We watch the grandfather, in close-up, contemplating death, while we listen to a discussion of the estate Elizabeth has left. In another scene, we are paying attention to Fanny and Georgie arguing when, from off-screen, comes the voice of the Ray Collins character complaining about noise and finally saying, "I'm going to move to a hotel."

Welles is extremely conscious of the mechanisms of attention. Early in *Kane* there is a scene of Thompson, the reporter, after his unsuccessful attempt to interview Susan. Just before he leaves, he makes a call from a telephone booth in the extreme foreground. He should be the center of attention, as we usually attend to that which is producing a sound. Furthermore, he is close to us, and he is heard in aural close-up. The nightclub music is in the background, partially shut out when he closes the door. Nevertheless, a substantial portion of our attention is drawn away from the sound, through the left window of the phone booth door, and across the room to Susan—where she slumps in a pool of light. If sound attracts our attention, so does light. The result is that we are unable to focus completely on either one of the stimuli presented to us. In this case, the two are compatible: the telephone call has to do with Susan. Furthermore, one is completely visual and the other is completely aural, as Thompson is in a shadow; there isn't too much competition between them. In *Shanghai* and especially in *Evil* there is often so much confusion and competition between the elements within the frame that the audience finds itself unable to organize and process it normally. Consider the scene immediately after the explosion in *Evil*. There are many people, all being introduced to one another and to us talking and milling about. Characters critical to the narrative pop onto the scene and, just as quickly, disappear. We aren't given any signals as to what we should attend. The result is a diffusion of our faculties—and a feeling of relief when we finally leave with Vargas' wife.

In a later scene the fragmenting is done somewhat more delicately. In the scene where Vargas is talking on the blind woman's telephone, his turning away does bring the sound to our attention. We think about what an unnecessary movement he has made. By calling attention to itself it works reflexively, so we become aware of the film medium. At the same time another part of our attention is drawn out the window, where we see Menzes and Grandi. These two characters are seen in long shot, fussing and arguing with one another. The elements in this example, and the previous one, work against each other to split our focusing abilities.

When Welles does give us something to concentrate on in *Shanghai* and *Evil*, it is often something that seems peripheral to the narrative. The water glass and pills, in *Shanghai*, are forced on us well before they play any part in the narrative. Similarly, in *Evil*, the camera is on Vargas while Quinlan is interrogating his suspect about "finding" the dynamite. It's a critical moment until we realize that it's Vargas' reaction to this evidence that's important. We are continually left mildly disconcerted and dislocated by the conflicting demands on our attention.

Welles doesn't limit himself to psychological means when it comes to playing with our perceptions. He takes advantage of other, more complex social responses. We can't help but attend to Bannister as he laboriously leaves the witness stand in *Shanghai*. How often are we allowed to stare unabashedly at someone who is crippled? We are hardly aware of the calling of his wife, even though the prosecuting attorney who calls her is standing in the extreme foreground. His words carry the plot forward, and ordinarily his voice and position in the frame would be attention-getting devices, but Bannister steals the show. There's also the ringing telephone in the judge's chamber as O'Hara fights to get away. That's a sound to which we have a conditioned response, and Welles uses that response to assure our diversion—and a certain building up of tension which is turned to comic relief when the judge reacts for us and answers the phone.

Persons suffering from schizophrenia complain of being bombarded by sensations, and of a lack of control over their consciousness. Paranoid types often believe that outside forces have taken over their thought processes. Such claims would not be totally irrational for the moviegoer— especially if he's watching a movie by Welles. In such a situation his perception of reality is torn apart. Sound no longer defines space. Unable to focus his attention, he becomes dislocated within the narrative. If art is a re-experiencing of our mental and emotional conditions within a new context, Orson Welles is one of the world's supreme artists.

Citizen Kane, The Great Gatsby, and Some Conventions of American Narrative

ROBERT CARRINGER

I T IS widely thought that what finally characterizes American literary narratives is a preoccupation with Americanness. If the "great theme" of European fiction has been "man's life in society," Walter Allen writes in *The Modern Novel*, "the great theme of American fiction has been the exploration of what it means to be an American." The best American film narratives also seem to bear out this proposition, especially those of the great American naturals like Griffith and Ford and Hawks, and most especially Orson Welles' *Citizen Kane* (1941), regarded by many as the greatest American film. Welles' film belongs to that category of narratives which take a prominent figure from contemporary American life (here William Randolph Hearst) and use him to stand for what are conceived to be representative traits of the collective American character. Understandably, then, there are many general resemblances in the film to other well-known stories of American entrepreneurs, magnates, and tycoons. Long before the flourishing of tycoon biographies in the American sound film, well before F. Scott Fitzgerald or Sinclair Lewis or Theodore Dreiser, before even Henry James, certain conventions and associations had become well established in stories of this type. The up-and-coming young American was shrewd and practical, an image of compulsive energy, a man with his eye always on the future. His Americanness also consisted of such traits as enterprise, indomitable idealism, a certain naturalness and openness to experience, and a relentless will to succeed. His geographical origin could be made to carry moral force, and he or another character who equated American commercial *noblesse oblige* with universal morality could be a useful thematic touchstone.

But in one instance the parallels between *Citizen Kane* and a well-known literary narrative seem to be more than simply a case of variations on standard formulas and types. There are striking similarities in characterization and idea, even occasionally in specific images and details, between Welles' film and Fitzgerald's novel *The Great Gatsby*, another portrait of a rich and powerful American who finances gaudy, elaborate entertainments and harbors sentimental ties to his youth in the West. Some of these may be the result of direct borrowing from *The Great*

From *Critical Inquiry* 2 (Winter 1975):307–25. Reprinted by permission of the University of Chicago Press.

Gatsby by Herman J. Mankiewicz, the principal screenwriter on *Citizen Kane*. But the symmetry of the parallels between the novel and the completed film seems to suggest a broader implication: that novels and films on explicitly American subjects may undergo analogous processes of formation, receiving the same basic impulses directly from the ambience of American life, and drawing from the same storehouse of accomplished narrative forms and characterizations to give shape to their materials; and to this extent at the least they may be said to belong to a common mainstream tradition of American narrative.[1]

<h1 style="text-align:center">I</h1>

Except for a few obvious resemblances, *The Great Gatsby* and *Citizen Kane* seem an unlikely pair. Though both protagonists are characterized as representative Americans, they seem to represent very different faces of America. Gatsby is a man outside the law, a big-scale bootlegger, a social climber, a perennial adolescent who uses his ill-gotten gains in an effort to bring maudlin storybook romances to life. Kane, on the other hand, is in the mainstream of American corporate and political life, a wealthy publisher with enough clout to influence (even bully) the president of the United States, and seemingly enough wealth to strip Europe of its transportable artistic treasures. But in certain key features of their personalities, in certain key facts and events which are presented as constituting the most significant details of their lives, and in the way the essential nature of their failings is defined, the stories of Gatsby and Kane contain a number of startling similarities.

Both works are in the form of retrospective narratives set a short time after the deaths of their protagonists. Both men were wealthy and given to open displays of their wealth and power; they were controversial figures whose stature and flamboyance evoked mixed feelings of distrust and awe in the public mind. Yet surprisingly little was known about the private life and private feelings of either man. People speculate about Gatsby's past— it is rumored that he was in the war and that he went to Oxford, and there are rumblings of various shady deals past and present, but no one really knows about any of these things for sure. Of Charles Foster Kane, the newspaper giant, about all that is known is what one reads in the newspapers. In each story a person sets out to gather evidence about his subject's private life. His aim is to collect relevant details to be assembled into a definitive portrait of the man; his mission is to discover what his subject was *really* like.

In the novel, Nick Carraway, Gatsby's former confidant and a stern moralist, brings strict judgments to bear on the subject of his attention, pronouncing him a corrupt scoundrel but, at the same time, totally incorruptible in his boyish innocence. In the film, one of the several accounts of the central figure is given by a "New England schoolmarm" type, who also makes harsh moral judgments on the former confidant he held in awe, and also sees his essential failure as idealism corrupted. The protagonist of the novel as a young man in the Midwest was at just the right place and time when an accident occurred and so was enabled to get into the good graces of an American tycoon—a connection which, as it turned out, most influenced what he eventually became. The protagonist of the film, another young Westerner, came under the tutelage of another great American capitalist as a result of equally capricious circumstances, and again this proved to be the connection that made his fortune. The protagonist of the novel continually thinks everything could be all right again if he could go back to an earlier point in his life, to that "secret place above the trees."[2] The protagonist of the film gazes at an object representing freedom from mature responsibility and dotes on his childhood. The stern moralist of the novel is continually reminded by his subject of a forgotten word or phrase of conversation or dialogue which, if he could recall it, would probably be a definitive explanation of that man. On his deathbed, the protagonist of the film utters a word which sends everyone scrambling in search of a definitive insight into his life. In the novel, we are told that just before the protagonist's death, his lifelong dream had "broken up like glass" against the cold, hard rock of real facts (p. 148). In the film, just as this protagonist dies, we see him lose his grasp on a symbol of his dream of childhood innocence and it falls and smashes to pieces on the marble floor.

Chance similarities? Or yokings together of things similar in one superficial aspect but in essence not really comparable? When considered together with a number of other parallels and associations, they seem to become something more. Of special interest are the central figure's attachment to an object that represents his past and the fashion in which this central figure is presented.

Nick Carraway's first glimpse of Gatsby is of him staring at a green light on the end of a dock across a bay. Our first glimpse of Kane is of his staring at "one of those little glass balls . . . sold in novelty stores all over the world . . . contain[ing] . . . a snow scene . . . a too picturesque farmhouse and a snowman."[3] As it turns out, these two symbols carry a remarkably similar pattern of meaning not only for the two protagonists but also for the two figures charged with the responsibility of providing a definitive view of them. The green light is on Daisy and Tom Buchanan's dock; Gatsby, Nick learns, is thinking of Daisy. But as Nick learns more and more about Gatsby, he comes to the conclusion that Gatsby is not thinking of the Daisy who lives across the bay at all, but of a Daisy he once knew, and in thinking of her, he is really trying to recover something in himself he once lost. In fact, Nick concludes, Daisy stands for Gatsby's lost innocence—that state of freedom from adult anxieties and responsibilities he associates with his childhood in the Midwest. Gatsby senses that somehow he lost it when he first met and fell in love with Daisy. Nick guesses that Gatsby's problem is his wish to remain forever in that preadolescent state in the clouds or above the trees or back in a Midwest that never was—in short, that resistance to growing up which such critics as R. W. B. Lewis and Leslie Fiedler have said is at the heart of American narratives and presumably also therefore at the heart of American life.[4] The green light, then, really represents what Gatsby thinks he is trying to recover—an ideal state which, Fitzgerald reminds us in the striking metaphor of time that closes the book, is in future tense, not past: a condition we yearn for and often mistakenly associate with a point in time somewhere behind us.

At least three times in *Citizen Kane* we see the little glass globe. Once, if we look carefully, we can see it in the litter on Susan Alexander's dressing table in the "love nest." Later, after he smashes up Susan's room when she leaves him, Kane picks up the globe and whispers the word "Rosebud." Kane's last act is to whisper "Rosebud" while gazing at the little glass ball. As in *Gatsby*, the little glass ball is associated specifically with the loss of a woman. But, as we recognize when Rosebud is identified at last, this object stands for the same complex of associations in Kane's experience as in Gatsby's. The glass ball is also generally a sign of Kane's childhood in the West and what it represents to him: maternal security and love but, above all, freedom from the chief burdens and responsibilities of his adult life—wealth, and the compulsion of the wealthy to possess, to dominate, and to control; and relationships with others which call upon one to give as well as to receive. Glass objects, "very simple things," mean at least three virtually identical things in *Gatsby* and *Kane*—the loss of a woman, childhood innocence versus adult experience, and the ideal West versus the corrupt East.

These two symbols also turn out to function in practically the same way for the two gatherers of evidence, Nick Carraway and Thompson, the reporter in *Citizen Kane*. In both narratives the small glass object is the first clue to the private life of the main character. In both it also provides the initial impetus of the plot. Nick Carraway and Thompson both start from the premise that, if they can discover the meaning of this clue, the information will eventually lead to the definitive understanding of the subjects they are both after. In both cases the manner in which the evidence gatherer proceeds has major implications for the ultimate result of the undertaking.

Both narratives are organized chronologically according to the experience of the evidence gatherer. The "foreground" story, then, is strictly sequential. Nick Carraway tells, in order, how eighteen months ago he went East, moved next door to Gatsby, renewed his acquaintance with the Buchanans, went to a party at Gatsby's, had lunch with Gatsby and Meyer Wolfsheim, arranged for a meeting between Gatsby and Daisy, became

Gatsby's confidant, spent a disastrous afternoon in New York with Gatsby and the Buchanans, stayed by Gatsby after the motor accident, oversaw arrangements for Gatsby's funeral, and, finally, in moral outrage and disgust, came back home again. The reporter in *Citizen Kane* received an assignment from his producer, and he travels around interviewing people who might be able to provide a clue to the meaning of Rosebud. If the foreground stories are neat and uncomplicated, the inner, but central, stories are sequentially and temporally disjointed. Whatever information comes to light about the principal figure is revealed in piecemeal fashion, in scattered and apparently unrelated fragments. It is the task of the gatherer of evidence to arrange these fragments into a composite view of the subject.

Characteristic of this narrative strategy is that it involves the reader or viewer as an active participant in the "discovery" of the subject. This is as true of *Gatsby* as of *Kane*, even though Nick Carraway stands in a different relationship to his subject from Thompson's relationship to his. (Nick is retelling past events he already knows the outcome of, while everything Thompson learns is all new to him.) Nick is extremely ambivalent toward Gatsby and his whole experience in the East. As he tells us at the beginning, one of his purposes in setting down his experiences is to discover how he really feels about Gatsby. Like Thompson, Nick is sorting through evidence in an effort to arrive at a fresh and clear interpretation of it. Narrators involved in the process of discovery have set better in an age of uncertainties than narrators who know and tell all. In the characteristic use of the discovery narrative in modern times (as by Conrad and Faulkner), the narrator has usually found his search for a definitive perspective to be frustrated or thwarted. This outcome is partially inherent in the nature of the form itself: since all informants (like all mediums generally) are inherently distorting, in the absence of any mechanism or principle of authority or mediation, all that the evidence gatherer can ever arrive at is a version of the truth, not the thing itself. A search for authority is undermined by the very process of searching.

This is precisely what happens in both *Gatsby* and *Kane*. The more Thompson learns about Kane, the less confident he becomes of his mission: to uncover the clue that will give him the definitive perspective he needs for his newsreel summary of Kane's life. At the end, just before Rosebud is revealed at last—to the audience alone—Thompson not only discounts his boss's guess that Rosebud might be such a clue but also rejects the more fundamental premise on which it is based—that a man's life can be summed up in epigrams and all-inclusive generalizations. When a colleague remarks, "if you could have found out what Rosebud meant, I bet that would've explained everything," Thompson replies:

> No, I don't think so. No. Mr. Kane was a man who got everything he wanted, and then lost it. Maybe Rosebud was something he couldn't get or some-

thing he lost. Anyway, it wouldn't have explained anything. I don't think any word can explain a man's life. No, I guess Rosebud is just a piece in a jigsaw puzzle, a missing piece. [*Citizen Kane Book*, pp. 419–20].

Nick, on the other hand, does learn what Gatsby's green light stands for, and at the last, in one of the most eloquent passages in American writing, is allowed that definitive vision and understanding of Gatsby and himself that had puzzled and eluded him up until then. Yet despite this difference in the turn of specific events, Nick's final attitude toward his mission and his subject is very similar to Thompson's. For what Nick finally says about the green light is that it represents not only a person, Daisy Buchanan, not only a personal past, Jay Gatsby's, but the entire complex experience of a whole society. The green light is multiform and complex and no more capable of being summed up in a neat formula than Gatsby himself. To rescue a man after he is gone from simplistic explanations, and to preserve a sense of his mystery and ultimate complexity—that, according to Nick Carraway, is also what he owes Gatsby, as he tells us in a famous passage at the outset of his narrative:

> Only Gatsby, the man who gives his name to this book, was exempt from my reaction—Gatsby, who represented everything for which I have an unaffected scorn. If personality is an unbroken series of successful gestures, then there was something gorgeous about him, some heightened sensitivity to the promises of life, as if he were related to one of those intricate machines that register earthquakes ten thousand miles away. This responsiveness . . . was an extraordinary gift for hope, a romantic readiness such as I have never found in any other person and which it is not likely I shall ever find again. No—Gatsby turned out all right at the end; it is what preyed on Gatsby, what foul dust floated in the wake of his dreams that temporarily closed out my interest in the abortive sorrows and short-winded elations of men. [*The Great Gatsby*, p. 2]

If Nick had never discovered the relationship between the green light and Daisy Buchanan, *Gatsby* would have contained very different events. But essentially it would have been the same story, and Daisy would have been a piece in a jigsaw puzzle—a missing piece. If Thompson had stayed on and had just happened to turn up Rosebud, there is little to indicate that his final pronouncement would have been any different—"it wouldn't have explained anything. I don't think any word can explain a man's life."

To summarize: in both stories,

1. A gatherer of evidence sets out to reveal what the private life of a well-known figure was really like.

2. He proceeds by assembling fragments of information from various sources.

3. He begins with the known public facts.

4. He also has one clue to the man's personal life, an object which represents something very special to that person. (In both cases it is a small glass object, "a very simple thing.")

5. Progressively this clue leads him into more and more intimate and personal details about the man.

6. As it turns out, this clue stands for a complex of associations in the man's mind—a woman he lost, his childhood innocence, and the pastoral American West.

7. Ultimately, the gatherer of evidence rejects a basic premise he started from—that a significant incident, detail, or object can provide a unifying and definitive perspective on a man's life.

II

The predominance of "auteur theory" in recent film criticism—the principle that creative responsibility for a film can be traced ultimately to one man, the director—was probably responsible for the habit of attributing everything in *Citizen Kane* to Orson Welles. Thanks to Pauline Kael's research which culminated in "Raising Kane," however, we are now more conscious that others—especially the screenwriter, Herman J. Mankiewicz—also made important contributions that influenced the final design of the film. There is no doubt that it was Welles who finally shaped all the elements of a collaborative enterprise into the unified "vision" of *Citizen Kane*. Nor is there any doubt that Welles was in full control of the production. On the other hand, there is strong evidence to suggest that in at least one area—the early stages of the actual scripting of the film—Welles' involvement may only have been intermittent. Mankiewicz went into seclusion at Victorville, California, with John Houseman, a former Welles associate in the "Mercury Theatre," to prepare the script while Welles stayed behind in Hollywood. Welles was often in touch by phone, and on occasion he visited Victorville. There is disagreement as to the amount of direct influence he exerted on the first draft of the script. Pauline Kael argues that the first draft screenplay, called simply *American*, is almost wholly the work of Mankiewicz. John Houseman, an old arch enemy of Welles, confirms this. Peter Bogdanovich, a Welles partisan—indeed the would-be Boswell to Welles' Johnson—calls it a malicious fabrication. Welles himself partly concedes Kael's point but counters that at the same time he was writing a first draft script of his own, into which *American* was subsumed at a later stage.[5] Welles has not made this script available for inspection, however, and without it there is no way to arrive at a definitive resolution of this dispute. On the other hand, *American*, the screenplay over which Mankiewicz and Houseman labored for almost three months, has survived.[6] *American* contains additional material resembling *The Great Gatsby* which was deleted in subsequent versions of the screenplay and does not appear in the film.

Specific parallels between *American* and *The Great Gatsby* begin with the rejection of a natural father. James Gatz, Jr., rejected his father for his shiftlessness and lack of ambition. Although the separation scene in the film is somewhat ambiguous, *American* is perfectly clear: Kane's mother made the arrangements with Thatcher to get young Charles out from under the influence of his shiftless father, Charles Sr., who spends his days hanging around a livery stable. In *Gatsby*, considerable attention is devoted to the gaudy crowd who hang out at Gatsby's, an odd assortment of social climbers, actresses and producers, effeminate young men, tramps, college boys, alcoholics, and debutantes. In *American*, Thatcher visits Kane on his twenty-fifth birthday at his Renaissance palace in Rome and finds him surrounded by an equally disreputable crowd of hangers-on—"pimps, Lesbians, dissipated Army officers, homosexuals, nymphomaniacs and international society tramps." Kane himself is "draped along the fireplace, talking to a hideous woman, under five feet in height and weighing three hundred pounds, who is sixty-five years old and trying to look twenty-five" (*American*, p. 47). In *Gatsby*, Nick Carraway finds out that the entire hullabaloo at West Egg was set up just for Daisy, in hopes of attracting her attention and drawing her to one of the goings-on. In *American*, Kane in his later years almost always had some elaborate entertainment going on at Xanadu (or "The Alhambra," as it is called in some parts of *American*). Hearst entertained this way at San Simeon, of course, but in a moment of rare candor Kane tells Bernstein that he puts the whole thing on just for Susan's sake. In *Gatsby*, Nick was awed that Tom Buchanan could be wealthy enough to bring "a string of polo ponies" with him from Chicago when he moved East (p. 6). In *American*, there is a visitor at Xanadu, Jerry Martin, who loves polo ponies and who also—like Tom Buchanan in every instance—is arrogant, self-satisfied, and involved in an affair with another man's wife (he is Susan's lover). At one point he remarks ironically to Susan that if Kane knew of his fondness for the sport he would probably "have a building put up by next Monday just for polo ponies[,] fully equipped—with two hundred of South America's best" (*American*, p. 277).

One overall similarity between Gatsby and Kane is stronger in *American* than in the film. The theme of the film seems to be that Kane was perhaps all the things said about him, perhaps none—"it depends on who's talking about him," as Welles puts it, "so that the truth about Kane, like the truth about any man, can only be calculated, by the sum of everything that has been said about him."[7] In order to shape the film's meaning in this way, Welles seems deliberately in some cases to have obscured Kane's motivations where they were perfectly clear in Mankiewicz's script.

In *American*, Kane's tragedy appears to have been, like Gatsby's, a case of idealism which became progressively tainted. Gatsby set up a pure and incorruptible ideal and pushed doggedly ahead in pursuit of it, unmindful and uncaring as the means he used to pursue it became more and more corrupt. In *American*, several scenes of Kane running his newspaper (all but a very few later deleted) reveal that the nature of his failure was very similar. He set out with noble goals to build a big circulation daily totally committed to the pursuit of truth regardless of the personal or professional consequences. As time passed, however, he gradually lost the ability to discriminate between this lofty ideal and the shallow sensationalism he used in its service. But—again like Gatsby—to the end he retained his tragic innocence of the implications of his actions. There is also a close parallel in the way the moral corruption of the two characters is exposed and defined. Nick Carraway, it will be recalled, is able to preserve his moral credibility by turning down Gatsby's offer of a "connection"—an offer Nick knows could make his fortune for him. In *American*, Bradford Leland (later to become Jedediah) is Kane's strongest critic and the agent by which the nature of his corruption is defined. Like Nick Carraway (and other Fitzgerald narrators), Leland, a Midwesterner from a well-to-do family, is a curious mixture of libertinism and stern morality. He and Kane are constantly off to the theater or expensive restaurants. He dreads being sent on assignment to Cuba because "they tell me there isn't a decent restaurant on the whole island" (*American*, p. 180). He and Kane are both fond of loose women, and at one point they appear together in a brothel. Yet, in the long run, Leland, like Nick, is able to summon up the strength finally to resist the corrupting influence of Kane's wealth and power. In the film, Leland starts a bad notice of Susan's Chicago debut but is too drunk to finish it (Kane finishes it for him); later he does return Kane's $25,000 severance check. *American*, on the other hand, is not nearly so morally equivocal in regard to Leland. The parallel event is when Kane's assistant Reilly informs Leland of a promotional scheme to use dramatic reviews in advertising. If Leland's review is favorable, it will be carried; if it appears too unfavorable, another man's more favorable notice will be substituted. Outraged, Leland refuses to go along even though it means a rift with Kane, his employer and oldest and closest friend. As a result, again like Nick, he departs for the Midwest and a new moral vantage point from which to pass judgment on the object of his simultaneous disgust, reverence, and awe.

Do all these parallels add up to anything? If it were a problem in literary studies, that peculiar contorted quality and elusiveness about most of the parallels would probably be taken as a sign of the weakness of the case. But with screenwriting, special circumstances make many of the ordinary assumptions of literary studies inoperative, and those same traits may even become a supporting link in what appears to be a strong circumstantial case. Screenwriting is ordinarily an assembly line operation. The making of *any* story involves interplay between invention and precedent, but the relative importance of precedent generally increases when personal authorial self-respect is not at stake. Keeping an eye over one's shoulder was a writer's way of life in old Hollywood. Hollywood writers "collaborated all over the place and backward in time," as Pauline Kael colorfully puts it; "they collaborated promiscuously, and within a few years were rewriting the remakes of their own or somebody else's rewrites" ("Raising Kane," p. 18). But legal departments were also a part of this way of life. A story was a "property," and unauthorized or unpaid borrowing from someone else's story property was as much a case of stealing as it would have been to carry off props or costumes. Story litigation was commonplace, sometimes reaching a point where it involved just a few circumstances or gestures in one or two scenes. Hollywood screenwriters were always just behind the lines in such combat. Constantly in a rush against tight production schedules, they did not have time for luxuries of ordinary writers such as temperamental or artistic crises. To keep on schedule, *anything* was fair game to salvage a scene or a character, so long as the final product kept the studio off a legal hook. In short, a good screenwriter simply would not leave his work vulnerable to charges of infringement or plagiarism. If plagiarizing was a well-developed art, so too was the art of covering one's tracks.

One of Hollywood's most durable writers, unquestionably also one of its best read, Herman Mankiewicz was also something of a master at the art of covering tracks. In *John Meade's Woman* (1937), a tycoon biography that was probably one of his testing grounds for *Citizen Kane*, a lumber baron in his middle age (Edward Arnold) meets an outspoken young woman and marries her on impulse. There is a young assistant to the tycoon who advocates, of all things, reforestation. At one point the tycoon is seen discussing a swindle with some associates. Those who have seen another Edward Arnold tycoon picture of the previous year, *Come and Get It*, may detect a ring of familiarity in all this. But when one begins to track down the parallels they have ways of suddenly veering off course—the young woman is a kind of suffragette, not a dance hall girl; the progressive young man is just an employee, not the boss's son. Mankiewicz also seems to have developed a habit of lifting material from his own scripts as he went from one studio to another. The first scene of *John Meade's Woman* (Paramount) is set in the Chicago Opera House, a premonition of *Citizen Kane* (RKO); a post-*Kane* script for Universal, *Christmas Holiday* (1944), involves a broken-down singer in a second-rate nightclub relating her past in flashback to an inquisitive stranger, a circumstance suspiciously like something in *Citizen Kane*.

Mankiewicz and Scott Fitzgerald were personal friends for many years, and he was especially fond of *The Great Gatsby*.[8] Most of the parallels between *Gatsby* and *Kane* are curiously wrenched in the same way as the parallels between the scripts. And well they had better be: a fifteen-year-old best seller would still be a valuable commercial property, and its author still lived in Hollywood. But the elaborateness of the parallels makes it seem to me a reasonable inference that Mankiewicz's familiarity with *The Great Gatsby* proved helpful to him as he worked on the script of *Citizen Kane*. It is possible that this material crept into his script unconsciously. (John Houseman cannot recall *The Great Gatsby* being mentioned during the period they worked on *American*.) But even if its use were conscious and deliberate, the end result would still have had something of the same look of not having been. For Mankiewicz would have used *Gatsby* in the same way he would have had to use any recognizable material still protected by copyright: not as a writer working alone would borrow from another work to add resonances or complexities to one of his own, but as a screenwriter—working obliquely and peripherally, picking and choosing here and there as an aid to working out specific plot situations and character motivations, but, as in the series of examples from his other scripts, always being careful to twist and contort and conceal.[9]

III

With John Houseman, Mankiewicz delivered *American* to Welles at RKO in Hollywood on May 27, 1940. As this script underwent revision prior to the beginning of shooting in July, a number of new hands and "Mercury Theatre" voices became involved. But from this point on, the controlling voice was that of the director. The final shooting script, which more clearly reflects Welles' intentions, and the film itself show fewer, rather than more, suggestions of indebtedness to *The Great Gatsby* than the early script does. Nevertheless, the completed version of Charles Foster Kane follows logically in every major respect from the rough outlines of Mankiewicz's treatment. Revision involved the inevitable pruning and shaping, but it also seems to have involved steady progress toward a kind of mythic clarification. The finished portrait of Charles Foster Kane is in striking consistency with other portraits of the representative American as an entrepreneur, magnate, or tycoon.[10] Jay Gatsby, of course, and for obvious reasons I will continue to use him as the basis of comparison. But for many of the comparisons it would also be possible to use a number of other American protagonists, from Benjamin Franklin to Christopher Newman to Frank Cowperwood to Colonel Thomas Sutpen. This consistency with type is all the more interesting in view of Welles' career. Though he has never really renounced his American past, he has spent the better part of his adult life abroad and has taken careful pains to insure that he is regarded as a kind of international citizen, partaking of the best of various national heritages and traditions but finally answerable to none.

He will not be the first expatriate American artist, however, whose works turn out to be founded on fundamental American traits.

"I am, have been, and will be only one thing," Charles Foster Kane declares—"an American" (*Citizen Kane Book*, p. 316). In Nick Carraway's final summation into the Long Island night, Gatsby is also explicitly identified with what Nick conceives to be certain original, quintessential traits of America. In the mainstream of American narrative, the concept of a "Representative American" has denoted a loose but distinguishable complex of traits—in effect, a group of narrative conventions—used to define explicitly American characters. In *Great Gatsby* and *Citizen Kane*, identical conventions are used to identify and define the Americanness of the central figures. Both protagonists were fortunate to have been born and spent their early lives in that amorphous territory out beyond the eastern mountain ranges, circumstances traditionally represented in American narratives as somehow associated with (perhaps even responsible for) strength of will and character. Both possessed the magic gift of "relinquishment"—the capacity to discover a fortuitous moment and the strength to act on it by renouncing everything in the past and beginning all over again. The crucial event in both lives was just such a moment, when in youth they suddenly and dramatically rejected their former selves and re-created themselves in new identities. One day while walking along the shore of Lake Superior, promising himself that *I will be rich* and *I will be somebody*, James Gatz became Jay Gatsby. On his twenty-fifth birthday, Charles Foster Kane, away in Europe living off the fat of his estate, decided suddenly, almost as on a whim, *I think it would be fun to run a newspaper!* Both saw themselves as having been singled out to fulfill special destinies, and both were possessed with a restless compulsion to succeed against superior or overwhelming odds in bringing those exalted ends about—Gatsby the commoner (as one of Nick's metaphors has it) to become the prince who would win the golden princess's hand, Kane to take a dying newspaper and build it into the linchpin of the world's biggest, most powerful newspaper empire. Both had the self-discipline to shut out everything else but that one all-consuming ambition. Both also possessed that predilection for forging ahead without regard for precedent—that pragmatic genius and innocent faith that all things will turn out well which are sometimes said to be the fundamental traits of the American character. The approach of both to practically all situations is never a question—not "How has it been done?" or even "Can it be done?"—but always a declaration, "It will be done!" The persistence of this trait is one of the things that impresses Nick most deeply about Gatsby. It is even at the root of his most colossal illusion: "Can't repeat the past?" Nick says Gatsby said to him once. "Why of course you can!" (p. 111). Kane wills that *The Inquirer* will be a great newspaper. One of the most memorable sequences in the film shows him taking over, cleaning house, and beginning to run things not as professional newspapermen would run them but on sheer force of will, and almost wholly by personal instinct. One of the most saddening is the time when Kane decrees, after Susan's disastrous debut and contrary to all good evidence, that she *will* continue her singing and become a great star.

The characteristic American protagonist, Quentin Anderson argues, is a Gatsby or a Kane. He is fatherless—that is, free of that archetypal symbol of the transmission of a cultural heritage. Unlike, say, Tom Jones or Stephen Dedalus, whose stories involve the search for a father as the search for an identity, Gatsby and Kane proceed in the Emersonian mode, creating themselves in their own best images. If the passage about Gatsby springing from his "Platonic conception of himself" seems to contain ironic echoes of Emerson's "transparent eyeball" experience, there is also a conscious homage to American traditions at Kane's new beginnings. Leland, his alter ego, remarks, about Kane's Declaration of Principles, that for all the hullabaloo it might as well be another Declaration of Independence. And while the European protagonist starts from the premise "What place am I to occupy?" American protagonists start (like Gatsby and Kane) from the premise "What world am I to conquer?" American narratives are typically stories of strength and energy expended in the pursuit and acquisition of or extension of control over geographic areas or political enterprises—the creation, in short, of symbolic but concrete private worlds.[11] Nick Carraway finally concludes that, in the general corruption and immorality of Gatsby's world and his times, only Gatsby possesses these same traits he associates with men of integrity who rescued a wilderness and created a new world. Kane's is also a story of the possession of America: of a man who renounces European ways, throws himself into a new, modern American line (mass circulation newspaper publishing), and becomes one of the most influential personalities of his time. Whitman and Emerson spoke of a man standing at the center, with widening concentric circles radiating outward from him over the American continent. In *Citizen Kane*, it is a map in a newsreel, showing the widening concentric circles of the Kane empire spreading over America, while a booming voice on the soundtrack speaks of "an empire upon an empire," and "dominion" (*Citizen Kane Book*, p. 313).

Gatsby and Kane have in common a relentless strength of will, a force of total commitment to a goal, an exalted image of themselves, and an exaggerated capacity for idealism. Their phenomenal outward successes are largely attributable to these traits and so, it is implied, is the phenomenal outward success of America. But it is not the problem of succeeding in American life that we see depicted in either story. In both cases the emphasis in the action is upon the later phases of careers, after their fortune, power, and fame (or, in Gatsby's case, infamy) are secure, and in both cases we get only fragmentary glimpses of the up-and-coming young

men they once were. Neither Gatsby nor Kane is a figure of original creation, building his own original world in a primal American setting, like,
say, youthful Ben Franklin or the protagonists of Dreiser: that role in both
stories is fulfilled by mentors of a previous generation such as Dan Cody
or Walter P. Thatcher. Nor, despite the emphasis in the action, are they figures of adjustment like the *older* Benjamin Franklin, telling how he spent
the second half of a lifetime learning how to live among the neighbors he
spent the first half trying to outdo; or the businessman protagonists of
James, off in Europe in search of more enriching forms of self-fulfillment
than American commercial enterprise can offer. Rather, Gatsby and Kane
are figures of defeat. The linear, open-ended biographical forms of
Franklin and Dreiser reflect their underlying themes, the unlimited capa-
bilities of the self and the infinite diversity of American experience. *Gatsby*
and *Kane* are both set chronologically *after* the deaths of their American
protagonists, and their closed retrospective forms are circular, beginning
with accomplished tragedy, tracing their way backward to early hopes and
forward again to hopes frustrated and to ultimate defeat, and finally back
to the starting point.

What causes lie behind the personal tragedies of these two men? The
closing of the frontier? adult reality? the modern *Angst*? In both cases, the
immediate cause—the catalyst, really—is the loss of a woman. After everything Gatsby did to win her back, Daisy went back to Tom Buchanan in the
end. After everything Kane did for Susan—building an opera house, pushing her career, building Xanadu, even hosting a kind of perpetual social
marathon like Gatsby—she finally walked out on him. Each man seems to
lay the blame on the generally corrupt state of things in the East: each
dotes to the end on his little glass object, a symbol that somewhere back
there in the West and in the past everything was all right. But internal critical perspective in each story points to another explanation.

Gatsby's most private room, Nick says, was practically bare except for a
plain dresser set of pure dull gold. At the core of Kane's mystery is nothing
but a little glass trinket, representing a childhood toy. The chief misfor-
tunes of both men seem to stem not so much from an inability to keep
public and private apart as from there being practically nothing private to
separate. The defect seems to be ultimately traceable to their American
personae. An all-consuming persona inevitably also consumes its wearer;
the mask eventually becomes inseparable from the face. Gatsby and Kane
are both compelled to carry over into their personal relationships those
same traits that made possible their public success, and this is the root
cause of their private miseries. To Gatsby, Nick realizes, Daisy is less a real
person than a symbol of his exalted conception of his destiny. His total
immersion in this ideal allows him to avoid accepting or facing anything
that doesn't fit into his scheme—in particular the cold, hard fact that Daisy
isn't worthy of his tributes and sacrifices. It also permits him his special

form of moral blindness. Doggedly he pursues his ideal future, totally oblivious to the moral implications of his present. Toward the end, when his golden princess has become visibly tarnished even to him, he persists in his colossal illusion. In a final formal gesture, Gatsby continues his vigil, even though he is keeping watch, Nick tells us, over nothing at all. Charles Foster Kane sets out at the beginning determined always to settle only for the best, whatever the effort or cost. His ruling passion is his compulsion to acquire on the grand scale, his need to reach out and possess whatever interests him and make it a part of one of his collections. He begins his rise in the newspaper game by collecting the staff of a rival newspaper, *The Chronicle*. He spends his vacation seasons looting Europe of its artistic treasures. His Noah's Ark on a Florida mountaintop is one final colossal attempt to collect together all the makings of a private, self-sufficient little world. Inevitably, Kane comes to treat those who are close to him in the same way he treats his possessions. It was her good-natured innocence, plus the fact that she didn't recognize him, that first attracted him to Susan. Yet his deepening interest, it soon becomes apparent, is less in her as a person than in the prospect of collecting and exhibiting an operatic attraction. Her entire operatic career is little more than a monument to himself, just like the giant opera house he built for her to sing in. When she is about to leave him for good, she wavers momentarily—until he makes reference to the harm her leaving will do his public image. He was incapable of giving love except on his own terms, Leland says—which is to say he was incapable of giving love at all. Like Gatsby, he is a victim of his own blinding innocence. He never understands why people are not as malleable and undemanding as his statues. Alone at last amid the lifeless treasures of Xanadu and holding himself guiltless, he persists to the end in his total commitment to an abstract ideal of personal innocence.

The stories of Jay Gatsby and Charles Foster Kane illustrate the inevitable consequences for anyone who would use an exalted conception of personal destiny as a release from personal responsibility. But both stories gain their special poignancy and point from the American paradox on which they are founded, and they belong to the same species of characteristic American tragedy. Both men are preeminently suited by temperament to succeed at the tricks, twists, and turns played by the game of American life. Yet those very traits which make possible their phenomenal public successes serve at the same time to insure that they will be privately miserable. In winning the game, they lose; in arriving at last at those positions of wealth and power always cherished so dearly in official American culture and therefore redeeming the official aspirations of their society, they also sacrifice themselves. In winning their worlds, Gatsby and Kane also lose their souls. American narrative is filled with tragic figures of this sort: Yankee pariahs who, in calling up the inner resources to meet the expectations set by their society, lay the groundwork for their own undoing, an inevitable and irrevocable alienation from the community of men. In the first generation, they were figures of epic magnificence even when they failed, American Adams engaged in the original creation of a new world. In a later generation, they were forced to adjust to the disillusionment of dead ends; and as their idealism degenerated into the gaudy fantasies of a big-scale bootlegger or the childish regressiveness of a once-powerful old man, the sons of American Adams became figures bearing the guilt of their cultural heritage, American Cains.

IV

The best stories of explicitly American characters have usually been a blending together of headlines, personal observation, and the accomplished characterizations and distilled wisdom of a continuing tradition. Clearly this generalization also extends to the best film story of an American, *Citizen Kane*. William Randolph Hearst was the original model for Kane; this is more evident in *American* than at later stages. But as the character gradually evolved away from this specific model and toward a kind of composite of the collective American character—as this American became *the* American—precedent played a formative role. Jay Gatsby, it appears, was used at early stages. There are hints that Mankiewicz may also have drawn on other classic American works for his early portrait. Another of his favorite modern writers, William Faulkner,[12] is closely associated with the structure Mankiewicz used in *American* (and in other unproduced scripts about Dillinger and Aimee Semple McPherson), having the main subject evoked in retrospect through a series of testimonies. Gerald Mast has observed that the intricate structure of Citizen Kane "resembl[es] nothing so much as Faulkner's *Absalom, Absalom!*"[13] The central character's life in both cases is reconstructed piecemeal by persons of varying degrees of closeness in time and emotional involvement to him. Both works are about boys of humble origin who rose to become American Titans and built imposing architectural monuments in honor of themselves, and both are centrally concerned with a theme implicit in the narrative technique, whether the subject's essential reality can ever be dependably reconstructed. The portrait continued to emerge along well-worn lines even after the script fell into new hands. It is also evident that in these later stages the shaping of the portrait continued to be a mixture of invention and precedent. In the first revised draft, for instance, Jed Leland is written into the sequence (later scrapped) at Kane's Renaissance palace in Rome. Just before the momentous step that will take Kane back to America and an American destiny, Leland appears among Kane's entourage of decadent Europeans, reciting lines from, of all sources, early Walt Whitman.[14] Despite the collaborative nature of the enterprise, the completed portrait of Charles Foster Kane is entirely consistent with

Mankiewicz's rough sketch, and it also bears startling resemblances to another second-generation American tycoon figure, Jay Gatsby, and clear family resemblances to earlier portraits in the line.

Nor is *Citizen Kane* an isolated instance of how film stories of typical Americans are partially shaped by the influence of traditional narrative materials. Many of the best American films show clear evidence of aware-ness of the central documents of American literary history. The screen persona of Fred Astaire (for instance) is a continuation of a well-worn stereotype, the typical American as a carefree, spontaneous, pragmatic fel-low, perennially an optimist and demonstrably more natural and less fet-tered by tradition than his European counterpart. Among Astaire's most endearing films are the musicals he made at RKO with Ginger Rogers in the thirties. Four of these are based on another timeworn American premise—a band of American innocents facing hardships abroad and having to exercise their American resourcefulness to keep from being swallowed up by Europe. One customarily does not look for literary indebtedness in such an unlikely place as a popular musical. But what other explanation is there for touches such as Astaire playing a Midwestern innocent named Huck; Rogers playing a bogus countess who is really Lizzie Gatz from back home in the Midwest; Rogers, in their most popular film, knowing only that Astaire is an American and calling him "Adam" (an American Adam in Paris?); or Astaire in the same film saying (like Thoreau said of Americans) he has the Saint Vitus Dance. Howard Hawks' *Red River* (1948), one of the very best efforts in that most charac-teristic of American genres, the Western, is another story of a proud and ambitious American who appropriates virgin land and builds his own empire. As is the custom, through cold calculation and hard work, the undertakings of this American prosper. But suddenly, when he is at the height of his power and seemingly just on the threshold of seeing his fondest ambitions realized, the heir apparent in this frontier dynastic line rebels against his (surrogate) father's wishes and sets off on a course of his own. In a desperate attempt to avert the shattering of his dream, the father proposes to a woman that they test-mate: if she is able to bear him a male heir, he will share his property and position with her. The general motifs are the stock-in-trade of American narratives at all levels, but who can fail to see the *specific* echoes of Colonel Thomas Sutpen? In another of the undoubted classics of American popular genre films, a big-time bootlegger is out to win another man's woman; he invites her to his place to show off his flashy new things; in his bedroom he takes out piles of expensive new shirts and excitedly displays them to her; the woman is named for a flower. Can anyone doubt that in scenes like this in *Scarface* (1932), a Capone film filled with conscious ironic homages to the American self-help tradition, Howard Hawks and his writer Ben Hecht were reworking material from *The Great Gatsby*?

Such eminent critics of American narrative as D. H. Lawrence, Richard Chase, and Leslie Fiedler have said for years that artists in America always share a common starting point, the need to evolve original narrative forms to do justice to the complex and paradoxical experiences of their American subjects; and that genuinely American narratives, in whatever medium or period, take shape along certain lines common to them all. There is a whole body of noteworthy criticism devoted to illustrating and substantiating these themes in American literary narratives but practically no consideration of the possibility that they may also extend to narratives in the new visual forms of the twentieth century. Yet, in at least one instance, there are remarkably extensive structural and conceptual parallels between masterworks in two mediums. It may turn out that the *Great Gatsby/Citizen Kane* relationship is just a special case, or it may turn out that there are general patterns of this sort to be uncovered in American films. In any case, it is something that ought to be considered.

Notes

1. Recent criticism has been characterized by efforts to establish a narrative ancestry for *Citizen Kane*. The most conspicuous of these is "Raising Kane" (reprinted in *The Citizen Kane Book* [Boston, 1971]), in which Pauline Kael attempts to show that many streams in American films of the thirties fed into *Citizen Kane*, among them *Mad Love* and the tradition of Gothic melodrama; *The Front Page* and other films of newspaper reporters in search of stories; tycoon biographies such as *The Power and the Glory* and *A Man to Remember;* and Paramount-style comedy, with its snappy dialogue and well-oiled plots. ("Raising Kane" is also an effort to restore what Kael sees as a rightful share of credit to Herman Mankiewicz for his work on the script. It has seemed to many to take *too much* credit away from Welles.) Also see Charles Higham, *The Films of Orson Welles* (Berkeley, 1970), pp. 10–14; and Tom Shales, "Antecedents of *Citizen Kane,*" *The American Film Heritage: Impressions from the American Film Institute Archives* (Washington, D.C., 1972), pp. 127–34. An attempt to establish literary ancestry is Hubert Cohen's "The *Heart of Darkness* in *Citizen Kane,*" *Cinema Journal* 12 (1972): 11–25. (Welles' first Hollywood project was to have been an adaptation of Conrad's novel. The "Mercury Theatre of the Air" had done a radio drama of it.) The idea of comparing *The Great Gatsby* and *Citizen Kane* was first suggested to me by a remark of Ronald Gottesman in his introduction to *Focus on "Citizen Kane"* (Englewood Cliffs, N.J., 1971). p. 6. I thank Professor Gottesman and Professors Warren French and Alan Rose for their generous assistance and advice.

2. *The Great Gatsby* (Scribner Library ed.), p. 112. Quotations are from this edition.

3. Herman J. Mankiewicz and Orson Welles, shooting script of *Citizen Kane,* in *The Citizen Kane Book,* pp. 95–97.

4. R. W. B. Lewis, *The American Adam: Innocence, Tragedy and Tradition in the Nineteenth Century* (Chicago, 1955); Leslie A. Fiedler, *Love and Death in the American Novel,* revised ed. (New York, 1966).

5. Kael, "Raising Kane"; John Houseman, *Run-Through: A Memoir* (New York, 1972), pp. 447–61; Peter Bogdanovich, "The Kane Mutiny," *Esquire* (October 1972), pp. 99–105, 180–90; Orson Welles, "The creation of *Citizen Kane*" (Letter to the Editor), London *Times,* November 17, 1971, p. 17.

6. There is a photocopy of *American* in the Theater Arts Library at UCLA (see *Motion Pictures: A Catalog,* Theater Arts Library, UCLA; Boston, 1972, 1:514). I thank Professor

Howard Suber and the UCLA Theater Arts Library for making this copy available to me. I also thank Pauline Kael for her assistance.

7. Orson Welles, "*Citizen Kane* Is Not about Louella Parsons' Boss," *Friday* 2 (February 14, 1941): 9; reprinted in Gottesman, *Focus on "Citizen Kane,"* pp. 67–68.

8. Sara Mankiewicz, letter to the author, June 6, 1973.

9. Houseman, letter to the author, June 25, 1974. Samuel Rosenberg, author of the Conan Doyle book *Naked Is the Best Disguise* and former plagiarism expert for Hollywood studios, writes in reaction to my discussion of borrowing by screenwriters: "You are onto something very important in the film industry: the wholesale cannibalizing of trashy and profound material for the mass of pictures made under terrific competitive pressure. . . . The method of self-and-other plagiarism you describe was so widespread that it even had a name: 'switcheroo'" (letter to the author, June 27, 1974). As a related point of interest, in 1947 the author of *Imperial Hearst* brought suit against the makers of *Citizen Kane* for copyright infringement. Mankiewicz insisted that he had known *firsthand* material about Hearst that had appeared *in print* only in *Imperial Hearst*. After copies of the book turned up on an inventory of Mankiewicz's library, the trial ended with a hung jury, and RKO settled out of court (see "Raising Kane," pp. 81–82).

10. Houseman (*Run-Through*, p. 457) says he remembers the exact date because that same evening he listened to the broadcast via short-wave of the capitulation speech of the King of Belgium. I have examined Revised Final Script 6/5/40 (in the Theater Arts Library, UCLA), Second Revised Final 6/24/40 (in the Film Study Center, Museum of Modern Art), and Third Revised Final 7/16/40 (also at UCLA), plus other special scripts assembled by Professor Suber at UCLA and listed in *Motion Pictures*, 1:514.

11. Quentin Anderson, *The Imperial Self: An Essay in American Literary and Cultural History* (New York, 1971). Also see, among others, Lewis, *American Adam;* Tony Tanner, *The Reign of Wonder: Naivety and Reality in American Literature* (Cambridge, 1965); Richard Poirier, *A World Elsewhere: The Place of Style in American Literature* (New York, 1966).

12. Sara Mankiewicz, letter to the author, June 6, 1973.

13. Gerald Mast, *A Short History of the Movies* (Indianapolis, 1971), p. 310.

14. Revised Final Script 6/5/40.

The Great Diptych: Geology and Relief

ANDRÉ BAZIN

THE OBSESSION WITH CHILDHOOD

BEFORE CONTINUING the artistic biography of Orson Welles, this would seem a suitable moment to pause over his work and reflect on its critical significance. There is little doubt that even if he had directed only *Citizen Kane* and *The Magnificent Ambersons*, Welles would have a major position in the history of the cinema. It is not to diminish the importance of his later films if I assert that, at least on a formal level, the essence of what Welles brought to the cinema is already present in his first two films.

Analysis and reflection reveal, above all, a stylistic unity. Within the context of Welles' filmography, these two works constitute a vast aesthetic land mass whose geology and relief justify simultaneous study.

Let us take up their orientation first. *Kane* and *Ambersons* together form what might be called the social realist cycle, to distinguish it both from the Shakespearean cycle composed by *Macbeth* and *Othello* and from the "ethical entertainments" comprising *The Lady from Shanghai* and *Mr. Arkadin*. "Entertainment" should not be understood here in a pejorative or even a restrictive sense. But it is obvious that these two latter films imposed an overall sense of amused contrivance on their thriller conventions. In other words, the seriousness of the message filters through the apparent futility of the game.

Kane and *Ambersons*, on the other hand, are the cinematic equivalents of realistic novels in the tradition of, say, Balzac. On one level they appear to be powerful, critical testimonies on American society.

But one must pass beyond this first level of significance, where one soon reaches, beneath these social deposits, the crystalline mass of moral significance. From this point of view, Welles' *oeuvre* is one of the least debatable in the history of the cinema, and takes its place beside the great spiritual landscapes created by Stroheim, Chaplin, Eisenstein, Renoir, Flaherty, Rossellini. Rather than pursue an exhaustive description and analysis of this message, we shall try to isolate one of the major themes of Welles' imagination as it is revealed in a very special way in his first two films: the obsession with or, if one prefers, nostalgia for childhood. Kane's lust for social power and George Minafer's pride are deeply rooted in their childhoods—that is, in Welles' childhood. We have seen, however, that it was a happy childhood *par excellence*, but nonetheless one that was possibly—and paradoxically—incomplete by virtue of its very happiness. Too many good fairies hovered over his cradle, not leaving the child time enough to live his childhood. So it is not surprising that *Citizen Kane* and *The Magnificent Ambersons* could finally be a matter of a childhood tragedy. The last wish of Kane, the superman, the supercitizen who squanders his fabulous wealth playing with and against public opinion, his "fundamental project," as the existentialists would say, is completely contained in a glass ball where a few artificial snowflakes fall at will on a little house. This grizzled old man, whom no one dares to admit is senile, who almost held in his hand the destiny of a nation, grasps this childish souvenir before dying, this toy that was spared during his destruction of the doll's room belonging to his wife Susan. The film ends on the word with which it began; "Rosebud," whose significance in Kane's life the investigation seeks in vain, is nothing but the word written on the surface of a child's sled. When pride and the alibis of success have loosened their grip, when this old man, on the threshold of death, forgets himself so far as to let slip the most secret key to his dreams in a last reverie, his legacy to history is only the word of a child. Isn't it with the sled, whose perhaps unconscious memory will haunt him until his death, that he violently strikes, at the very outset of his life, the banker who has come to tear him from his play in the snow and his mother's protection, come to snatch him from his childhood to make him into Kane the citizen? "A great citizen"—Kane indeed becomes this because his fortune condemns him to it; but at least he takes revenge on the frustration of his childhood by playing with his social power as a monstrous sled, allowing himself to be intoxicated by the dizziness of wealth or striking in the face those who dared to question the moral grounds of his acts and his pleasures. Unmasked by his best friend and by the woman he thought he loved the most, Kane admits before dying that there is no profit in gaining the whole world if one has lost one's own childhood.

If one had any doubts, on the evidence of a single film, about the obsession with childhood in Welles' work, *The Magnificent Ambersons* would provide a decisive confirmation. Although the screenplay this time was not original but one based on a novel whose plot was imposed on him from the outset, Welles succeeded in infecting the principal character, played by Tim Holt, with the same obsession as Kane. Not that George Minafer is in any way a duplicate of Kane. The social context, the historical moment, the biographical conditions in which the Amberson heir evolves, give his personal drama a completely different character. But his tyrannical attachment to his mother and his opposition to Eugene Morgan—the industrialist who loves her and who represents both economic and social change—form a similar egotistic "fixation" on the universe of his childhood, where he was king (the scene where the young George, dressed in a curious Louis XIV outfit, refuses to apologize is highly significant).

But even more strongly than this superficial reading of the scripts' underlying meaning suggests, the profound authenticity of the theme of childhood in *Citizen Kane* and *The Magnificent Ambersons* is revealed more persuasively by the introduction in the story or *mise en scène* of significant and visibly unpremeditated details, which have imposed themselves on the author's imagination by their affective power alone. For instance, the repeated use of snow, characteristic of childhood fantasies (the snowballs of *Les Enfants Terribles*). Nostalgia for snow is connected to our earliest games (to which should doubtless be added the specific symbolism of snow, whose threatened whiteness, auguring the mire to come, is particularly suited to the guilty innocence of childhood). In *Ambersons*, a fall in the snow becomes the pretext for the first lovers' kiss between George and Lucy. Another detail, this time from the dialogue: the affair between Kane and Susan dates from a meeting when Kane was going alone on foot to a warehouse on the edge of the city to look at some things that belonged to his mother. Indirectly linked to the theme of childhood by way of egotism and the need for social approval is Kane's taste for statues, through which he is obviously pursuing the impossible project of becoming a statue himself.

Once again, this interpretation, which we might call existential, does not pretend in any way to exhaust the meanings of Welles' first two films, whose labyrinths could be traced by other threads. What matters is that one should be no less sure of meeting the Minotaur there. Welles' *oeuvre* is a haunted one—that is all that it was necessary to demonstrate.

THE INTUITION OF THE SEQUENCE SHOT

But more than the intellectual and moral message—which will become more precise and perhaps richer later on, in the subsequent films—it is their formal brilliance, their overwhelming originality of expression, to which *Citizen Kane* and *The Magnificent Ambersons* owe their historical importance and the decisive influence they have had on cinema all over the world. We can analyze the technique of the *mise en scène* in either film, for despite considerable variations between their styles, the essential aspects of their means of expression are the same. This likeness is all the more revealing in that the technical crew, and the cameraman in particular, are different. Certainly one must not underestimate the merits of Gregg Toland, who, before and after his collaboration with Welles, has shown himself to be a cameraman of genius, to whom the tyro director undoubtedly owed a great deal; but the refined and somewhat sophisticated elegance of Stanley Cortez's photography is at opposite poles to the rugged frankness of Toland's. Nevertheless, the construction of *The*

Magnificent Ambersons is founded on the same principles as *Citizen Kane*, principles which therefore certainly originated with Welles. When one has seen and absorbed *Citizen Kane* and meditated, however briefly but without prejudice, on its *mise en scène*, the accusations of plagiarism or of gratuitous eccentricities designed to *épater le bourgeois* soon appear absurd. There are so many inescapable connections between the formal approaches adopted and the film's significance that a desire to astonish and attract attention appears infinitely less probable than a need to recreate a language capable of expressing new realities on the screen. Let us try to reconstruct one of these logical progressions from intention to form.

It is plausible, for example, to suppose that Welles, as a man of the theatre, constructs his *mise en scène* on the basis of the actor. One may imagine that the intuition of the sequence shot, this new unit in film semantics and syntax, grew out of the vision of a director accustomed to placing the actor within the décor, who experienced traditional editing no longer as a fluency or language but as a loss of efficacy, a mutilation of the spectacular possibilities of the image. For Welles, each scene to be played forms a complete unit in time and space. The acting loses its meaning, is deprived of its dramatic blood like a severed limb, if it ceases to maintain a living and responsive connection with the other characters and the décor. Furthermore, the scene charges itself like an electrical condenser as it progresses and must be kept carefully insulated against all parasitic contacts until a sufficient dramatic voltage has been reached, which produces the spark that all the action has been directed toward. Take, for instance, Welles' favorite scene in *The Magnificent Ambersons*: the one in the kitchen between Fanny and George and, later, Jack. It lasts almost the length of an entire reel of film. The camera remains immobile from start to finish,[1] facing Fanny and George; the latter, having just returned from a trip with his mother, has rushed into the kitchen to gorge himself on strawberry shortcake prepared by his aunt. Let us distinguish what one may call "the real action" and "the pretext action" in this scene. The real action is the suppressed anxiety of Aunt Fanny, secretly in love with Eugene Morgan, as she tries with feigned indifference to find out if George and his mother traveled with Eugene. The pretext action—George's childish gluttony—which floods the entire screen, submerging Aunt Fanny's shy but distressed vibrations, is deliberately insignificant. For these two actions there are two dialogues: the real one, made up of a few insidious questions, camouflaged in a certain way by the other, crudely banal, in which Fanny advises George not to eat too fast and asks him whether the cake is sweet enough. Treated in the classic manner, this scene would have been cut into a number of separate shots, in order to enable us to distinguish clearly between the real and the apparent action. The few words that reveal Fanny's feelings would have been underlined by a close-up, which would also have allowed us to appreciate Agnes Moorehead's performance at that precise moment. In short, the dramatic continuity would have been the exact opposite of the weighty objectivity Welles imposes in order to bring us with maximum effect to Fanny's final breakdown, exploding brutally in the midst of this insignificant dialogue. Wasn't it more skillful to ease us gradually into this intolerable tension, created from moment to moment, between the real feelings of the protagonists and their outward behavior? Fanny's pain and jealousy burst out at the end like an awaited storm, but one whose moment of arrival and whose violence one could not exactly predict. The slightest camera movement, or a close-up to cue us in on the scene's evolution, would have broken this heavy spell which forces us to participate intimately in the action. We shall have occasion, returning to Welles' construction from another point of view, to analyze scenes built up in exactly the same manner. It is obvious that this shot was the only one that allowed the action to be set in such relief. If one wished to play at each moment on the unity of the scene's significance, and construct the action not on a logical analysis of the relations between the characters and their surroundings, but on the physical perception of these relations as dramatic forces, to make us present at their evolution right up to the moment when the entire scene explodes beneath this accumulated pressure, it was essential for the borders of the screen to be able to reveal the scene's totality. This is why Welles asked his cameraman to resolve this difficult problem. In the same way, throughout the wonderful sequence of the ball at the beginning of *Ambersons* (a sequence whose construction, moreover, is very close to that of the chase in *La Règle du Jeu*), several centers of interest are perpetually crossing the screen, compelling us to leap from one to the next, regretfully abandoning each preceding one.[2]

THE TECHNIQUE OF WIDE ANGLES

But the clarity of the scene in depth was not enough for Welles' theatrical approach; he also needed a "lateral" depth of focus. This is why Gregg Toland used very wide-angle lenses, bringing the angle of the shot close to that of the eye's normal vision. These wide-angle shots are perhaps even more characteristic of the style of *Citizen Kane* than the depth of focus (in *The Best Years of Our Lives*, Gregg Toland seems mainly to have used "long focal lengths," giving a narrow angle and a "telephoto" effect). Initially, it was because of the exceptional openness of this angle of vision that the presence of ceilings became indispensable to hide the studio superstructures. Their installation must have singularly complicated the lighting problems, especially as with very reduced iris stops a strong light was necessary, which was the origin of the high contrasts in the images. This must have been counteracted on several occasions by using false netted ceilings which permitted light to come across.[3] Wide-angle lenses also have the effect of distorting perspective appreciably. They give the impression of a stretching of length, which accentuates the deep focus even more. I won't risk the hypothesis that Welles planned this effect; but in any case he has turned it to his advantage. The stretching of the image in depth, combined with the nearly constant use of low angles, produces throughout the film an impression of tension and conflict, as if the image might be torn apart. No one can deny that there is a convincing affinity between this physical aspect of the image and the metaphysical drama of the story. As for the ceilings, expecially in *Ambersons*, they help situate the characters in a closed universe, crushed on all sides by the décor. In a remarkable and indispensable study of space in the cinema,[4] Maurice Scherer[5] has demonstrated conclusively the role of the spatial structures of the film image. Indeed, the significance of directions of movement has long been recognized in painting, and everyone now agrees in marveling at the famous vertical distortions in El Greco. Why, then, should what one proclaims to be full of meaning and high aesthetic value in a traditional art instantly cease to be a valid process as soon as it is used in cinema? Why should Orson Welles be nothing but a show-off and a sensation-monger when he imprints the same formal characteristics on all his work? Certainly Orson Welles is neither the inventor of low angles nor the first to use ceilings, but when he wanted to play with technique and astonish us with a dazzling formal display, he made *The Lady From Shanghai*. The persistence of the low angle in *Citizen Kane* means, on the contrary, that we quickly cease to have a clear awareness of technique even while we continue to submit to its mastery. Thus it is much more likely that the method corresponds to a precise aesthetic intention: to impose a particular vision of drama on us—a vision that could be called infernal, since the gaze upward seems to come out of the earth, while the ceilings, forbidding any escape within the décor, complete the fatality of this curse. Kane's lust for power crushes us, but is itself crushed by the décor. Through the camera, we are capable in a way of perceiving Kane's failure at the same time we experience his power.

CONSTRUCTION IN DEPTH

Up to this point I have been attempting to account for the choice of technique employed by Welles on the basis of his creative psychology, in relation to his past and his tastes. But let us abandon this subjective point of view, at the risk of limiting the scope of our analysis. Whatever Welles' intentions were, conscious or not, his films remain, independently of what we know about their author. The influence of *Citizen Kane* on the evolution of cinema—its importance as a model—goes far beyond the admirable lesson in dramatic direction which I have tried to analyze. Beyond the new way of developing a particular scene, it was the very structures of film language—such as they were almost universally practiced around 1940, and in most cases still are today—that Welles came along to upset.

I shall deliberately not dwell on the narrative originality of *Citizen Kane*, on the decomposition of time and the multiplicity of points of view. Welles is not really the inventor of this in the cinema, and the procedure was obviously taken from novels. But he perfected its use and adapted it to the resources of cinema with a comprehensiveness that had never yet been achieved.

But I shall pass lightly over these aspects of Welles' films, since they offer no difficulty for even the uninitiated spectator, provided he shows a little good faith. A bit of attention and reflection is sufficient.

In short, it would be better to spend some time on more specific innovations, where a certain familiarity with film analysis is perhaps necessary if one is to be able to distinguish them from the unity of the *oeuvre*. We shall see, moreover, that they are directly dependent on the subjects and their treatment.

We have seen that the value of deep focus, so passionately contested by some, probably lay for Welles in a certain way of placing the décor and characters. But it involves many consequences in addition to the construction of ceilings and a denser style of acting. To begin with, its technical demands make shot transitions more difficult. In any case, Welles was not the sort of man to stop at such a difficulty, even though the decision to have the whole scene played in the camera's distinct field of vision was contradictory to the classical practice of shot transitions. Better still, Welles quite often reinforces the maintenance of this dramatic unity by refusing to use camera movements that would in fact reestablish, by the succession of new framings, a hypothetical breakdown into shots. But we must perhaps recall here, for greater clarity, what we mean by breakdown into shots.[6]

Whatever the film, its aim is to give us the illusion of being present at real events unfolding before us as in everyday reality. But this illusion involves a fundamental deceit, for reality exists in a continuous space, and the screen in fact presents us with a succession of tiny fragments called "shots," whose choice, order and length constitute precisely what we call the film's *découpage*. If, through a deliberate effort of attention, we try to see the ruptures imposed by the camera on the continuous unfolding of the event represented, and try to understand clearly why we normally take no notice of them, we realize that we tolerate them because they nevertheless allow an impression to remain of continuous and homogeneous reality. In reality we don't see everything at once either. Action, passion or fear makes us proceed to an unconscious *découpage* of the space surrounding us. Our legs and neck didn't wait for the cinema to invent the tracking shot and the pan, nor our attention to contrive the close-up. This universal psychological experience is enough to make us forget the material lack of verisimilitude of *découpage*, and enables the spectator to participate in it just as he does in a natural relationship with reality.

In contrast, let us examine a typical Welles scene: Susan's attempted suicide in *Citizen Kane*. The screen opens on Susan's bedroom seen from behind the night table. In close-up, wedged against the camera, is an enormous glass, taking up almost a quarter of the image, along with a little spoon and an open medicine bottle. The glass almost entirely conceals Susan's bed, enclosed in a shadowy zone from which only a faint sound of labored breathing escapes, like that of a drugged sleeper. The bedroom is empty; far away in the background of this private desert is the door, rendered even more distant by the lens' false perspectives, and, *behind* the door, a knocking. Without having seen anything but a glass and heard two noises, on two different sound planes, we have immediately grasped the situation: Susan has locked herself in her room to try to kill herself; Kane is trying to get in. The scene's dramatic structure is basically founded on the distinction between the two sound planes: close up, Susan's breathing, and from behind the door, her husband's knocking. A tension is established between these two poles, which are kept at a distance from each other by the deep focus. Now the knocks become louder; Kane is trying to force the door with his shoulder; he succeeds. We see him appear, tiny, framed in the doorway, and then rush toward us. The spark has been ignited between the two dramatic poles of the image. The scene is over.

To really understand the originality of this *mise-en-scène*—which may appear natural, so effortlessly does it achieve its goal—one must try to imagine what anyone else but Welles would have done (give or take a detail or two).

The scene would have been split up into at least five or six shots. For instance: a close-up of the glass and the pills, a shot of Susan sweating and breathing heavily on her bed (at this moment, the off-screen sound of the knocking on the door), a shot of Kane knocking on the door, creation of suspense by brief cross-cutting, that is, a series of shots first inside, then outside the room, leading up to a shot of Kane forcing the door open. At that moment, another shot of Kane from behind, rushing toward the bed; and to end, perhaps, a close-up of Kane leaning over Susan.

It is evident that the classical sequence composed of a series of shots, analyzing the action according to the way the director wants us to see it, is resolved here into only one shot. So that Welles' *découpage* in deep focus ultimately tends to absorb the concept of "shots" in a *découpage* unit which might be called the sequence shot.

Naturally, this revolution in the conventions of *découpage* is of interest less in itself than for its implications. To simplify, let us say that this synthetic language is more realistic than traditional analytical *découpage*.

More realistic and at the same time more intellectual, for in a way it forces the spectator to participate in the meaning of the film by distinguishing the implicit relations, which the *découpage* no longer displays on the screen like the pieces of a dismantled engine. Obliged to exercise his liberty and his intelligence, the spectator perceives the ontological ambivalence of reality directly, in the very structure of its appearances. Reconsidered from this point of view, a scene like the static shot of the kitchen in *Ambersons* is particularly significant. It seems that during the entire sequence, the camera obstinately refuses to come to our assistance, to guide us in the perception of an action that we feel is gaining momentum, even though we don't know when or where it will erupt. Who knows if it may not be just when we are looking at George that a revealing expression will cross Fanny's face? And during the whole scene, objects, outrageously irrelevant to the action yet monstrously present (cakes, food, kitchenware, a coffeepot), solicit our attention without a single camera movement conspiring to diminish their presence.

Contrary to what one might believe at first, "*découpage* in depth" is more charged with meaning than analytical *découpage*. It is no less abstract than the other, but the additional abstraction which it integrates into the narrative comes precisely from a surplus of realism. A realism that is in a certain sense ontological, restoring to the object and the décor their existential density, the weight of their presence; a dramatic realism which refuses to separate the actor from the décor, the foreground from the background; a psychological realism which brings the spectator back to the real conditions of perception, a perception which is never completely determined a priori. In opposition to this "realistic" *mise en scène*, proceeding by "sequence shots" seized by the camera as blocks of reality, Welles frequently uses an abstract metaphorical or symbolic montage to encapsulate lengthy sections of the plot (the evolution of the relationship between Kane and his first wife; Susan's career as a singer). But this very old procedure, which the silent cinema abused, finds a new meaning here, in precise contrast to the extreme realism of the scenes in which events are respected integrally. Instead of a crossbred *découpage*, in which the concrete event is partially dissolved into abstraction by shot transitions, we have two essentially different narrative modalities. One can see this quite clearly when, after the series of superimpositions encapsulating three years of torture for Susan and ending on a light going out, the screen thrusts us brutally into the drama of Susan's attempted suicide. Jean-Paul Sartre pointed out very aptly in an article in *L'Écran Français* that this was the equivalent of the frequentative form in English: "For three years he obliged her to sing on all the stages of America. Susan's anxiety would grow, each show would be an ordeal for her, one day she could no longer stand it . . ."[7]: Susan's attempted suicide.

A STYLE THAT CREATES MEANING

All great cinematic works doubtless reflect, more or less explicitly, the moral vision, the spiritual tendencies of their author. Sartre wrote in reference to Faulkner and Dos Passos that every novelistic technique necessarily relates back to a metaphysics. If there *was* a metaphysics, the old form of *découpage* couldn't contribute to its expression: the world of Ford and Capra can be defined on the basis of their scripts, their themes, the dramatic effects they have sought, the choice of scenes. It is not to be found in the *découpage* as such. With Orson Welles, on the contrary, the *découpage* in depth becomes a technique which constitutes the meaning of the story. It isn't merely a way of placing the camera, sets and actors [*mettre en scène*]; it places the very nature of the story in question. With this technique, the cinema strays a little further from the theatre, becomes less a spectacle than a narrative.

Indeed, as in the novel, it isn't only the dialogue, the descriptive clarity, the behavior of the characters, but the style imparted to the language which creates meaning.

Far from being—as some persist in saying, assuming inattentiveness in the spectator—a return to the "static shot" employed in the early days of cinema by Méliès, Zecca and Feuillade, or else some rediscovery of filmed theatre, Welles' sequence shot is a decisive stage in the evolution of film language, which after having passed through the montage of the silent period and the *découpage* of the talkies, is now tending to revert to the static shot, but by a dialectical progress which incorporates all the discoveries of *découpage* into the realism of the sequence shot. Of course, Welles is not the only promoter of this evolution, to which Wyler's work also gives testimony. Renoir, for example, in all his French productions, did not cease to work in the same direction. But Welles has brought to it a powerful and original contribution which, like it or not, has shaken the edifices of cinematic tradition.

Notes

1. To dot the *i*'s and cross the *t*'s somewhat, the shot runs for four minutes and twenty-five seconds and contains two brief pans—one at the beginning and another at the end. (*Trans.*)

2. In an article about *The Magnificent Ambersons* for *L'Écran Français* (November 19, 1946), Bazin also noted: "Thanks to the depth of field, all of the actors participate in the action and the entire set, including the ceilings, encloses them in its presence. In *Ambersons*, the house's interior architecture seems to be completely and continually on the screen, just as one sees the street in its entire length several times, either directly or through the reflections in the shopwindows. The care taken by Orson Welles not to crack this dramatic crystal led him to break with the usual practice of construction by using static shots of vertiginous duration (that of the kitchen dialogue between Aunt Fanny and George), but it would be a simple matter to show that the extended tracking shots arise from the same concern to follow an event in all its developments. It is not so much camera movements as

actors' movements within the décor and the variations of lighting which serve the narrative." Bazin explored this latter point more fully in "*L'Apport d'Orson Welles*," an article printed in *Ciné-Club* (May 1948): "Choosing examples from *Kane* and *Ambersons*, it would be easy to demonstrate that the dramatic and technical construction, even though it didn't radically upset basic filmic matters, testified to a singular inventive power that already was in the *mise en scène*. In particular, the frequent use (remarkably subtle and assured in *Ambersons*) of what one could call the counteremphasis of the subject has never been pushed so far. I mean by this the refusal to let the spectator see the climactic events of a scene. This dramatic procedure should in no way be confused with ellipsis, which is cited, perhaps incorrectly, as the basic rhetorical figure of cinema; it should be linked, rather, with litotes [understatement]. With Welles, the entire film is partially pulled out of our reach, and all the action seems to be surrounded by an aura of inaccessibility. In *Ambersons* particularly, the lighting of Cortez, the cameraman, probably serves in one respect to restore the ambiance of gaslight, and in another respect, enables Welles to let the actors evolve in a luminous heterogeneous space, where the alternations of clear and shadowy areas restore, within the immobility of the sequence shot, a sort of *découpage* and dramatic rhythm. But it will frequently be noted that Welles takes paradoxical care to have the most important lines uttered precisely when the actor is least visible. Thus the strong moments in the action escape us at the very instant when our desire to grasp them is most acute. The famous kitchen scene in Ambersons between George and Aunt Fanny can be partially explained in relation to this. The *refusal* to move the camera throughout the scene's duration, particularly when Agnes Moorehead has her emotional crisis and rushes away (the camera keeping its nose obstinately glued to the strawberry shortcake), is tantamount to making us witness the event in the position of a man helplessly strapped to an armchair." (*Trans.*)

3. "None of the sets was rigged for overhead lighting, although occasionally necessary backlighting was arranged by lifting a small section of the ceiling and using a light through the opening"—Gregg Toland, "How I Broke the Rules in *Citizen Kane*," *Popular Photography*, June 1941. (*Trans.*)

4. *La Revue du Cinéma*, No. 14.

5. A pseudonym used by Eric Rohmer. (*Trans*)

6. Bazin's term here is *découpage*, a word translated variously as "construction," "cutting" or "breakdown into shots," depending on the context. For a detailed account of the separate meanings and uses of this word, cf. the first chapter of Nöel Burch's *Theory of Film Practice* (Praeger, 1973). (*Trans.*)

7. The third and fourth verbs have been adapted here to English frequentative forms to suit the context. (*Trans.*)

The Inaccessibility of *The Lady from Shanghai*

MARK GRAHAM

ONE OF André Bazin's most provocative comments on Orson Welles' films is that "With Welles, the whole film is somehow partially inaccessible to the grasp; nothing that happens can altogether be gotten to."[1] As I shall argue, the sense of inaccessibility is central to *The Lady from Shanghai* (1946) and to our experience of the film. For this work continually shifts and shimmers, its pieces refusing to stay still long enough to coalesce into a durable and unified pattern. As a result, we are repeatedly baffled in our attempts to gain a firm and reliable perspective, whether visually, mentally, or emotionally.

The film's ungraspability operates on multiple levels—narrative point of view and structure, visual style, settings, plot, and theme. But on whatever level, it generally involves two distinctive features: first, a radical instability that results in a splitting of perspective; and second, a seductive and tantalizing lure, a misleading suggestion that we can at last get a grip on the film. Typically, this lure serves to increase our desire for, and expectation of, accessibility and then—once the lure proves false—to heighten our sense of inaccessibility.

Much of the elusiveness of *The Lady from Shanghai* results from the treatment of narrative point of view. Of all the characters that Welles plays in his own films, only Michael O'Hara is both voice-over narrator and a major participant in the action.[2] As such, Michael is unique in that he is both observer and observed, subject and object, as well as the only character in this director's work who is centrally engaged in commenting upon his own visually rendered past.

To begin with, Michael's dual role creates several temporal instabilities that constantly alter our perception of the film's narrative and structural framework, and thereby greatly contribute to the overall sense of inaccessibility. These instabilities are introduced in the first few minutes of the film, culminating in the striking transition from Michael's voice-over narration to his first lines of synchronous on-screen speech. The narrator, referring to Elsa Bannister, remarks: "'Good evening,' says I, . . ." and "I asked her if she'd have a cigarette." Then comes a close-up of Michael saying to Elsa, who is off-screen, "It's my last one. I've been looking forward to it, so please don't disappoint me."

Reprinted by permission from *Film Criticism* 5 (Spring 1981).

This clearly marks a shift from present to past, but it is a rather tricky one. On the one hand, the narrator's use of reported speech in the past tense indicates that the visualized events occur in the past and that it is the narrator's temporal standpoint that places them there. On the other hand, that Michael's first on-screen lines are delivered as direct address in the present tense dramatizes the fact that these ostensibly past events are rendered aurally and visually as though in the present.

Indeed, throughout the film, the spectator must adapt his focus to two distinct, juxtaposed, and asynchronous presents—the one the narrator inhabits and the anterior present on the screen. Often what we see seems to be happening in an unqualified present, largely because the images themselves are so powerfully immediate, but also because during the lengthy stretches without any voice-over narration we tend to forget the temporal perspective created by the narrator. But whenever we are made aware of this perspective—whenever for example, the narrator resumes his commentary after a considerable silence—we once again must adjust our perception of the time frame of these events.

Another temporal instability introduced in the opening scenes involves our inability to determine whether what we see represents actual occurrences as they originally happened or merely the visualized projections of the narrator's memory of those occurrences. The film begins with a series of shots of water, followed by the more specific, though still general, views of the East River and Central Park; then a shot of a moving carriage in the park, with Elsa soon becoming visible, seated in the carriage; a shot of Michael walking alone, a two-shot of Michael and Elsa, a close-up of Elsa, another two-shot, and then the close-up of Michael speaking his first on-screen lines. The way these images become increasingly specific and narrow in their focus suggests the sequence of establishing shots, medium shots, and close-ups which is traditionally used to introduce "realistic" narratives, that is, narratives whose action, although fictional, is supposed to be occurring objectively. But this progression and these images can also be regarded as authorized, indeed generated, by the narrator himself. For they suggest a gradual homing in of the narrator's memory through a visualized chain of mental associations (water/East River/Central Park/the carriage/Elsa/the first encounter with Elsa). Such an interpretation is supported by the fact that, until the last of these images, the only voice we hear is that of the retrospective narrator, unaccompanied by any on-screen dialogue or even by any appreciable on-screen sound.

In fact, everything that we see in this film can be regarded alternately as constituting either an objective occurrence or a mentally evoked recurrence. Consequently, we often have the hallucinatory sense that the compelling physical solidity of these events is illusory, not only because of the suggestion that what seems to be happening in a continually unfolding present has, in fact, already happened and therefore no longer actually exists, but also because these events may represent not physical but mental phenomena—that is, the manifestations of the narrator's memory. By the same token, the presentness of these events can be attributed either to their actually occurring in their own autonomous present or to their being vividly and indeed literally present to the narrator as memories.

Now the transition in the first scene from voice-over narration to on-screen speech clearly serves to notify us that the speaker in both cases is virtually the same character. In fact, at this transition the narrator and participant seem to converge and even to merge, as though the narrator were imaginatively re-entering his own past. Once this implied re-entry is accomplished, it becomes increasingly evident that the relationship between the narrator and his past is essentially circular. For the narrator is engaged in relating and reliving the past experiences that lead up to and determine his present, in which, of course, he is engaged in relating and reliving those same experiences—and so on, as though Michael were trapped on a temporal merry-go-round.

As a result, the film's linear structure, in which past leads to present, is subsumed by its circular structure, which involves a doubling back of present to past. Though the sense of an endless temporal loop is implied throughout the film, it is most clearly confirmed at the conclusion. In the final shot, we see Michael leaving the Crazy House and the dying Elsa and walking towards the ocean, visible in the distance. Near the end of this shot, the narrator utters his last lines, which refer to Elsa: "Maybe I'll live so long that I'll forget her. Maybe I'll die trying." But as the film we have just seen *proves*, Michael cannot forget Elsa or his past with her, and the conclusion is indeed ironic. For although the final shot seemingly shows Michael's liberation from his long ordeal the spectator suddenly realizes retrospectively that Michael is heading not towards freedom, but rather only back towards the reliving and recounting of his past—back, that is, to the beginning of the film and the beginning of his narration of the circumstances that, in turn, lead to the final shot.

The film's overall circularity is emphasized by being geographical as will as temporal. The narrative proper progresses from the East River south around the Panama Canal and then north to San Francisco Bay. This watery circuit is completed by the implied continuity between the final shot and the first shots of the film—in other words, between the San Francisco oceanfront towards which Michael is walking in the last shot and the initial shots of water, followed by the view of the East River in New York. In this continuity, the initial water shots suggest a visualized intermediate phase in the narrator's mental transition back to his past. First of all, these initial shots, unlike the final shot and the shot of the river, are unidentified as to any specific place or time. Second, the wave that unexpectedly breaks in the last of these shots may represent a link between the ocean waves visible in the film's final shot and the wake from the passing barge in the river shot. Finally, the lighting of these initial shots indicates a time of day somewhere between morning—when the last shot takes place—and evening, the time of the shots of the East River and Central Park.

As we have seen, all the temporal instabilities created by Michael's dual role involve a splitting of perspective—between present and past, between the narrational and filmic present, between objective occurrence and subjective recurrence, and between a linear and a circular structure. The overall result is a kaleidoscopic fragmentation of vision. However, as we watch the film we are generally aware of only one perspective at a time, and we are lured into believing that this is conclusive and therefore that what it discloses is accessible. But whenever we are made conscious of the multiplicity of temporal viewpoints, our confidence dissolves, leaving us with the suspicion that none of these is final or can supply a solid hold on the film.

Michael's double role is responsible for throwing several additional monkey wrenches into the works. For it contributes to the sense of inaccessibility in other ways, which likewise entail a radical instability and a false suggestion of accessibility. One such way concerns what might be called the dynamics of intimacy and distance, which function so that what may seem near and available at one moment can suddenly seem remote and elusive at the next. For example, the narrator may suggest intimacy in that he seems to be addressing the audience in a shared temporal present, but he is also distanced because disembodied, heard rather than seen; and though he seems to be speaking in the here and now, he is, in fact, unsituated as to any precise place and time. We know neither where the narrator is speaking from nor exactly when he is speaking in relation to his visualized past.

On the other hand, Michael as participant is indeed physically present, visible as well as audible. He also might seem intimate in that he exists within the visual immediacy of the filmic events. Yet both participant and events are distanced by being consigned to the vanished past by the narrator's commentary. And though this commentary may give us an intimately personalized view of these events, it also tends to make them seem remote by filtering them.

A related point is that while Michael may seem intimate inasmuch as we are apt to regard him as being essentially one character, though represented at different periods, we also often have a strong contrary impression that there are two distinct Michaels. Granted, the participant and narrator may seem unified by sharing the same experience and by speaking with the same voice and improbable brogue. And they do seem to converge during the transition in the opening scene, and perhaps again during the final shot. However, they are effectively separated from one another by several factors—for example, by time, by their disparate degrees of knowledge regarding the meaning and outcome of the action, by the fact that the narrator is invisible while the participant is not, and by the narrator's frequent reflexive irony, which distances him from his past self (and from his present self as well). That we experience narrator and participant more or less simultaneously, with the voice of the former superimposed upon the experience of the latter, merely dramatizes the paradox whereby one character seems to divide into two. This paradox involves a splitting of perspective, first, between Michael viewed as one character and as two characters, and, then, between each of the two Michaels. Because of this focal bifurcation, Michael no longer seems graspable as a unitary figure, but rather tends to become abstract, remote, and ultimately inaccessible.

Now insofar as we can regard Michael as a single unified character, we are encouraged to believe he is the protagonist and central consciousness of the film and, therefore, that both he and the film are comprehensible in terms of conventional cinematic narrative. But this suggestion of accessibility proves to be yet another false lure. For as soon as there seem to be two separate Michaels, the viewer becomes disoriented, the film elusive, and Michael's centrality highly problematic. Can we consider that the narrator and participant are somehow both the central character, jointly and equally? Or does only one of them really fit that role? Or is it, perhaps, neither of them?

We might reasonably suppose the narrator is the true center of consciousness and that the film focuses on his experience and response to that experience. After all, he mediates the action, and he alone is endowed with a retrospective view, a critical distance. However, the narrator is decentered, first of all, by the fact that, while his commentary is concentrated at the beginning and end of the film, in between the voice-over remarks are rather brief, sporadic, and infrequent. After the Central Park sequence and until the Crazy House sequence at the conclusion, the narrator speaks only six times and generally not more than a few sentences each time. (These comments occur during the following scenes: (1) at the hiring hall, (2) when Michael returns Bannister to his yacht, (3) later on the yacht, (4) just before the picnic, (5) when the launch docks in Sausalito, and (6) just after Michael's arrest). For fully half the film—that is, from after the voice-over comment that precedes the picnic sequence and up to the Crazy House sequence—the narrator speaks only twice. And in this portion of the film particularly, but elsewhere as well, there are several key scenes that are unaccompanied by any voice-over narration whatever (e.g., the scenes in Acapulco, at Grisby's office, the Aquarium, during the entire evening of Grisby's murder, at the trial and the Chinese theater).

Second, when the narrator does speak, his comments are remarkably reserved, unrevealing, and general, almost never describing the specific content of the images. In fact, he cannot strictly be said to narrate the action, which we surely could not envision if we had to rely solely on his sparse and sketchy remarks. Indeed, we often feel he is cut off and distanced not only from his past self, but also from the visualized past events, whose course he is unable to alter, and which frequently seem to be occurring independently of his narration.

Then perhaps the other Michael, the participant, is the film's protagonist. He is, on the whole, chivalrous, idealistic, poetic though no sissy, potent in combat, and the only likely candidate for the male romantic lead. He not only takes part in the action, while the narrator is separated from it, but he is also the only principal character who seems to learn something from his experience, though we may not be sure exactly what. But his status as the film's hero is made wobbly by all that is questionable, unconvincing, and even silly about his character—that is, about his motivations as well as his action.

The fact is that, in *both* his roles, Michael begins to be decentered quite early in the film. In the opening park sequence, Michael is indeed central in that, as participant, he is featured dramatically and visually and, as narrator, he comments almost continually. However, during the following sequence, in the garage, the narrator is silent and the participant, though still prominent, is eclipsed somewhat by the mysterious presence of Grisby and Broome. The next sequence begins with the narrator saying,

> I don't like a girlfriend to have a husband. If she'll fool a husband, I figure she'll fool me.
>
> Now New York is not as big a city as it pretends to be. So I spent the next day at the hiring hall waiting for a ship. That way, big boob that I am, I thought I could escape her.

These lines, the last ones the narrator speaks until this and the following sequence, in the bar, are over, seem almost totally unrelated to what we see on the screen: a long tracking shot of a man, not yet identified as Bannister, painfully limping across the hiring hall. In fact, despite the narrator's self-referential comments, we do not see Michael during Bannister's entrance or his exchange with the two sailors, Goldie and Jake. When Michael finally does join this group, he and Bannister share the spotlight, though Michael here seems to dominate the situation. However, in the next scene, in the bar, Bannister and Jake do most of the talking, while Michael merely sits by passively, observing and listening (during this scene, he chortles audibly once and utters only one word, "True").

As this summary suggests, Welles has centered the narrator in the park sequence, only to decenter him gradually afterwards by making the voice-over commentary so general and infrequent. Further, in the beginning of the hiring hall sequence, we have the first instance of shots that decenter Michael the participant by the fact that he is absent from them and does not take part in the events they depict. Such shots also decenter the narrator, since he clearly could not have witnessed these events. These shots are so numerous and often so crucial that the spectator cannot help sensing the overall effect of this decentering. However, especially in a first viewing, the spectator may fail to notice anything anomalous about such shots. This is largely a result of the way we are led to accept and assimilate them as being part of a conventional narrative. For whenever we temporarily forget the narrator's perspective, we tend to regard the film as a sort of cinematic equivalent of third-person omniscient narrative, a form that permits the depiction of events from which the protagonist is excluded and of which he may be entirely ignorant. On the other hand, whenever we do become aware of the narrator's perspective, the film seems to be a first-person quasi-autobiographical narrative. Even then, the spectator may not find anything terribly amiss about these shots, since, as Wayne Booth points out (citing Ishmael in *Moby Dick* as an example), a retrospective first-person narrator may occasionally report incidents that, realistically, he could neither have seen nor heard.[3]

Nonetheless, in some recess of his mind at least, the viewer may well wonder how to reconcile fictional verisimilitude and credibility with the fact that we are shown so many important events that the narrator himself could never have witnessed.[4] The only plausible explanation involves what is first suggested in the film's opening sequence: that everything that happens on the screen represents the narrator's imaginative reconstruction of the past. All the filmic events would then constitute his subjective synthesis, some of which may have an objective basis in actual fact, and some—including the shots in question—merely a speculative basis on the part of the narrator.

One problem with such an explanation is that these shots can also be regarded as wholly objective, since they tend to validate the actual occurrence of all that takes place independently of Michael and his personal point of view. Partly because of the uncertainty created by this splitting of perspective, the entire film becomes a strange mélange of subjectivity and objectivity, neither of which dominates as the decisive focus. This obviously makes it hard, if not impossible, to determine the status of the image at any point. Is what we are seeing a subjective vision, centered in, and authorized by, the narrator himself, or is it an objective and more or less impersonal rendering of events? And if it is subjective, then how accurate—in a sense, how objective—is the narrator's version of the past?

The bar sequence, in which Michael is present but not central, offers the first example in the film of another major decentering technique. Later, there are far more striking instances of scenes where Michael is peripheral visually as well as dramatically (the most notable is surely the trial sequence; some others are the scene at the Chinese theater and the final duel between Elsa and Bannister). In such sequences, Michael's diminished importance and de-emphasized presence suggest not only the extent to which he has lost control over events, but also that he may be, if not quite marginal, then merely secondary in terms of the overall action and the entire film. These scenes, therefore, raise several crucial questions. Is Michael to be regarded as the film's protagonist and a major initiator of the action or merely as a rather passive victim, an incidental and convenient patsy? Is he the center of consciousness or only the Ishmael—like witness to, and sole survivor of, a disastrous chain of circumstances? Is the real focus of the film Michael's subjective experience, or is it, instead, the objective world he enters when he first meets Elsa and the internecine strife that finally destroys Elsa, Bannister, and Grisby? Is this, in short, his film or theirs? (The fact that Michael is absent from numerous shots may lend weight to the latter possibility.) Whenever the viewer becomes aware of this double focus, involving two equally valid though mutually contradictory perspectives, both Michael and the film seem ever more problematic, shape-shifting, and ungraspable.

A third decentering technique, though one not employed in the opening scenes, involves those shots that are from the point of view of characters other than Michael. For example, when Elsa is called to testify at the trial, there is a shot of her that seems authorized not by Michael, but by Bannister and the District Attorney; and when Michael escapes from the courthouse, we see him from the point of view of Goldie and of Bessie, the Bannister's maid. Undoubtedly, the most conspicuous shots of this type are those representing Grisby's point of view as seen through his spyglass. I am referring to the two series of masked shots, the first, of Elsa diving and sunbathing, and the second, of the principal characters arriving at the picnic.

This third decentering technique is potentially the most disorienting of all. For while the other two techniques that I have discussed may challenge the spectator's belief in Michael's centrality, they do not absolutely negate such a view. The shots in which Michael is absent may, after all, represent part of his mental reconstruction of the past; and the scenes in which he is peripheral just may be authorized by his presence and by his own sense that events have gotten out of his control. The shots from the point of view of other characters clearly allow the spectator no such interpretational loophole.

But since the film does encourage us, to a considerable degree, to regard Michael as central, all three decentering techniques—and especially this third one—create a sort of schizoid severance of experience from the ostensible experiencer, namely Michael. And so they all help heighten the feeling of inaccessibility by making the film seem eccentric in every sense of the word.

The close-ups of Elsa and those of Grisby are some of the most memorable and intense shots in *The Lady from Shanghai*. They express almost emblematically the visual world of the film, and they exemplify several major ways in which this work visually produces a sense of inaccessibility. To begin with, these close-ups display the film's characteristic combination of fascination and impenetrability. All the dazzling surfaces that comprise this hallucinatory world compel our attention and then refuse to render their meaning. Rather they remain somehow opaque, cryptic, both illusive and elusive. Indeed, their impenetrability may be partly what arouses our fascination.

The shots of Elsa are amazing, fantastic in every sense, luminously beautiful and, as Charles Higham notes, "banal and emptily glossy"[5]—and they are so largely because Elsa herself is all these things. While seductively attracting the viewer's gaze, Elsa's face continually thwarts all attempts to pierce the enigma of its beautiful bland surface. The close-ups of Grisby are as dazzling as those of Elsa. Just as her face fascinates us by its cold beauty, composure, and inexpressiveness, Grisby's face rivets us by being so wonderfully repellent and wildly demonic. These shots similarly invite and frustrate our scrutiny, and so thoroughly that, as Joseph McBride puts it, "Grisby remains an absolute befuddlement."[6]

Traditionally, such intense and emphatic close-ups serve to portray the characters' inmost thoughts and feelings. This is what one critic means by the term "portraiture shot."[7] The close-ups of Elsa and Grisby, however, might properly be called "anti-portraiture shots." For though they may promise such a revelation, they never fulfill that promise. They not only pointedly fail to give any glimpse into the the characters' interior, they also offer no sense that there really is an interior or any psychological depth and complexity.[8] What these shots do offer is another false and misleading suggestion of accessibility.

The close-ups of Elsa and Grisby also exemplify the intense visual stylization of *The Lady from Shanghai*. Elsa's face is filtered through a shimmering soft focus, while Grisby's is distorted by an equally transforming hard focus and by a wide-angle lens that makes his face seem to protrude from the screen. In both cases, the effect is bizarre and masklike—Elsa's "mask" being that of an unapproachable goddess and Grisby's that of a leering gargoyle. Such stylization causes the two characters, their faces, and the shots themselves to seem even more inaccessible, because abstract and fantastic, transcending the dimensions both of realism and the merely human.

In general, the close-ups of Elsa and Grisby seem to express Michael's own sense of these characters—his dismay in response to Grisby and his mystified and mesmerized wonder towards both Grisby and Elsa. The visual stylization also serves this end, the strange masklike effect suggesting Michael's point of view as an outsider, his subjective and necessarily external perspective. Indeed, throughout *The Lady from Shanghai*, Michael's response to the stunning visual world that he encounters mirrors our own—and in this respect at least, he can be considered central. Like Michael, we find this world "all very rich and rare and strange." Like him, we are seduced, overwhelmed, dazed and deceived by its hypnotic surfaces[9] and must attempt to construe it solely on the basis of outward appearances. Finally, we, too, seek the inner meaning beneath these surfaces, only to discover that this meaning is unattainable—if indeed it exists at all.

The dynamics of intimacy and distance, which I discussed earlier in another context, also function visually in the film. In the close-ups, for instance, our sense of the compelling immediacy of those shots is often countered by a correspondingly strong sense of distance caused by the impenetrability of their surface and the inaccessibility of their inner meaning. Then we have the related dynamics of presence and absence, by which what is present may suddenly seem to vanish and what we may have believed absent can unexpectedly materialize. This alternation, like that of intimacy and distance, involves a splitting of perspective and a radical instability, and it similarly leads to a feeling of elusiveness. To use the close-ups again as examples, while the faces of Elsa and Grisby may seem very much present in the way they fill the screen, these shots also convey a sense of spiritual absence by suggesting that there is really nothing behind the visual surfaces and that both Elsa and Grisby are empty, insubstantial, and soulless. But perhaps the culminating example occurs in the final shootout, when the apparent presence of Elsa and Bannister repeatedly turns out to be merely their reflection in the various mirrors.

Moreover, throughout *The Lady from Shanghai*, certain characters have a way of appearing or disappearing almost magically. In the garage, for example, Broome pops out from behind a pillar as unexpectedly as he appears later on the yacht when Michael first arrives, in Acapulco when spying on Elsa and Michael, and at the Bannister home when Grisby confronts him.

But it is Grisby who seems especially associated with the dynamics of presence and absence, perhaps because, of all the characters, he is the most volatile and the most clearly linked to the preternatural. It is Grisby, after all, who says that he wants people to think he has disappeared while actually being present on a South Seas island, and that he hopes by this means to escape annihilation in a nuclear holocaust, when everything present would instantly be absent. Grisby's unexpected presence at the garage startles us (and Elsa, too) as does the abrupt way he exits from the scene. We are also surprised when we see him spying on Elsa through his telescope; when we (together with Michael and Elsa) learn he has not left the yacht as anticipated but has been there eavesdropping all along; and when, after making his proposition to Michael on top of the precipice in

Acapulco, he suddenly departs, leaving both Michael and the spectator dumbfounded.

Aptly, Grisby is involved in one of the film's key scenes of presence and absence. I mean the sequence in which Michael, surrounded by a swarm of policemen, is apprehended for Grisby's murder. In a few highly compressed moments, we as well as Michael discover that Grisby is unexpectedly present, but as a cadaver, the ultimate form of presence and absence, and then, while Grisby is quickly wheeled off-screen on a stretcher, thus becoming visually as well as vitally absent, that Bannister, whom we thought murdered, is really alive and present. Finally, Elsa's unforseen arrival caps off this scene.

With its complex reversal of expectations and ceaseless, confused activity, this sequence offers us so much information so quickly that it is hard to assimilate it all. This is true of the entire film, because of the density and complexity of the individual images and the rapidity with which they succeed one another. Our need to decipher and digest this visual flurry causes us to be intensely involved in the film. But, at the same time, we tend to be distanced by the way the images assault us, making reflection difficult and meaning elusive.

The film's prevalent sense of onrushing speed and of visual flux, fragmentation, and instability is also the result of such factors as the rapid and frequent cutting; the great variety of camera angles, many of which are extreme and disjunctive; and Welles' characteristic employment of a moving camera to film moving characters (a technique that can make even stationary objects seem to move, as happens, for example, to the pier on which Michael is running after firing Grisby's revolver). Moreover, the accelerated pacing of the visuals is fully matched by that of the incidents which they depict. It is amazing to consider, for example, that the time supposed to have elapsed between the yacht's arrival in Sausalito and Michael's arrest is little over a day, and that within that period Michael meets Grisby at his office and then Elsa at the Aquarium, accompanies Grisby to Bannister's home where Broome is shot, rams into a truck, helps stage the fake murder, and is arrested for the real one.

The film's images and events are divided into roughly a dozen principal sequences, each a bravura set piece, dramatically complete and self-contained, and with its own distinct style. These sequences are one and all so overwhelming visually that a kind of episodic intensification results. Whichever scene we happen to be watching absorbs our attention completely. And perhaps only at the transitions between the episodes can we observe clearly how the preceding scene gradually recedes from our awareness as it is eclipsed and, in a sense, cancelled by the one just starting—which, in turn, will itself be eclipsed by the following scene. Such episodic intensification adds greatly to the feeling of elusiveness, and not least because it makes any overview or synthesis very difficult for the spectator.

The major episodes of *The Lady from Shanghai* are generally referred to by their settings. Hence we speak of the Aquarium sequence, the Crazy House sequence, and so on. This is more than just a convenient and conventional means of designation. Rather it reflects the importance of the settings in this work. Through Welles' remarkable treatment, the settings are largely responsible for giving each episode its distinctive character and, more significantly, for creating the film's overall sense of inaccessibility.

Visually and often aurally, the settings are highly distracting, deflecting our attention away from the dialogue and doings of the central characters and from the plot. The sequences in Acapulco (especially when Michael and Grisby climb the hill and when Michael and Elsa wander around the town), in the courtroom, the Crazy House, and, above all, the Aquarium and the Chinese theater—all these provide fairly obvious instances of this distraction. But it can also operate less noticeably, as during the long talk between Elsa and Bannister outside the courtroom, when we are subtly diverted from their dialogue by the shadows of the passing legal officials, by Bannister's exchange of greetings with these officials, and even by the fact that a "No Smoking" sign is clearly posted behind the smoking couple.

Welles himself has said that the Aquarium sequence is the classic example of his tendency to have the visual elements in a scene become more compelling than the dialogue. Drawn willy-nilly to watch the strange creatures swimming in the background, we are apt to miss parts of the discussion between Elsa and Michael, though this, Welles claims, is "the marrow of the film."[10] Whenever we return to the dialogue—whether dutifully, dazedly, or anxiously—we feel that something important may have irretrievably escaped us, perhaps some crucial bit of information, all because of our involvement with the background. Nonetheless, our gaze soon wanders back to the swimming creatures, then we return once again to listen to the dialogue, and so on. This feeling that we may have missed something essential through our involuntary inattention occurs frequently and helps make the film seem as strange and slippery as the creatures in the Aquarium.

In view of the film's centrifugal nature, such distraction seems appropriate. After all, the root meaning of "distraction" is "a pulling or drawing apart." The word can also signify amusement, confusion, and madness. Now the distraction caused by the settings is surely entertaining—diverting in every sense. As at a three-ring circus, our attention is drawn by several simultaneous attractions and, unable to take them in all at once, we heed now one, now another, in an embarrassment of riches. Moreover, the settings themselves are so delightful that—to alter my big-top metaphor slightly—the sideshow soon becomes more arresting than the supposed main attraction, the narrative. As for distraction in the sense of confusion and madness, the restless shifting of our interest greatly intensifies the general impression of chaotic movement; and, as Phyllis Goldfarb points out, the viewer's experience thereby comes to resemble the atomized world of the schizophrenic, who is unable to order the sensations that bombard him, helter-skelter, from all sides.[11]

This distraction clearly involves a radical instability and, by dividing our focus between setting and story, a splitting of perspective. The circularity and decentering that I discussed earlier also function, although in a somewhat different manner, at the level of the settings—the circularity, in the recurrent alternation of our attention, and the decentering, in the distraction from the narrative.

Moreover, a false lure of accessibility lurks insidiously in the settings. Often the background fascinates us partly because it seems to offer a clue of some sort as to how we should interpret the narrative situation with which it is juxtaposed. Yet this implicit premise of clarification is at least somewhat misleading. For while setting and situation may at first seem entirely incongruous, then somehow related, we ultimately are unable to find any clear-cut, point-for-point correspondence between them. For example, the fish and other marine creatures in the Aquarium sequence are often said to be objective correlatives of some kind; but do these creatures represent the statements that Michael and Elsa make in their dialogue, their unspoken thoughts or feelings, the various characters that are mentioned, or the increasingly strange and "fishy" atmosphere in which Michael finds himself—or all or none of the above? And in the theater sequence, what precisely does the ritualized Chinese drama symbolize, if anything? This setting seems loaded with significance, but try as we may, we can never ascertain exactly what it is.

As is true of the entire film visually, the settings fascinate us, yet withhold their meaning. And not only are the mute fish and the Chinese drama pointedly unintelligible, they also convey the essential incomprehensibility of the film. Moreover, through Welles' stylized treatment, the settings transcend the role generally accorded to them. In *The Lady from Shanghai*, they are no longer subordinate to the tale. Rather than being merely background, at most atmospheric or illustrative, the settings here seem to have an independent and irreducible identity of their own. And even though we may be uncertain at times about the relationship between setting and narrative situation, we nonetheless do relate them, simply because they are juxtaposed and because we revert from one to the other. The result is a richly ambiguous and suggestive interaction, a dynamic counterpoint that creates a further dimension. The linking of setting and story comes to evince an odd, often inexplicable, appropriateness as well as a surrealistic and absurdist wit. This linking gradually takes on an abstract quality that is apt to distance us somewhat from the narrative, while immersing us ever more deeply in the dreamlike atmosphere of the film.

Characteristically, when a plot discloses new information, one must go back mentally in order to revise the provisional patterns one has formed regarding the meaning of the action thus far. The plot of *The Lady from Shanghai* makes us perform such retrospective circlings continually, but for the most part they prove less than helpful and we return none the wiser from them. A fairly minor example will serve to indicate how pervasive this precess is: when we see Grisby for the second time—that is, when the yacht is in the Caribbean—we are meant to recall having seen him before, at the garage; but his second appearance entirely fails to account for his first, which, incidentally, is one of the many things that are never explained. More significant are the instances in which we seem to be offered full or partial clarifications of past events—for example, Grisby's "explanations" to Michael at the Sausalito bar and at his office, which are intended to deceive us as much as Michael about Grisby's behavior and motives; the discussion between Elsa and Bannister outside the courtroom; and the supposedly conclusive revelations in the Crazy House sequence. All such clues represent a false lure of accessibility, since they ultimately raise more questions than they ever resolve about this complicated and bewildering tale.

At times, we are also deliberately made to revert to a past anterior to the events of the story. This narrative pluperfect entices us into further fruitless but hopeful circlings. For example, we may vainly try to understand Elsa better through her enigmatic allusions, early in the film, to her shady past in Shanghai, Chefoo, and Macao. Similarly, during the picnic sequence, we are led to speculate as to what past events have enabled Bannister to blackmail Elsa into marrying him, and also as to what skeletons in Grisby's and Bannister's past furnish the basis of their present relationship and, indeed, of their characters. And what implications, we ask ourselves, might there be in the fact that Elsa's parents were White Russians or that Bannister's mother was a Manchester Greek? What outrage did Grisby commit to get himself kicked off the Social Register? We also conjecture about the impact upon Michael of what—to judge from his uneasy reaction to Grisby's probing—is the chief shadow in his life, his murder of a Franco spy. But conjecture as much as we will, we can determine neither the precise circumstances surrounding all these pluperfect events nor their significance in terms of the action and characters.

We have all been conditioned to expect that a plot will serve as a vehicle of meaning, that it will give coherence and itself be coherent. I think Welles counted on our having similar expectations regarding the plot of this film. Paradoxically, the fact that this plot is so confusing throughout strengthens our belief that there will eventually be a decisive resolution to all our perplexities, that the culmination of the story will somehow explain everything, and that the film's meaning will finally be accessible. Other factors help fuel this belief. First of all, the action develops through a fairly traditional dramatic structure, with a clearly defined beginning, middle and end; and it does lead to a truly spectacular climax and denouement. The action, consequently, seems to have a strong headlong thrust and a sort of crazy inevitability. This momentum is maintained in spite of the frequent disruptions caused by the distracting elements in the settings and by other factors, such as the stylized close-ups, that similarly create a sense of abstraction and of a stoppage of time. The completeness of each episode also leads us to anticipate a unified and self-contained tale, as does the existence of a first-person retrospective narrator, who even refers to his visualized experiences as constituting a story ("That's why I start out in this story a little bit like a hero"). Moreover, throughout the film there are several lines that suggest completeness by stressing beginnings and endings. For example, when Grisby asks if he thinks the world is coming to an end, Michael replies, "There was a start to the world someplace, so I guess there'll be a stop." When Bannister asks if he is glad he joined the cruise, Michael says, "I never make up my mind about anything at all until it's over and done with." At the Aquarium, Michael, referring to his spurious confession, tells Elsa, "Read the last part. That explains the whole of it." And during the Central Park sequence, the narrator declares, "If I'd known where it would end, I'd never have let anything start."

It is ironic that Michael should speak the above lines, since, as we know by the end of the film, he is unable to make up his mind about his experiences and, consequently, they are never over and done with. Instead, they seem to recur obsessively: for, as I have already suggested, although the film does indeed have a certain linear continuity, this is subsumed by the implied circular structure arising from Michael's reflexive dual role. I bring this up again here because this circularity (which is analogous in some respects to the spectator's retrospective circlings) is one means by which the film's apparent finality breaks down into unresolved ambiguity.

But the chief culprit in this regard is the plot, which not only is full of false leads, but is itself a major false lead. First of all, the plot leaves innumerable strings untied at the end, many contradictions intact, and much accumulated confusion. Second and more important, the plot in no way "explains" the essential mystery of this world of stunning, inscrutable surfaces—a mystery which it finally enforces rather than dispels. Instead of a coherent plot, what we are presented with is a welter of plotful incidents, which results in an abstract effect that one might term "plottiness."[12] And what this conveys is not the meaning but the incomprehensibility of a world whose parts refuse to add up, to make sense.

Bazin writes that,

Citizen Kane: Mr Kane (Harry Shannon), Thatcher (George Coulouris), Mrs. Kane (Agnes Moorehead), the young Charles Foster Kane (Buddy Swan), and the sled.

Museum of Modern Art/Film Stills Archive (New York)

Citizen Kane: The Kanes at breakfast: Welles and Ruth Warwick.

Museum of Modern Art/Film Stills Archive (New York)

The Magnificent Ambersons: Jack Anderson (Ray Collins), Fanny Minafer (Agnes Moorehead), and George Amberson Minafer (Tim Holt).

Museum of Modern Art/Film Stills Archive (New York)

The Lady from Shanghai: The famous "Crazy House" mirror scene, with Elsa and Arthur Bannister (Rita Hayworth and Everett Sloane), and Michael O' Hara (Welles).

Museum of Modern Art/Film Stills Archive (New York)

Macbeth: Banquo (Edgar Barrier) and Macbeth (Welles).

Museum of Modern Art/Film Stills Archive (New York)

The Third Man: Welles as Harry Lime, in the sewers of Vienna.

Museum of Modern Art/Film Stills Archive (New York)

Touch of Evil: Joe Grandi (Akim Tamiroff) and Hank Quinlan (Welles).
Museum of Modern Art/Film Stills Archive (New York)

Othello: Othello (Welles) and Iago (Micheál MacLiammóir).
Museum of Modern Art/Film Stills Archive (New York)

Mr. Arkadin (Confidential Report): Welles as Gregory Arkadin.
Museum of Modern Art/Film Stills Archive (New York)

The Trial: Welles as the Advocate, Hastler; in the background are Joseph K. (Anthony Perkins) and Joseph's Uncle Max (Max Haufler).

Chimes at Midnight (*Falstaff*): Doll Tearsheet (Jeanne Moreau) and Falstaff (Welles).

Lacking a well-constructed plot, *The Lady from Shanghai* nevertheless reveals an action of uncommon—one might even say subterranean—force. The thriller plot serves as little more than a pretext.[13]

And,

The Lady from Shanghai is paradoxically the richest in meaning of Welles' films in proportion to the insignificance of the script: the plot no longer interferes with the underlying action, from which the themes blossom out in something close to their pure states.[14]

Bazin here seems to imply that the incoherence of the plot is merely a fortunate defect, a happy accident. But I believe it is functional in itself and largely intentional. For through this incomprehensibility, Welles expresses one of his principal thematic motifs: that of life as a mystery without a solution and a labyrinth without an exit. Associated with this idea in the film are some of his other recurrent themes—for example, that of the entrapment in the past, a past, moreover, that is at once irremediable, determining, and elusive; the irreducibility of experience; the fickleness of appearances and the protean ungraspability of the truth; and the consequent inevitability of illusion and self-delusion.

In a revealing and pertinent passage, deleted from the final version of *The Trial*, Welles was to have delivered the following lines:

Opinions differ on this point, but the error lies in believing that the problem can be resolved through special knowledge or perspicacity—that it is a mystery to be solved. A true mystery is unfathomable and nothing is hidden inside it. There is nothing to explain. It has been said that the logic of this story is the logic of a dream. Do you feel lost in a labyrinth? Do not look for a way out. You will not be able to find it. There is no way out.[15]

Of course, a labyrinth leads one to seek and exit, just as a mystery leads one to expect a solution. Similarly, the plot of *The Lady from Shanghai* seems to promise eventual accessibility, but instead what it offers throughout is "the logic of a dream"—very fitting for a film characterized by what Raymond Borde and Etienne Chaumeton call a "frenzied oneirism."[16]

Refering to Welles' films James Naremore writes of "a hopeless, centerless labyrinth."[17] Now, the original Labyrinth (whose designer Daedalus, like Welles, himself became caught in his own creation) did have a way out as well as a center, for it led to the devouring Minotaur. But in *The Lady from Shanghai*, the maze is hopeless not just because there is no exit, but also because where the center should be we find only a void. The principal false lead is that we are made to believe, first, that Grisby is the archvillain, and then Bannister. Only in the theater sequence do we know that behind all the murderous machinations and deception stands Elsa, the seductress as man-eating Minotaur. However, knowing that she is at the root of all the intrigue still doesn't explain her, the world she inhabits, nor the film—for Elsa remains the central, inaccessible void. Or—to use a phrase with which Welles once described someone—she is "the vacuum in the heart of a tornado."[18]

Elsa proves that while nature may abhor vacuums, Welles is fascinated by them. She belongs to that distinguished group of characters—including Kane, Quinlan, Arkadin, and Clay—whose imposing exteriors conceal an inner emptiness which leads ultimately to their collapse and self-destruction. What is true of these characters is also true of their environment. All of Welles' work Maurice Bessy writes, "is the sumptuous, hallucinogenic and baroque re-creation of a world in the process of disintegration."[19] Elsa herself merely personifies the unreality and elusiveness of a world whose hypnotic surfaces shimmer over an endless void.

We can glimpse this void when, for example, Grisby, having made his proposition, abruptly departs, and Michael as well as the viewer seem vertiginously suspended ever the rocks and glittering water far below. We can also sense it when, in the Crazy House sequence, as the narrator says, "I was the fall guy," the floor gives way and Michael hurtles down the chute; and when, in the Mirror Maze, we have an infinite recession not of reality but of illusion.

For this film is literally much ado about nothing. It is an elaborately constructed, convoluted, suspenseful and, finally, hilarious shaggy dog story, an enormous joke. This is hinted when Grisby explains the legal absurdities involved in his fake murder: Michael asks what will happen to him after this event and Grisby replies, "Nothing. That's the joker." And this comic scene ends with Grisby saying, "Silly, isn't it?" Later, when they are actually staging the would-be murder, Michael asks Grisby why he is laughing, to which Grisby, speaking his final line, responds, "Wait and see." We, too, must wait and see. For the viewer, like Michael, is the butt of a prolonged practical joke. Yet, unlike Michael, we don't mind at all. Since we are not personally involves in the same way he is, we are in a better position to enjoy the culminating confusion and zaniness. Now not only does a joke involve a triumph of nonsense, a liberation from logic, an explosive deflation, and a temporary acceptance of and escape from our own labyrinth, it is also, Freud tells us, an outlet for aggression. And so, though we may see through Michael's eyes, we are purposely never made to care much about him. For in this wonderful celebration of the incomprehensible and the absurd, Michael is finally our straight man, our scapegoat, and our fall guy as well.

Notes

1. André Bazin, "L'apport d'Orson Welles," *Ciné-Club*, No. 7 (May 1948); rpt. in Maurice Bessy, ed., *Orson Welles*, trans. Ciba Vaughan (New York: Crown, 1971), p. 148.

2. Welles delivers the voice-over narration of *Mr. Arkadin*, *The Trial*, and *The Immortal Story*, but not as Arkadin, Hastler, and Clay, the characters he plays in these films.

3. Wayne Booth, *The Rhetoric of Fiction* (Chicago: Univ. of Chicago Press, 1961), p. 60

4. The following is a partial list of the occasions on which Michael is absent: at the picnic, when Broome speaks confidentially to Bannister and also during the conversation of Bannister, Elsa and Grisby before Michael joins them; in Acapulco, when Elsa flees her husband at the night club; when Grisby shoots Broome and, shortly afterwards, when he doubles back to the Sausalito dock as Michael is calling the Bannister home; during the dying Broome's exchange with Elsa at her home; during Elsa's arrival at the courthouse in her convertible as well as her long talk with Bannister outside the courtroom; in the judge's chambers, both when the judge is told the jury has reached its verdict and also during the mayhem following Michael's escape; when Elsa tracks Michael to the Chinese theater and goes backstage to call her servant Li; when Li listens to the news of Michael's escape over the radio and when he receives Elsa's call—and so on.

5. Charles Higham, *The Films of Orson Welles* (Berkeley: Univ. of California Press, 1970), p. 112.

6. Joseph McBride, *Orson Welles* (New York: Viking, 1972), p. 102.

7. William Simon, Professor of Cinema Studies at New York University, introduced this term during one of his lectures.

8. Grisby is particularly inexplicable in psychological terms. If Elsa seems coldly inhuman, Grisby seems *non*-human. He strikes one as being purely a force of nature—or rather, of the unnatural. In any case, he is surely wonderful and a prize creep.

9. Clearly, it is through his visual fascination with Elsa that Michael is first seduced by this world. During the Central Park sequence, this fact is emphasized by the voice-over remark when Michael as well as the viewer first glimpse Elsa: "Once I'd seen her . . . *once I'd seen her*," the narrator significantly repeats, "I was not in my right mind for quite some time."

10. Orson Welles, in an interview with Juan Cobos, Miguel Rubio and José Antonio Pruneda, "Voyage au pays de Don Quixote," *Cahiers du Cinéma*, April 1965; my translation.

11. Phyllis Goldfarb, "Orson Welles' Use of Sound," in *Focus on Orson Welles*, ed. Ronald Gottesman (Englewood Cliffs, N.J.: Prentice-Hall, 1976), p. 95.

12. Maurice Bessy has quoted Welles as saying he likes a certain "quality of abstraction" in a film; and Bessy then refers to the "abstraction that pervades *The Lady from Shanghai*. . . a film whose raw materials were the absurd, the irremediable, the incomprehensible" (*Orson Welles*, p. 24).

13. André Bazin, *Orson Welles: A Critical View*, trans. Jonathan Rosenbaum (New York: Harper and Row, 1978), p. 93.

14. Bazin, *Orson Welles*, p. 94.

15. Quoted in James Naremore, *The Magic World of Orson Welles* (New York: Oxford Univ. Press, 1978), p. 236.

16. Raymond Borde and Etienne Chaumeton, *Panorama du film noir Amèricain* (Paris: Editions de Minuit, 1955), p. 163; my translation.

17. Naremore, p. 234.

18. Quoted in Naremore, p. 229.

19. Bessy, p. 60.

The Study of Corruption: *Touch of Evil*

PETER COWIE

"A policeman's job is only easy in a police state, Captain . . . Who's the boss, the cop or the law?"

—*Mike Vargas in* Touch of Evil

PLOT OUTLINE

MIKE VARGAS, narcotics investigator for the Mexican Ministry of Justice, is honeymooning in the frontier town of Los Robles when the millionaire Linnekar is killed by a time-bomb planted just as he crosses the border into the United States. The local police captain, Hank Quinlan, agrees truculently to cooperate with Vargas on the case. Joe Grandi, an underworld figure who owns the lonely motel at which Vargas's wife, Susan, is staying, is keen to ruin the Mexican's reputation, because he (Vargas) has nabbed his brother (the real gang boss) on a narcotics charge. Unexpectedly, Quinlan helps Grandi to kidnap Susan because he is enraged at having been caught by Vargas while planting dynamite on Linnekar's potential son-in-law, Sanchez. Vargas discovers further that Quinlan has falsified evidence throughout his remarkable career. Quinlan meanwhile murders Grandi, arranging the scene so that the drugged Susan seems to be responsible. Then Vargas manages to sway Quinlan's old associate, Menzies, to his side, and the latter contrives to record Quinlan's drunken confessions on a tape recorder. Quinlan discovers this, shoots Menzies, and is in his turn shot by his dying accomplice. As he dies, news arrives that Sanchez has in fact confessed, vindicating Quinlan's intuition but not his methods.

Touch of Evil marked a brief return to America for Welles in the late Fifties, and the film was shot mostly on location at Venice, California, an old coastal town about fifteen miles from Hollywood. At first he was only asked to act in the picture. He refused. Then the producers approached Charlton Heston, who agreed to appear only if Welles would direct. And so Welles accepted the project—with two and a half weeks to go before production was due to start. "When I make this sort of picture," he has said, "for which I can pretend no special aptitude or interest—it is not 'for

---

Reprinted from Peter Cowie, *A Ribbon of Dreams: The Cinema of Orson Welles* (San Diego: Oak Tree Publications) [1973].

the money' (I support myself as an actor) but because of the greedy need to exercise, in some way, the function of my choice. I have to accept whatever comes along from time to time or accept the alternative of not working at all."

All Welles's leading figures are lonely in themselves, often nursing some secret grudge against society and turning to immoral methods to gain the power they feel to be their due. Like the principals of classical tragedy, they are doomed to nemesis. But Welles has never deserted the contemporary world and its problems although he casts his films in a tragic mould. Justice is an ideal that he pursues, without success, in *The Lady from Shanghai, Touch of Evil,* and *The Trial.* "I firmly believe that in the modern world," he says, "we have to choose between the morality of the law and the morality of basic justice. That is to say between lynching someone and letting him go free. I prefer to let a murderer go free than to let the police arrest him by mistake." Welles's belief clarifies many points in *Touch of Evil* (and, of course, in *The Trial*). The Hank Quinlan whom he portrays so convincingly is a policeman who will do anything to "crack the case" and to add to his string of successful arrests. So, when an American millionaire is blown up by a time-bomb on the Mexican border, Quinlan immediately arranges to frame the lover of the dead man's daughter, by planting two sticks of dynamite in his apartment. The fact that in the final seconds of the film this Sanchez apparently confesses to the crime matters little to Welles; the means, if not the end, are wrong. "He's wrong despite everything," asserts the director.

The Mexican investigator, Vargas, is Welles's mouthpiece throughout the film, much as Michael O'Hara is in *The Lady from Shanghai.* He has his suspicions about Quinlan from the start. "What makes you so sure it was dynamite?" he asks warily. One can sense the conflict beginning between these two men, just as one can between O'Hara and Bannister (who, significantly, moves like Quinlan in the manner of some loathsome reptile). Welles rounds off this opening sequence with Vargas's smiling, "Captain, you won't have any trouble from me!" and Quinlan's reply, loaded with menace, "You bet your sweet life I won't."

Each man uses a person close to the other as a weapon. Quinlan arranges for Grandi, one of a family that rules Los Robles, to incriminate Vargas's wife as a dope addict; and Vargas eventually persuades Quinlan's lifelong henchman, Pete Menzies, to destroy his master by concealing a microphone under his coat and luring him into a confession of his illegal manoeuvres. Each man is shown to be sensitive and sentimental beneath a rugged exterior. It transpires that Quinlan's fanatical, ruthless approach to his job dates back to the day in 1917 when his wife was strangled (by "that half-breed, of course [Grandi]") and the killer escaped forever. Like Arkadin and even Kane, he is a slave to a past he cannot forget and only when Grandi has been throttled does the debt to the past appear to have been paid. Vargas ostensibly neglects his newly-wed wife while the investigation into Linnekar's death gets under way, but he loses all control when he learns that Susan has been drugged and framed by Quinlan; he wrecks Grandi's bar and beats up his nephews. And, finally, he resorts to underhand tactics himself to bring down his adversary. As Gilles Jacob has suggested, "Vargas is tainted by his contact with Quinlan . . . he has been stung, as it were, by the scorpion on his back [a reference to *Confidential Report*]." This theme of the duel to the death runs like a fugue through all Welles's work. It is similar—to take an analogy dear to his heart—to the *corrida*.

Quinlan is, visually, the most memorable Wellesian character. With his vast paunch, his limp, wide-brimmed hat, his fancy for cigars and candy bars, his half-closed eyes, he resembles a monstrous toad whose touch and presence besmirch everything about it. Yet the curiously disgruntled look on his ill-shaven face provides a glimpse of the human being beneath the corruption. When he visits the aging prostitute Tanya in her bordello, the sound of the player piano arouses memories of some vanished past, and his expression assumes a wistful, almost childlike radiance. He loses his words in his throat. "Almost all serious stories in the world are stories of a failure with a death in it," says Welles. "But there is more lost paradise in them than defeat. To me that's the central theme in Western culture, the lost paradise."

Quinlan sees Tanya twice, once at the beginning and once at the end of the film. On both occasions there is a moment of genuine simplicity that recalls other meetings in Welles's world—between Kane and Susan Alexander on that wet evening outside 185 West Seventy-fourth Street, between Van Stratten and Sophie, between Joseph K and Block . . . When Quinlan asks her to foretell his future from her cards, Tanya replies steadily: "Your future is all used up," and suddenly through his besotted mind flits an inkling of his fate, almost as if Quinlan had consciously decided to abdicate by entering this stretch of Grandi territory, to drop his guard and accept whatever the Fates have in store for him now that his wife has been avenged. It is the moment of truth that always comes to Welles's heroes just before their end. Unlike Kane, Quinlan's ruthlessness has not stemmed from material ambitions. As he says to Menzies in the final sequence, "I could have been rich . . . after thirty years . . . all I've got's a turkey farm." For Quinlan, power over money is secondary to power over people.

As he lies dying in the turgid river, Quinlan hears Schwartz, the D.A.'s assistant, turn to Tanya and say, "That was a great detective all right." "And a lousy cop," she answers. "Is that all you have to say for him?" asks Schwartz. "He was some kind of a man . . . what does it matter what you say about people?" comes the reply. The bald defence of Tanya's final remark recalls de Sade's dictum: "In a criminal society, one must be a criminal." Quinlan, like Arkadin or Iago, distorts reality because he believes that beyond its superficial appearance reality conforms to his notions. Sanchez is guilty because Quinlan wills him so; as Jean Domarchi has pointed out, if Lady Macbeth can suggest to her husband the idea of a murder, it is because she knows that Macbeth is *already* a murderer. The irony of *Touch of Evil* is that Quinlan is shot finally by his faithful accomplice. As he dies he mumbles how this is the second time he has stopped a bullet for Menzies (the first being when he had saved his life some time before—hence his limp). "Quinlan is the god of Menzies. And, because Menzies worships him, the real theme of the scenario is treason, the terrible impulsion that Menzies has to betray his friend." His first pangs of conscience come in the records room, as Vargas uncovers the trials so skillfully and ruthlessly rigged by Quinlan; and misgivings develop into conviction when he finds the police chief's cane in the room where Grandi has been strangled. Unwillingly he allows himself to deceive his master, and Henri Agel has aptly compared the hand Menzies has in Quinlan's death with the shooting of Harry Lime by his friend Holly Martins.

If Quinlan and Vargas dominate the stage in *Touch of Evil*, the film would hardly be the convincing, disturbing thriller it is without those minor characters whom Welles, like Pieter Bruegel, always manages to place in the background of his work. The slavish Grandi, with his wig and unlit cigars, given to petty harangues and moments of malevolent humour, dancing around Quinlan's shuffling bulk like some fish around a barracuda; the various nephews and nieces who comprise his brother's gang, terrorising Susan in the isolated motel or tracking Vargas through the streets; and Menzies, the Sergeant, whom Quinlan calls "pardner" with more than mere familiarity, watching with ashen face the piecing together of Quinlan's corruption in the records room. Then there is the sinister blind woman in the shop where Vargas telephones his wife; one has the impression she is absorbing all the gentle love phrases he whispers to Susan, and is twisting them foully in her mind. And, perhaps drollest of all, the receptionist at the Mirador motel: nervous, beetle-like, eyes expanding in panic behind the spectacles, mumbling incoherently, he calls to mind the stunted clowns of the Shakespearian theatre, whose very ridiculousness supplies a sharp comment on the action. "He seems to crystallise the chaos . . . like the drunken groom in *Miss Julie* . . . a kind of powerless chorus that reflects to the maximum the tragic insecurity of this night." The role was completely improvised.

But, as always, it is not only the characters and their actions that convey the full impact of a film by Orson Welles. *Touch of Evil,* although apparently edited behind its director's back (with a series of comedy sequences omitted), is much less disjointed than *Confidential Report,* and shows Welles's imagination at its most breathtaking. The opening shot, lasting well over three minutes, must have been incredibly difficult to set up. "It took us all night to get it," recalls Janet Leigh. It starts with a close-up of a time-bomb being set and then, as Henry Mancini's tense, low-pitched score tock-tock-tocks on the soundtrack, the camera cranes up sharply to show the bomb being planted in the boot of Linnekar's car. Almost immediately the unsuspecting millionaire and his floosie emerge from the background and drive out through the streets towards the border. The camera travels back, on a high crane, in front of the car, and descends gently as Vargas and his wife cross the road at some traffic lights while Linnekar is held up. Welles then tracks alongside and in front of the couple as they stroll towards the control post, and cranes up again as Linnekar eases his car alongside them and halts for the formalities. A few words pass between Vargas and the customs official about the Grandi brother whom Vargas has just sent for trial, and then the camera moves beside the Mexican and his wife as they walk over the border. Suddenly, there is a blinding explosion as the time-bomb goes off, and Welles completes the shot with a close-up of the blazing car followed by a short zoom into the wreck. These three minutes are made suspenseful by the presence of the bomb, of which only the audience is aware, and at the same time the uninterrupted fluidity of the shot suggests the peace that is to be so rudely disturbed when the millionaire is killed. The effect is rather blunted in the finished film, because the producers insisted on superimposing the credits on the left of the screen, thus diverting one's attention from the action and, conversely, preventing one from absorbing the credits themselves. Originally, they were to have appeared as Tanya walks away across the bridge at the end.

There are several other long takes, but none compares in virtuosity with this initial shot. Often unnoticed are two four to five minute takes in Sanchez's apartment that must have been extremely tricky to film because of the presence of anything up to eight actors in a ceilinged set. Yet had Welles adhered to convention and broken up these scenes into fragments, they would have lost irremediably in both tension and claustrophobia. Again and again throughout his career Welles has demonstrated that the long take, as opposed to the syncopated montage of Eisenstein, allows the audience to immerse itself in the action happening on the screen.

In *Touch of Evil* Welles was for the first time able to rely principally on the 18.5 mm lens. This is ideal for the scenes such as that in which Vargas is trailed by Grandi's nephews and strides towards the camera at right of frame, while the youths follow silently in the distance; or when Menzies finds Vargas in the long, high-walled records room and walks uneasily back and forth. The wide angle provides a vision greater in range than the human eye, which can focus on only one particular point at a time; in *Touch of Evil* it foreshortens and elongates perspectives by turns, thus mirroring the contortions of the action itself. Welles uses close-ups sparingly in this film, and when they do appear they fulfil a clear purpose, such as the close-up of Quinlan while—sinking fast—he listens to his confession being played back on the tape recorder, or of the black glove that he draws on before throttling Grandi (significantly, the glove in the foreground blots out the face of its terrified victim in the background). This entire scene of Grandi's death is, in fact, one of the very few in the film that was untouched by the producers. It takes place in the hotel room of Susan Vargas as she lies drugged on the bed. Quinlan asks Grandi to put out the light; he does so, and the only illumination comes from the neon sign that flashes on and off outside the hotel with inexorable regularity. Then Quinlan dons his black gloves and, drawing a gun on Grandi, tells him to telephone Menzies at police headquarters. After a brief conversation he hangs up, locks the door of the bedroom and then advances like a human steamroller on the quivering Grandi, who tries desperately to attract attention by smashing the window above the door. But Quinlan drags him savagely down and strangles him just as his own wife had been strangled forty years earlier. The brightening and fading of the reflected light on the action provides a similarly scarifying effect to the swinging lamp in the store-room where Joseph K sees the police officers being whipped in *The Trial*.

As in *The Trial*, too, the last scene is among the most powerful of all. Menzies walks with the inebriated Quinlan across a landscape as weird as any conceived by Kafka: spidery derricks pierce the night sky, oil pumps rise and fall with a rhythmic insistence, gigantic, silvery tanks squat in the background, and the metallic croak of Quinlan's voice as it ricochets out of the recording machine held by Vargas overlays the scene with a nightmarish confusion. Vargas himself clambers after the two men, finally wading beneath a bridge to keep within range of the microphone hidden in Menzies's clothing. When Quinlan senses the presence of Vargas, and his friend's complicity, he shoots Menzies. Symbolically, he tries to bathe his hand free of blood in the slimy, cluttered water in which Vargas has just been standing. One thinks of the moment in *The Lady from Shanghai* when Grisby smears his blood over O'Hara's clothes to incriminate him more effectively.

This sequence, like the first one at the border, and the murder of Grandi, takes place at night. *Touch of Evil* is essentially a film of the darkness; the blend of shadow and silhouette emphasises the vague, intangible nature of the intrigue itself, and the darkness offers a cloak for crime and revenge. As Gilles Jacob has argued, "What does it matter if the shadow is arbitrary, if the lighting is arbitrary; all that counts is the dramatic illusion thus attained."

Seen in the context of Welles's other work, *Touch of Evil* is a most revealing film. Sergei Gerasimov, the Soviet director, has said of it: "This depressing, and I would say most amoral film had all the characteristics of present-day decadence in art. In the realm of ideas it flaunts lack of faith in man, a squeamish aversion for him, while in the sphere of artistic form it shows a morbid confusion, a shift of realistic concepts towards meta-physics, towards the dissecting room and the 'aesthetics' of filth and blood." But surely the point of Welles's view of the world is that goodness can be perceived through evil? For all his grotesqueness, Quinlan is more human a figure than any Gerasimov has created, and *Touch of Evil* runs true to the great tragedies of literature, from Sophocles and Euripides to Shakespeare and Marlowe. The study of corruption is no less valid than the study of innocence.

Welles is aware that one of his major themes is "the struggle for dignity. I absolutely disagree with those works of art, those novels, those films that, these days, speak about despair. I do not think that an artist may take total despair as a subject: we are too close to it in daily life." While this may sound as arbitrary as Gerasimov's remarks, it shows that like all great artists Welles is eager to cut his moorings and let his fancy free—to escape from everyday reality and yet help one to bear with it through contact with a world of the imagination.

Echoes of Art: The Distant Sounds of Orson Welles

DUDLEY ANDREW

ENTER A "body of work," a "corpus of films." Orson Welles, decadent individualist that he is, illegitimate son of European high art traditions, knew the *auteur* theory in advance and set out to make a series of films whose variety would make sense to later critics intent on their unity.

At the center of this body, then, what? A soul, a spirit, an animating force, a world view, a style? Welles' opus as well as his personality invites a descent into the core, into the heart of darkness pumping blood into the miles of images for which he has been responsible. In this, *Citizen Kane* is exemplary: a film to peel, to unlayer and explore. It is arranged in separable skins: the title, the rising camera invading Xanadu's grounds, the word "Rosebud" spoken from inside a dying man, a newsreel of his life, a series of separate interviews, a final omniscient camera summary, and the credits at the end. What is at the center of this onion? The plot reveals to us the glass ball and the sled, the privileged symbols of a man's last and, it is argued, his perpetual obsession.

Critics turn away from this "find" as "dollar-book Freud" only to posit another core, one that satisfies not the plot of Kane's past but that other plot, the one of discovery and detection, the plot of the search for Kane's past. The center of this detective tale is given and remarked upon: it is the jigsaw puzzle. No matter that it bears a meaning of failure and incoherence, the symbol itself is absolutely coherent. Planted, like the glass ball, at several points in the film, the jigsaw puzzle as explicator comes to relieve Thompson who sums up his search in a final phrase ("I guess Rosebud is a piece in a jigsaw puzzle, a missing piece") just as the name on the sled is about to be revealed, solving the question opened by the film's first word. How can we be satisfied with either?

"Rosebud," a glass ball, a sled . . . our dissatisfaction with these is our refusal of metaphor, of the single sacred signifier capable of clarifying the full life of a man. The jigsaw puzzle and the missing piece . . . our rejection of this cliché is a refusal of metonymy, of the progressive unraveling of a truth. The hollowness of both these solutions points to the hollowness of the cinema, that medium made up of image and tale, of metaphor and metonymy intermixed. Thus the film collapses under its own success,

From Dudley Andrew, *Film in the Aura of Art* (Princeton: Princeton U.P., 1984), pp. 152–71. Reprinted by permission of Princeton University Press, 41 William Street, Princeton, NJ 08540.

leaving us to meditate on the unrepresentable, on the mystery or emptiness of life.

Nearly all of Welles' films move like *Citizen Kane* toward cloying parables or metaphors that threaten to explain in a few words the delicious problem we expect to savor for two hours. There is the tale of the scorpion in *Mr. Arkadin*, which some critics have used to ground their sense not only of that film but of Welles and all his work. Then there is the patently oversimplified Holinshed's Chronicles providing a clear but hopelessly meager view of life in England in Falstaff's time. *The Magnificent Ambersons* moves to its denouement once Lucy can recite her parable about the sad fate of the Indian brave, Vendonah.

It is no wonder critics have credited to Orson Welles the sections of *The Third Man* in which he appears, since the film's key scene places Welles and Joseph Cotten high atop a ferris wheel where Welles as the mysterious Harry Lime can summarize the moral problem of the film in his characteristically parabolic manner ("Look down there. Would you really feel any pity if one of those dots stopped moving forever?"). The wheel itself is a complex metaphor for the action and the milieu, just the kind of temptingly explicit backdrop against which Welles could indulge his penchant for clever aphorisms. Finally, and with extreme self-consciousness, Welles (in *F for Fake*) threatens to sum up his whole career by laying out his major insights as sleight of hand. This film concludes with the extended "Picasso" parable on authenticity.

What is the function of these parables? First of all they serve as central nodes in the onion structure of the films. Dramatic resting points, they reflect back and forth across the intrigues that they directly interpret. Even as these explanations fail we sense the rightness of the attempt and we experience in the film the doubleness and distance that so define the world of Orson Welles. The parable is, in short, a peculiar but integral part in the engine of Wellesian drama.

The ostentation of aphorisms, parables, and metaphors gives to the "thought" of his films the same flamboyance that characterizes the "spectacle," to use Aristotle's language. Not only is Welles a magician in the realm of special effects, editing, and mise-en-scène, the ideas his films ask us to entertain are striking, troubling, unforgettable. And if he is subject to charges of empty bravura, of eclecticism, and even of plagiarism in his panoply of dramatic tricks, and in his parade of cinematic styles, so we must cast a skeptical eye on the "serious ideas" each film develops. The insufficiency of the parables is an index to the overall hollowness of the intellectual body of his work, to its eclecticism, to its derivative, often faddish origins. Welles organizes these ideas not for their truth or consistency but for their sheer effect. It is all dollar-book Freud, or Kafka, or Nietzsche, or Shakespeare.

And so in both its outward appearance and its inner soul *Citizen Kane* (like all his films) demands our admiration, evokes our astonishment, only to leave us with a feeling of emptiness and fraud. This is the vapidity of paradox from Zeno to Nietzsche, and Welles is only too proud to extend this tradition, adding to it the specifically illusory dimension of moving pictures.

Welles is not the first director to express the emptiness of appearances and to question the solidity of the world or ideas he so forcefully images. As a master of the long take and the tracking camera he engages a cinematic aesthetic ruled by the great names of F. W. Murnau, Kenji Mizoguchi, and Max Ophuls. If Welles obtrudes from this company we must blame his ostentation. Next to the delicate realism of Murnau, the refined rigor of Mizoguchi, and the relentless irony of Ophuls, Welles stands out as gaudy, even inauthentic.

One is tempted to blame this on production conditions. Only his first two films approached the budget, studio support, and independence routinely accorded Murnau and Mizoguchi toward the end of their careers. But even Welles' first films exemplify a cloying cleverness that cheapens the artistry while it draws attention directly to itself. Here, despite all his efforts to mask it, Welles shows himself the quintessential American. His lack of good, or even sustained, taste gives him away, especially beside the authentically cultured Murnau, the thoroughly disciplined Mizoguchi.

Mizoguchi and Murnau spent whole lifetimes in the pursuit of a style and theme they could rely on. They studied, experimented, and repeated their experiments until they achieved a stance from which to peer out at the moral vistas that attracted them. Welles has never trusted his footing, has never struggled long enough to earn one. He expects to accomplish by cleverness and energy what others gain through artistic instinct or prodigious labor.

We have already encountered one of Welles' cleverest devices in the parable. The parable is a false discourse not only because it is a logical magic trick but because it is a set piece lodged within the very situation it purports to explain. It is a conditioned discourse posing as unconditioned truth. Welles' own relation to these "truths" is the most troubling aspect of his narrational tone. Does the magician believe in the tricks that bear away the faith of his audience? This is the subject of *F for Fake* which spoofs artistic originality.

The issue of authenticity and certitude has always been at the center of his films, as though his world view is a distrust of, or nostalgia for, integral views. Welles' parables promise integral views but come to us through the fractured prisms of his films. There may rest a truth deep in the parable but the parable itself lies so far down in the film that we cannot reach or listen to it directly. And the voice which speaks it so pompously does so with the echo of great distance or with the cackle of ironic smirking.

Would Welles trade his cleverness, his ability to manipulate, for talent or wisdom? Would he trust the perceptions arising from either? Clearly he admires the integral vision of a Shakespeare or even an H. G. Wells; but his obsession with adaptation reveals more certainly a crisis in his own perception and in that of his age. Never has he sought merely to reproduce an earlier vision for our times, nor even to amend or supplement the sources he admires. The original work (*The Trial, Othello, The Magnificent Ambersons*) maintains its integrity by virtue of tradition, by its name or that of its author, while Welles employs it for one or more of its obvious effects. And the employment is qualified by other effects such as acting, lighting, sets, and camera angle which purport to deliver the message of the original to us.

In the adaptations as in the parables, an authoritative voice of a previously formulated truth issues from the center of the films; and yet no voice or truth comes to us purely or directly. Welles has caged Shakespeare, Kafka, Isak Dinesen. They are the rabbits he conjures out of his hat. He lets us believe they are his intimate friends whom he is generous enough to put on display for our edification, whereas in fact he calls upon them to remind himself of the paucity of his own vision. The strength of their voices betrays the insecurity behind the stentorian style of his cinematic delivery. The power of Shakespeare, like that of Kafka's parable of the law courts, fills us with awe, but it is a power removed from us, vitiated in the labyrinth of the films. The flesh and blood at the center of these films is seen only as an array of images in a hall of mirrors, each shatterable, each but a centimeter thick.

A scheme of multiple narrators accomplishes this project of embedding each film's values as mirages inaccessibly deep inside the magic box of the work. Once again, *Citizen Kane* provides the best example of this strategy. Six versions of Kane's life are told, some of which explicitly question the possibility of a uniform or total view. The subject of these narratives and of the film as a whole, Charles Foster Kane, recedes into the center of a narrative maze; the more we search, the more paths we find we must take and the less certain we become of what we see. The giant Kane is at once magnified and dissolved by this technique: magnified as the focus of multiple views and concerns, yet dissolved into the inevitable forgetfulness of the past. He is irretrievable except in story, and every story is qualified by its neighbor.

Certainly Welles' apprenticeship in radio taught him the possibilities of the framed story, of qualifying introductions, and of nested tales. So thorough is his taste for this structure that his fullest rendition of Shakespeare, *Chimes at Midnight*, is consciously re-presented rather than directly staged for the camera. Holinshed's Chronicles set the scene but only after

Falstaff and Master Shallow have stared into the camera, full of age and memory, declaring "We have heard the chimes at midnight." The film might properly be thought of as a retrospective gaze.

Stephen Heath has convincingly shown[1] that the key dramatic movement in *Touch of Evil* as well as that film's central moral drama involve neither the murder during the opening credits nor Charlton Heston's search for justice, but rather concern Hank Quinlan's past, told to us in bits and fragments. The dramatic lulls in Tania's place are symptoms of the real story the film encases, that of Hank Quinlan's trauma years ago and his subsequent obsessions and decline. There at the center of the film, in a neutral, quiet spot between Mexico and America, the real tragedy is laid out to reverberate forward and back through the plot, until Tania can conclude the film with her famous line, "He was some kind of a man."

Of course, certain of Welles' films make embedded stories the very subject of their interest. One could say this of *Mr. Arkadin*, which begins with a double flashback and features a search for an event lodged years earlier still in Poland, an event whose disclosure has the power to shatter a life and an empire, yet an event whose real existence depends completely on its inclusions in the stories of the past that the characters tell each other.

In its very title *The Immortal Story* is a fable about fables. James Naremore writes, "The film as a whole has been structured like a nest of boxes containing a story within a story and reminding us, with constant references to Welles' previous films, that the director himself is like Clay (the main character). Thus Welles strives to create fictions that will live, standing outside his actors like a puppet master, always aware of his mortality."[2] Where *F for Fake* shows all art to be inauthentic, *The Immortal Story* shows that in the power of artifice lies the chance for the only authenticity available to man. Clay literally brings to life a story that no one otherwise would believe. The intermeshing of art and illusion goes no further in Welles' work. The fragility of appearance here attains the palpability of fact even though it is set ("nested") in an infinite regress of tales and tellings. Man is mortal but the lies of fiction never end. The multiple mirrors around Clay's head at the outset of the film signal this in a single image. Truth lies in the telling, in the reflections, rather than in the mirage of what is there seen.

Welles' narrational tone is one of calculated bravura. The parables he infatuates us with are insufficient to explain the moral situations of the films. The rhetoric of the great authors he adapts reminds us of a seriousness and authenticity that the films as a whole lack. At no time in all dozen films do we feel a weakness of purpose or slovenliness of presentation. Everything is presented as powerfully as possible, often with a technical and stylistic flare that comes near to being haughty. Ultimately we are impressed by the vanity of such presentations, sickened by the emptiness of the rhetoric.

This tone of narrative voice takes its cue from the obsessive theme that dominates every film, that of disintegration. Like the structure of paradox discussed earlier, the narrative structure presents us with an impressive façade sliding into decay and oblivion. Characters, knowledge, entire ways of life are undermined and collapse over the course of his films.

This two-step method (creating an appearance of solidity, then permitting it to crumble before our eyes) is most visible in his treatment of the wax museum of characters everyone knows by heart, a museum Welles heats to the melting point: Charles Foster Kane, Hank Quinlan, Macbeth, Othello, Gregory Arkadin, Falstaff, Joseph K. It concerns as well the decline of gentility in *The Magnificent Ambersons*, of Merrie England in *Chimes at Midnight*, of rationality in *The Trial*, of story-telling in *Immortal Story* and of authorship in *F for Fake*.

Everything is made important and sacred in Welles' world only the better for him to deride the important and to question the sacred. This not only controls the overall rhythm of each scenario, it permeates the inner fabric of the mise-en-scène directing the presentation of the scenes themselves. André Bazin was the first to notice this method, coining the term "blocks of reality" to describe the molecular units at the core of *Kane* and *Ambersons*.[3] All the key scenes of *Ambersons* are rendered in single take, giving them a solidity unknown up to that time in the Hollywood cinema. Each scene, Bazin claims, is a block that stands before us with unquestionable authority. Welles' artistry consists of preparing these blocks before filming and in arranging them in a dramatic rhythm during editing. But the scenes themselves unroll of their own accord, the camera recording (rather than constructing or even representing) the scene as though it were a building or territory to be rendered. Even such a lengthy and edited sequence as that of the ball in *The Magnificent Ambersons* attains substantial body through the distance of the camera, its refusal to enter the scene via cross-cutting or subjective view of any sort, and most memorably through the solemnity of its rhythm which outwaits the confident music of the ball, holding every shot beyond its dramatic significance, until the characters finally realize that the evening is over. Far from being the romantic dream of a debutante, this ball is the concrete realization of an epoch celebrating himself. Because of its density, it will later stand unforgettable as a memory node, lodged in everyone's mind, a communal image the reality and disappearance of which we have witnessed.

The inevitable dissolution across that film's range of characters and their way of life is only the most obvious method Welles has of tearing down what presents itself as confident. Transitions occur continually in individual scenes. The end of *Ambersons* offers a succession of devastating scenes each of which crumbles before our eyes: Isabel's carriage ride back to her home and to her deathbed in which her profile subsides into ever darker shadows; Eugene's attempt to see her which is thwarted by Georgie, Fanny, and Jack standing on increasingly higher landings of the great staircase so that Eugene's romantic presence and straightforward good will is made ridiculous; Isabel's death rendered with the simple falling of a mottled shadow across her face, the final curtain pulled while Georgie's silhouette turns away in sadness. Now comes the film's shortest and most experimental scene. In the darkness of an antechamber the Major pushes himself toward the camera; he turns screen right and we follow him while we hear Aunt Fanny sobbing. A figure then cuts between the camera and the Major so abruptly that we turn to follow it until Fanny whirls in from screen right to embrace Georgie coming back the other way muttering, "She loved you, George; it was you she loved." Never in the era of Hollywood cinema has a camera been so ungrounded, so at the mercy of hushed but whirling character emotions. The scene, like the characters, flies away from the camera, dispersing itself so that there is nothing to hold onto, nothing to photograph. Unremittingly Welles pursues this anxiety in the Major's mad ramblings about the origin of the world and the place of man ("The sun; it must be the sun"). Again without a cut we watch him stare blankly at us as the shadows of a fire flicker across his troubled face. Finally, as though to lighten the atmosphere, Welles gives us the parting of Jack from Georgie at the train station. This seemingly ordinary and obligatory scene nevertheless sustains the mood of the film by the severe manner of its presentation. Georgie utters not a word as Jack alternately excoriates and coddles him in front of a smoky set so painterly and still that it looks like a cheap backdrop. When Jack suddenly turns to run to catch his train, however, this cardboard set is shown to be real, swallowing up the figure which diminishes in the rear plane while Georgie looks on, forlorn.

Jack's exit is multiplied endlessly across all the films of Orson Welles, the close-up figure leaving to the rear, pushed to nothingness by a wide-angle lens. Welles' space is a vast tunnel. Seldom do characters enter or leave from the wings; more often the lens and lighting accentuate their feebleness as they pass out of view, even, indeed especially, after they have delivered an impressive speech in close shot. A dark wind ushers everything out the back of the frame so that the great baroque world of Kane, the splendor of the Ambersons, the palpable pleasure of the Boar's Head, are all blown away from us out the window of the screen, dispersed into the infinite nothingness of an expanding universe. Shot after shot insists on this as close-up figures gradually or suddenly lose their control of the scene in favor of the space behind them, space that refuses to amplify their sentiments, swallowing them up instead.

Citizen Kane is full of such scenes, almost defying the spectator to guess the full size of the set. Bernstein reads a legal document in close-up; when he puts the pages down, Thatcher is shown to be sitting across a table from him in midshot; only then do we hear Kane's voice as he moves from a tiny figure by the window at the back of the room toward the desk to properly compose a three-shot. Earlier Kane as a young boy is photographed with his sled in standard medium shot, exterior. Gradually the camera begins to pull back to reveal first his mother at the window, then Thatcher, then his father, the adults retreating with the camera to an interior room where they discuss the fate of the tiny boy still visible through the small rectangle of the window. At the end of the film, of course, we have the much reproduced static shots of Susan Alexander in Xanadu, building her puzzle on a set designed inhumanly by Citizen Kane himself.

Such a spatial structure permits first of all a pervasive irony to color both *Citizen Kane* and *The Magnificent Ambersons*, as central characters are "put in their place" after dominating the frame. The opening sections of *Ambersons* trades on this tone, so much so that we are led to believe the film will be a comedy of manners or a satire. The off-screen narrator situates quaint images for us, and (once little Georgie graces the screen) the images themselves are composed for comic effect, as when the boy runs down a man planting his garden.

Such easy ridicule continues into the ball sequence where Georgie's pretensions are mocked by the long shots that contain them. But at the end of the ball a new, more serious tone is signaled by Bernard Hermann's dark score rising up behind the hushed urgency of all the characters saying their good-byes. Isabel leads the camera to the exit where she is silhouetted against the door's leaded glass while we see Georgie and Lucy engaged in making arrangements for tomorrow. At the same time, on the side of the screen Fanny and Jack whisper, watching Eugene take his leave of Isabel. The multiple desires and restrictions at play here are uniformly qualified by the somber lighting and by the dissolution that the decentered, mobile composition implies. No longer is the comedy of the film so pure as it had been. Georgie, Jack, Wilbur, and Fanny all say good night to each other poking good-natured jibes into one another's weak spots, but a deadening silence outlasts their chuckles. Moreover, deep shadows against the huge ceilings and voices yelling out distantly "Will you shut up in there" put us in a sepulchral space. Fanny and Georgie whisper loudly as one might at a funeral. Even the glorious sleigh ride which follows succumbs in the end to a dark iris closing down on the sleigh and all its passengers as it passes by a lone tree atop the distant hill. The iris is as quaint and as winning as the tradition of the sleigh ride itself. The technique and the tradition are both lost; indeed the technique signifies the loss. As if to seal this point Welles fades in next with the leaded door we saw at the end of the ball. This time shadowy figures approach from the outside. This time it is Wilbur's wake, not a Christmas ball, which is celebrated. In this, the film's first death, we are returned to the tomblike space of *Citizen Kane* and to a certain metaphysical seriousness which ridicules the pretensions of the characters and even overwhelms the narrator himself and his irony. "George Amberson Minafer had got his comeuppance"; so does every viewer who thought to laugh at this boy and at this era from the enlightened distance of modernity. Welles would hurl all of us, all boys and all eras, into a space of doubt and inevitable loss.

These hints of darkness are fulfilled toward the film's end in one of Welles' most frightening and masterful scenes. Fanny's latent madness finally overbrims itself as she confesses her destitution to Georgie and her fear that he will "leave her in the lurch." This once proud woman sinks to the floor in complete despair. Georgie, befuddled at her loss of strength, tells her to stand up, not to burn herself against the boiler she is leaning up against. "It's not hot. It's cold," Agnes Moorehead blurts out. No music moderates the abrasiveness of this ugly scene, as Georgie finally pulls the woman down a corridor through two sets of doors and into the great drawing room where now all the furniture stands covered in white sheets. Fanny's helpless sobbing brings an era and a film toward its close, even as Georgie tries fruitlessly to comfort her. The scene as a whole expresses in full pathos the disintegration and loss that has obsessed Welles in all his films. And the tenacious camera which stays with the entire scene imitates this process of decay as we are pulled without a cut from the floor by the dirty boiler through the house we have come to know so well and, in a final whirling gesture, into an inhumanly distant view of Georgie and his aunt lost in the deep shadows of the hollow drawing room.

The seriousness of this scene sits badly with the glossy sentimental ending repudiated by Welles.[4] And no wonder! This was the director whose very first project was the scuttled *Heart of Darkness*. His has always been a cinema of penetration, not of surfaces. His very first images as a filmmaker announce this ethos as the camera takes us ineluctably forward toward Kane's eerie castle while deep chords set a nearly metaphysical tone. This film, and all his subsequent work, we suspect, will be about mysterious penetration into a horrifying depth. Comedy, irony, parody, and satire will enter, but all will be buckled under the framing chords of the "power music,"[5] and the preternatural movement of the camera. Even in the silliest and safest episodes, we stand ready to be taken away by the music and the solemn crane of the camera.

The opening and closing of *Citizen Kane* are exemplary in figuring the plunge into a drama and the plunge of that drama. In a single movement they figure the strategy of *transition* by which a massive façade is penetrated to its hollowness, a strategy we have seen elaborated in the tactics of mise-en-scène, of narrative structure, and of character development. If Welles' narration (what we have termed his bravura) strikes us at first as pompously loud, it is only so he can hear its echoes pathetically die away.

"I wrote and directed this film; my name is Orson Welles." His voice leaves the most lasting impression even as the image of the microphone swings away from us at the end of *The Magnificent Ambersons*. Welles' voice is resonant and voluminous, satisfyingly thick. It is, as much as possible, the voice of God, confident because omniscient, demanding that we hearken to it and interpret our situation in relation to its message. If this feeling is greatest in *The Magnificent Ambersons*, where paradoxically he hides behind the camera, it emanates just as surely from his other films: the booming voices of Kane, Hank Quinlan, the Advocate, and Gregory Arkadin; the subtly modulated roles which that voice adopts in the Shakespeare films where he would render up to eight different parts. Because of the genius of his own voice and the experience this gift opened up for him first in the theater and then in radio, Welles was able to break decisively with Hollywood sound practice and to give to his films a new tone bearing an unaccustomed feeling.

Welles' sound practice is first perceived as a problem to be overcome. Particularly in his European films, dialogue is so muffled that in many instances it is incomprehensible at first hearing. This has always been attributed to the cheap post-synchronization his budgets required. Yet we find already in the RKO films the first seeds of a conception of sound necessitating increased audience acuity. Dialogue overlaps would seem to be the key to this new method, but more central is Welles' practice of microphone placement in conjunction with the overlaps. *Citizen Kane* and *The Magnificent Ambersons* abound in examples in which a close-up voice will unexpectedly smother a conversation taking place at mid-distance, or where a boisterous exchange will be followed by whispering or sobbing. Altogether these oppositions produce a veritable audio space in which events take place. Obviously adopted from the techniques spawned by dramatic radio production, this spatializing of the sound track is built up through throat-miking for whisper effects, apparent directional sound, reverberation, and high-level ambient noise inclusion. Such extended space is put into play in conjunction with a heightened use of the conventional "sound off." In the Amberson mansion voices emanate from unseen rooms (the good-night scene after the ball) and huge doors echo when pushed closed off-camera. Sound so dominated Welles' conception of this film that most sequences are designed to integrate audio information with the fewest possible camera positions. We have mentioned already the single-take sequences in the kitchen, at the train station, and of the Major before the fire. These are static scenes, readily accessible to the single angle. Welles goes beyond this in certain action scenes where one couple walking in conversation will pass out of view urging the camera to pick up what the sound track is already giving to us, a second conversation of a second couple. It is the flow of conversation that dictates the rhythm of this film and the role of the camera. Doubtless, over the course of ninety minutes a much larger, more atmospheric space is represented than we are accustomed to, thanks to which this comedy of manners, this satire, can affect us with unusual power.

Touted for his expressionist visual sense, Welles' most signal moments come to us from devices realized on the sound track. When placed counter to the image, the voice delivers rhetoric or irony, as in the haughty recitation of the Holinshed Chronicles or in the narrator's judgment toward the end of *Ambersons*: "George Amberson Minafer had got his comeuppance, had got it three times full and running over." On other occasions the sound track, far from smugly commenting on what we see, is the very vehicle of pathos: Welles' most outrageously authoritative voice screaming, "You can't do this to me Gettys. I'm Charles Foster Kane," the murmurs following Isabel Amberson's death, the train whistle calling Jack away after her funeral, the phone call Tania makes prefiguring the downfall of Quinlan, Quinlan's own voice betrayed by a walkie-talkie in the final moments of *Touch of Evil*, Joseph K. pleading for justice to a raucous courtroom in *The Trial* and the pathetic ditty sung as he awaits the blast of the dynamite. Added to all these scripted effects is the continual friction of ambient noise and choral voicing which thicken the image, dragging it toward its slow decline.

Welles' fascination with the possibilities of sound culminates in his *Chimes at Midnight*. Perhaps the greatest adaptation of Shakespeare that the cinema has yet produced, this is also the adaptation most difficult physically to hear. Lines are delivered at lightning speed, often over the shoulder, mixed with the dialogue or laughter of other characters, by quick turns bellowed, then murmured. Some viewers find it maddening to find our greatest poet left to the mercy of Welles with his bizarre sense of sound mixing and of pace. They prefer the Olivier films where every speech is directed to the audience, amplified by the closed shell of its decor, separated from neighboring speeches by studied silences if not actual changes in camera setup. In this way we miss not a line; indeed we might think of *Henry V* or *Hamlet* as films based on Shakespeare's *writing* whereas *Chimes at Midnight* is tied to the actor's *voice*. *Henry V*, especially, with its Duc de Berry sets, is an embellishment of a sacred text, truly a manuscript illuminated by the three-strip Technicolor filmstock and by the bright light of the projection arc. In contrast, Welles violated the sanctity of the manuscript, piecing and patching a single film from the fragments of five different plays. Instead of a *text* which comfortingly remains behind the scenes and outlasts the film, Welles gives us a *voice* disconcertingly disappearing over time. Welles has taken as his model not the immortal Bard but "a poor player that struts and frets his hour upon the stage and then is heard no more."

Shakespeare, even Shakespeare, cannot outlast deterioration in time and diminution in space. Once again Welles has put forth an immense power, here the greatest dramatist the world has known, only to listen to it echo away inconsequentially in an infinitude of natural space and time. The effect is the more disturbing for the simplicity of its means. Whereas the techniques of transition, of embedding, and of parable all depend upon the magician's panoply of tricks, Welles also knows how to devastate through sheer sound recording.

Far from betraying theater, cinema here bestows upon it a most intimate gift, to let its cultured speeches contend with the wind of a truly open space, to test human struggle in the vast stretches of inhuman time. Recall Gielgud as the king in his cold, enormous castle, Hotspur spewing forth heroic epithets on the windy hill, or Falstaff discoursing white-robed in the birch forest . . . the words of all these die out as we hear them, are carried away by the wind they cannot hush. Thus, the nostalgia expressed in the prologue ("Where have they all gone? Dead, all dead") comes through the sound track to haunt every moment of the film. Only the Holinshed Chronicles, read imperiously by Ralph Richardson, pretends to outlast the events it comments on. Yet this is precisely that official view of history and of life satirized by the human life of the Boar's Head, by the flesh of Shakespeare's verse, and by the raspiness of the actors delivering that verse. Despite its victory over impersonal monumentality, such realism pays a price, the price of transition, deterioration, and mortality. Welles' great reverberating laugh is locked within the body of Falstaff borne off in a box at the end to be lowered deep into the earth.

Despite his background in theater and the evident theatricality of his personality, Orson Welles is fully a man of the cinema, if by this we mean someone whose most profound realizations are made possible in this medium. The illusory quality of the image, the magic-trick effects of motion picture technology, the depth of sound, and the shallowness of the screen all contribute to the expression of Welles' meditations on authenticity, mirage, impermanence, and loss.

First Bazin and now Roland Barthes have written evocatively of the relation of photography to death.[6] The image is the trace left by an object gone before us in time. More than representing that object, it expresses its absence. And yet the animating power of motion confers on the cinema a vibrancy missing from the still photograph. Barthes recognized this in his classic formulation: "Film can no longer be seen as animated photographs: the *having-been-there* gives way before a *being-there* of the thing."[7] Popular criticism supports Barthes' distinction. Movies are thought of as the artform that captures life, brings to life, animates our dreams, and so on.

Welles is one of those few directors (Truffaut is another) whose overriding obsession with the past and death goes against the grain of the medium even while it is best expressed in that medium. How does he distort the moving image to make it figure its own demise? We have already encountered his most calculated strategy for this in the embedded story. By consigning his images to a teller, especially when that teller is representing a past event, Welles manages to frame what we see like an expanded still photograph. The images of Kane at the newspaper office or at the opera or at Xanadu may affect us greatly but part of what we feel about them is their distance from us. Unable to break out of the temporal boundary constructed for them, they are the property of the teller who recounts them. Once again Welles plays with the tension between power and debility, this time between the strength of living pictures and our realization that these are of the past.

Doubtless this tension gives to *Chimes at Midnight* a sentiment absent even from the Shakespearean original. Not only is the life at the Boar's Head contrasted with the tomblike empire at the court, that life has already been put into the realm of memory by the rueful preface where two old men reflect upon the days that they have seen, all gone. The film then operates under two time schemes, that of the eternal history of the Plantagenets as chronicled in the heroic language of Holinshed, and that of the mortal history of Falstaff and the common folk, livingly expressed in the human verse of Shakespeare. We must add to this that other nostalgia for Shakespeare himself which Welles is able to inject into the film, a regret for a time now gone when life and history could be so completely and satisfyingly represented.

In all his films the images arrange themselves in such a way as to embody the notion of loss and death. They obliterate themselves in the characters' flow away from the camera, in the deep shadows that settle on them, in the contrived quaintness of their presentation, and of course in the architectural structures that dominate the compositions (sepulchral rooms, old castles, timeless and inhuman spaces).

We watch Welles' films not as living artifacts emerging into our present, but as traces of a power that once was. We want to be astounded by the strength of that power even while the greater power of time reduces this strength to dust, to memory. While it is true that Welles indecorously promotes this reading of his films through overt references to death and loss lodged in the dialogue or contributed by the morbid voice of the narrator, the tone of the past and of things passing is constantly maintained by the work of the sound track. For an image is always potentially graspable, sight being, as Walter Ong urges, a most possessive sense as it seizes views like postcards.[8] But sound is the sense of hearkening, of vocation. Its source remains outside us, profoundly in the Other. When, as in Welles, this source retreats from us, we are left with a nostalgia for the full-throated presence left in its echo on the sound track. In short, unlike the simple pastness of the still photograph, Welles' films are simultaneously grand and gone; we are present to their fading.

To characterize this effect critics have called upon a series of spatial metaphors: the cavernous volume of his images, the screen as window onto a vanishing point which swallows up the figures that had loomed so large. Our meditation on sound and on temporality suggests other, potentially corrective metaphors. These films do not dwell on something that once was close and now is far away; instead their source, like some original vibrating chord, is settled deep within them, producing a tone which, through successive borrowings, modulations, usages, and distortions, is transformed into the gaudy surface of the films. But the inauthenticity of this showman's technique still serves as a great volume for the vibrations of life within it. In other words, the very hollowness of Welles' personal world view, the emptiness of his paradoxes, his characters, and his tricky plots, prepares us for the sound of something in its core.

Although unrecoverable in literal fact, it is wrong to suggest that this something (this authentic feeling or formulation) is utterly lost in the past. For the tense of Welles' films is never that of the simple past, but of the historical preterite. No event in his film floats free; all are bound up in an historical account which Heidegger would call "recollection in care."[9] And even when, at his most relentless, as in *Chimes at Midnight* or *The Magnificent Ambersons*, he questions the very histories that hold the past so dear, Welles effectively encloses time in the giant box of his narration. He may no longer feel able to touch the real life of Merrie England, nor that of Shakespeare, but he can allude to them, or rather (to maintain our metaphor) he can permit something of their sound to vibrate the empty space he has fashioned around them.

He has, in both senses of the term, *related* something to us. In this way his films are repetitions of a care about mortality, repetitions to which we can now add our own meditation which is related to and relates his subject. The cultural extension this produces is, Ricoeur would suggest, an artistic compensation for the essentially nontransferable character of death.[10] If our criticism is a mere echo of his films, Welles' corpus itself issues up an echo of art and through art the tremolo of something feeble but authentic by which we sense both feeling and life.

Notes

1. Stephen Heath, "Film and System; Terms of Analysis," *Screen*, 16, no. 1 (1975), 7–77.

2. James Naremore, *The Magic World of Orson Welles* (New York: Oxford University Press, 1978), p. 293.

3. André Bazin, *Orson Welles* (Paris: Editions du Cerf, 1972), pp. 62–70.

4. The interested reader may learn more about the making of this and all of Welles's films in Charles Higham's *The Films of Orson Welles* (Berkeley and Los Angeles: University of California Press, 1970). Naremore's book is full of other details as well and is highly recommended.

5. Naremore, *Magic World*, p. 77.

6. André Bazin, "The Ontology of the Photographic Image," *What is Cinema?* (Berkeley and Los Angeles: University of California Press, 1967), pp. 10–15. Roland Barthes, *Camera Lucida* (New York: Hill and Wang, 1980).

7. Roland Barthes, *Image, Music, Text*, trans. Stephen Heath (New York: Hill and Wang, 1977), p. 44.

8. Walter Ong, *The Presence of the Word* (New Haven: Yale University Press, 1967), pp. 166–68.

9. Martin Heidegger, *Being and Time*, trans. Macquerrie and Robinson (New York: Harper & Row, 1962), pp. 437, 438.

10. Paul Ricoeur, "Narrative Time," *Critical Inquiry* 7 (Autumn 1980), 188–90.

Welles' Farewell, *The Other Side of the Wind*

KEVIN C. BRECHNER

ONE OF Orson Welles' last films as a director was *The Other Side of the Wind*. In March and April of 1974 a portion of the film was shot at Southwestern Studio and in the town of Carefree in the Arizona desert forty miles north of Phoenix. I had the opportunity of spending three days on the sets. The last two days I brought an old Leica IIIf and was allowed to shoot anything from the sides and the lighting catwalks above, as an observer-participant only. What information I gained came from talks with the cast and crew; it must be considered hearsay information and taken with a large grain of salt. However, the overall *mise-en-scène* does give an indication of the way Orson Welles was working at that point in his career.

The Other Side of the Wind has not been released. Excerpts of the film were shown on the telecast of the 1975 American Film Institute's tribute to Orson Welles (*American Cinematographer*, April, 1975). It revealed some magnificent photography and editing. The cast list of the film is rather impressive in itself. Included among the players are John Huston, Oja Kodar, Peter Bogdanovich, Edmond O'Brien, Lilli Palmer, Norman Foster, Mercedes McCambridge, Dennis Hopper, Paul Stewart, Susan Strasberg, Claude Chabrol, Stephanne Audran, Robert Random, Paul Mazursky, Henry Jaglom, George Jessel, Cameron Mitchell, Benny Rubin, Pat McMahon, Frank Marshall, Curtis Harrington, Dan Tobin, Larry Jackson, and Stafford Repp. Many others play small roles and bits or serve as extras.

Most of out knowledge of the film comes from accounts written during or after the filming. A recent interview with the filmmaker Henry Jaglom described *The Other Side of the Wind* as "A brilliant film he (Welles) made about Hollywood that's been locked in a vault in Paris because of a complicated legal suit." Joseph McBride's book *Orson Welles* (Viking Press, New York, 1972) gives a description and photographs of the early stages of filming. A newspaper account by Joyce Haber in the *Arizona Republic* (March 21, 1974) describes the role of Peter Bogdanovich. Three recent books on Orson Welles by James Naremore (Oxford University Press, 1978), Barbara Leaming (Viking Press, New York, 1985), and Charles Higham (St. Martin's Press, New York, 1985) discuss *The Other Side of the Wind* at length. John Huston described his involvement in his autobiography, *An Open Book* (Alfred A. Knopf, New York, 1980).

From *American Cinematographer* (July 1986): 34–38. Reprinted courtesy of American Cinematographer Magazine.

My involvement in *The Other Side of the Wind* resulted from a phone call made to the secretary at Southwestern Studio. The studio was all but shut down due to a lack of business. Only a skeleton crew remained consisting of the studio management, Tom Brodek and Mark Lambert, a secretary, the operations manager, and a couple of guards. Southwestern Studios had three large soundstages, production offices; facilities for makeup, dressing and editing; a tour department and a 125 acre back lot with Western street. Although the studio was well outfitted, it had seen better days as the network television home of *The New Dick Van Dyke Show* which ran for three seasons on CBS. The studio also housed production offices for Hugh Downs and had been used for several network pilots. The studio or back lot had been used for part or all of several feature films, including *Zabriskie Point* (1969), *Cancel My Reservation* (1972), *Pocket Money* (1972), *Man and Boy* (1972), and the short feature *Time River* (1973). But by 1974 lack of work had caused the tour department and all but the most vital functions to be closed down. After that I periodically phoned the office to keep in touch. It was one such call that got me involved in *The Other Side of the Wind*.

When asked what was going on at the studio, the secretary said, "Oh, not much . . . It's pretty quiet here . . . Oh, . . . Orson Welles is back on Stage One working on a film . . . they're having trouble finding extras . . . maybe you could help." Trying to remain calm, I forced out a reserved, "Well, . . . maybe I could find some time." A Phoenix newspaper earlier had run Joyce Haber's article announcing that Welles was filming at an undisclosed location in the Phoenix area. The city was abuzz with rumors about where that might be. The secretary gave me the phone number of Rick Walzer, a production assistant on the film. When I spoke with him he said that they did indeed need extras because of the studio's remote location. I arranged to gather together some friends, mostly film enthusiasts and graduate psychology students, to travel the 40 miles north into the desert the next evening to be "extras in an Orson Welles movie." Incidentally, some of the extras those nights have gone on to prominence in other fields such as psychologists Dr. Avril Thorne of Wellesley College and Dr. June Flora of Stanford, and social economist John Cook of the University of North Carolina.

I drove up to Carefree a little earlier than the eight o'clock call to find the sound stage set up but empty of people except one technician. It was not until about nine o'clock that the cast and crew began to come in. Bit-by-bit from questions directed to the crew I gained a mosaic of what the film was about and it seemed every bit as incredible in concept as *Citizen Kane*.

The Other Side of the Wind tells the story of an aging film director, Jake Hannaford, played by John Huston, who is having trouble finding financing for his current film. The principal action takes place at a birthday party for Hannaford attended by various Hollywood types: actors, actresses, directors, critics—those on the way up and those on the way down, a few going nowhere. A group of young filmmakers are following Hannaford wherever he goes, documenting his life.

The scene being shot that evening was being made on the abandoned main set built for *The New Dick Van Dyke Show*. Originally the set had represented the kitchen and living room of a desert house. Adobe brick columns surrounded windows looking out to a painted desert backdrop. A small alcove contained a bar and was adjoined by an unusual fireplace shaped like a rounded cone. It looked a little like the bread ovens built by Pueblo Indians.

Welles' set however looked entirely different than *The New Dick Van Dyke Show*. The lighting of director of photography Gary Graver did not resemble the bright situation comedy lighting designed by Richard H. Kline, ASC for the Van Dyke show. It was dark and moody, with pools of light around tables and chairs. Kline had used scores of 10Ks and 5Ks to illuminate and completely wash the large set in soft modeled light. Welles and Gary Graver took what was left of that set and changed the visual look entirely. Most of the lighting was done with 1, 2, and 5Ks. Often only five to ten instruments would be used in a large scene. In some of the later scenes shot in the house in Carefree, only one or two 1Ks would be used to light a scene with two people. While this economy in the use of lighting instruments was in part due to the low budget, it also led to very dramatic lighting where the principals would be haloed in light and the shadows would go to black. This probably helped them match this set to previous sets they had filmed, and it also was reminiscent of the lighting in *Citizen Kane*.

It is impossible to describe accurately the sensation when Orson Welles arrived on the set. The three nights I was in attendance, the "day's" filming began at about 10 pm and ended the next day at about 6 am. Usually the small crew of about ten people arrived first. The crew consisted of the director of photography, one camera operator, two production assistants, a gaffer, and grips. Then the extras and cast filtered in. Messrs. Huston and Welles arrived about the same time. Actually, Welles' voice arrived first. Most everyone is familiar with his deep, commanding voice. But, when he came through one of the doors of the large sound stage and spoke to someone as he entered, it was as though a huge electrical switch had been thrown that suddenly energized the whole building. *Everyone* became alert, even the veterans. Most seemed to sense that they were participating in an extraordinary experience. The atmosphere was electric.

Most of the time, perhaps because of his great bulk, which must have been pushing 300 pounds, he chose to sit while directing. From a chair on the side of the set he would give directions to Gary Graver and camera operator Bill Weaver. Sometimes Welles would operate one of the two cameras. One crew member mentioned that if the director of photography thought a different camera angle was needed he would secretly move Orson's chair to the new angle when Orson took a break.

Production assistants Rick Waltzer and Neil Canton simultaneously filled the roles of assistant directors, associate producers, clapper-loaders, gofers, and continuity. Rick Waltzer also acted in the picture. Neil Canton has gone on to co-produce the smash hit *Back to the Future* and at the time of this writing is working on *Witches* at Warner Brothers. Welles would speak quietly to the actors, often individually. Several of the scenes involved interactions of John Huston with Bogdanovich, Norman Foster, veteran actors Dan Tobin and Stafford Repp, and a young blonde actress, Cathy Lucas. When Welles did choose to stand up to make a point, or direct a camera movement, the point was emphasized by the sheer presence of his bulk and his commanding voice. It seemed curious how different the aging Welles looked from the way he had projected the aging Charles Foster Kane.

We were told that only one copy of the script existed and Mr. Welles had it. Later we saw it as a typewritten script held in a black leather binder. The script had been written by Welles with assistance from Oja Kodar. Unfortunately, being an extra did not grant one the privilege of strolling over and thumbing through the script.

What seemed incredible about *The Other Side of the Wind* was that the fine line that exists between the reality of the "real world" and the unreality of the "reel world" disappeared. The aging film director was played by aging film director Huston. The rising young film director was played by rising young film director Bogdanovich. The older pitchman was played by older director Foster, who surely must have made many pitches in his day, including when he directed Welles in *Journey Into Fear* (1942). The beautiful young actress in Hannaford's film was played by a beautiful young actress Oja Kodar (co-author of the script). A Hollywood critic was played by the actress Susan Strasberg who looked lovely and who surely must have grown up a critic by living in the household of her father, Lee Strasberg. We were told that Dennis Hopper and Paul Mazursky had been filmed earlier portraying themselves. The pattern followed all the way down to the extras. The group of cinema enthusiasts and onlookers wandering around the party scene were all played by cinema enthusiasts. None of them were getting paid. Perhaps the story line did not follow the actors' real lives; nevertheless, the ensemble could only be regarded as an extreme example of typecasting.

The documentary filmmakers, led by Larry Jackson, were recording the party with still cameras and an empty Eclair Camaflex camera, which Welles owned. The actual film was running through two hand-held 16mm Eclair NPR's, also owned by Welles. Other scenes had been shot with an Arri 2C, Super 8, and still cameras. As the real cameras flowed through the party scenes, they occasionally caught sight of the other cameras real and unreal. It didn't seem to matter because the story and the filming of the story at that point became the same thing. (Larry Jackson has gone on to become the vice president of international acquisitions for Samuel Goldwyn Productions.)

Many times it was difficult to distinguish a difference between the actions and dialogue of the participants when the cameras were rolling and when they were not rolling. The dialogue between the actual takes was every bit as interesting as that of the film. Imagine Welles, Huston, and Bogdanovich, three giants of filmmaking, in the same room, trading off barbs and comments. It is unfortunate that these conversations were not recorded, because most of the comments have faded from memory. I do remember John Huston sliding up to Graver while the latter was directing the placement of a lighting instrument, and saying, "Well, Mr. Toland, do you think that was the right choice?" In sort of a backhanded compliment, John Huston placed Gary Graver in the same class as Gregg Toland, ASC, the legendary cinematographer of the likes of *Tugboat Annie* (1933), *Les Misérables* (1935), *The Goldwyn Follies* (1938), *Wuthering Heights* (1939), *The Grapes of Wrath* (1940), *The Westerner* (1940), and *The Best Years of Our Lives* (1946). In 1941, Toland teamed with Welles in what is generally considered one of the greatest of films, *Citizen Kane*. Graver, who appeared to be in his late twenties, just smiled.

Graver also filmed *F for Fake* (1976) and an educational film on *Othello* for Orson Welles. After *The Other Side of the Wind*, he went on to photograph *The Attic* (1980) for director George Edwards with Ray Milland and Carrie Snodgrass. He wrote and directed *Texas Lightning* (1980) and *Trick or Treat* (1982). He has recently completed *Love Leads the Way* (1986) for Disney and the remake of *Stagecoach* (1986).

During the filming of the party scenes, for what reason I know not, Welles selected Jack Boyce, who I had brought as an extra, and me to deliver single lines of dialogue. Whether we made it past the cutting room floor is not as important as the experience itself. Boyce was so affected by the experience that his first child, a boy born a few months later, received the middle name Welles.

The line I delivered was, "Fascist, shall we define our terms?" I had absolutely no idea what it meant or how it fit into the story line. I asked Welles some lame question like, "What is my motivation?" He pointed to Bogdanovich and said, "He'll tell you . . . Peter, help him with his line." Bogdanovich, who had just finished *Paper Moon* (1973) and *Daisy Miller* (1974) following the success of *Last Picture Show* (1971), and was beginning *At Long Last Love* (1975), took me over to the script. I saw that my line was typed under the heading of a character called "Cineaste." Later I looked it up in a dictionary and found out the word *cineaste* means cinema enthusiast. I, too, had been type cast in my small role. I read the line from the script a few times. Bogdanovich said, "That's fine." Welles came over and said to Bogdanovich, "Do you think he can say the line?" The shot went very fast. I delivered the line while totally confused about what it meant. Bogdanovich crossed in front of me and delivered some response which I cannot remember. My enthusiasm was tempered later when I read in Joseph McBride's 1972 book *Orson Welles* how honored he felt to have been picked to deliver a line in *The Other Side of the Wind*. His event occurred in 1970. Mine was in 1974. This will give some indication of how long the film was in production. Who knows how many people during those years were pulled to deliver one liners?

Financing for this film seemed to fit perfectly into the image of Welles as a maverick who could not get funding through the Hollywood studios. The crew members, who were all very young, mostly in their twenties, said that the financing was "coming from France." One said that none of the crew had received their salary for several weeks. There was of course no pay or screen credit mentioned for any of the extras. The second night I was at the studio, at about 3 a.m., a young woman dressed in a flowing black cape arrived on the soundstage with a gush of French words, "Oh, Orson, mon ami . . .!" Welles disappeared with her for a few moments. I was told by one of the crew members that the payroll had just arrived in cash from France. Information in Barbara Leaming's book on Orson Welles leads me to believe that the caped woman was Dominique Antoine, who arrived *without* the cash. That same night Oja Kodar spent the evening on the set, although she did not appear in any of the scenes. Besides being a co-author on the script, Leaming describes Ms. Kodar as a co-financer of the film.

The third evening I was in attendance was not at Southwestern Studio, but in a private mansion in the nearby town of Carefree. The large house was perched on a desert hillside and built into the huge round stone boulders. In order to preserve secrecy, one of the crew members had posed as a vacationer renting the house for an extended holiday. Welles was said to be staying in the house during the Arizona portion of the filming. Again, not having a copy of the script, we had no idea of how the scenes fit into the story. The size of the rooms made the event much more intimate than on the sound stage. The original group of extras dropped in size due to conflicting commitments or lack of interest. The hard-cores made the long trek out from Phoenix.

Most of the shots that evening were dialogue between John Huston and Cathy Lucas. Huston's gravelly voice, free spirit, and lumbering, slightly-bent-forward walk charmed everyone.

It was a pleasure to see him take direction from Welles. Welles had him retake one difficult scene in particular several times. After the third take, Welles said softly, almost with tears in his eyes, "That couldn't be done any better!", to which Mr. Huston replied, "Perhaps." Huston provides a long description of his participation in *The Other Side of the Wind* in his autobiography *An Open Book*. He mentions that Orson caught him studying his lines for his party scenes, and said, "John, you're just causing yourself unnecessary agony. Just read the lines or forget them and say what you please. The idea is all that matters." Huston also related a humorous incident that occurred during the filming of an exterior scene that required Jake Hannaford to drive recklessly. Huston, who does not generally drive, unintentionally gave them more than they asked for. With the car jammed with Welles, the crew and a rolling camera, Huston managed to steer the automobile the wrong way on a freeway into oncoming traffic. Then he jumped the curb, crossed the median, and eventually got the car aimed in the right direction. The passengers reacted with a stony silence followed by a heavy sigh. Orson said, "Thanks, John, that'll do."

After the third night our services as extras were no longer needed, and *The Other Side of the Wind* became a great memory for many of us.

A recent interview with Henry Jaglom stated that *The Other Side of the Wind* is tied up in a Paris vault. David A. Cook in *A History of Narrative Film* (Norton, New York, 1981) reported from another source that as of 1979 the film was 96 percent completed. Barbara Leaming's book *Orson Welles* describes at length the complications associated with the film that have involved financing from a relative of the former Shah of Iran and the disputes that resulted when the Ayatollah took over. According to Gary Graver at a recent meeting, the film is completely shot, except for a few pick ups. It is partially edited. Oja Kodar now has control of the property. Gary Graver said that he and Ms. Kodar currently are working to complete the film.

Whether we shall ever get to see this last major work of one of the world's greatest filmmakers is uncertain. Perhaps the film forever will remain unfinished or unreleased, like Eisenstein's *Que Viva Mexico* (1930–32) or Josef von Sternberg's *I, Claudius* (1937). The excerpts of *The Other Side of the Wind* that have been shown publicly so far show magnificent photography, fine acting, and a truly unique concept. We can only hope that Graver and Kodar can complete the project. Bogdanovich, quoted in Joyce Haber's news article says, "I think this is Orson's most exciting film since *Citizen Kane*."

Chimes at Midnight from Stage to Screen: The Art of Adaptation

ROBERT HAPGOOD

Most of the best Shakespeare films have a stage production in their background. Examples come readily to mind: Olivier had performed on stage all the plays he made into films; Kozintsev had directed both *Hamlet* and *King Lear* for the theatre before he made films of them. Zeffirelli's film of *Romeo and Juliet* put the same accent on youth as had his Old Vic production; the Peter Brook/Paul Scofield film of *King Lear* was a revised edition of their stage version. Yet this theatrical lineage of the films has received remarkably little comment. In general, film commentators have tended to play down the ties between film and theatre (they are more inclined to see parallels with narrative literature) precisely because the two are so close, theatre came first, and the commentators are concerned to maintain the integrity of film as an independent art-form.[1] That it is. Yet much can be learned from exploring the relations between the two forms of drama, as indeed Allardyce Nicoll, André Bazin, and Roger Manvell have already shown.[2] They, however, have considered the subject in general terms and have not focused on particular films and the stage productions to which they were related, whether the plays were by Shakespeare or other playwrights. Admittedly, a prior stage production may not always be an asset for a film. Most critics have felt that, on film, Olivier's portrayal of Othello would have been better if it had not so directly reflected his stage performance; what was bravura classic acting on the stage seems stagey on the screen. A stage production should not be in the foreground of a film. But in general a stage background seems to have been an asset for most Shakespeare films, making for a maturely considered and fully crystallized interpretation. The study of this background should thus help to illuminate the film interpretation.

I

Orson Welles's film *Chimes at Midnight* is an especially interesting case in point. It has justly been praised as a 'masterpiece' or a 'near masterpiece' (flawed by a poor soundtrack) by the authors of books both on Shakespearian films and on Welles's films in general. It was preceded by

From *Shakespeare Survey* 39 (1987): 39–52. Reprinted with the permission of Cambridge University Press.

two stage incarnations, neither of which was itself a success yet both of which made important contributions to the film.

The first was *Five Kings* (1938), which traced in a single, very long evening the whole career of Harry Monmouth from Prince Hal cavorting with Falstaff in the tavern to King Henry V wooing Katherine after his victory at Agincourt.[3] At twenty-three, Welles was nearing the height of the Boy Wonder phase of his career. He had already scored successes on stage with his fascist *Julius Caesar* and voodoo *Macbeth* and was about to film *Citizen Kane*. For *Five Kings* he adapted the script (selecting, condensing, and rearranging relevant portions of the two parts of *Henry IV* and *Henry V*, plus preliminary materials from *Richard II*), directed the production, and played the role of Falstaff. The result was to have been performed in tandem with a similar reworking of materials drawn from the first tetralogy of history plays. (As a schoolboy Welles had adapted and played the role of Richard III in just such a compilation called 'The Winter of Our Discontent.')[4] Hence the promise of five kings in the title. The second project was never realized. In *Five Kings* reviewers found much to praise, especially Welles's own performance as Falstaff and his imaginative use of a revolving stage. The latter was a source of practical difficulty (its misadventures are entertainingly recounted by John Houseman),[5] but integral to Welles's conception of a 'world in motion'.[6] The production as a whole, however, could not be called either a critical or a financial success. After try-outs in Boston, Washington, DC, and Philadelphia, it folded without reaching New York.

In 1960 Welles tried again with a stage production called *Chimes at Midnight*, which played in Belfast and Dublin for a month.[7] It had much in common with *Five Kings*. The use of a narrator continued, but with material drawn exclusively from Holinshed and without additional choruses from *Henry V*. In both versions, essentially the same portions were selected from the *Henry IV* plays: Hotspur was given an important role, his farewell scene with Lady Percy was included, Worcester's role as villain was developed somewhat; but other aspects of the civil wars were totally omitted—Glendower and Douglas did not figure at all, nor did the rebels in *Part 2* apart from occasional mention of Northumberland. All of the tavern scenes were kept, as were most of the scenes involving the king at court and on the battlefield. In both versions, newspaper reviewers agreed, the emotional highpoint was the rejection of Falstaff. Reviewers also consistently found more sadness than humour in Welles's Falstaff.[8]

What was chiefly different about the Irish version was its stronger focus on Falstaff, 'being' (as the programme put it) 'the adventures of the Fat Knight and the Prince of Wales.' As adapted by Welles, its first act was essentially an abbreviation of *Part 1* of *Henry IV*. Welles wrote to Hilton Edwards, who staged it: 'the shape and form of Part One is well nigh perfect . . . not only as a whole play, but as *an act*': hence 'in general terms, the shape of our Act One simply must have the basic shape of Shakespeare's Part One.' Welles's second act was a reworking of materials in *Part 2*, for which he did not have so high a regard: 'The scenes in Part Two are often superior to Part One . . . but the shape is less good, and, thus, our cutting is going to actually help.'[9] Only Falstaff's death was included from *Henry V*.

The staged *Chimes at Midnight* was a critical success, with London as well as Belfast and Dublin reviewers, but a financial disaster. Welles himself regarded it as a 'flop' and did not take it on a contemplated tour to London and Paris.[10]

The filmed *Chimes at Midnight* (originally distributed in the United States under the title *Falstaff*) was released in 1965. It was adapted and directed by Welles, who played Falstaff. For it Welles made essentially the same selection of materials from *Henry IV* as for the two stage versions. In content, it resembles the Irish version in drawing its text almost entirely from the two parts of *Henry IV*, without the large concern of *Five Kings* with *Henry V*. In structure, however, it resembles the treatment of *Henry IV* materials in *Five Kings*, taking *Part 1* as its basis and drawing on portions from *Part 2* to fill out that structure and add an extended coda to it.

In matters of detail, the film is especially close to the Irish stage production. Many of the film script's stage directions are verbatim from the stage script.[11] For instance, the film's introduction of the Percys one by one as the narrator mentions them comes directly from the Irish version. Keith Baxter played Prince Hal in both, and with the same mixture of the 'young man with a taste for practical jokes and the serious young prince aware of his own destiny'.[12] The slowly tolling bells which are a motif in the film serve the same function as did the death-march drumbeats which sounded through much of the Irish production.

It is fascinating to see how certain features in the film emerged as Welles moved from version to version. One of the funniest moments in the film comes in the midst of the prince's battlefield lament over 'dead' Falstaff (*1 Henry IV*, 5.4.102–10).[13] No sooner has he said 'I could have better spared a better man' than he sees the vapour of Falstaff's breath coming through his visor: 'Embowelled will I see thee by and by,' he taunts and goes his ways. In the Irish version, the lines between 'better man' and 'Embowelled' were cut, but without motivation. In the film script, the cut was prompted by the prince's noticing 'an involuntary heave' in the 'corpse'. In the film, the tell-tale vapour makes the effect unmistakably graphic and comic.

The successive versions show Welles practising a growing economy of means. At first he apparently felt it necessary to dramatize his use of Holinshed by showing the audience a copy of the *Chronicles*. On-stage in Ireland the narrator took a large book from a stand and read from it; in the film script: 'the screen is filled with a section of a page from

"Holinshed's Chronicle History of England" showing the same words as those spoken by the narrator'. The actual film dispenses with this fuss: the titles conclude with 'Narration based on Holinshed's Chronicles as spoken by Ralph Richardson', at which we hear Richardson's voice describing the murder of Richard II as the camera shot descends from the sky to reveal Pomfret Castle.

At times, Welles may have overdone his economies, becoming so elliptical as to be obscure. In the stage *Chimes at Midnight* he took elaborate pains to introduce the prince to the audience. He had the king ask, 'Can no man tell me of my unthrifty son?' (*Richard II*, 5.3.1–12) to which Westmoreland replied, 'The prince will, in the perfectness of time, / Cast off his followers' (*2 Henry IV*, 4.4.74–9). The Chorus then put in, 'Now for the king's son':

> [*Enter Prince Hal*] Lord Henry prince of Wales . . . Indeed he was youthfully given, grown to audacity, and had chosen companions with whom he spent the time in such recreations, exercises and delights as he fancied . . .
> [*Falstaff, awakening, pops his head up from behind a rostrum or chest*].

This may have been too explicit an introduction, but in the film Welles goes to the other extreme. After Hotspur has wished that his rival might be 'poisoned with a pot of ale', the image dissolves to show Hal finishing a pot of ale—and that is the extent of his introduction. The effect is direct and vivid, to be sure, but it is one of the reasons the film often seems made for an audience that already knows the plays.

Considering the closeness of the film to the stage productions, Welles was remarkably successful in respecting the idioms of the two dramatic forms. In the film, he avoids the use of stage conventions. He has all Shakespeare's soliloquies spoken as dialogue in the hearing of other characters; he gets around the convention of impenetrable disguise by making Poins and Hal hidden eavesdroppers on Falstaff in the tavern rather than presenting themselves as pantlers. In his own performance as Falstaff in the Irish stage version, Welles made the most of the live situation, playing up a sense of community with the audience. As his own script writer, Welles let Falstaff in on secrets that in the original are at first known only to the audience. (He realized in advance that it was the prince who had picked his pocket and who was disguised as a pantler.) In turn, Welles as actor let the audience in on Falstaff's secrets. Reviewers delighted in the way he would confide certain of his speeches, 'sitting down with his legs dangling over the front of the stage, chatting to the audience'.[14] Appropriately, none of these stage familiarities carried over into his screen performance.

To focus so neatly on the two stage productions and the film is untrue, however, to the fecundity of Welles's response to the history plays and the fluidity of his creative process. By all accounts, *Five Kings* was in a continual state of redefinition, especially of ruthless cutting, during its time on the road. Of the Irish production, Thelma Ruby, who played Mistress Quickly, has recalled that the cast was still rehearsing at the end of the run, trying new arrangements of the material.[15] For instance, Welles experimented with taking Mistress Quickly's report of the death of Falstaff from the very end (where a reviewer had found it 'anticlimactic'),[16] and introducing it at the very beginning, thus interestingly anticipating the retrospective effect the film creates by putting the 'chimes at midnight' exchange between Falstaff and Shallow before the titles.

Beyond the examples already given, Welles's original film script differed significantly from the version that reached the screen. There were good things in the script that got lost. The 'quite symphonic' snoring that Welles called for when Falstaff is first presented is hardly more than a snuffle on the soundtrack. Falstaff was to have gone to Gadshill on a 'huge shire horse to match his size'. In the script Welles made the prince the bearer of the good news to his dying father that the rebels had been defeated; hence his initial jocularity to his weeping brother ('How now? Rain within doors, and none abroad?'—2 Henry IV, 4.5.9). In the film his bearing of the good news does not appear, leaving his jocularity a puzzle, especially after his solemn final departure from the tavern. Other omissions, however, were positive benefits to the film, such as the cutting of the extended treatment of Falstaff's debt and breach of promise to Mistress Quickly, which the film script had taken over bodily from the Irish stage version.

Welles's process of redefinition did not stop with the shooting of the film. Keith Baxter has pointed out that only after editing the film did Welles begin talking of it as a lament for the loss of Merrie England.[17] In this respect and others Welles's *Sight and Sound* interview about the film, which has been highly influential upon subsequent commentators, can thus be read as still another refashioning of the *Henry IV* materials.[18] For instance, James Naremore has rightly observed that Welles's claim in the interview that he intercut the famous battle scene so that 'every cut seemed to be a blow, a counter-blow, a blow received, a blow returned' does not in fact fit what we see on the screen.[19] Welles seems never to have tired of ringing new changes on the Shakespearian themes, and his film is best understood as part of this continuum of interpretation.

II

Amid these permutations, certain hallmarks of Welles's style as an adapter of Shakespeare stand out, both in his scriptwriting and directing:

(I) *Expansion/contraction*. Obviously, the initial impulse for all the adaptations is Welles's desire to encompass as much as he can of Shakespeare's large scope but render it within a shorter form: to tell the story of Harry Monmouth in one play rather than three. Such expansive-

ness is to be seen at every stage of his adaptive process. Throwing back to
Five Kings, Welles's film script called for an opening section drawn from
Richard II; it gave an abbreviated treatment of Richard's deposition and
Exton's delivery of his corpse to the horrified new king. Reportedly, Welles
also shot footage of Bolingbroke's arrival from banishment.[20] All this preliminary matter was eventually omitted, thus illustrating Welles's ability to
counteract his own expansiveness when it was excessive.

(2)   *Dynamism*. A related impulse is Welles's desire to have more
going on per dramatized moment than he found in his source. By his own
acknowledgement Welles was himself 'easily bored'. Presumably he felt (as
is true) that the first time we see Prince Hal and Falstaff together not very
much happens beyond talk and preparation for the Gadshill incidents. In
Five Kings he moved the pantlers episode in *2 Henry IV* up to fill this vacuum, even though the tone of the latter passage is much less playful than
that of the Gadshill high jinks. The film much more successfully moves the
pocket-picking (*1 Henry IV*, 2.4) up instead. And by making a single
episode of the pocket-picking, which Shakespeare rather thinly spreads
out over two separate scenes, Welles is able to follow through on the
action to its conclusion. The incidents in the Gadshill adventure are similarly combined into a single uninterrupted sequence. Here, however,
Welles overdoes the fast pace of his story-telling; his Poins never gives the
audience the pleasure of hearing in advance the details of the trick to be
played on Falstaff.

(3)   *Pointing/counterpointing*. In general, Welles seeks an intenser
impact than he finds in his Shakespeare materials. In *Five Kings* some of
the vignettes suggest 'black-out' sketches.[21] At the end of the pantler
episode, for example, when Falstaff is defending his dispraise of the prince
to the wicked and expatiating on the wickedness of his associates, especially the Hostess, Welles cleverly stitches on Falstaff's give-and-take with
the Hostess from *Part 1* (3.3.115–30) so that her 'Thou or any man knows
where to have me' becomes the punchline that ends the scene.

Often Welles rearranges dialogue for climactic emphasis. In both the
stage and the film *Chimes at Midnight* he reversed the order of *2 Henry
IV*, 3.1, so that the scene would end with the king's 'Uneasy lies the head
that wears a crown'. In the Irish stage version he put Falstaff's praise of
sherris sack (*2 Henry IV*, 4.3.86–125) at the end of the battle scene in
which he had claimed credit for killing Hotspur. Confided to the audience,
it made an effective end to the first act. In the film, Welles keeps the
speech in this same position but to very different effect; it has become an
appeal to Hal to renew their tavern conviviality, which the prince walks
away from, dropping his cup as he goes.

It is very like Welles when he actually shot the lead-in to the opening
credits of the film to go beyond his script's scene of 'trees like black skele-

tons against a leaden sky', amid which are seen some 'old gentlemen walking together in the winter orchard, talking over old times'. The film brings
the talkers indoors from the orchard, past a contrastingly hot fire in a
round stove, to seat them in front of a still larger fire in a huge fireplace.
Welles then goes on to contrast the stasis of the reminiscers recalling the
chimes at midnight with the rush of a troop of horsemen riding to wild
music through a street, as the titles begin.

(4) *Knitting*. Shakespeare himself likes to create a tissue of cross-ref-
erences, which Welles delights in underlining. As early as *Five Kings* he
went out of his way to take the prince's protestation of virtue amid bad
influences ('by this hand thou thinkest me as far in the Devil's book as
thou, and Falstaff—*2 Henry IV*, 2.2.45–60) and juxtapose it with Falstaff
protesting to Bardolph, 'Company, villainous company hath been the spoil
of me' (*1 Henry IV*, 3.3.1–33). In the film script, the king's 'Uneasy lies the
head that wears a crown' (*2 Henry IV*, 3.1.1–31) dissolves into the prince
telling Poins that 'Before God, I am exceeding weary' (2.2.1). The film
itself not only includes this link but begins the scene that follows with
Falstaff telling Bardolph, 'I am as melancholy as a gib-cat or a lugg'd bear'
(*1 Henry IV*, 1.2.74). The three moments are further knit by brooding
background music scored for strings.

The film threads together numerous motifs. The mourning bells that
sound during the lead-in before the credits are heard at intervals throughout and turn to 'joy-bells' (as they are described in Welles's scene direction) at the coronation. Troops of horsemen repeatedly ride by, usually
suggesting the imperious claim of public duty on private lives. Scene after
scene ends with someone watching someone else leave, whether it is
Falstaff watching the prince ride away, or Lady Percy watching her husband ride away, or Falstaff—on foot—being seen off by Doll (with kisses
blown) or Justice Shallow. At the very end, after the rejection, the page
watches as Falstaff, deserted by his other associates, makes his slow way
out of the courtyard; after Falstaff's death, Mistress Quickly watches as his
huge coffin is laboriously pushed away on its cart.

(5) *Narrative coherence*. In addition to such interstitching in the texture of his adaptations, Welles seeks to tighten the loose narrative patterns
he finds in the original. This is especially notable in act 2 of the staged
Chimes at Midnight. Having removed from it the political scenes in *Part 2*,
with which Shakespeare alternates the adventures of Falstaff, Welles makes
a virtuoso rearrangement and integration of what remains, resulting in a
little story about Falstaff's day. First we see Hal and Poins plotting to disguise themselves as pantlers (2.2) and trick Falstaff. We are then given a
further promise of problems to come for Falstaff as Mistress Quickly
appears, instructing Fang and Snare to arrest him (2.1.1–37). At last
Falstaff himself appears in the street, talking of how he has led his raga-

muffins to where they were 'pepper'd' (*1 Henry IV*, 5.3.35–8). 'And I,' he continues, 'am I not fallen away vilely since this last action?' (*1 Henry IV*, 3.3.1–10). His servant appears, giving the doctor's report on his 'water' and leading into his remark that 'I am not only witty in myself, but the cause that wit is in other men' (*2 Henry IV*, 1.2.1–9). His servant replies, 'Sir John, you are so fretful you cannot live long' (*1 Henry IV*, 3.3.3–11) and Falstaff maintains that he is 'as virtuously given as a gentleman need to be' (ll.12–17). Then follows the first encounter between Falstaff and the Lord Chief Justice (*2 Henry IV*, 1.2.61–192), considerably cut and with Falstaff's 'gravy, gravy, gravy' (l.161) transposed as a punchline to give him the last word. Then the Hostess 'dashes onto the scene' with Fang and Snare. Unaware of their arrival, however, Falstaff instructs his servant to bear various letters, including one 'to old Mistress Ursula, whom I have weekly sworn to marry since I perceiv'd the first white hair of my chin' (ll.237–42). At this the Hostess breaks in, 'Thou didst swear to *me*' (2.1.86–92). She then urges the beadles into action and the Justice intervenes very much as in the original, except that Welles highhandedly omits all the lines reconciling Falstaff and Mistress Quickly, apart from his 'Come hither, Hostess.' Despite the urgent news of the arrival of the prince and the king, Falstaff limps toward the tavern brooding, 'A pox of this gout, or a gout of this pox' (1.2.242–8). As he proceeds there, we see the Hostess consoling Doll (2.4.22–30), who has drunk too much canaries. Falstaff arrives, then Hal and Poins in disguise, and then Pistol. Unlike the original, Welles thus has Hal and Poins present during the Pistol episode; they in fact take the lead in driving Pistol away. Doll then babies Falstaff as in Shakespeare (ll.208–25) but Welles adds to this passage the later one in which Falstaff laments 'I am old' (ll.271–9). By doing so, Welles tightens the connection between Falstaff's insults about the prince and Poins (ll.236–54) and their discovery (ll.283–4), which thus follows immediately. The story of Falstaff's day then ends as in Shakespeare with Falstaff sending for Doll, and Quickly hurrying her off.

Much of this is in the film script, but little of it appears in the film. In the film Welles is nonetheless much concerned with small narrative continuities. He likes to develop a second ring for his circus so that by crosscutting he can tell an incidental story, such as the repeated knocks at the door during the play-within-a-play of which the Hostess alone seems to be aware or Falstaff's visit to the water-closet ('Empty the jordan'–*2 Henry IV*, 2.4.34), which is linked to his page's report on his 'water' (1.2.1–5). Welles never lets us forget the presence of onlookers, each time showing them in a different aspect—as with the whores at the play or Poins and the prince eavesdropping from a loft on Falstaff: in separate glimpses, they 'shh' an attendant to silence, Hal bumps his head on a rafter, they spy through slats in the floor, almost fall out of the loft, before swinging down to identify themselves.

Welles is especially intent on sustaining a fluidity between scenes. In *Five Kings* he made the most of the revolving stage to keep a steady flow of action. Martin Gabel describes how Falstaff learns that Hal has been made king and sets off for the palace:

> The revolve was also going, in the opposite direction . . . Finally, the palace comes into view, and there's Falstaff outside the gate with all the mob (as many people as Welles had). The guard tries to keep Falstaff out, but he gets through with his one henchman. Now, the palace courtyard is raked, and as the stage revolves to bring it in front of you, two rows of nobles, all clad in ermine, come out of the coronation. The courtyard now occupies virtually the whole stage . . .[22]

One can see why film proved so congenial a medium for Welles. In Ireland there was no revolve, but transitions were enhanced by music and lighting. Here is the way Welles envisaged the moment after the king's soliloquy ending 'Uneasy lies the head that wears a crown':

> Lights dim as the king exits . . . The slow death-march beat of distant drums is heard and then in time to this (but *double* time)—a chorus of male voices offstage begins a drinking song. The tune is fierce and coarse (like 'Let me the canniken'). There is a burst of raucous laughter and a woman's shrill scream . . . A small gang of vaguely military young men tumbles forward out of the darkness in pursuit of a girl . . . The prince and Poins follow the group on-stage . . . The girl is cut off by one of the soldiers and turning runs into the prince's arms. He kisses her a bit absent-mindedly and lets her go. She runs off pursued by the others except for Poins, who is left downstage looking at the prince sardonically. (The drinking song continues off but fades throughout the following scene, leaving only the muffled death-march drum beat) . . .
>
> *Poins.*—Is it come to this?
> *Prince.*—[*with a slight laugh*]: Before God, I am exceeding weary.

The production notebook indicates that this transition was in fact made in just this fashion.

In dialogue as well as in plot, Welles seeks a rapid, conversational flow. He not only drastically cuts long speeches but reworks the order of speeches for comic or dramatic effect. In the arrest of Falstaff in the Irish stage version, for example, he has Fang twice interrupted by Falstaff ('Away varlets') and the Hostess, who is continuing her aggrieved account of Falstaff's breach of promise (*2 Henry IV*, 2.1.93.101–2), before he can get out 'Sir John, I arrest you at the suit of Mistress Quickly' (45). Welles adds emphasis to the king's question, 'But wherefore did he take away the crown?' (*2 Henry IV*, 4.5.88) by having him address it not to the court but directly to the prince and immediately before he gives his explanation:

KING. But wherefore did you take away the crown?
PRINCE. God witness with me, when I here came in,
   And found no course of breath within your Majesty,
   How cold it struck my heart! (ll.149–51)

This kind of reworking is more and more pronounced in Welles's successive versions.

III

All these features can be seen as bringing Shakespeare's text into line with the general idiom of modern drama, tightening its unity and coherence, sharpening its emphasis, speeding its pace. Welles is not so different from contemporary directors, who are not as scrupulous as he to label their work as adaptations. After all, he uses only Shakespeare's dialogue, although he may occasionally change a word or speaker. What distinguishes Welles is his boldness and flair and the extreme freedom he takes in transposing parts. He thus occupies a middle area between a director given to interpretative cutting and a free adapter (such as John Barton, Charles Marowitz, or Tom Stoppard), who writes a good deal of his own dialogue.

The feature in Welles's adaptations that most stands out is another modern preoccupation, a strong emphasis on psychology. Both stage versions were centrally concerned with the personal relationship between the prince and the fat knight. The film gives greater prominence to the king, and to the inner workings of the resulting triangle, than do the stage productions. Welles was brilliantly right in telling Kenneth Tynan:

> The richness of the triangle between the father and Falstaff and the son is without parallel: it's a complete Shakespearean creation. The other plays are good stories borrowed from other sources and made great because of what Shakespeare breathed into them. But there's nothing in the medieval chronicles that even hints at the Falstaff-Hal-King story. That's Shakespeare's story.

There is truth, too, in Welles's assertion: 'My film is entirely true to the story, although it sacrifices great parts of the plays from which the story is mined.'[23]

Visually, the film constantly contrasts the king and his court with Falstaff and the tavern. The king is spare, shaven, sharp-featured (as emphasized in profiles); Falstaff is enormous and round of body and beard. The king's ambience is vertical (full of vaults and spears), stone, stark, where Falstaff's is horizontal (low-ceilinged), wood-and-plaster, full of things and people. Welles repeatedly juxtaposes the half-timbered tavern and the walls of the fortress. Like Shakespeare, he shows an all-male court whereas the women are in the tavern, but Welles underlines the contrast by filling the tavern with whores, who at exciting moments come running déshabillé from their rooms.

In body language, too, court and tavern contrast. The king is physically remote, cold (his breath vapourizes when that of his courtiers does not—as if he were surrounded by an aura of coldness). He is often very still and indeed most effectively exerts his royal authority through a prolonged level gaze at his adversaries. When he moves it is in straight lines. His attending armed soldiers always stand in long lines. Light in his court is visibly angular, as sunlight is spotlighted through high windows. Only once does the king reach out in affection to his son.

In the tavern, light is diffused. Tavern people move in circles (as does the camera in places), often spinning around. When we are introduced to Hal he spins from whore to whore before he runs up some steps to join Poins, who, after announcing 'I've picked his pocket,' does a slow twirl around a post. When the prince is making his last exit from the tavern (now walking purposefully in a bee-line to his horse), Falstaff as he hurries after him is caught by dancers who take him arm-in-arm and swing him in circles. Falstaff is associated with touching (he and Hal often embrace), and with warmth, making especially ironic Mrs Quickly's lament that the dead Falstaff is 'cold as any stone.'

The resulting effect approaches expressionism, so graphically do the contrasting filmed worlds project the inner attitudes of their inhabitants. Thinking literally, one might marvel at the scene in which Hotspur uses his weapon-room as a place to bathe. But in the idiom of the film the scene is a visual pun on his nickname: he is not only hot but steaming from his bath, not merely fitted with spurs but surrounded by spears and complete coats of armour—and then hurried off to the battlefield by carefully climaxed calls of one, two, four, six buglers.

Welles seems to have a special feeling for Hotspur. As he explained in a note to Hilton Edwards,[25] he sees Hotspur as more sympathetic than the prince, whom he regards as 'beady-eyed and self-regarding.'[26] Gabel, in his recollections of *Five Kings*, describes Hotspur's final battle:

> the stage had started circling. Finally, upstage, half-hidden behind a mound, you saw Hal deliver the death-blow to Hotspur. At this point, the revolve stopped; the music stopped; and there was a great moment of silence. Then, slowly, the revolve brought Hotspur around in front where he delivered his last words.[27]

Along with Hotspur, the audience must have felt that 'time, that takes survey of all the world, / Must have a stop.' In the film there is a comparable overlap of inner and outer worlds when the prince mistakenly assumes that the king is dead. At this moment, Welles interposes shots of monks in the court and sounds of their chanting, as if indeed they were already mourning the dead king.

Subtextually, the film carefully traces a straight line in the relationship between the king and the prince. In Shakespeare the king repeatedly zigzags between mistrust and trust of his son—he needs continually to be won over—as in their first interview and Hal's battlefield rescue of his father in *Part 1* and Hal's premature taking of the crown in *Part 2*. Welles cuts the battlefield rescue in all three versions. *Five Kings* simply reflected the king's other vacillations. In the staged *Chimes at Midnight* the king 'suddenly embraced' his son at 'A thousand rebels die in this' (*1 Henry IV*, 3.2.160). Welles then took care to motivate the king's renewed suspicions by inserting a choric passage from Holinshed concerning rumours of Hal's designs on the throne and his consequent banishment from court. In the film Welles cuts the 'thousand rebels' line from their first interview and the king remains distant throughout the scene. As the stage direction in the script reads: the king is 'still bleakly unconvinced,' and he gives the order 'coldly': 'Harry you shall set forward.' The word 'cold' recurs three times in the stage directions and is applied to both speakers. After the battle is won and Falstaff has made his claim of killing Hotspur, the king makes an unspoken rejection of his son in the series of looks that are exchanged. The stage directions in the script make clear what is not so clear in the film; Falstaff has said, 'I look to be either Earl or Duke, I assure you':

> Silence as the king moves to the body of Hotspur . . . He looks from the dead hero to his son . . . Then to Falstaff (who is, for once, a bit abashed and keeps silent) . . . Now the king turns back to the prince . . . Hal meets his father's eye, but makes no reply to the unspoken question, stubbornly refusing to spoil Falstaff's joke . . . Then suddenly weary disappointment in the king's face touches him . . . But it's too late; the king has turned away . . . Hal wants to go with his father, but stands paralysed by the hopeless distance stretching between them . . .

Only after the crown has been returned and his death is near does the king express love for his son and put his hand on his shoulder.

The prince's attitudes toward his responsibilities as heir apparent are no less carefully charted. Each twinge of conscience is motivated. In the film script his 'I know you all' speech is prompted by Falstaff's question (interpolated from earlier in the scene), 'I prithee sweet wag, shall there be gallows standing when thou art king?' The prince does not answer, being 'lost in a sort of dream.' 'Do not thou, when thou art king, hang a thief,' Falstaff goes on. The prince responds to this but makes the joke 'with an absent air': 'thou shalt have the hanging of the thieves and so become a rare hangman.' He moves to the door:

> Hal turns back, looking at Falstaff . . . What he now says is deadly serious,
> but he covers it with a very slight sweetening of self-parody—almost as
> though he were quoting some other, some more virtuous prince . . .

Although the film is not entirely clear, the script confirms that Welles intended that Falstaff should at least half overhear the prince's words. After 'unyoked humour of your idleness,' Falstaff raises his wine cup 'in ironic salutation.' After 'be more wonder'd at': 'Falstaff watches him with a grin, but behind the twinkle in the old man's eye there is a faint shadow of foreknowledge.'

The actual film points Hal's motivation still more strongly. It substitutes for the 'hanging of thieves' speech Falstaff's ruminations about the squires of the night's body (ll.23–9). This speech not only includes a reminder to Hal about his future 'when thou art king', but also refers to 'men of good government.' It is at this last phrase that Hal's expression turns sober.

Welles commented that the farewell of the prince to Falstaff is 'performed about four times during the movie.'[28] But this is not simply a series of reluctant farewells; they reflect his growing revulsion towards his low-life associates. At a crucial turning point, Hal makes explicit his distaste for Poins, and by extension for Falstaff. Welles's treatment of this feature in the film evolved through the successive versions. In *Five Kings*, Hal's rejection of Poins was confined to a single scene (*2 Henry IV*, 2.2). In it Welles gave the rejection prominence by rearranging the dialogue so that Hal's strongest words of repudiation came at the very end of their exchange (this is true of all later versions as well): 'By this hand thou thinkest me as far in the Devil's book, as thou, and Falstaff for obduracy and persistency. Let the end try the man.' Since, in this version, the pantler-disguise episode had been transposed to the very first encounter between the prince and Falstaff, the prince never did make a final return to the tavern.

In the stage *Chimes at Midnight* this serious omission was rectified. Welles restored the pantler episode as in the original, and the prince made his exit upon hearing Peto's report that the king 'is at Westminster,' and after reflecting, 'I feel me much to blame / So idly to profane the precious time.' As for the prince's earlier repudiation of Poins, Welles's stage directions suggest the tone he desired:

PRINCE. Shall I tell thee one thing, Poins? [*There is something hard and dangerous in his tone, but Poins puts a good face on it, and plays up gaily.*]

POINS. [*with hollow-heartiness*] Yes, faith; and let it be an excellent good thing.

PRINCE. [*with an icy smile*] It shall serve among wits of no higher breeding than thine.

In the film script, Welles sees Poins as less on the defensive, almost asking for his own repudiation:

PRINCE. Doth it now (*sic*: apparently a typographical error for 'not' that is spoken thus in the film) show vilely in me to desire small beer?

POINS. [*playing up, but with a cruel undertone in his joking*] How ill it follows, after you have laboured so hard, you should talk so idly! Tell me, how many good young princes would do so, their fathers being so sick as yours at this time is? [*Silence . . . (Poins, feeling his days numbered, has been committing a kind of social suicide) . . . The prince looks at him . . .*]

PRINCE. What a disgrace is it for me to remember thy name! . . . Or to know thy face tomorrow! [*Then the prince laughs—quite nicely—and Poins is quick to join the laughter*] Do you use me thus, Ned? must I marry your sister?

POINS. God send the wench no worse fortune—[*quickly*] but I never said so.

The passage ends with Poins '[bowing with a sour smile]': 'I am your shadow, my lord; I follow you . . . '

In the film most of the speeches of repudiation are transferred to the prince's last tavern visit. After Poins and Hal have revealed themselves and had their fun with Falstaff about his dispraising them before the wicked, Falstaff rambles on about how vilely he is fallen away (*1 Henry IV*, 3.3) and hears from his page that his 'water' shows he might have more diseases than he knew of (*2 Henry IV*, 1.2). The prince's mind is elsewhere; he reflects solemnly 'how idly I do profane the precious time'. He then talks to a wickedly grinning Poins about his father's sickness, much as in the original text (*2 Henry IV*, 2.2.35–60) except that their lines are counterpointed against Falstaff's all-too apposite comments about wisdom crying out in the street (*1 Henry IV*, 1.2.83–8) and how men should take heed of their company (*2 Henry IV*, 5.1.75–8). Thus Falstaff is audibly linked by Welles with Poins in the prince's disgust.

For Hal's last words, the soundtrack makes a refinement on the script. In the script the prince replied to Poins's 'I would think thee a most princely hypocrite', with 'It would be every man's thought; and thou art a blessed fellow to think as every man thinks . . . Never a man's thought keeps the roadway better than thine.' On the soundtrack this part is cut, leaving the prince's final 'Every man would think me a hypocrite indeed' an unsoftened, *self*-rebuke. He gives Poins a long level look worthy of his father: 'Let the end try the man', and heads off hurriedly.

Thus Welles totally internalizes the prince's final departure from the tavern. He has made the bold choice of cutting Peto's report that the king has come to Westminster, the external factor with which Shakespeare prompted the prince's departure. In the film, this prompting is solely the result of the prince's feeling for his father in his illness, his revulsion towards his tavern associates, and his resolve to reform his own behaviour.

IV

Since Welles's rearrangements suggest different choices that Shakespeare might have made, they can provide a fresh perspective on the original text. From this vantage one is first of all struck by how much less overtly psychological Shakespeare is than Welles, and how much more political. As has just been discussed, the psychology of the prince's choice between his father and Falstaff is suggested in Shakespeare but less often than in Welles and less explicitly. Daniel Seltzer aptly writes in this respect of 'Welles' dramatization of the plays' *sub*text'.[29] In the original *text* the prince's decisive assumption of his regal responsibilities comes later than his last visit to the tavern, in act 5, scene 2 (a scene that Welles omitted from all his adaptations). Shakespeare's timing is more external than Welles's (Henry IV is actually dead and Henry V all but crowned), and his context is more political (the young king affirms the rule of law and the Lord Chief Justice's adherence to it).

In general, Shakespeare is much more interested in the civil wars than is Welles. The battle is of course one of the high points of the film, but not because it shows a meaningful struggle between the two sides. Through most of it, it is impossible to tell who is winning and who is losing. As Welles shows the increasing brutality and squalor of the fighting, indeed, his chief point seems to be the political meaninglessness of it all. This is true even of the hand-to-hand victory of the prince over Hotspur, which comes after Hotspur has driven the prince to the ground and is taken off guard while coming in for the kill. Contrast Shakespeare, where by an adversary's account the prince's 'swift wrath beat down / The never-daunted Percy to the earth / From whence with life he never more sprung up' (*2 Henry IV*, 1.1.109–11).

Other features of the original stand out in contrast to Welles's adaptations. Shakespeare's delight in local colour is an instance, as in the exotic Welsh court and the Cotswold talk of Shallow and Silence. Welles's amalgamations tend to level the striking differences between the two parts of *Henry IV*, the muse of *Part 1* being youthful while that of *Part 2* is aging, verging on senility.

Yet, outweighing these and other differences, the chief insight into Shakespeare that is yielded by Welles's work is a point of resemblance. The film and the stage adaptations make one see anew the genius of the core of the *Henry IV* plays: Shakespeare's treatment of the four-way conflicts of the king, the prince, Hotspur, and Falstaff as they move the action through the contrasting worlds of court, tavern, and battlefield. Welles did not come to a fully successful treatment of this core until he had tried tipping Shakespeare's balance in alternative directions—towards the prince in *Five Kings*, towards Falstaff in the stage *Chimes at Midnight*. Through trial and error in these stage adaptations he worked his way back to a balance in his film that is, ironically, very close to Shakespeare's own. Yet this process was not unproductive, for through it Welles gained not only a deeper insight into the original but a freer hand in reworking it and a surer touch in placing his distinctive psychological emphasis upon it.

In his 'Defense of Mixed Cinema', André Bazin argues that 'Far from being a sign of decadence, the mastering of the theatrical repertoire by the cinema is on the contrary a proof of maturity. In short, to adapt is no longer to betray but to respect.'[30] A key word in Bazin's very hopeful declaration is 'mastering'. Not all Shakespearian films show the necessary mastery. *Chimes at Midnight*, however, does. As it emerged from its stage versions to its final realization on screen, Welles's adaptation achieved, in essentials, that difficult double feat that Bazin envisages: it respects its Shakespearian theatrical original while also respecting its modern film idiom—and in such a way that, when it is at its best, Welles's vision and Shakespeare's coincide.

Notes

1. Susan Sontag, *Against Interpretation* (New York, 1972), pp. 242–5.

2. Allardyce Nicoll, *Film and Theatre* (London, 1936); André Bazin, *What is Cinema?*, trans. H. Gray (Berkeley, 1974); Roger Manvell, *Theatre and Film* (Rutherford and London, 1979). See also Andrew Horton and Joan Magretta, *Modern European Filmmakers and the Art of Adaptation* (New York, 1981).

3. For details of the script of this production I have consulted the typescript bearing the name of Millie Davenport, who did the costumes for *Five Kings*, in the Billy Rose Collection of the New York Public Library at Lincoln Center.

4. Richard France, *The Theatre of Orson Welles* (Lewisburg and London, 1977), pp. 24–6. As France discusses (pp. 72–3), Welles's film of *Macbeth* derives in many ways from his prior stage versions.

5. John Houseman, *Run-Through* (New York, 1972), pp. 414–28. See also Jean Rosenthal, 'Five Kings', *Theatre Arts Magazine*, 23 (1939).

6. France, *Theatre of Orson Welles*, p. 161.

7. For details of the script of this production, which has been virtually ignored by previous commentators, I have consulted the typescript by Welles and the three booklets of production notes by Hilton Edwards in the Gate Theatre Archive, Special Collections, Northwestern University Library. These resources—along with other materials in the Archive—have not to my knowledge hitherto been brought to bear on Welles's work.

8. An appendix of *The Theatre of Orson Welles* lists numerous reviews of *Five Kings*. I have consulted the following newspaper comments on the stage *Chimes at Midnight* in 1960: *Belfast Telegraph*, 20, 22, 24 February; *Belfast Newsletter*, 23, 24 February; *Northern Whig*, 24 February; *The Times*, 25 February; *Daily Mail* (London), 22, 24, 25 February; *Daily Express* (London), 25 February; *Irish Times*, 1 March; *Evening Mail* (Dublin), 1 March; *Evening Herald* (Dublin), 1 March; *Irish Independent*, 7 March.

9. From a note 'about essentials' in the file of Edwards's correspondence with Welles in Northwestern University's Gate Theatre Archive. As here Welles often uses '. . . ' as a mark of punctuation; in my quotations from Welles I have avoided use of three dots as a mark of ellipsis.

10. Barbara Leaming, *Orson Welles* (New York, 1985), p. 448.

11. For details of this script I have consulted the copy in the Gate Theatre Archive.

12. Betty Lowry, *Belfast Telegraph*, 24 February 1960.

13. All line references are to *The Riverside Shakespeare*, ed. G. B. Evans et al. (Boston, 1974).

14. H. R. Jeans, *Daily Mail*, 25 February 1960.

15. In conversation with the author, July 1985.

16. Lowry, *Belfast Telegraph*.

17. Deborah T. Curren Aquino, '*Chimes at Midnight*: Retrospectively Elegiac', *Shakespeare on Film Newsletter*, 4 (1979).

18. Juan Cobos and Miguel Rubio, 'Welles and Falstaff', *Sight and Sound*, 35 (1966).

19. James Naremore, *The Magic World of Orson Welles* (Oxford, 1978), p. 271.

20. Cobos and Rubio, 'Welles and Falstaff,' p. 161.

21. France, *The Theatre of Orson Welles*, p. 168, connects Welles's 'black-out' techniques in *Five Kings* with those Pauline Kael sees in *Citizen Kane*–in *The Citizen Kane Book* (Boston, 1971).

22. Quoted by France, p. 167.

23. Kenneth Tynan, 'Interview with Orson Welles', *Playboy*, 14 (1967), 56.

24. For the Irish *Chimes at Midnight*, Welles outlined in a memo to Hilton Edwards a re-blocking of the battle between Prince Hal and Hotspur. The memo was accompanied by a set of sketches, . . . The new staging was designed to permit Welles, who had a long history of back trouble, to have off-stage assistance with picking up Hotspur's corpse. In archive correspondence, Edwards at first expressed resentment at Welles's re-staging but later recanted. Although the sketches were originally catalogued as the work of Edwards, they are clearly by Welles, who as a youth aspired to be a painter, and reflect the energy of his visual imagination.

25. In the note 'about essentials' in the Gate Theatre Archive.

26. Tynan, 'Interview', p. 56.

27. Quoted by France, *The Theatre of Orson Welles*, p. 167.

28. Cobos and Rubio, 'Welles and Falstaff,' p. 159. See Samuel Crowl, 'The Long Goodbye', *Shakespeare Quarterly*, 31 (1980).

29. Daniel Seltzer, 'Shakespeare's Texts and Modern Production', *Reinterpretations of Elizabethan Drama*, ed. Norman Rabkin (New York, 1969), p. 109.

30. Bazin, *What is Cinema?*, p. 69.

"Every Third Word a Lie": Rhetoric and History in Orson Welles's *Chimes at Midnight*

MICHAEL ANDEREGG

*C*HIMES AT MIDNIGHT has come to be recognized, over the last decade or so, both as one of the most intelligent and imaginative of films adapted from Shakespeare and as one of Orson Welles's finest achievements, a film at least equal in energy and brilliance to *Citizen Kane* and *The Magnificent Ambersons*.[1] The chorus of praise occasionally includes a few sour notes, however; as so often with Welles's post *Citizen Kane* films, various qualifications temper even highly enthusiastic assessments.[2] Criticism tends to center on the sound track and on the uncertain relationship between sound and image: the recording is technically faulty, Shakespeare's words are frequently unintelligible (Welles's Falstaff, in particular, is difficult to understand much of the time), several sequences are poorly synchronized, and, disconcertingly, a number of the minor actors have been dubbed by Welles himself—all signs that inadequate financing forced artistic compromise. Additionally, critics find fault with Welles for the film's haphazard continuity and for a general inattention to detail, especially in the casting and playing of the secondary roles. In short, *Chimes at Midnight* is often discussed in terms that remind us of Shakespeare's Sir John Falstaff himself: attractive, vibrant, large, complex, but, withal, so deeply flawed as to negate many of its virtues.

In this essay, I would like to place both the unquestioned successes and the supposed defects of *Chimes at Midnight* within the context of what I take to be the film's governing strategy: the rewriting of Shakespeare's text, a rewriting that includes an attempted erasure of writing, a critique of rhetoric, an undermining of language itself. Taking up what is undeniably present in Shakespeare—no writer shows more awareness of the dangerous seductiveness of words—Welles carries the questioning of language much further than Shakespeare, whose primary resource was language, ever could. *Chimes at Midnight* centers squarely on a conflict between rhetoric and history, on the one hand, and the immediacy of a pre-linguistic, pre-lapsarian, timeless physical world, on the other. This conflict comes to us primarily through the actions and character of Falstaff, as we might expect, but it informs as well the texture and style of each moment of Welles's film. With remarkable boldness, Welles has made a

Shakespearean film in which poetry itself seems to undergo a rigorous devaluation.

To a certain extent, of course, Welles had to rewrite Shakespeare as part of the process of adaptation: no Shakespearian film reproduces Shakespeare's text in its entirety (nor, for that matter, do most stage productions). But Welles's editorial decisions nevertheless aim at a particular end and have a specific focus. He compresses and reshapes his source material at will, reducing it to a bare minimum of words. Drawing primarily on *Henry IV*, Parts I and II, adding a few lines from *Richard II, Henry V,* and *The Merry Wives of Windsor*, Welles gives Shakespeare's story of a prince's coming of age a single plot line and a new emphasis. Critics have often noted that *Henry IV*, Part II, in many ways recapitulates, albeit in a different key, the structure and theme of Part I: Shakespeare presents two scenes of reconciliation between Hal and his father, two military engagements (Shrewsbury and Galtree Forest), two moments when Hal realizes his destiny, and so forth. Welles, while doing away with much of this repetition, shifts scenes and parts of scenes around at his convenience, placing Falstaff's recruitment of soldiers in Part II, for example, before Part I's battle of Shrewsbury. Although Welles's refashioning of Shakespeare's text(s) has a number of consequences, the primary effect is to shift the thematic emphasis away from Hal and towards Falstaff, or, to put it another way, away from history and towards satire.[3]

The critique of history in *Chimes at Midnight* completes a process already begun by Shakespeare, but Welles's attack is harsher, his conclusion far less optimistic. "History," for the purposes of my argument, includes the whole world of kings and politics, of war and chivalry, as well as the language, the rhetoric, which is that world's chief expressive medium. Shakespeare's Henriad comprehends a set of binary oppositions—Court/Tavern, Honor/Dishonor, Hotspur/Falstaff, Henry IV/Falstaff, Time/Timelessness, Word/Being, Serious/Non-serious—where either the first term is the privileged one or where both terms have been suspended in an uneasy equilibrium, leaving to Hal the task of determining which to choose, or if indeed a choice has to be made at all. In Welles's film, these paired alternatives are unbalanced, diminished, reversed, or exploded. Shakespeare's Hal has always already made the choice, though he appears to be choosing all the time. For Welles's Hal, the choice poses genuine and insoluble problems.[4] The various embodiments of "positive" values, what I have simply termed "History," have little exemplary force in *Chimes at Midnight*, tending at times to degenerate, at the level of language, into the incoherent babbling of poseurs, cynics, and fools. At the same time, any attempt to abolish language, to ignore the power of words, leads inevitably to destruction. Here, Falstaff stands as the cautionary figure, and his desire to abolish language and put sheer physicality in its place becomes the tragic fulcrum upon which Welles's film turns.

Welles's strategy for undermining history and rhetoric only begins with the process of adaptation. His tactics are primarily stylistic. History and (verbal) rhetoric are constantly displaced, replaced by Welles's nervous, erratic, decentered, unstable visual and aural style, a flow of images and sounds that thoroughly dismantle Shakespeare's text, peeling away layers of strategically placed and carefully joined verbal and thematic checks against disintegration. In this context, the supposed problems with the sound track become less a matter of technical flaws (though flaws there are, as Welles has publicly lamented), and more a question of Welles's intentions and methods.[5] In some shots, for example, the actors deliver their lines as they, or the camera, or both, are in rapid motion. Or a character will make an important speech from the depth of an extreme long shot, depriving us of lip movement and facial expression, both important cues for the understanding of unfamiliar language and syntax. Furthermore, Welles constructs jarring editing patterns that easily distract from the spoken word. At several points, even what Welles has structured to resemble continuity editing turns into something unexpected. A simple reverse shot, for example, may involve illogical changes in time and/or space. These and other stylistic idiosyncracies help to explain why we can follow the sound track of *Chimes at Midnight* more easily if we keep our eyes closed. In effect, Welles generates a constant tension between what we see and what we hear, a tension that points to the ambiguous status of language in its relation to action.

Welles further exhibits his ambivalence towards rhetoric in his handling of soliloquies. In his previous Shakespearian films, Welles had already suggested some discomfort with filmed soliloquies, resorting to a variety of voice-over techniques in *Macbeth*, and in *Othello* having some of his actors deliver soliloquies and speeches with their backs to the camera. In *Chimes*, Welles virtually does away with soliloquies as such by not allowing anyone to speak directly to the camera or to be truly alone: Hal's revelation (in Shakespeare, to the audience only) that his madcap humor is primarily for show ("I know you all") is spoken in Falstaff's presence; Falstaff delivers both his catechism on honor and his later dissertation on the virtues of sherris-sack directly to Hal. Even King Henry is not allowed a true soliloquy. His famous meditation on sleep, to choose a notable instance, though filmed in a single, uninterrupted take and in close-up, becomes an address to his courtiers; he is not, as he is in the play, alone. All soliloquies have thus become, at least implicitly, attempts at conversation, at communication within the diegetic universe, and not, as soliloquies can be, privileged moments where language provides a more or less unmediated access to thought.

We can see Welles's strategy ideally realized at that moment when Hotspur—whose bath has been interrupted by the pressing demands of history—cries "That roan shall be my throne" and simultaneously drops the towel in which he has draped himself and turns away from the camera, revealing his bare behind. Hotspur's towel falls in the midst of a highly rhetorical gesture, a wide sweep of the arm that serves as punctuation for his words. Welles comically undermines Hotspur's rhetoric, lays bare his linguistic bravado, and ridicules his historical pretensions, his (partly unconscious) desire for the English throne. Hotspur's words have already been mocked throughout this scene by the trumpeters who echo his belligerent posings with elaborate, comic fanfares. The trumpets say as much as he does, and are equally meaningful as rational statement. Hotspur's dropped towel suggests an additional meaning as well, one contiguous with that just described: for a moment, Hotspur reveals the physical he tries to deny or push aside in the semi-playful, semi-serious exchange with his wife, Kate, that follows this scene. The dropped towel signifies the return of the repressed, cancelling Hotspur's attempt to replace sensuality with rhetoric (war, history, etc.), to deny the body by asserting the word.

In what is perhaps the most remarkable sequence in *Chimes at Midnight*, the battle of Shrewsbury, Welles presents us with another kind of history—a history stripped of all rhetoric, denuded of language, and at the same time supremely eloquent. Here, the rhetorical dismemberment of the body politic, the scenes of accusation and counter-accusation between the royal party and the highborn conspirators, becomes displaced and mocked by the literal dismemberment of the body physical. Welles's style forcefully underlines the brutal, unheroic character of hand-to-hand combat in a nervously edited mosaic of varied shots, some photographed with a handheld camera, some filmed with wide-angle lenses, some in slow motion, some speeded up, some shots static and others that employ swish pans or other kinds of rapid movement, together with a complex, many-layered sound track of shouts and screams, of the clash of sword against sword, armor against armor, of grunts and cries and cracking bones. Welles conjures up Armegeddon, a nightmare vision of destruction which points up the futility of this or any other war. By the end, both armies have become one huge, awkward, disintegrating war machine, a grotesque robot whose power source slowly begins to fail and finally comes to a frozen halt. Verbal rhetoric—language itself—seems, for the moment, both irrelevant and obscene.

In this context, the highly verbal King Henry IV, the only character in the film whose words and speeches are allowed their full Shakespearean weight and style, stands in ironic counterpoint to the carnage of Shrewsbury. As John Gielgud plays him, and as Welles directs his scenes, King Henry is reduced to a nearly disembodied voice. The most "poetic" and rhetorical figure in Welles's film, he is also the most ethereal. Cold, pinched, ascetic, photographed sitting on or standing near his throne set on a high stone platform, his face illuminated by a harsh, white light, he is an isolated, distant figure of overbearing but brittle authority. As Falstaff seems to be all flesh, Henry seems all words. But even the king's voice fails him: he can neither govern his son with it nor tame the rebels, who refuse to credit his verbal promises. Henry's highly rhetorical manner, meant to gloss over his insecurities and fears, finally serves to reveal them. His voice becomes an object of parody: at various points in the film, Hotspur, Hal, and Falstaff all imitate Gielgud's immediately recognizable vocal characteristics. The "beauty" of Henry's speech only serves to place in an even harsher light his asceticism, coldness, and largely self-imposed isolation; a supreme poseur, he cannot see beyond his role. Although never really alone, Henry seems to speak only to himself.

King Henry's dependence on words becomes ideally focused in a scene Welles has totally refashioned from Shakespeare. After the battle of Shrewsbury, Falstaff takes credit for killing Hotspur, spinning another one of his outrageous lies for Hal's benefit. Welles gives the scene a special emphasis by having King Henry present as Falstaff tells his tale. The king, for once, says nothing, and Hal, too, is silent, but their faces tell a clear enough story. Earlier, Hal had told his father that he would redeem himself for his bad behavior "on Percy's head / And in the closing of some glorious day, / Be bold to tell you that I am your son, . . ." Now is the moment when this prophecy should come true, when the moving rhetoric should be realized in action. But Hal fails to make good on his promise. Unwilling to expose Falstaff, he refuses to say the words his father so much wants to hear, and the moment slips by. The silence, emphasized by a series of static close-ups, takes on precise thematic significance. We can tell, from Henry's expression, that he knows very well who killed Hotspur, but the knowledge, without the words, is not enough. We see, too, the conflict within Hal. And, finally, we can read in Falstaff's face his understanding of what the other two are thinking. For all three as well as for us, silence acquires a rhetorical force ordinarily reserved to speech.[6]

If the world of kings overvalues words, the tavern world fatally undervalues them. In the tavern world, which for my purposes includes the Justice Shallow scenes, words are acknowledged to mean very little. Falstaff's notorious lies, and the ease with which everyone sees through them, are symptomatic, but many of his cohorts share his linguistic deviance. Shallow constantly reminisces about the old days, but "every third word" he speaks, according to Falstaff, is "a lie." Falstaff's hanger-on, Ancient Pistol, is perhaps the most unintelligible character in the film. In Shakespeare, he is already rhetorically tedious; his primary function is to cast in ironic light, through highflown speeches and outrageous behavior, the chivalric code. But in a world where rhetoric and history are so constantly and thoroughly brought into question, Welles takes the extreme course of reducing Pistol to little more than noise. Against Pistol's meaningless bombast, we have Silence's inability to say anything at all. Welles afflicts him with a stutter so severe that he cannot complete his sentences.

Shallow must speak for him, must become in effect his voice (a nice joke in a film where so many characters are clearly dubbed). Words are interchangeable, attach themselves to no one in particular, have no individual meaning. Speech, in short, appears to be as debased through undervaluing in the tavern world as it is debased through overvaluing in the court world.

The difficulty of penetrating language, of determining the truth and weight of words, of reading history, comes to be, in especial, Falstaff's dilemma. Falstaff distrusts words; in a sense, he himself has nothing to say, certainly nothing with which to answer King Henry, who is all speech, all words, the very incarnation of logos. Falstaff's own words are frequently unintelligible, or nearly so, because he wants to deny the efficacy of language. (Welles the actor here exaggerates his post-*Citizen Kane* tendency to downplay the orotund and avuncular qualities of his vocal delivery by deliberately "throwing away" words and lines and even entire speeches.) But, though words may be questioned, subverted, and parodied, they cannot be abolished. Falstaff's refusal to credit words at all leads to his undoing. Even Hal's words—especially Hal's words—mean little to Falstaff, though Hal is at great pains throughout to make his motives clear. Welles's presentation of Hal, an attractive, appealing prince as played by Keith Baxter, runs counter to some modern, especially theatrical, views of the Henriad which condemn Hal as a cold, hypocritical careerist who cynically uses Falstaff for his own ends. Instead, Welles deliberately distorts Shakespeare's text at several points in order to stress Hal's straightforwardness. I've already noted that Hal's revealing "I know you all" meditation is no longer a soliloquy in the film; it is delivered in Falstaff's hearing, the second half of it spoken directly to him. Similarly, when Hal, speaking as his father at the end of the famous play scene, tells Falstaff that he will indeed banish him ("I do; I will"), he gives the words a moving, elegiac tone that render their meaning unmistakable to anyone not as bent on self-deception as Falstaff is.

Against language, Falstaff posits being, presence, physicality. We are made aware, throughout Welles's film, of Falstaff as sheer physical mass. His huge figure—sometimes just his face alone—often dominates the frame. Although he enters the film in the depth of an extreme long shot, a small, round object on the horizon, he gradually moves toward the camera until his head alone fills over three-fourths of the image, leaving what remains to his companion, Shallow. In the play scene, two men and a boy must help Falstaff onto his makeshift "throne." Before the battle of Shrewsbury, his followers valiantly attempt to raise him to his saddle with block and tackle, only to drop his armor-encased body to the ground. At the Boar's Head tavern, stairways and corridors seem too narrow for his passage. The point is made most strikingly in the Gadshill episode, where Falstaff's monk's robe transforms him into a huge white tent which sharply contrasts with the thin, black trees that surround him. Falstaff's girth is, of course, a running joke in Shakespeare, but Welles goes out of his way to elaborate on the theme; he seems intent on suggesting the extent to which Falstaff's world is physical, corporeal, of the flesh. Falstaff's relationships are expressed in predominently tactile ways, his rotund figure giving others, especially Hal and Doll Tearsheet, something to grasp, to hold on to, or—in Doll's case—to climb on.

Although Welles has said that, for him, Falstaff was "the greatest conception of a good man, the most completely good man, in all drama,"[7] *Chimes at Midnight* presents a far more ambivalent portrait of Falstaff than these words suggest. We cannot doubt that Welles sympathizes, both as director and as actor, with Falstaff's desire to bypass language and thereby gain access to an unmediated reality. At the same time, we know, and Welles knows, that in a fallen world, such a desire is folly. And we know as well that, like many Wellesian heroes, Falstaff longs for an Edenic world only because he has long since forfeited it. Welles's Falstaff is far from the jolly knight seen in various theatrical interpretations of the role. Rather, he seems more the corrupt, gross "misleader of youth" that Hal and others claim he is. Some readers have seen two Falstaffs emerging from the two parts of *Henry IV*, the second considerably less pleasant than the first. But whether the Falstaff of Part II is really a different character from the Falstaff of Part I, or whether he evolves naturally in the course of the two plays, Welles chose to combine both Falstaffs in his performance. Welles's Falstaff is, in Beverle Houston's felicitous phrase, a "Power Baby," an "eating, sucking, foetus-like creature"[8] whose benignity is an illusion. Pre-linguistic, he is forever locked in the imaginary world of infancy. Like Kane, like Arkadin, like Quinlan, like Clay, Falstaff is fundamentally, irredeemably corrupt. A larger-than-life figure flawed by hubris, he tragically collaborates in his own destruction.

Falstaff's defeat has a specifically linguistic dimension: Hal's rejection of him is a rhetorical act, the new king of England's maiden speech, the son's entrance into the symbolic world of his father. (By staging this scene in the midst of the coronation ceremony, Welles puts the emphasis as much on Hal's humiliation as on Falstaff's.) Falstaff's response to Hal's elaborate, majestic, and witty rebuke is nonverbal: we must read it in Welles's expression. What we see are emotions in conflict: awe, perhaps pride (this is *his* king, after all), and a wistfulness not unmixed with cunning (is he already thinking of a "starting hole," a way out?). The dominant emotion, however, is disbelief: Hal's words cannot be meaningful, they are rhetoric only; Falstaff sees through and beyond them. Shakespeare's Falstaff, we feel, indulges himself in sheer bravado when he tells Shallow "This that you heard was but a color . . . I shall be sent for soon at night."[9] For Welles's Falstaff, these words suggest not bravado so much as a deeply felt hope, a nearly desperate attempt to render words meaningless. But Hal not only means what he says, he now has the power to turn words into deeds, and his words and deeds kill Falstaff.

In keeping with his method throughout the film, Welles strips even Falstaff's death of easy sentiment. Mistress Quickly's description of Falstaff's last moments functions as a piece of information for a clearly unmoved Poins; spoken with Falstaff already in his coffin, her words lack the immediacy they have in Shakespeare's *Henry V*. Welles barely prepares us for this crucial finale: one moment Falstaff is alive, if crushed; the next moment he is dead. No illness, no tears, no bedside scene as in Laurence Olivier's film of *Henry V*. Only a final irony: words continue to fail Falstaff, even after death. In a complete departure from Shakespeare's text, Welles concludes his film with the image of Falstaff's coffin passing away in the distance while on the sound track Ralph Richardson recites a passage from Holinshed's *Chronicles of England, Scotland, and Ireland*, a passage in praise of King Henry V, who, we are told, "was so humane withal that he left no offense unpunished or friendship unrewarded."[10] Whatever we may think of the truth or justice of Holinshed's words, one irony, at least, is certain: in *Chimes at Midnight*, a film that thoroughly reveals the hollowness of kings and their fine words, language and history stubbornly abide when all else is gone.[11]

Notes

1. See, for example, Joseph McBride, *Orson Welles* (New York: Viking Press, 1972); James Naremore, *The Magic World of Orson Welles* (New York: Oxford University Press, 1978); Samuel Crowl. "The Long Goodbye: Welles and Falstaff," *Shakespeare Quarterly*, 31 (Autumn, 1980), 369–380; and the comments by David Bordwell ("*Citizen Kane*," *Film Comment*, 7 (1971), 38–47) and Brian Henderson ("The Long Take," *Film Comment*, 7 (1971), 6–11); both of these essays have been reprinted in *Movies and Methods*, ed. Bill Nichols (Berkeley and Los Angeles: University of California Press, 1976).

2. Most of the negative points are summarized by Jack Jorgens in *Shakespeare on Film* (Bloomington: Indiana University Press, 1977); Jorgens, however, provides a generally positive analysis. See also Charles Higham, *The Films of Orson Welles* (Berkeley and Los Angeles: University of California Press, 1970); Higham writes of Welles's "impatience with detail and finalization that, combined with [his] tragic perennial lack of funds, have left the work just short of the triumph it should have been" (p. 177).

3. Samuel Crowl, cited above, convincingly demonstrates that "Welles's overriding visual and structural emphasis is to signal farewell, to say a long goodbye to Falstaff, rather than to celebrate Hal's homecoming to princely right reason and responsible rule" (p. 373).

4. For a sensitive discussion of Hal's role in Welles's film, see Leland Poague, "'Reading' the Prince: Shakespeare, Welles, and Some Aspects of *Chimes at Midnight*," *Iowa State Journal of Research*, 56, 1 (August, 1981), 57–65.

5. Dudley Andrew's comments on the nature of Welles's sound track in *Chimes at Midnight* and in other films closely parallel my own observations. See *Film in the Aura of Art* (Princeton, NJ: Princeton University Press, 1984), pp. 164–168.

6. John Gielgud later recalled that "we never did the scene at all. On the last day Orson said, 'There's a close-up I have to do of you, just look down there, that's Hotspur's

body, now look up at me'" (Gyles Brandreth, *John Gielgud: A Celebration* (Little, Brown and Company: Boston, 1984), p. 152).

7. Juan Cobos and Miguel Rubio, "Welles and Falstaff," *Sight and Sound*, 35 (Autumn, 1966), 158–163; 159.

8. "Power and Dis-Integration in the Films of Orson Welles," *Film Quarterly*, 35 (Summer, 1982), 2–12; 2.

9. Henry IV, Part II, 5.5.85–6 and 89–90, cited from *The Arden Edition*, ed. A.R. Humphreys (London: Methuen, 1966).

10. Stanley S. Rubin discusses Welles's use of Holinshed as a narrative device in "Welles/Falstaff/Shakespeare/Welles: The Narrative Structure of *Chimes at Midnight*," *Film Criticism*, 2 (Winter/Spring, 1978), 66–71.

11. By the end of Welles's film, Andrew McLean notes, "An epoch has passed, a world view has altered, and a new historical consciousness has been born" ("Orson Welles and Shakespeare: History and Consciousness in *Chimes at Midnight*," *Literature/Film Quarterly*, 11 (1983), 197–202; 202).

Orson Welles, Brazil, and the Power of Blackness

ROBERT STAM

I T IS well known that Orson Welles's ill-fated attempt to make *It's All True* formed a pivotal and in some respects a disastrous turning point in his career, playing a role analogous to that of *Que Viva Mexico!* (1930–32) in the career of Eisenstein. But quite apart from its negative consequences for Welles's career, the *It's All True* project forms the point of convergence of a constellation of issues at once political, cultural, and aesthetic. Of interest both for the parallels and the contrasts it offers with Welles's other films, *It's All True* would have been the only Welles film with a popular focus to be conceived, as it were, from "the bottom up." The Brazilian episodes, taken together, from what we know, would have formed a generic synthesis of city symphony film (about Rio de Janeiro), Flaherty-style documentary (the *jangadeiro* episode), musical, travelogue, social consciousness film, and cinematic essay. As the filmic equivalent of what Welles himself designated a "magazine feature story," it would have anticipated *F for Fake*, whose title ironically reverberates against the veracious thrust of *It's All True*. The completed film would have condensed typical Wellesian themes and strategies: the melange of documentary/fiction (already characteristic of *Citizen Kane* and reaching its paroxysm in *F for Fake*) and the fascination with parties, carnivals, and the carnivalesque (with corollary themes of masks, costumes, fantasy, and disguise); in other ways, it would have constituted a radical new departure.[1]

Whatever its beginnings as a project assigned to Welles owing to the vicissitudes of international geo-politics, the *It's All True* project ultimately became a passionate cause with Welles, a project close to his heart and even, it might be argued, to the wellsprings of his enthusiasms and creativity. Considerable evidence points to Welles's devotion to, indeed, his obsession with the film. We know that Welles, although a well-paid celebrity director at the very peak of his career, was willing to continue filming in Fortaleza with minimal equipment, without RKO backing, working even with his own money. For years, Welles made strenuous efforts to recuperate the Brazilian footage and to fashion it into a finished film. "Too much effort and real love went into the entire project," Welles wrote to Brazilian friend Fernando Pinto, "for it to fail and come to nothing in the end. I have a degree of faith in it which amounts to fanaticism, and you can

Originally published in *Persistence of Vision* 7 (1989) special issue on Orson Welles: 93–112.

believe that if *It's All True* goes down into limbo I'll go with it." In the same letter, Welles expresses his desire to finish the film, not in the name of Hollywood executives and his own career, but in the name of the relatively obscure raftsmen—*jangadeiros*—who traveled more than a thousand miles to present their social grievances to Brazilian President Vargas. "I cannot remember you with simple pleasure," Welles writes his friend Fernando, "because no thought of you can exist without some feeling of responsibility unfulfilled to you—responsibility to our common respect for the heroes of the beach, and specifically Jacare's family." (This last reference was obviously to Jacaré, the leader of the *jangadeiros*, who drowned during the filming.)[2]

Despite Welles's dedication, the *It's All True* project became hounded by hostile rumors and negative publicity, which were to shadow Welles throughout his filmmaking career. My task here will not be to reconstruct all the events surrounding the making of *It's All True*, or to counter in detail the tendentious versions proposed by some of Welles's biographers and critics. Rather, I would like to offer a kind of "view from Brazil" of the *It's All True* experience, stressing four interlinked issues: 1) the reciprocal affection between Welles and his Brazilian hosts and collaborators; 2) the audacity of the project in cultural, aesthetic, cinematic, and racial terms; 3) Welles's relation to Afro-Brazilian culture and his working relationships with black Brazilians; and 4) the racial subtext of some of the opposition to *It's All True*, a subtext recapitulated, I will argue, in the discourse of many latter-day Welles critics.

THE CONVENTIONAL ACCOUNT

The conventional version of what is often dismissively labelled the *It's All True* "adventure," as presented by such critics as Charles Higham and John Russell Taylor, has generally been hostile to Welles.[3] Higham's account, less a biography than a relentless and morbidly selective indictment, shows us a profligate Welles, swayed by tropical temptations and incapacitated by a pathological terror of completion, as himself largely responsible for the film's demise. His incessant partying and womanizing, his financial extravagance, his unseemly behavior (throwing furniture out of hotel windows), and his irrational reluctance to mold his materials into a conventional story with box-office appeal, climaxed by the accidental death of the crucial actor/personality Jacaré, a death for which Welles was not directly responsible but for which he was partially blamed, together with the negative reception of *The Magnificent Ambersons* and a change of leadership at RKO, all led to the acrimonious non-completion of the film. The language and tone of the Higham account, largely echoed by other commentators, is moralistic and at times even prosecutorial. Welles's behavior is repeatedly described as "erratic," his decisions as "foolish," and, in the cases where

Welles quarrelled with others, it is almost invariably assumed that Welles's interlocutors were right. Within the classical "rise and fall" trope which informs Higham's narrative, the *It's All True* episode clearly marks the beginning of the "fall." And within the Social Darwinist binarism of success or failure, Welles the precocious genius is virtually fated to suffer a meteoric decline. It is as if for Higham the *It's All True* experience formed a microcosmic exemplum further confirming the overriding parable orienting his observations and stated in the final paragraph of *Orson Welles: The Rise and Fall of an American Genius*: "Some perverse streak of anti-commercialism drove him; he was the brilliant architect of his own downfall."

Richard Wilson, George Fanto, and other direct participants have already countered such prejudicial accounts, pointing to the responsibility of others (the new RKO management, the Brazilian Department of Press and Propaganda, Production Manager Lynn Shores) for the non-completion of the film.[4] What interests me here, however, is something rather different. For in the case of *It's All True*, the general indictment of Welles's personality—projected as irresponsible, arrogant, power-hungry, narcissistic—is accompanied by a distinct cultural dimension. A kind of isomorphism links the censure of Welles and the implicit critique of a Brazilian culture at that time (and to some extent still today) very much misunderstood and undervalued. A common hostility embraces both Welles and certain features of Brazilian culture, a hostility subtended, I would suggest, by the implicit racial conventions of ethnocentric discourse. The Rio de Janeiro sequence of *It's All True*, for example, was intended to be an enthusiastic homage to the gregarious spirit and protean energy of Rio's carnival, yet a striking feature of the critical discourse is a pervasive, almost visceral, anti-carnivalism. A metonymical "contamination" links Welles's personality and his carnival subject; the bill of particulars against Welles echoes the perennial accusations against carnival itself—debauched, dissipated, dissolute. The "tragedy" of Welles's "fall" must entail a tragic flaw, and that flaw has a name: carnival and its attendant vices. John Russell Taylor's account of *It's All True* fairly reeks with a puritanical distaste for carnival and for what he calls Welles's "living it up," all superimposed on implicit hommages to the Anglo-Saxon work ethic. While Robert Wise and others were "struggling on with *Ambersons* and *Journey into Fear*," we are told, "their leader, incommunicado, was having the time of his life in Brazil."[5] The censorious and somewhat voyeuristic emphasis on Welles's riotous pleasures conveys the distinct impression that Welles's hedonistic "excesses" were somehow responsible for the final scuttling of the film; its non-completion was the "punishment" for Welles's self-indulgent immersion in the ludic irresponsibilities of the tropical feast. Here film criticism switches genre and becomes cautionary tale. We sense a kind of ill will, a barely disguised pleasure or *Schadenfreude* in the comeuppance of the boy genius who wanted to have it all, work hard and also have a fabulous time. "Even when he got home," Taylor tells us in the language of the ledger-book, "he did not fully realize the harm the Brazilian adventure had done his career . . . This was the painful bottom line to Welles's six wasted months in Brazil." The critics thus play the role of policemen-Malvolios at Welles's carnival, throwing a wet blanket over the filmmaker's Brazilian "party" in the name of conventional story-telling, efficiency, and the bottom line.

I would like here to propose a radically different perspective on the *It's All True* experience. For to first read the accounts of Welles's critics and then to immerse oneself in the primary documents generated by Welles and his collaborators, or in the accounts published by the Brazilian press or expressed in interviews with Welles's Brazilian interlocutors, is to enter two distinct and largely incompatible worlds. To someone adopting a Brazilian perspective, Higham's accounts, for example, sound more like a North American critic's ethnocentric nightmares than anything which actually transpired. Here, for example, is Higham's description of the filming: "Second units went into villages and jungle areas, capturing the frenzied excitement of a nation afire with violent erotic rhythms, voluptuous and pulsating."[6] Quite apart from the extreme unlikelihood of Welles ever having filmed in any "jungle areas," what is symptomatic is Higham's manner of seeing Brazil through the deforming grid of the "exotic," and specifically as mediated through the caricaturing formulae of the "darkest Africa" films, with their ethnocentric orchestration of primitivism, percussion, menace, and eroticism. Or, here is the Higham account of Welles filming in the *favelas*, which Higham describes as those "hideous slums that crawled up the hills over Rio": "Shooting amid piles of garbage, and wading through excrement thrown down the hillside, haunted by vultures overhead and surrounded by rats and roaches, Welles and his crew were jeered and pelted with beer bottles by slum inhabitants who resented having their misery recorded on film." The passage calls for a number of comments. First, interviews with Welles's close collaborators, such as Richard Wilson and George Fanto, as well as with Brazilian participant-witnesses (Alex Viany, Edgar Morel), as well as a perusal of Brazilian press accounts from the period, reveal no evidence whatsoever that Welles and his crew were ever "jeered and pelted" by slum inhabitants. Indeed, there is considerable evidence to the contrary, that Welles was well received and even cheered in the *favelas*, and this quite apart from the fact that his presence brought with it jobs, money, and a certain prestige for the *favelados*. Secondly, one might psychoanalyze the need, on the part of the critics, to put Welles, as it were, "in the shit." Barbara Leaming, for example, tells a similar tale about Welles in Fortaleza, evoking an incident which Welles's closest collaborators claim never took place. Thirdly, while *favelas* are indeed in some respects socially degraded places, hardly to be idealized as they were in *Black Orpheus*, they are not "seamy"—as Welles himself hastens to emphasize in his "Hello Americans" show broadcast from Brazil.

Higham's account is more evocative of the social nightmares of the first-world bourgeois than of anything actually experienced by the Welles team. A phenomenon beyond mere reporting, then, seems to be occurring here, something having to do with metropolitan fantasies concerning the "peripheral" world, exactly the kind of fantasies that Welles himself, as well shall see, hoped to combat.

WELLES AND BRAZIL: A CASE OF RECIPROCAL AFFECTION

In his travels through Latin America, Welles took very seriously his responsibilities as a roving ambassador for Pan-Americanism, a role in perfect accord with his own personal sympathies and his left-leaning politics. In lectures, broadcasts, and press conferences, Welles stressed the historical-cultural links between North and South America and was appreciated by Latin Americans as someone who understood their problems and perspectives. Welles was highly conscious of the negative legacy of North American ignorance and condescension toward the inhabitants of what was sometimes contemptuously called America's "backyard." In a collective interview shortly after his arrival in Rio, Welles told journalists that nothing offended him more than the "confusion and ignorance" which led many North Americans to believe, for example, that Brazilians spoke Spanish. "I come to Brazil," he said, "hoping to reveal it both to those who judge it badly and to those who do not yet know it."[7] Apart from any political-diplomatic motives behind what might be regarded as the formulaic discourse of the eager-to-please politician emphasizing all possible connections to the locale where he happens to be, considerable evidence suggests that Welles was sincerely enthusiastic about Brazil. In interviews, Welles constantly reiterated his affectionate feelings toward the country, describing himself as an "enthusiastic fan" of a "friendly people" who "made us feel completely at home."[8] The Brazilian press accounts of Welles's visit emphasize his apparent happiness, his constant laughter, his enthusiasm for Brazilian culture, his efforts to learn Portuguese and even the latest slang. One Rio journalist describes him as "perfectly identified with our language [and aware] of the most up-to-date slang, [which he] attempts to use in all his sentences, in a demonstration that he is au courant of all the latest popular sayings."[9] By April 1942, a *Cine-Radio Jornal* reporter tells us, Welles was getting along in Portuguese: "Welles insisted on speaking Portuguese, with great effort, but almost always managing to communicate."[10] This insistence on linguistic reciprocity, a leitmotif of Welles's Latin American radio broadcasts as well, is significant not only because it was so rare among North American visitors—especially celebrity visitors—but also because in Welles's case it was emblematic of a more pervasive sense of Pan-American equality and confraternity.[11]

Throughout his stay in Brazil, Welles was fond of telling reporters that he was "almost a Brazilian," since he had narrowly missed being born in Brazil, where his parents had been vacationing during his mother's pregnancy. "And, I, who had been conceived in Brazil and would have been born in Brazil," Welles told journalists, "thus acquired the United States as homeland. But I never stopped feeling great sympathy for Brazil . . . Now I am eager to know Brazil close up, from very close up, to know the people that were to be my people and the things which were to have been my things."[12] The psychoanalytically inclined might be tempted to read this projected conjunction of a Brazilian conception and a quasi-accidental birth in the United States as a kind of national "family romance," a desire to adopt an alternative parent-nation, possibly linked even to a dissatisfaction or disappointment with his real national parents as having disallowed the full flourishing of his genius and capacities. But even apart from such psychoanalytic flights of interpretation, a look at the Brazilian materials reveals a powerful sense of affinity between Welles and Brazil, completely reciprocated by the Brazilians. A telegram from Tom Petty to Herbert Drake on February 11 describes the Brazilian sentiment: "Press reaction one of delight. Stories described him altogether different from any other Hollywood visitor. Franker, brighter, more sympathetic." Celestino Silveira in *Cine-Radio Jornal* contrasted Welles's scintillating and provocative presence with that of the other "mediocre specimens," such as Tyrone Power, sent by Hollywood. A May 27, 1942, letter from the "Brazilian Division" to the Coordinator of Inter-American Affairs stressed that the Brazilian press and many private sources had credited Welles with being "the one visitor who most quickly understood Brazil, its problems, and its people." A February 19 letter from Phil Reisman to John Hay Whitney of the CIAA, credits Welles with a "magnificent job" and adds: "To give you some idea of Welles's popularity: he seems to be especially great with the masses; he has mingled with them and danced with them, and wherever we go in the car, the children yell out his name and applaud."

Brazilian journalists, for their part, were almost unanimously enthusiastic about Welles. And while it is true that Brazilian journalists, especially those associated with entertainment journals such as *Cinearte* and *A Cena Muda*, were traditionally adulatory toward Hollywood and its stars, in this case there was an important distinction in that many commentators took the unprecedented step of symbolically adopting Welles as an honorary Brazilian. In an article entitled "Orson Welles: Carioca Citizen Kane," Celestino Silveira wrote that "this enormously sympathetic big boy who's being seen around the streets of our metropolis is without a doubt an authentic first-rate Carioca."[13] Victor Jose Lima calls Welles "a perfect example of the democratic spirit . . . He's like us and he enjoys being like us."[14] Vinicius de Moraes, then a film critic but later to become poet, dramatist, composer, and popular singer, went so far as to call Welles a "great Brazilian." Watching Welles at work in the Cinedia studios in Rio, Vinicius wrote:

> What energy, what vitality, what ubiquity there is in this great Brazilian! Brazilian, yes; Orson Welles is beginning to know Brazil, or at least an important side of the soul of Brazil, better than many sociologists, novelists, critics, and poets. His vision is at times raw, but he never sins through injustice. Orson Welles has known better than anyone how to understand our character, our foibles, our easy-going ways, our so-to-speak "negative" qualities . . . Welles has felt Brazil and the character of the Brazilian people in a deeper and richer way than the vast majority of foreigners who have lived among us.[15]

Vinicius, who became fairly close to Welles, made many observations about Welles's character, claiming, for example, that Welles was capable of exaggeration but never of outright lying. He describes Welles as combining "tremendous passion with great tranquility," all tempered with a "good-humored capacity for self-criticism." He speaks of Welles's perfectionism, his attention to detail, his constant reworking of an evolving script, as well as his kindness to the Brazilian performers: "If the reader could see how he treats his actors, always playing with them, always helping them, never leaving them nervous or embarrassed." More important, Vinicius trusted Welles to represent Brazil adequately by generating "the most impressive propaganda yet created in favor of our national values." And this faith in Welles, as Heloisa Buarque de Holanda points out, has less to do with his technological know-how than with "the transgressive and dialogic profile of his work and personality."[16]

Vinicius' portrait of Welles is especially fascinating given Vinicius' own artistic affinities with Welles. Fond of describing himself as the "blackest white man in Brazil," Vinicius too became involved in artistic projects involving blacks. In his contemporaneous chronicle in *A Manha* concerning Welles's visit, Vinicius speaks of the "high cultural values" of black Brazil, and his own *Black Orpheus* (1959), first staged as a play in 1955 and subsequently adapted to the screen by Marcel Camus, can be seen in some ways as a direct descendant of Welles's "Voodoo" *Macbeth*, in that both superimpose classical culture—Shakespearean tragedy in *Macbeth*, antique classical Greek myth in *Orpheus*—on black performance. In another sense, the Vinicius play prolongs and "fulfills" Welles's ambitions in *It's All True*, i.e., to create a spectacle centered on Rio's carnival, which would treat its black participants and black culture with respect and affection.

WELLES'S METHODS: THE CONTRAST WITH HOLLYWOOD

Although Andrew Sarris describes Welles in a recent *Village Voice* as having blundered into "Hollywood's Carmen Miranda syndrome," in reality Welles's production methods and aesthetic stand in striking contrast to the conventional Hollywood approach to Latin America.[17] As the heir of "Manifest Destiny" and the Monroe Doctrine, Hollywood premised its political and cultural paradigms on the political incapacity and cultural nullity of Latin America. In terms of cultural portraiture, Hollywood films were capable of the most elementary and inexcusable gaffes, presenting Mexicans as "greasers" and Latin America generally as a kind of vast extension of Tiajuana. When Hollywood, shortly after the advent of sound, attempted to make alternative Spanish versions of its films, it offended (and amused) Latin Americans by mingling, to ridiculous effect, the most diverse Hispanic accents. Even the Hollywood attempts to audio-visually implement the Good Neighbor Policy by "positive images" of Latin America, in such films as *Down Argentine Way* (1940), foundered on the shoals of studio ignorance and condescension; *Tropical Serenade*, for example, provoked riots in Buenos Aires and had to have some scenes refilmed by Fox. In later years Hollywood was quite capable of mismatching language with country: Mervyn Leroy's *Latin Lovers* (1953) had its "Brazilian" characters, when they were not speaking English, address each other not in Portuguese but in Spanish.

Brazilian commentators were quick to note the difference between Hollywood orthodoxy and the Welles approach. One journalist observed that Hollywood, "which used to persist in sending us pretty faces and absurd films about our country, now seems to have realized that the Brazilian people deserve something better," citing Welles as an example of the new trend.[18] Welles, for his part, was consciously marking off his difference from the usual Hollywood treatment. In an April interview with *A Noite*, Welles remarked: "If I had wanted to make a carnival film in the way in which Hollywood usually portrays the customs and scenes of strange lands, I wouldn't have even had to leave the United States."[19] Welles wanted to paint a more knowing and intimate portrait of Rio de Janeiro that that offered by such films as *Flying Down to Rio* (1933) and *That Night in Rio* (1941). In his first press conference, Welles complained that "Rio de Janeiro has not been given its due" by most motion pictures: "I come here with the intention of showing to the United States and to the world the truth about this city and about Brazil."[20]

A mere desire to move beyond stereotype and caricature, however, is hardly sufficient; information is as essential as openness and good will. And in this sense, Welles's approach in *It's All True* constituted a radical departure both from Hollywood modes of production and from Hollywood norms of representation. Welles showed himself to be hungry for the most diverse kinds of information—geographical, linguistic, political, economic, musical. Brazilian journalists were impressed by Welles's devouring curiosity, his relentless questioning about all features of Brazilian history and culture, and his astonishing capacity to remember what he had learned. Celestino Silveira comments on Welles's "prodigious memory"; for example, he could remember not only the melodies but also the lyrics of countless Brazilian songs.[21] But apart from informal questioning, Welles commissioned research by a number of Brazilian writers—Alex Viany, Clovis de Gusmao, Ernani Fornari, Luiz Edmondo, Aydana Couto Ferraz, Rui Costa, Ayres de Andrade, Jr.—researchers whose knowledge of Brazilian customs provided the filmmakers with ready and authoritative reference.

The research commissioned by Welles, and the indications of his own reactions to and absorption of the materials, tell us a good deal about Welles, about Brazil, and about what a completed *It's All True* might have looked like. There are a number of striking features about this research. First, Welles asked for Brazilian views rather than for the opinions of Hollywood "experts." Second, the range of the subjects covered—sugar culture, coffee culture, rubber culture, *vaqueros*, gauchos, mining, Brazilian heroes, social conditions, the diverse races, slavery, folklore, festivals, and political institutions—is quite astonishing. Third, one is struck by the open non-finalized nature of the discussion, the lack of dogmatism about conclusions. Welles and his partners sought a multiplicity of viewpoints on every subject; the emphasis was on polyphony and debate, on lively differences of opinion which were to enter the film via the commentaries of Welles and others. Fourth, the orientation is toward Brazilian popular culture and more particularly toward popular liberatory movements: the anti-slavery rebellions, the black fugitive slave republic of Palmares, the millennial movement led by Antonio Conselheiro, and so forth. Welles saw the *jangadeiro* episode, for example, as part of an ongoing tradition of popular Brazilian resistance to oppression, since the *jangadeiros* in the past had been instrumental in the struggle against slavery, and in the present were capable of articulating popular demands, as in the case of their epic journey by raft from Fortaleza to Rio in order to present demands for better living conditions to President Vargas. Jacare, who was to have been the key figure in the *jangadeiro* episode, was himself a political and syndical leader, whose death is said to have been celebrated with champagne toasts by his political enemies, the owners in the fishing industry.

In his interest in the Northeast, in the *cangaceiros* (rebel bandits), in millennial cults, in popular culture and rebellions, Welles managed to anticipate many of the themes subsequently taken up by Brazilian Cinema Novo in the Sixties and after: the Northeast (theme of such early Cinema Novo films as *Barren Lives*, 1963, and *The Guns*, 1964), black culture in Bahia (subsequently explored in *The Given Word*, 1962, and *Barravento*, 1962), *cangaceiros* (treated in Glauber Rocha's *Black God, White Devil*, 1964, and *Antonio das Mortes*, 1969), and the black rebellions of Palmares (theme of *Ganga Zumba* in 1963 and *Quilombo* in 1984). The *jangadeiro* sequence, from what we know of it, clearly anticipates, in both theme and treatment, the documentary-inflected but formally rigorous lyricism of

Rocha's *Barravento*, released exactly two decades later, another documentary-inflected film about *jangadeiros* and social oppression. Both films form odes to Africanized, mestizo communities surviving in harsh conditions but somehow sustaining energy and optimism. Both films stress the communitarian side of *jangadeiro* life, as well as the oppressive role of the fishing industry owners, and both develop a quasi-Eisensteinian formal lyricism. Speaking more generally, *It's All True* foreshadowed the social audaciousness of Cinema Novo, its willingness to explore the life and culture of the *favellas* and its melange of documentary and fiction, and can be seen as pointing not only to what Rogerio Sganzerla calls the "beach verismo" of *Barravento* but also to the urban neo-realism of Nelson Pereira dos Santos' *Rio 40°*. Indeed, Brazilian filmmaker Rogerio Sganzerla pays homage to Welles in his documentary/fiction feature, *Nem Tudo e Verdade* (*It's Not All True*, 1985), where he recreates Welles's Brazilian experience through a sound-image collage combining documentary-style material (footage from *It's All True*, footage of Welles in Rio, citations of *Citizen Kane* and *The Lady from Shanghai*, newspaper accounts, with staged reconstructions in which an Orson Welles look-alike encounters Brazilian celebrities and studio executives). Sganzerla portrays Welles as the rebellious victim of the studio system, the press, and North American and Brazilian politicians. Welles's utopian dream of real industrial and artistic collaboration between North and South America, Sganzerla suggests, violently challenged the neo-colonial assumptions of the time.

In Brazil, Welles was touched by what later came to be called "underdevelopment." A Mercury memorandum calls attention to the arduous nature of filmmaking in Brazil: "Making a picture in Brazil means working day and night. It means working several days on a problem which an organized studio in Hollywood could cope with in a few hours." But if the American filmmakers found filmmaking in Brazil difficult, the Brazilian filmmaking milieu was astonished at the wealth and technical resources of the North Americans, and more than one commentator remarked that witnessing the technical and financial advantages of the Americans might help Brazilians appreciate the sacrifices of their own filmmakers, who, with roughly one-twentieth of the Welles budget, might have made ten features. After Welles was officially abandoned by RKO, however, with the published notification on July 20, 1942, that the studio would not be responsible for any debts incurred by the *It's All True* production team, Welles was forced into filmmaking circumstances not unlike those confronted by Brazilian filmmakers. Indeed, the image of Welles and his five-person team struggling with inadequate equipment in Fortaleza, with George Fanto working without dollies, improvising cranes, fixing broken cameras, and constructing makeshift darkrooms, can be seen as proleptic, in some ways, of the artisanal anti-industrial, and collaborative production methods of Cinema Novo and its "aesthetic of hunger."

TEXT AND PARATEXT

All discussion of *It's All True* spirals around an absent center—the missing text. Given the evidentiary status of the film, we are obliged to rely on the scant material now visible, on production stills, on production team memoranda, on memorabilia, on the reminiscences of the participants and witnesses, and on such para-textual materials as the research documents and even the contemporaneous Welles radio shows from Latin America. Indeed, much of the material contemplated for *It's All True* made its way into the radio broadcasts. These shows—"President Vargas' Birthday," "Pan-American Day," and a series of "Hello Americans" shows broadcast from Latin America—give us a glimpse of Welles's intentions in *It's All True*. In these shows, Welles transcends his role as a roving ambassador representing the North American "Good Neighbor" policy to become a veritable advocate for the Latin American countries. The broadcasts from Brazil, for example, proliferate in subtle and not-so-subtle critiques of North American ethnocentrism. Welles needles North American chauvinism, for example, by reminding his listeners that Brazil is the "largest republic in the world" and that "you could put the entire United States within the borders of Brazil and still have room for several American republics such as Paraguay, Chile, and Haiti." Welles also repeatedly uses the word "American" in its Latin American sense, as referring to all the Americas, calling Brazilian diplomat Oswald Aranha, for example, a "great American." Welles reminds listeners of the untranslatability of Brazilian words like *saudades*, or insists on the specialness of Brazilian festivity, calling the Casino de Urca one of the "last truly gay places in the world." He also warns listeners against stereotypical interpretations, for example, that "Brazilians do nothing but samba"—and again: "Don't think that the function of Brazilian music is to translate American hits into Portuguese." At times, Welles seems to take on Brazilian nationality, saying, for example, "Here in Brazil we say . . . ," or warmly reciting the lyrics of "Tudo e Brazil" (All Is Brazil): "I am a Brazilian. Oh, my Brazil."

One of the "Hello Americans" shows gives us an idea of the approach *It's All True* might have taken toward Brazilian music. Lauding Rio as "the loveliest city in our hemisphere." Welles describes the city in implicitly class terms, contrasting the urbane sophistication of the elite southern beach neighborhoods with "another side" of Rio, embodied in the music. That music, which "throbs in the streets . . . called samba . . . comes rolling down from the hills"—the "hills," in a Brazilian context, referring to the *favelas* or shanty-towns hanging on the hills surrounding Rio. In the broadcast, Welles recasts the information gathered by his researchers in the typically dialogical form of a debate. Welles's claim that samba came from the hills is immediately followed by a counter-claim that samba did not come from the hills. Welles then introduces, in a quasi-didactic manner, all the percussion instruments, placing special emphasis on the notion of polyrhythm, and making cross-cultural comparisons to American instruments and musical traditions. He calls attention to the extraordinary musicality of the Brazilian people. "Brazilian babies can beat out samba rhythms before they can talk," Welles tells us, "and they can dance to the samba rhythm before they can walk."

To deepen his own vision of samba and Brazilian music, Welles commissioned research into its roots. In his "The Genealogy of Samba and Other Aspects of an Unquiet Life," Welles's special assistant Robert Meltzer speaks of the pedigree, ancestry, and roots of samba, but notes that opinion on the subject is still "in suspension," untouched by the "crystalizing effects of critical prose." (Indeed, some Brazilian observers claim that Welles was the first to call for serious erudite studies of samba and popular culture.) The commissioned essay by Ayres de Andrade, Jr.—"The Story of the Rio de Janeiro Carnival"—traces the historical origins of carnival to the *entrudos* (water battles), then speaks about the gradual Africanization of carnival via such African-derived dances as the *maxixe*. Andrade informs us about the custom of throwing confetti, of squirting ether through lanca-perfumes, and of decorating streetcars, as well as about transvestitism ("every boy goes out as a girl and vice versa"). All in all, the commissioned research covers a wide spectrum of topics linked to Brazilian music and carnival: the origins of the circle dance (*roda*), the nature of *capoeira*, the African-derived dance/martial art, and the derivation of carnival's percussion instruments, whether African (e.g., the friction drum called the *cuica*) or indigenous "indian" (the bead and bean percussion instruments originally used in chants and religious ceremonies).

Welles himself acquired a certain intimacy with samba songs and rhythms. One of the "Hello Americans" shows, broadcast immediately after Welles's return from Brazil, features Welles himself, along with Carmen Miranda, singing the Brazilian song, "Tabuleiro da Baiana," in excellent Portuguese. Vinicius de Moraes describes Welles as a "master of our carnival," familiar with "its mannerisms, rhythms, instruments," and Alex Viany, a Brazilian filmmaker and critic commissioned to do research for *It's All True*, claims that Welles mastered samba rhythms "better than any foreigner." At times, when Welles would disappear and people would have to search for him all over Rio," they would finally find him in the *favela*, playing the [percussion instrument] *pandeiro* and drinking *cachaca* [rum]."[22]

THE CENTRALITY OF MUSIC

Music was absolutely fundamental to the Wellesian conception of *It's All True*, making it virtually impossible to appreciate the film on the basis of music-less rushes. "Music is the basis of our picture," Welles writes in his script-presentation of the film, "and it is our very good luck that our music is samba." The United States, Welles points out, is only now becoming aware of the samba's "incomparable danceability," and while the United

States has rhumba, conga, and tango orchestras, "the samba can only be recorded in Brazil." The very aesthetic of *It's All True*, Welles writes, "is based on the conception of an illustrated musical constructed of Brazilian popular tunes." The music, he goes on to say, is not incidental, but of "primary importance": "Music had to do more than complement the picture— it must dictate what was to be seen." "In the interests of veracity," Welles goes on, "our music had to be native and truly of carnival, and our picture had to be true to the music. We had to discover what samba was before we found an architecture for our film. Samba, we learned, comes from the hills, so our picture had to be oriented to the hills." (This "preferential option" for the hills and for blacks, as we shall see, got Welles into considerable trouble.)

Although on one level Welles intended in *It's All True* to downplay individual talents in favor of the collective phenomenon of carnival itself, on another level he hoped to promote Brazilian performers. In contrast to most North American films set in Latin America, Welles was uninterested in displaying North American stars against "exotic" backdrops; rather, he was seeking and promoting local talent. Welles and his collaborators solicited the participation of well-known Brazilian performers such as Linda Batista, actress and singer from Brazilian cinema; Emilinha Borba, a singer-star from Urca and from the *chanchadas* (the so-called "carnivalesque films"); along with some of the best carnival orchestras (Chiquinho, Fon-Fon, Dede), instrumentalists, and composers (for example Pixinguinha, the black flautist and composer of "Carinhoso"). One of the key performers was to be the brilliant black actor Sebastiao Prata (generally known as "Grande Otelo"), whose role would be to "personalize" the carnival sequence. Welles repeatedly characterized Grande Otelo as one of the world's preeminent comic actors and a "multi-talented performer." Already well known in Brazil as a theatrical and night-club performer as well as an actor in *chanchadas*, Otelo subsequently played in well over a hundred films ranging from Burle's *Moleque Tiao* (1943), a film based on his own life, to Joaquim Pedro de Andrade's *Macunaima* (1969), through Herzog's *Fitzcaraldo* (1982), and indeed has figured prominently in all the crucial phases of Brazilian cinema since the Thirties. In his script-presentation, Welles introduced the black actor with the Shakespearean name as follows: "His name is Othello. Remember that name. It belongs to the performer himself and this isn't the last time you'll encounter it. This is only his first American picture, and he's a big hit in it for sure. Othello likes to be compared to Mickey Rooney, but he's closer to a young Chaplin." (Significantly, Welles does not racially categorize Otelo; nor does he feel compelled to compare Otelo only to other black actors.)

Again in contrast to Hollywood practice, Welles collaborated with, and planned to give full credit to, a number of Brazilians. One of his collaborators was Herivelto Martins who, apart from being a samba composer and samba pageant organizer, was also a union leader: consequently, he had excellent relations with people in the *favelas*. His background in the cinema both as actor and composer also facilitated his collaboration with Welles. According to both Grande Otelo and Herivelto Martins himself, the twosome would spend many nights conversing with Welles about the samba life and carnival, and in the following days their ideas would be realized or, as they put it, "idealized" by Welles. Martins describes Welles as voracious in his search for information about Brazilian culture: "He would ask about everything: what people in the *favelas* did when they weren't doing the samba, what the *porta bandeira* (the standard-bearer of the samba group) was like, if there were fights. He wouldn't take notes, but then he would tell everything to his assistant, and the assistant would note it all down." It was thanks to the information provided by Herivelto and Otelo that Welles reconstructed Praca Onze (the square through which carnival traditionally passed from the *favelas* into the city) inside of the Cinedia studios. "He reproduced everything," Herivelto tells us, "exactly as we described it." Welles also gave Herivelto considerable control over all aspects of filming the samba. Thus Herivelto worked both as a kind of co-scriptwriter with Welles, the script here taking oral form and then re-elaborated by Welles, and as a kind of production director for the samba school scenes. Both Otelo and Herivelto insist that Welles respected Herivelto's word on all filming of the samba. "It had to be done as we wanted . . . There were grandiose scenes, with three or four hundred extras, with all the Technicolor lights lit, four or five cameras filming, and when he finished shooting, he would ask: 'Okay?' and if I said 'no good,' he would do everything all over again."[23]

Especially impressive in Welles's work in Brazil is his concern with understanding and respecting Brazilian cultural codes, his desire for the truth about the samba, and his felt responsibility toward the Brazilians themselves. Welles understood the spirit of the country, its ironic self-mocking humor, its love of irreverent play, characteristics especially amplified and exalted in Rio's carnival. Although Barbara Leaming portrays Welles as not being particularly fond of carnivals, Welles's collaborators in Brazil, such as close associate Richard Wilson and filming coordinator Jose Sanz, claim that in fact Welles "loved" carnival. In his script-presentation, Welles describes carnival very much along Bakhtinian lines, as a privileged moment of "free and familiar contact," when "cariocas think only about dancing, singing, and making love to one another," and where individuals, according to Welles, "set aside their self-consciousness and timidity and reticence." Welles also calls attention to Brazilians' "unaggressive good humor," and the "unpoliced good behavior of carnival mobs." Carnival's "hilarious congestion," Welles writes, "exists in the very hottest latitudes of human hilarity," and is as yet "uncharted and unexplored." Hollywood, Welles explains, "has never before exploited any part of its color or atmosphere. A dozen carnival pictures may be made this year in North America,

but none of them can possibly have anything to do with the real thing."
The sheer immensity of Rio's carnival, Welles writes, "defies studio representation" and "is hopelessly beyond the scope of any Hollywood spectacle." The suggestion that any spectacle might be beyond the scope of
Hollywood, and indeed that the supposedly underdeveloped Brazilians
might put on a better show than Hollywood itself, is typical of Welles's
penchant for needling Hollywood pretensions and reversing established
cultural hierarchies.

FILMING A STORM

Filming carnival, however, was far from easy. In his communiques with
RKO and with the Coordinator of Inter-American Affairs, Welles compares
shooting carnival to "filming a storm," and inventories the challenges and
obstacles. Quite apart from the difficulties occasioned by the war (such as
shortages of fuel and film), Welles cites: inadequate equipment, insufficient information, the ephemeral and dispersed nature of carnival activities, the lack of appropriate lights for filming at night (Welles ultimately
had to depend on lights provided by the Brazilian army), the virtual
impossibility of recording carnival music and sound effects with any completeness or accuracy, and the impossibility of seeing rushes, a situation
which Welles compared to transporting pay dirt around the world and
only then getting out the gold. In a document entitled, "Problems of
Photographing Carnival," Welles offers very concrete advice to his crews,
such as: 1) film in black and white with small cameras, and film people
before they know they're being photographed; 2) use a decoy camera to
distract attention from the large technicolor camera; and 3) when filming
ranchos, i.e., very large groups of carnival revellers, ask the Brazilian
Department of Propaganda to turn the whole area over to the company so
as to limit access to the performing group, avoiding all bystanders.

The seeable footage from *It's All True* shows samba school pageants,
high society balls, street carnival, "art nouveau" and "art deco" buildings,
and *blocos* playing at carnival in Copacabana, Rua do Ouvidor, Praca
Maua, and Cinelandia. We see balls at the Teatro Municipal, the *terreiros*
of the samba schools, Grande Otelo singing and dancing, along with shots
of Corcovado, Sugar Loaf, and other attractions. There was, reportedly,
technicolor footage from the Casino de Urca, Teatro Municipal, and the
Tennis Club. Despite Robert Wise's (reported) judgment that Welles's
Brazil footage was "simply a jumble of what was essentially travelogue
stuff," it is not so difficult to discern a coherent overall intention in the
carnival sequence. The goal was to create a pedagogical fictive-documen-
tary-entertainment, a Pan-American musical without Hollywood stars and
without a conventional story, which would initiate the spectator into the
world of the samba. A didactic succession of shots would introduce the

instruments, not as background decor as in *Black Orpheus*, but for their own sake. The film would speak of their origin, their function, how they were made and played (material, once again, that made its way into the "Hello Americans" radio show Welles performed with Carmen Miranda). Since the samba is not "a beat immediately understandable to the uninitiated ear," Welles tries to ease the North American into the music by making cross-cultural comparisons, comparing the Brazilian song, "Praca Onze," for example, to "Old Kentucky Home" and "The Beautiful Ohio." By acting as mediator or facilitator of cultural dialogue, Welles was performing precisely the task assigned him by the Coordinator of Inter-American Affairs, but he performed that task, as we shall see, with too much enthusiasm for official taste.

Welles's approach to carnival is striking in its awareness of social differences. Welles recognized that carnival is what Bakhtin calls a "heteroglossia," a many-languaged phenomenon, lived differently depending on one's race and class. The narration and images were intended to highlight the differences between the popular street samba and the more fashionable and exclusive balls (*bailes*), exploring the diverse locations where carnival was celebrated and the kind of crowds that frequented them. The Teatro Municipal, for example, featured swanky balls for the elite, while the Teatro da Republica hosted balls for the middle class, and so forth. The film would also emphasize what Bakhtin would call the "erasure of the boundaries between spectator and spectacle." In carnival, wrote Welles, the people "entertain themselves and others almost without let up." Welles wanted it all to be "tremendously alive, and, we use the word advisedly, sexy." The goal, for him, was "to leave our audience as open-mouthed and google-eyed as we were who shot the action."

Apart from the general outline of the story of the samba and the lament for the passing of Praca Onze, Welles planned what might be called micro-sequences intended to convey the cheerful rituals and atmosphere of carnival. The emphasis was to be less on spectacle per se than on carnival's myriad forms of human interplay, between performing musicians and responding audience, among groups of revellers (the throwing of confetti and streamers), between lovers or lovers-to-be, and even between competing samba groups. The memoranda also list specific close shots and sequences of shots: a woman throwing ether into a man's champagne glass, a woman kissing a man with a mask, then pulling back the mask to discover she has kissed the back of his head, streamers falling into a bourgeois man's meal. The emphasis, in these micro-sequences, is often on the playful upsetting of pomposity, in a manner reminiscent of another carnival documentary film, Vigo's *A Propos de Nice* (1929–30). Welles's purposes, however, were less satirical and more sympathetic. He hoped to initiate the spectator into the typical gestures of carnival and into the codes of Brazilian culture; he would show festive groups singing and beating out samba rhythms, girls messing up their boyfriends' hair, men fanning women and vice versa, and lots of Brazilians in affectionate greeting. (This last emphasis catches a major Brazilian cultural characteristic, i.e., the naturalness with which Brazilians, on any occasion and without any formal pretext, kiss, embrace, or caress one another.) The complaints from studio observers that Welles was just filming people throwing confetti completely miss the point, for what mattered always was not the activity per se but rather the contagiously ludic, interrelational quality of carnival—what Bakhtin would call the "in-between" of carnival's "free and familiar contact" and "gay relativity."

Welles warned studio executives away from watching the apparently disjointed rushes of *It's All True*, since the ultimate effectiveness of the material would derive not so much from the compositional beauty of the individual shots as from the relation between the montage and the music. A percussive montage, for example, would convey the overwhelming sensation of the *batucada* rhythms: "A drumbeat sounds. Eyes turn; toes twitch. The drummer enters the scene, beating a slow rhythm, but since it is a rhythm, nobody can sit still. They start to rise, one by one, and then in hundreds . . . until everyone is dancing and singing." The film was also to feature a number of "magical" spatial-temporal matches and transformations. A "contrapuntal" musical montage, since become banal but relatively rare in 1942, would alternate shots of Linda Batista singing in the Casino de Urca with shots of Grande Otelo singing in Praca Onze, handled in such a way that the lyrics of her song would appear to be having a dialogue with the lyrics of his song: Linda Batista would sing, "I like to hear the rhythms from the hills / I like to hear the rhythms from the hills, ai ai ai," and Grande Otelo, as if in response, would sing, "That's because the rhythms are marvelous / That's because the rhythms are marvelous, ai ai ai."[24]

WELLES AND THE POWER OF BLACKNESS

The research commissioned by Welles would have alerted him, if he were not already aware of it, to the indispensable black contribution to carnival. Alex Viany's commissioned essay, "The Samba Goes to Town," describes Praca Onze as the square closest to the *favelas*, which became during carnival a kind of "Africa embassy," whose inimitable feasts were "the biggest social events for black cariocas . . . reminiscent of gigantic Harlem jam sessions elevated to the highest degree." Brazilian whites, Viany explains, had undergone a process of cultural Africanization: "Black slang came down from the hills and took over the city, democracy advanced a hundred years in ten, and the white man's acceptance of his colored brother was easy because he learned to speak the same language and sing the same songs." Viany describes Praca Onze during carnival as an ephemeral social utopia, the locus of "the most genuine freedom in thinking and speaking," and it is interesting to speculate on the reactions of Welles, as a fighter against racism from a largely segregated society, on encountering a society certainly not without prejudice, but where blacks and whites mingled with a celebratory ease relatively unknown in the United States.

In his chronicle for *A Manha* (February 10, 1942), Vinicius de Moraes speaks of Welles's prior involvement with black culture and blacks in North America. The Orson Welles who went to Brazil in 1942, it is important to remember, was already well attuned to the power and intelligence of what Robert Farris Thompson calls "black Atlantic civilization," and was therefore well prepared to appreciate the black contribution to Brazilian culture. Even before his trip to Brazil, Welles had shown himself to be a person animated by a deep hatred of all that smacked of white supremacy and cultural apartheid. More than a "tolerant liberal," Welles was passionately anti-racist. Indeed, one might argue that Welles was a "premature anti-racist," much as one speaks of "premature anti-fascists." Retroactively, we see evidence of pro-black attitudes throughout Welles's career: going all the way back to an impromptu version of *Uncle Tom's Cabin* at Todd School, through his script for *Marching Song*, a depiction of John Brown as abolitionist prophet and warrior, to the various creative encounters with black performers and themes in the period immediately preceding *It's All True*. In a period of extreme anti-black racism, of Jim Crow laws and even lynchings, of segregation in the South and discrimination in the North, Welles was attracted to black themes and black performers, most notably in his "Voodoo" *Macbeth*, performed in Harlem in 1936. Indeed, the "Voodoo" *Macbeth* prepares the way, in many respects, for *It's All True*. Both treat black themes, one in a tragic, the other in a musical-documentary register. In both instances, Welles placed his confidence in performers untrained in the classical sense, yet rich in experience, performance smarts, and charisma. Asked in Brazil why he had called on black actors to represent Shakespeare, Welles responded by affirming the superiority of black actors: "In all my years of experience, I have concluded that black actors are more natural, more understanding, and more sure of themselves, even in the most difficult passages, than white actors, and that they perform the roles given them with more facility."[25]

Welles's theatrical adaptation of Richard Wright's *Native Son* constitutes another major encounter between Welles and blackness. The date, 1940, suggests that racial issues must have been very much on Welles's mind in the period immediately prior to the making of *It's All True*. Here, too, Welles's willingness to take risks on a black theme, and the Welles-Houseman approach of collaborating with the black community anticipates a similar approach in the case of *It's All True*. The nature of the project suggests that Welles's support for black causes went far beyond liberal do-goodism and patronizing efforts to "upgrade the underprivileged." Welles's language is surprisingly radical, in cultural as well as political terms. In his *New York Post* column (1945), for example, Welles recommended another Richard Wright novel, *Black Boy*, to those "white citizens who claimed to 'understand the negro.'" Such citizens, he said, should be "tied down with banjo strings, gagged with bandannas, their eyes propped open with watermelon seeds, and made to read *Black Boy* word for word."

Welles's other major engagement with black culture, prior to Brazil, was the Duke Ellington "Jazz Story" project originally slated to form the fourth episode of *It's All True*. The jazz episode, to be written by Ellington and Welles, directed by Ellington and Welles, with music written and performed by Ellington, was to tell the story of Louis Armstrong. Both Ellington and Welles were reportedly eager to work on the project, and indeed Welles's initial reluctance to go to South America derived from his reluctance to abandon the jazz project. It was only when he realized that samba was the Brazilian counterpart to jazz and that both were expressions of the African diaspora in the New World, that Welles opted for the story of carnival and the samba. A comparison of the projected jazz episode to what we know of the carnival sequence of *It's All True* reveals a series of paradigmatic substitutions. New Orleans as setting is replaced by another Africanized New World carnival city—Rio de Janeiro. Instead of the Afro-American music called jazz, we find the Afro-Brazilian music called samba. Songs such as "Didn't He Ramble" give way to Brazilian tunes such as "Bahia" and "Praca Onze," and performer-composers like Duke Ellington and Louis Armstrong make way for Pixinguinha and Grande Otelo.

The testimony of the Brazilian participants in the filmmaking tells us a good deal about Welles's relations with popular culture and with black Brazilians. Raul Marques, composer of the samba "Risoleta," who was charged with the responsibility of gathering the participants from the *favelas*, describes working with Welles as a "holiday," saying "people liked the movement" and "there were people who even slept there in the studio,"[26] an account which directly contradicts the Higham account of enraged *favelados* pelting Welles and his crew with beer bottles and tin cans. Herivelto Martins and Grande Otelo, for their part, describe Welles as extremely democratic, claiming that Welles liked them precisely because they showed no special servility toward him. Martins describes the communications between the three as follows: "Welles spoke Portuguese badly, I spoke English badly, and Otelo translated badly, but still we understood each other. He was very human, he liked common people, and lived with my son, Peri, on his lap."[27] As Otelo and Herivelto describe it, there was both camaraderie and real artistic collaboration between the two of them and Welles. The camaraderie took the form of drinking rum, of Welles sleeping at Herivelto's house, of frequent visits to the *favela*, and of playing with Peri, who Welles likes so much that he gave him a major role in the film. The artistic collaboration, as we have seen, took the form both of informal exchange of ideas and of assistance in directing scenes. We could not be farther from the methods and the racial conventions of Hollywood. Here we find not only fraternizing between the director and the "native" actors, but also a strong black creative direction in the film, both in the form of performing talent and through a kind of dialogic, conversational co-scripting.

Interestingly, Martins offers as an instance of Welles's "tempestuousness" what is in fact an exemplum of Welles's deep feelings about racism. He recounts an incident in which Welles was being honored at a party in the Casino de Urca, attended by RKO directors. "At that time," Martins tells us, "they didn't allow blacks into the casino, and after a while Welles began to ask: 'What happened to my friend Herivelto? Where's my friend Otelo?' In fact, neither I nor Otelo had been invited. When they told Welles that Grande Otelo wasn't allowed to join the party, Welles replied: 'If he can't come, then I can't stay,' and he left to look for us in the local bars. He finally found us, took off his smoking jacket and stayed there drinking with us until the bar closed at three in the morning. Everyone was looking for him, he was the guest of honor, but he stayed with us. Today, he said, today we will drink only black beer."

The incident reminds us, of course, of other similar incidents in Welles's career, of his *New York Post* open letter to Jack Benny protesting the segregation which prevented Benny from taking Eddie Anderson (Rochester) along on troop shows, or of the incident registered by Barbara Leaming in which Welles vigorously protested a suggestion by a production person on *Orson Welles's Almanac* that Duke Ellington be presented not as his "friend" but as his "servant." In the case of *It's All True*, Welles paid dearly for choosing black friends over the white elite. Edgar Morel, hired by Welles to research the *jangadeiros* material, describes Welles as an "anti-racist by formation" and attributed much of the hostility directed toward Welles to the fact that he enjoyed the company of blacks and that he became very close to Grande Otelo, who was almost always accompanied by what Morel calls a "black court" of followers. Just as racist critics subtly, and not so subtly, hounded Welles in the United States, so it was in Brazil, and this time the racism came from the Brazilian elite, from higher-ups in the RKO production hierarchy, and from the Rockefeller Committee of the Coordinator of Inter-American Affairs. A memorandum from the Rockefeller Committee to RKO recommends that the film "avoid any reference to miscegenation," and suggests that "sequences of the film in which mulattos or mestizos appear conspicuously"[28] should be omitted. There were also frequent complaints from RKO executives and, occasionally, from members of the *It's All True* production crew, that Welles was overemphasizing the black element and showing too much "ordinary social intercourse" between blacks and whites in carnival, a feature that might offend some North American viewers. A July 1942 letter from William Gordon of the production team of *It's All True* to an RKO executive, complains about Welles's "indiscriminate intermingling of blacks and whites in the Welles Brazilian film," something "which will be found objectionable south of the Mason-Dixon line in the United States, and in a good many countries of Latin America." Citing the example of Goldwyn's deletion of two close shots of two black members of Gene Krupa's orchestra in *Ball of Fire* (1941), he argues for the deletion of such shots. Lamenting the fact that he had been unable to control Welles in this matter, he remarks that Brazilians, while "completely lacking in race prejudice," may resent some of the footage "because it will tend to confirm the North American opinion that most South Americans belong to the African race."

The chief ethnic nay-sayer from within the Welles team was production manager Lynne Shores, an obscure artistic director of "B" comedies and musicals, now appointed as irritable "old hand"—some would say spy—in charge of monitoring what was seen as Welles's tendency to irrational behavior. In his letters and memoranda, Shores reveals, after only a few weeks in Brazil, intense hostility to Welles, to the project, and to Brazil itself.[29] Shores describes himself, in a letter to Walter Daniels back in Hollywood, as the defender of "law, order, morals and progress"—the language, again, is symptomatic—and his conception of "law, order, and progress" gives significant place to white supremacy. Indeed, Shore's letters provide an ongoing document of racism of the most noxious variety. Along with generally patronizing remarks about Brazil and Brazilians, Shores is especially obsessed with Welles's penchant for filming black people. Shores even came to conspire with certain officials of the Brazilian Department of Press and Propaganda. In an April 11, 1942, letter to Dr. Alfredo Pessoa, he complains:

> Despite repeated conversations with Mr. Richard Wilson . . . I still find myself unable to control the tendency of Mr. Welles to utilize our cameras in matters which I do not feel are in accord with the wishes of the Brazilian government and, I am sure, not in harmony with the feelings of our executives in Hollywood. The matter to which I refer is the continued exploitation of the negro and the low class element in and around Rio, specifically according to yesterday's shooting of films which occurred at these various points as itemized: the original Favela da Saude, the Cantagallo Favela, the Humayta Favela, the Praia do Pinto Favela. We have on top of these scenes, a schedule which calls for added filming in conjunction with the scenes already filmed at the Teatro Republica (the Teatro where blacks celebrate carnival), which I feel are all in very bad taste.

Claiming to represent the feelings of the majority of the working crew, Shores even implies the possibility of a kind of censorship or perhaps sabotage: "I am holding the negative of this film and not shipping it through for development until I can perhaps have a talk with you on this subject to be sure that I am not unduly alarmed over its possible consequences." On April 14, a Richard Wilson memorandum to Welles tells us that Dr. Pessoa called Wilson to his office to inform him that there had been many complaints about the filming in the *favelas*.

If Shores was euphemistic in his communications to the Department of Propaganda, he was more frankly and colloquially racist in his letters to Walter Daniels back in Los Angeles. In a letter dated April 14, the very day that Wilson was called in by the Department of Press and Propaganda, Shores complains to Daniels that "last Friday, he [Welles] ordered day and night shots in some very dirty and disreputable nigger neighborhoods throughout the city." And an April 30 letter to Daniels returns to the same racial leitmotif: "We had a very full week as far as shooting goes. However, the stuff itself is just carnival nigger singing and dancing, of which we already have piles." Unappreciative of Afro-Brazilian culture and of the nuances that Welles planned to emphasize, Shores sees nothing more than black people jumping around: "We are still pouncing on large groups of colored people doing exactly the same thing that has happened during the February carnival." Racism also affected the Fortaleza sequence. In September 1943, when there were still thoughts of recuperating the *It's All True* material, an RKO memorandum from Charles Koerner to William Gordon notes that "the heroes on the raft are referred to as Indians," a perspective that "will be impossible to sell to audiences, especially south of the Mason-Dixon line."

When the Brazilian press learned that Welles and Richard Wilson had witnessed the Afro-Brazilian *macumba* ritual and planned to integrate it into the film, the Brazilian establishment became quite alarmed. To understand this reaction on the part of a certain Brazilian elite, we must understand its context, not only in terms of a long history of subordination of blacks, but also in terms of a populist-fascist Vargas government, which tended to be intolerant of both black political expression and Afro-Brazilian cultural expression. As an ambiguous figure mingling vague pro-Axis sympathies with populism à la Roosevelt, Vargas was hardly progressive in racial matters. He banned the black activist group, "Frente Negra" (Black Front), in the late Thirties, and violently repressed Afro-Brazilian religious practices, such as *candomble*, a fact powerfully memorialized by the Triguerinho Neto film, *Bahia de Todos os Santos*, made in 1960 but focalizing events contemporaneous with the making of *It's All True*. We must also remember that the Brazilian official placed in charge of working with the Welles team was Assis Figuieredo, the head of the Department of Tourism, who was infinitely more interested in disseminating scenic clichés of Sugar Loaf and Corcovado than in exploring the deep social and cultural roots of the samba.

Welles and his closest collaborators, in contrast, saw it as absolutely vital to stress the origins of samba in the black culture of the hills of Rio, seeing the *favelas* as analogous to the brothels, back alleys, and streets of New Orleans, which spawned North American jazz. "For Welles," Richard Wilson tells us, "the carnival story was essentially a black story."[30] But when the filmmakers put this theory into practice, when they departed from the official program and started to film street carnival and popular balls, to visit popular bars, and to film in the *favelas*, RKO, DIP, and some elements in the press unleashed a campaign against Welles. Editorials politely suggested that the filmmakers limit themselves to touristic sites and leave aside unsavory scenes of squalor. Welles was accused of filming blacks, as if it were possible to film a real Rio carnival without filming the blacks who formed the vast majority of the samba schools (at that point roughly ninety percent black or mulatto) and of the Brazilian population as a whole.

A perusal of Brazilian press accounts from the period shows elite Brazilians becoming quite concerned with the filming of *favelas*. Around the time of Disney's earlier visit to Brazil, journalist Eneas Viany complained that Disney's hosts had taken him to the ceremonies of *macumba*, the Afro-Brazilian religion which Barbara Leaming mistakenly calls "voodoo." "Will anyone witnessing such scenes imagine that we also have a Carlos Gomes—(the reference is to a Brazilian operatic composer in the Verdi tradition)—who composes the marvel which is *O Guarani?*" And under the cheaply punning title of "Carioca Carnival Is Going to Be Very Dark on the Screen," a *Meio Dia* editorialist sneeringly comments on Welles's penchant for hiring black "artists" and "technicians" and "composers"—the words are placed in apologetic quotes—from the hills, and he protests the arrogance of two "colored technicians" who had the audacity to claim that Orson Welles is making a film such as had never been made in Brazil. Welles's informants, the editorialist complains, are committing an injustice by offering "cinema sequences in which only black people figure, as though Rio were another Harlem."[31] And a May 20, 1942, article by Gatinha Angora in *Cine-Radio Jornal*, which up to that point had been fairly sympathetic to Welles, expressed uneasiness with Welles's project:

> Each time the robust and handsome fiance of "del Rio" points his cameras at the so-called "picturesque" spots of the city, we feel a slight sensation of uneasiness . . . We must not let this perhaps unique occasion escape us of exploiting the prestige of Orson Welles, so much spoken of at the moment, to make our American friends feel the necessity of not distorting our aspect of a civilized nation . . . but what do his Brazilian advisors do? Instead of showing him our possibilities, they let him film to his delight, scenes of the hills, of no good half-breeds . . . and the filthy huts of the *favelas* which infest the lovely edge of the lake, where there is so much beauty and so many marvelous angles for filming; dances of negroes covered with maracatu feathers, reminiscent of the temples of the African wilds, as though our not always edifying street carnival were not already sufficient.

Then Angora goes on to lament the privileging of the *malandro* (street-smart trickster) figure, regretting that the filmmakers, set loose in such a marvelous city, "where there is already the rumble of great capitals," should call on "all the negative elements of our land," and that the representative of Brazil should be a "good-for-nothing in a striped shirt, dirty straw hat over his eye, who comes in dancing an out-of-joint samba."[32]

The democratic, anti-racist spirit animating Welles's project was antithetical to such colonized attitudes. *It's All True* was to emphasize not elite individual history but rather collective heroism and creativity. Welles wanted to show Brazilian heroes, not North American heroes, against Brazilian backdrops. The pivotal characters of both episodes were to be black (Otelo) or mestizo (Jacaré). That Welles could see a *sambista* from the *favelas* and a quartet of mestizo fishermen as authentic popular heroes speaks volumes about the distance that separates Welles from the ambient racism of his time. By choosing to focalize such a subject and privilege such characters, and by deciding to stay and complete *It's All True* with his own funds, Welles chose the margins over the center, even to the detriment of his own career. Welles's approach was neither miserabilist nor idealized; his intention was to show people who are poor but dignified, energetic, transforming their lives by art and activism. Many of Welles's critics and biographers, meanwhile, continue to peripheralize Welles. Welles was seen by his critics (both within the studio and outside it) at that time, and to some extent even today, not only as an artistic maverick and a rebel, but as a kind of ethnic renegade, rather like an anthropologist who, instead of maintaining the customary distance and superiority, has "gone native," who has loved the objects of his "study" just a little too dearly and too well.

Notes

1. I would like to thank the John Simon Guggenheim Memorial Foundation for providing me with the Fellowship that made this research possible. I would also like to thank two of the scholars most knowledgeable about the *It's All True* project: Catherine Benamou, who gathered many of the documents from the Lilly Library that served as a partial basis for this study; and Heloisa Buarque de Holanda (and her assistant Ana Rita Mendonca) for giving me access to what is most probably the most extensive archive of materials on *It's All True* and for generously sharing their perceptions concerning Welles's experience in Brazil.

2. Documents cited, when no other source is mentioned, are generally from the Welles collection at the Lilly Library.

3. See Charles Higham, *The Films of Orson Welles* (Berkeley: University of California Press, 1971) and *Orson Welles: The Rise and Fall of an American Genius* (New York: St. Martin's Press, 1985), and John Russell Taylor, *Orson Welles: A Celebration* (Boston: Little, Brown, & Co., 1986).

4. See both Charles Higham's article *"It's All True"* (*Sight and Sound*, Spring 1970) and Richard Wilson's response, "It's Not Quite All True" (*Sight and Sound*, Autumn 1970).

5. John Russell Taylor, *Orson Welles: A Celebration*, 64.

6. Charles Higham, *The Films of Orson Welles*, 87.

7. *Cine-Radio Jornal* (February 11, 1942).

8. *Cine-Radio Jornal* (March 6, 1942).

9. *Cine-Radio Jornal* (June 3, 1942).

10. *Cine-Radio Jornal* (April 22, 1942).

11. We find a similar insistence on linguistic reciprocity in Welles's radio broadcasts from Latin America. In "The Bad Will Ambassador," for example, a kind of *Ugly American* avant la lettre, Welles offers a satirical portrait of an arrogant American businessman who has trouble with "those strange Latin names." At one point, he asks of someone if he speaks English, to which his Latin American interlocutor replies, "No, Sir, only Spanish and Portuguese," provoking the American's comment: "That's all right. He'll have time to get an education."

12. Orson Welles ritualistically reaffirmed this notion in interviews with Brazilians, but for the first instance, see *Cine-Radio Jornal* (February 11, 1942).

13. *Cine-Radio Jornal* (February 11, 1942).

14. *Cine-Radio Jornal* (April 22, 1942).

15. *A Manha* (April 30, 1942).

16. From "Some Notes from a Research on Welles in Brazil," by Heloisa Buarque de Holanda with research assistance by Ana Rita Mendonca, notes sent as a contribution to the Welles Conference held at New York University in May 1988.

17. Andrew Sarris, *Village Voice* (May 5, 1988).

18. *Cine-Radio Jornal* (February 11, 1942).

19. *A Noite* (April 10, 1942).

20. *Cine-Radio Jornal* (February 11, 1942).

21. See, for example, *Cine-Radio Jornal* (June 3, 1942).

22. Taped interview with Alex Viany conducted by Heloisa Buarque de Holanda.

23. Interview with Grande Otelo and Herivelto Martins conducted by Alex Viany, available in the Rio de Janeiro Cinemateque, Museu de Arte Moderna.

24. It is interesting to think of *It's All True* as existing within the tradition of the Brazilian *chanchadas* or "carnivalesque films." Brazilians, after all, had been filming or staging carnival for decades prior to *It's All True*, first in documentary films, and later in fiction films. It was precisely Cinedia, the film studio where Welles chose to work, that had first developed the aesthetic formulae of the *chanchada*. Like *It's All True*, the early *chanchadas* based their appeal on the prestige of popular singers, and were intimately linked to the cultural universe of carnival itself. One of the *chanchada*'s functions, after all, was to disseminate the annual repertory of carnival songs, and the films were timed to be released exactly two weeks before carnival. If carnival fell at the end of February, for example, the screenplay was supposed to be ready in November and shooting completed by December. The parallel between the *chanchadas* and *It's All True* is more than speculative, furthermore, for although it is possible that Welles did not see any *chanchadas*, he did work with many collaborators linked to the *chanchada*: notably Adhemar Gonzaga, the founder and director of Cinedia; Lulu de Barros, director of a number of *chanchadas*, who helped Welles stage some of the scenes performed in the studio. Also Rui Costa, whom the Welles team commissioned to write about the history of carnival and the samba, had directed a number of *chanchadas* in the years immediately prior to the filming of *It's All True*. Grande Otelo and Herivelto Martins had both been linked to the *chanchada*, just as Welles's cameraman, George Fanto, had shot three films at Cinedia prior to his collaboration with Welles.

25. See *Cine-Radio Jornal* (February 11, 1942).

26. See *Jornal do Brasil*, Caderno B (1985).

27. Interview with Herivelto Martins and Grande Otelo conducted by Alex Viany, available in the cinemateque of the Museu de Arte Moderna.

28. Quoted by Servulo Siqueira, in "Tudo e Verdade," *Folha de São Paulo* (December 2, 1984).

29. One hears echoes of this early hostility in the present-day words of Reginald Armour, then executive secretary to George Schaeffer, as registered in the BBC documentary *The RKO Story*.

30. Wilson is interviewed in the BBC documentary *The RKO Story*.
31. *Meio Dia* (April 2, 1942).
32. Gatinha Angora, "Of Good Intentions," in *Cine-Radio Jornal* (May 20, 1942).

Orson Welles: The Semiotics of Focalization in *The Lady from Shanghai*

KAREN MARGUERITE RADELL

T HE NARRATIVE structure of the Orson Welles film, *The Lady from Shanghai* (Columbia Pictures, 1948), appears deceptively simple, much simpler than it really is, but this should not surprise us as one of its themes is the difficulty in distinguishing between appearance and reality and another is the unreliability of all human narrative. *The Lady from Shanghai* appears to be rooted, stylistically, in *film noir*; it has ". . . the voice-over and flashback devices which implicitly challenge conventionally linear narratives" as well as "the extended subjective camera sequence[s]" (Telotte 3). However, even in its obvious conventions it pursues the unconventional as this is a noir film in which the hero is *not* destroyed by the mysterious and deadly female in the story.

We know the hero/narrator has survived his encounter with the "lady" from Shanghai because his voice begins the film, which is one long flashback, and if he had not survived he would not be the narrator.[1] J. P. Telotte argues that *The Lady from Shanghai* "illustrates both [the] difficulties and the potential of an embracing voice-over/flashback" (58). He points out that the film's narrative pattern is one "that seems by turn rectilinear and cyclical, goal-directed like other classical narratives but also bound to the circular trajectory of desire," the desire to shape and order experience as well as the desire to "dwell on the pains and pleasures of the past" (58). In the first scene, we are introduced to the narrator, played by Welles himself, a sailor named O'Hara with a slight but charming brogue, and to the "lady" in question, Elsa Bannister, played by Rita Hayworth, an aloof icon of steely glamor who nevertheless beckons irresistibly to Michael O'Hara with her seductive and somewhat breathless voice. One critic has accurately noted that her deliberately stylized glamor is more contrived than sexual; in fact, she is so sexually aloof she seems "sexually lifeless" to some (Higham 116). However, even if we take her sexual attractiveness for granted, we must remember that "sex in *noir* is usually poisoned, presented characteristically not in a romantic context but a psychotic one" (Hirsh 186). Welles, ordered by Columbia's boss, Harry Cohn, to shoot several close-ups of Hayworth as they were considered essential to any "star" vehicle, responded "by making the close-ups of [her] the most banal and emptily glossy things in the film" (Higham 112).[2]

Reprinted by permission from *Journal of Narrative Technique* 22 (Spring 1992): 97–104.

In this way, of course, Welles as director achieves two important though unrelated results. First, he successfully debunks the self-reverential mythologizing of the Hollywood studio system while simultaneously appearing to cooperate in its process, and second, he makes these forced close-up shots contribute to the powerfully delineated topos of Elsa Bannister as "La belle dame sans merci" (Higham 114) which helps the film's visual subtext undermine the clarifying, ordering impulses of its narrative. Though the film is narrated by Welles the actor as Michael O'Hara, it is Welles the director (and Welles the screenwriter) who subverts the narration of his own character, controlling our responses to what happens, indeed controlling our very perception of what it is that does or does not happen to O'Hara in the film. In fact, in its narrative design, its accumulation of narrative tension, *The Lady from Shanghai* follows a pattern established by Welles' earlier films, including his masterpiece, *Citizen Kane* (Telotte 59):

> With its single voice-over/flashback, *Lady from Shanghai* pursues the same phantoms of desire as its famous predecessor and comments equally on the problems of narration. Of course, its protagonist, the sailor Michael O'Hara, is different—more innocent and obviously less powerful than Kane—and his narration affords a more stable, because singular, point of view. But the result is a similar analysis of the circular, almost self-consuming pattern of desire, accompanied by a similar shattering of the microcosm—or narrative—it tries to project in compensation (Telotte 60).

Welles, as director, has taken care to place the focalizer in this story *outside* the film, although on the surface of things and by conventional narrative standards the opposite appears to be true; after all, what is the point of the first-person narrator if he is not to function as the focalizer? I would argue that Welles has deliberately employed a first-person narration in order to undermine the process and validity of narration itself as a means of understanding. The narrator, Michael O'Hara, constructs or fashions a narrative for himself which seeks to explain the peculiar circumstances of his encounter with Elsa Bannister, her husband Arthur, a crippled and shrewd criminal lawyer, and the other "sharks" in the Bannisters' world, including George Grisby, Arthur Bannister's law partner, and a greasy looking detective named Broome who collects information for Bannister on his divorce cases. In this way, he hopes to understand this episode and at the same time to define himself as a survivor, someone morally superior to the dark forces working on him, someone who deserves to walk away, literally as well as figuratively, from the final act of destruction in which Elsa and Arthur Bannister fatally shoot each other in a fun-house hall of mirrors.

Michael O'Hara, then, is only the apparent focalizer of *The Lady from Shanghai*. If we examine the text of the film closely, we will find great dissonance between the naturally clarifying impulse of the voice-over narration and the film's visual subtext. Orson Welles, as director/auteur of the Michael O'Hara character, subverts O'Hara's position as focalizer, replacing it with himself. As director, he allows the subtext to deconstruct, as it were, the surface narrative. To confirm this we need to look at the film itself for the signs that point to the nature of Welles' intentions; we need to identify the signifiers of Welles' position as external focalizer. We will find these in elements of cinematographic language employed by Welles as director and co-editor.[3]

The importance of images articulated and patterns conveyed by cinematographic language cannot be overestimated, especially with regard to the tension produced in a film like *The Lady from Shanghai* when it is juxtaposed with a closed narrative pattern (one in which the end of the story is known at the beginning). It is "through its procedures of *denotation* [that] cinema is a specific language," rather than a langue (language system) argues Christian Metz in *Film Language: A Semiotics of the Cinema* (97). He insists that

> the concept of *diegesis* is as important for the film semiologist as the idea of art. The word is derived from the Greek [for] narration and was used particularly to designate one of the obligatory parts of judiciary discourse, the recital of facts. The term was introduced into the framework of the cinema by Étienne Souriau. It designates the film's *represented* instance . . . that is to say, the sum of a film's denotation: the narration itself, but also the fictional space and time dimensions implied in and by the narrative, and consequently the characters, the landscapes, the events, and other narrative elements, in so far as they are considered in their denoted aspect. (97–98)[4]

Metz talks further about what he identifies as "a kind of filmic *articulation* . . . which has no equivalent in photography: it is the denotation itself that is being constructed, organized, and to a certain extent codified (*codified*, not necessarily *encoded*)" (99). Metz reminds us that in photography "the denoted meaning is secured entirely through the automatic process of photochemical reproduction; denotation is a visual transfer, which is not codified and has no inherent organization" (98). We get something else entirely in the realm of the visual images of the cinema, where, Metz argues, "a whole semiotics of denotation is possible and necessary, for a film is composed of *many* photographs (the concept of montage, with its myriad consequences)—photographs that give us mostly only partial views of the diegetic referent" (98).

Metz's strongest argument, however, is the point that cinema can be considered a language "to the extent that it orders signifying elements within ordered arrangements different from those of spoken idioms . . . filmic manipulation transforms what might have been a mere visual transfer of reality into discourse" (105). It is this discourse, directed at the audience, that Welles creates and manipulates so superbly in *The Lady from Shanghai*, as distinct from the symbolic (on one level, connotative) elements in the film. This is not to say that the symbolism in the film is less skillfully manipulated; in fact it often draws attention to itself, as with the shark story told by O'Hara at the bizarre "picnic" on the beach or the famous hall of mirrors sequence which constitutes the penultimate scene, and it plays an intrinsic part in the development of the film's discourse.

Both the shark story and the hall of mirrors sequence operate as powerful metaphors in the story, the significance of which I will discuss after identifying some of the elements articulated in the film's visual subtext which form the filmic discourse Welles has constructed to convey his theme of the unreliability of human narrative. The opening of the film sets the scene for the beginning of O'Hara's narrative. We see Elsa Bannister riding alone in a carriage through Central Park and as the strolling sailor Michael crosses her path, we hear him telling us in the voice-over: "When I set out to make a fool of myself, there's very little can stop me." This line is delivered in an ironic, self-deprecating tone which suggests that the speaker, removed from the events of the story by time and space, now finds in its details a sense of wry amusement.

What is compelling is the manner in which the first images of Elsa Bannister are conveyed to us so that they undermine everything she says about herself, her hard-luck story about her parents being White Russian and her having to fend for herself in places like Shanghai. As Charles Higham points out:

> Close-ups of Elsa in the carriage shimmer with an extraordinary intensity, the light on her face even harder than William Daniels' arcs fixed on Garbo's, the hair bleached white, the cheekbones highly polished. The intercut shots of Elsa attacked by thugs have the casual, brutal look of a newsreel. Against this, Michael's lolling walk and the shaky movement of the carriage are matched in tracking shots so as to appear jerky, disconnected. (123)

There are many apparently disconnected elements in the world of the Bannisters, as the flirtatious and romantically inclined O'Hara discovers when he succumbs to the blandishments of work aboard their yacht which are offered him by the seemingly helpless woman he has rescued in the park ("I'll make it worth your while," she breathes at him in her most seductive pose before getting into her luxury convertible and driving away). Lurking behind pillars in the public garage where Michael delivers the rescued Elsa are two characters who keep surfacing later in the story, George Grisby, Arthur Bannister's partner, a man who lusts after Elsa the way Elsa lusts after money, and the ubiquitous Broome, who is employed by Bannister to ferret out information useful in the litigation of his divorce cases.

Lurking is the best way to describe the attitude and posture of Grisby, who floats around Michael and Elsa like a bad smell you can neither identify nor eliminate. His delineation in cinematic language is controlled and economical; in one shot, our very first close-up of Grisby, we know almost everything we need to about this loathsome creature. This first close-up is shot through the wrong end of a pair of binoculars as Grisby watches Elsa and Michael aboard the Bannisters' yacht. The shot establishes several different things at once without a word being spoken or a contrasting shot to establish context: Grisby is jealous of Michael's strength and youthful beauty—Charles Higham calls Grisby "the American hick incarnate" (114); Grisby lusts after Elsa himself; and perhaps most important, Grisby is a kind of voyeur. He contrives to be the extra pair of eyes peering into people's private moments whenever possible. Yet, in spite of his controlled "slimyness," there is a point in the film, when Arthur Bannister humiliates Grisby, that we actually feel some pity for him. (We also pity his clearly depicted but hopeless infatuation with Elsa Bannister, the ice-goddess.)

The denotation of the character of Broome, Bannister's divorce detective, is equally subtle and contributes even more to the deconstruction of the film's ordering narrative. If Grisby is like a bad odor haunting the private moments of Elsa and her reluctant wooer Michael, then Broome is like a bloodhound who will not give up the chase. He dogs the pair relentlessly, even on the yacht, where, dressed in white ducks he pretends to be the steward, and in the Bannister home, where, dressed in white jacket and black tie, he ostensibly carries out the duties of the butler. However, Broome, as we discover, is also part of the film's subtext which signals director Welles' discursive intentions; he is an important part of the confusion between appearance and reality that undermines the power of the narrative to order experience.

Another striking example of visual subtext which signals confusion or tension between reality and appearance is found in the Aquarium scene, where "wide-angle lenses were used for close-ups to achieve the deliberate distortion characteristic of the director's style" (Higham 112).[5] In a furtive rendezvous between Elsa and Michael at the public Aquarium, Elsa "declares" her love for Michael and easily draws him closer into her web of evil.[6] With her dialogue of passion and her arms around Michael, Elsa might also have convinced the viewer of her sincerity, except for the way Welles presents the visual images:

> In the Aquarium scene the lights came from sources simulating those in the tanks, while in fact the tanks were shot separately and matted in after enlargement to give a more striking effect. Welles, through this device, could match selected creatures to the character's thoughts. As Mrs. Bannister describes the murder scene, a shark glides behind her face; as she mentions the lawyer, a slimy conger eel writhes past her (Higham 112).

This same slimy eel repeatedly opens and closes its ugly, cavernous mouth while Elsa pledges her love to Michael, so that our attention is drawn to it rather than to Elsa, who addresses Michael, without a hint of tenderness, as "my beloved fool."

But it is Broome who finally provides a twist to the story, a Broome mortally wounded by a Grisby rendered nearly hysterical at the proximity of his goal of getting Arthur permanently out of the way, getting Arthur's money, and getting the woman he would kill for, Elsa. Grisby's greedy lust blinds him to Elsa's essential coldness. At this point in the film, Grisby's actions contain no surprises, but Broome's are nearly incomprehensible in conventional terms, that is in the terms of conventional narrative. Broome has been presented to us, his character denoted in ways that can only suggest he is a human species of an insect type, tenacious and dirty, boring into the soft underbelly of human weakness to make a living, and like a bug, completely amoral. Yet it is Broome who crawls across the kitchen floor and after calling a doctor (which will bring in the police), feels compelled to warn Elsa that a "real" murder is about to take place, probably her husband's. Broome does not suspect Elsa of being involved in any of the deceit and greed he and Grisby and Bannister flourish in. He does not seem to notice that she is rather indifferent to his serious wound and indeed offers no assistance to him other than to remark: "What's the matter Broome—are you sick?" Broome also pulls himself up to answer the phone when Michael calls, worried about Elsa, at which time Broome warns Michael about Grisby's intention to kill Arthur Bannister and let him, Michael O'Hara, take the rap.

Broome then, in spite of the outward depiction of his character, does not belong to the school of human sharks Michael refers to earlier when he tells the shark story at the Bannister picnic (again—appearance and reality are poles apart—Michael's voice-over tells us that "It was no more a picnic than Bannister was a man"):

> Do you know, once off the hump of Brazil, I saw the ocean so darkened with blood it was black, and the sun fadin' away over the lip of the sky. A few of us had lines out for a bit of idle fishin'. It was me had the first strike. A shark it was, and then there was another, and another shark again, till all about the sea was made of sharks . . . My shark had torn himself away from the hook, and the scent, or maybe the stain it was, and him bleedin' his life away drove the rest of them mad. Then the beasts took to eatin' each other; in their frenzy, they ate at themselves. You could feel the lust of murder like a wind stingin' your eyes, and you could smell the death, reekin' up out of the sea. I never saw anything worse, until this little picnic tonight. And you know, there wasn't one of them sharks in the whole crazy pack that survived?

This disquieting story within a story temporarily silences the unholy trio of Grisby and Arthur and Elsa Bannister. They clearly recognize the metaphor and find it an accurate though uncomfortable reflection of themselves. Later, when the mortally wounded Elsa is lying on the floor of the hall of mirrors, Michael alludes to it with: "Like the sharks, mad with their own blood. Chewing away at their own selves." Elsa Bannister has been chewing away at herself through the entire film.

The distorted, multiple reflections of Elsa and Arthur as they face and kill each other in the hall of mirrors reflect the distortions and contortions of O'Hara's narrative, his attempts to make sense of senseless things, of greed and violence, his attraction to a cold and venal woman (he remarks at the very end that he will probably die trying to forget her). As Bruce Crowther notes:

> Those distorted images revealed in the mirrors provide one of the most powerful visual interpretations in all *film noir* of the confusion between reality and imagination which lies at the genre's heart. (56)

This hall of mirrors sequence plays a key role in Welles' shaping of the film's discourse, a discourse that questions the nature and potential of all human narrative. Of course, as Foster Hirsh reminds us, "reflections in mirrors and windows are a recurrent aspect of *noir* iconography . . . as the double images suggest schizophrenia and masquerade" (90). In Welles' film, the hall of mirrors reinforces, in cinematic language, the point of view of the external focalizer, the director, who is making a narrative that not only lies beyond the normal parameters of narrative, but which, essentially, questions these parameters. When Michael leaves the broken images of the dead husband and the dying wife (without, as André Bazin puts it, "obeying the elementary rule that the heroine should be paid the courtesy of dying in the arms of the rugged sailor" [94]), and steps into the bright sunlight pouring down on the San Francisco Bay, we have an image, which in traditional or conventional cinematic terms suggests a positive resolution of tension, a metaphoric awakening, the surge of possibilities. But we know that this is false, that Michael O'Hara is still confused and circling, figuratively, around the events that brought him so close once again to the scent of death. The narrative he presents us in the film is one that shapes the memory rather than the reality of his encounter with the Bannisters. Welles as director and focalizer roots *The Lady from Shanghai* in what J. P. Telotte calls *film noir*'s "fascination with narration and a desire to speak of discourse's problems and potentials" (218), and offers us a film that, according to André Bazin, "is paradoxically the richest in meaning of [his] films in proportion to the insignificance of the script: the plot no longer interferes with the underlying action, from which the themes blossom out in something close to their pure states" (94). Welles has given us a nearly seamless piece of work in which form exfoliates theme; consequently, *The Lady from Shanghai* makes a valuable contribution both to the study of *film noir* and to the study of narratology. Like most *noir* masterpieces, the power of Welles' film lies in its "truly disconcerting" ability to strike at a fundamental level of existence, to reveal "the disturbing contradictions that mark the modern human experience" (Telotte 35).

Notes

1. The exception to this rule of nature is Billy Wilder's noir masterpiece, *Sunset Boulevard*, in which the dead writer's voice-over narration begins the film.

2. Joseph McBride, in his book *Orson Welles*, reports that Columbia Pictures was so appalled at what Welles had done to Hayworth's "star" image, it held up the film's release for two whole years.

3. Charles Higham, in *The Films of Orson Welles*, discusses in detail the problems Welles had in editing the final version of the film; he ended up reworking it piece by piece, with Virginia Van Upp, both on their hands and knees with the cutting continuity spread out on her office floor. This proved *not* to be the final version after a preview audience made damaging comments on their preview cards.

4. For a discussion of the concept of diegesis, see the Preface, p. 7, of *L'Univers filmique* (Paris, 1953), a collective work under the direction of Étienne Souriau. Cited in Christian Metz, *Film Language: A Semiotics of Cinema*.

5. Higham refers us to Herbert A. Lightman's fine analysis of the film in the June, 1948, issue of *American Cinematographer*.

6. Foster Hirsh, in *The Dark Side of the Screen: Film Noir*, identifies the predatory females of the *noir* terrain as "spider women."

Works Cited

Bazin, André. *Orson Welles: A Critical View*. Trans. Jonathan Rosenbaum. New York: Harper & Row, 1978.

Crowther, Bruce. *Film Noir: Reflections in a Dark Mirror*. New York: Frederick Ungar, 1989.

Higham, Charles. *The Films of Orson Welles*. Berkeley: University of California Press, 1970.

Hirsh, Foster. *The Dark Side of the Screen: Film Noir*. San Diego: A. S. Barnes & Co., 1981.

McBride, Joseph. *Orson Welles*. New York: Viking Press, 1972.

Metz, Christian. *Film Language: A Semiotics of Cinema*. Trans. Michael Taylor. New York: Oxford University Press, 1974.

Telotte, J. P. *Voices in the Dark: The Narrative Patterns of Film Noir*. Urbana: University of Illinois Press, 1989.

"A Really Great Man":
Myth and Realism in *Citizen Kane*

MORRIS BEJA

It isn't enough to tell us what a man did, you've got to tell us who he was.

Rawlston, *in* Citizen Kane

The trouble is, you don't realize you're talking to two people.

Charles Foster Kane

W HEN *Citizen Kane* first appeared, it seemed to be a breakthrough in the realistic presentation of American life in American film. Upon discovering the movie after the war in France, André Bazin classified it as part of Orson Welles's "social realist cycle," and as the cinematic equivalent of "realistic novels in the tradition of, say, Balzac."[1] One can see the accuracy of this emphasis: in the film's technique (both Welles and his cinematographer, Gregg Toland, have stressed that they meant their use of deep focus to correspond to how human beings really see things[2]); in its narrative approach, in which we feel as though we're learning things about Kane's life in much the same way we learn things in "real" life—in snatches, incompletely, and out of strict chronological order; and in its content—Kane is demythologized.

Maybe. Actually, as I hope to show, while Kane is "demythologized" in one narrow sense of the term myth, in a more important sense of that term—referring to tales and patterns of profound significance in a given culture or in all of human existence—Kane becomes a mythic hero to a degree that no one in the film fully perceives. It is perhaps on that level that we may understand Welles's otherwise cryptic response to an interviewer's query about how realistic the presentation of Kane's character is: "It's not a question of realism," he replied.[3]

Much of the effect of the film arises from a dichotomy within the presentation of the character of Kane, who is portrayed both "realistically" and "mythically." On the one hand, he is clearly based on a "real" (historical) figure, William Randolph Hearst; everyone, of course, knows that. Not so generally understood, however, is the way our response to the film is complicated by the overtones and undertones that give Kane the aura of a traditional mythic hero. The resulting tension largely produces the ambiva-

This essay was written specifically for this volume and is published here for the first time by permission of the author.

253

lence in our response to him, and it intensifies the fascination he holds over us, as well as over the other characters within the film.

Citizen Kane opens with that tension: we see a Disney-like fairy-tale castle in a Gothic, mysterious world, but we suddenly leave that world with no transition, as the scene is abruptly cut to the purportedly objective and journalistic approach of the documentary *News on the March*. The style of a documentary series such as De Rochemont's *March of Time* is carefully imitated—not so much parodied as used. *News on the March* epitomizes one of the two major elements in our sense of realism within *Citizen Kane*: verisimilitude, our impression that a real story is being pursued in a real way, as if by a real reporter.

The other chief element in our perception of the film's realism is our pervasive awareness that the life, career, and character of Charles Foster Kane have a real historical basis—in the life, career, and perhaps the character of William Randolph Hearst. The striking similarities cannot be denied, despite Welles's many understandable denials over the years, and we need not rehash here the important ways in which Kane's career echoes Hearst's (as in their acquisition of their first newspapers as young men, leading to an "empire" of many papers throughout the country; or their unscrupulous use of power, as in their fomentation of the Spanish-American War). There are numerous ironies in the relationship between *Citizen Kane* and actual history. Especially intriguing is the fact that when the film was made and released, Hearst was one of the most famous men in America, and the notoriety of the film came about largely because of its having been based on his career. Now, to many people—probably most—Hearst is best known as the fellow who served as the model for Kane.

Nevertheless, while our reaction to Kane is in large part controlled by our awareness of his historical model, it is not completely so. We are also aware that he is fictional. As Kane admonishes Walter Parks Thatcher, we must realize that Kane is "two people." Actually, by the time we get the various accounts from those who knew him, we recognize that Kane is more than just two. But for my purposes in this essay we can stick to that number: on the one hand he is William Randolph Hearst, and on the other he is the classic mythic hero of legend and folklore.

Later in his life Kane shows less insight about his own complexity and insists that, as he is quoted in a title within the news documentary, "I Am, Have Been, And Will Be Only One Thing—An American." Critics who have described him as "mythic" have taken his own lead and have tended to restrict themselves to viewing Kane as archetypally American. This view has been a running motif in criticism of the film, and when Kane is compared to heroes of the past, the comparisons tend to be with figures like Thomas Sutpen in William Faulkner's *Absalom, Absalom!* or, notably, F. Scott Fitzgerald's Jay Gatsby.[4] Such allusions are valuable, but they should not make us lose sight of the measure to which Kane shares the story of many more heroes than those comparisons imply, or the degree to which his story is indeed that of the "monomyth," to use the term Joseph Campbell borrows from James Joyce in describing how, "whether the hero be ridiculous or sublime, Greek or barbarian, gentile or Jew, his journey varies little in essential plan."[5]

Apart from Campbell, other scholars of comparative literature, myth, and folklore have of course discovered that throughout the world, in various societies and in many different ages, the story of the hero has tended to be strikingly similar. A work that was published shortly before *Citizen Kane* appeared and that I find particularly intriguing in regard to Welles's film is Lord Raglan's *The Hero: A Study in Tradition, Myth, and Drama* (1936). In a famous section of that volume, Raglan examines and compares some of the most well-known heroes of various tales and peoples— Moses, Oedipus, Arthur, Robin Hood, Jason, and so on—and comes up with a list of twenty-two events or situations that figure in the lives of such heroes. It is not that the stories of most heroes will have all of them; hardly any will in fact. But a hero's story will encompass many of them, maybe most, and some of the major heroes will have correspondences to almost all of them.

The following is Raglan's run down of the pattern of the story of the hero and its twenty-two components:

(1) The hero's mother is a royal virgin;

(2) His father is a king, and

(3) Often a near relative of his mother, but

(4) The circumstances of his conception are unusual, and

(5) He is also reputed to be son of a god.

(6) At birth an attempt is made, usually by his father or maternal grandfather, to kill him, but

(7) He is spirited away, and

(8) Reared by foster-parents in a far country.

(9) We are told nothing of his childhood, but

(10) On reaching manhood he returns or goes to his future kingdom.

(11) After a victory over the king and/or a giant, dragon, or wild beast,

(12) He marries a princess, often the daughter of his predecessor, and

(13) Becomes king.

(14) For a time he reigns uneventfully, and

(15) Prescribes laws, but

(16) Later he loses favour with the gods and/or his subjects, and

(17) Is driven from the throne and city, after which

(18) He meets a mysterious death,

(19) Often at the top of a hill.

(20) His children, if any, do not succeed him.

(21) His body is not buried, but nevertheless

(22) He has one or more holy sepulchres.[6]

In brief analyses of the stories of various heroes—male heroes, I am afraid it goes without saying—Raglan does not hesitate to "score" them with "points" from his list. Within British tradition, Robin Hood scores a respectable thirteen, Arthur, an impressive nineteen. In classical mythology, Apollo gets eleven, Zeus, fifteen, Theseus, twenty. Oedipus gets twenty-one out of twenty-two, the highest score Raglan grants to any figure, whereupon we notice that he rather pointedly never mentions Jesus—who, it might be argued, would score perfectly, or surely very highly. Biblical figures whom Raglan does discuss include Elijah, who scores nine, Joseph, who scores twelve, and Moses, who does exceptionally well with twenty.

As the reader will surely have guessed, I plan to explore how Kane stands up to such company. But first I should mention that while Raglan's paradigm is probably the best known, variations on it have appeared in the work of a number of other important scholars, before and after him, including Vladimir Propp, Otto Rank, and, again, Joseph Campbell. The latter pays much attention to one element that Raglan does not include in his list, but that may remind us of the role of Jed Leland in *Citizen Kane*: the presence of a friend or helper—or "stooge," as Leland calls himself.

Raglan's breakdown may not at first seem all that helpful to my thesis, since Kane cannot be connected with any of its first five elements. His mother (#1) is not a royal virgin. Nor (#2) is his father a king or (#3) a near relative of his mother. We have no reason to believe that (#4) the circumstances of his conception were unusual, and there are no hints that (#5) he is reputed to be the son of a god. In an extrapolation of what a "myth critic's interpretation" of *Citizen Kane* might be like, in which he presents a clever discussion of how "every leading character in *Citizen Kane* is the incarnation of a mythological figure," Bernard F. Dick suggests that Kane may be associated with Zeus, son of Cronus.[7] But while Dick's resulting connections are interesting, they are also—quite intentionally, surely—more narrow than they need be, for Kane and Zeus are both representative of pervasive patterns involving the mythic hero. In any case, I cannot see awarding Raglan's fifth phase to Kane, although of course "god" is not to be interpreted literally: it can refer to any unusually awesome or powerful authority figure. I shall in fact follow Raglan's example in interpreting the incidents in the pattern of the hero's life broadly—as when he awards Moses item #5 for being said to be the child of Pharaoh's daughter, or equates Robin Hood's death in "an upper room" with #19, death "at the top of a hill" (Raglan, 180, 184).

We can therefore connect #6, the attempt, usually by his father or maternal grandfather, to kill the hero, with the threats made by Kane's father out in the snow at the start of the boy's new life (though not at his birth). As Mrs. Kane says to her husband, it is because Mr. Kane thinks that "what that kid needs is a good thrashing" that the boy, as she puts it, is "going to be brought up where you can't get at him." Thus, (#7) he is spirited away and (#8) reared by foster parents (by Thatcher and by a bank acting as a "guardee-an") in a far country. We are told nothing of his childhood (#9), as we skip in superb match cuts right to Kane's adulthood, when (#10) he goes to his future kingdom or, in Thatcher's terminology, comes "into complete possession"—notably of the Inquirer. His victory (#11)—"over the reigning king," as Raglan expresses it at one point (Raglan, 191)—is over the rival paper, the Chronicle.

Such struggles often take the form of a battle against the father, and in that context we may be tempted to speak of Kane as being victorious over the father-surrogate Thatcher. The feeling that he is the enemy is surely connected in Kane's case with he fact that it was Thatcher who took his mother's love from him, or took him away from her, as fathers and father-surrogates are wont to do.[8] (For his part, according to Leland, Kane "always loved" only his mother.) Kane's rebellion against Thatcher and all he represents is thus all the more understandable: as Otto Rank puts it in *The Myth of the Birth of the Hero*, the rebellious hero "is originally a disobedient son, a rebel against the father."[9] That description entails God-the-father as well; and in the shooting script, although not in the final film, Kane confesses to Thatcher that he used to believe "you were omnipotent."[10] But while Kane may no longer believe in Thatcher's omnipotence, that is not the same as being victorious over him. Indeed, as psychoanalysis (or Franz Kafka, as in *The Trial*, which Welles later adapted into a film) has shown us, the father—the Law of the Father—is too powerful ever to be truly defeated.

Thatcher retains his awesome power even as he is seen to be ridiculous (or think of Welles's portrayal of the advocate in *The Trial*). In contrast, Kane remains childish or reverts to childhood. Our first word of him as an adult after *News on the March* is that he is getting himself a new toy, since he thinks "it would be fun to run a newspaper"; then we see him playing at war—and, as he puts it in his telegram to Wheeler, he even provides the war. He plays house on a grand scale at Xanadu; and he marries a Kewpie doll and makes her sing as if she were a windup toy. (He has wooed her by wiggling his ears and playing shadow games with his fingers.) We see him being rolled around in old age as if in a baby stroller, and he dies with a childish paperweight in his hand, muttering the name of a childhood sled. The trappings surrounding Walter Parks Thatcher, however, retain a sense of his power and authority even after death. If Rosebud is the "dol-lar-book Freud" Welles has accused it of being,[11] and yet more than that at the same time, so is Kane's comment to Thatcher that his own wish in life would have been to be "everything you hate." Another strong figure against whom rebellion turns out to be futile is Gettys—"Boss" Jim Gettys: in a scene witnessed by Kane's wife and mistress, Gettys humiliates him and makes him seem impotent.

One of those two women, Emily, corresponds to the person in Raglan's item #12, the princess whom the hero marries and who is often the daugh-ter of his predecessor: Emily is the niece of the President of the United States—whom Kane intends, although he does not carry it off, to succeed. The other woman, Susan, also serves as representative of the kingdom to which he aspires: she is, Leland reports Kane as saying, "a cross section of the American public." In addition, poor Susan is cast in a role for which she has no inclination, and which, although it does not figure in Raglan's list, is important in many stories of the hero: that of the Woman as Temptress, who lures the hero from his proper road or quest and who leads, directly or indirectly, temporarily or permanently, to his fall.

In item #13, the hero becomes king. Kane is repeatedly described as living in a "castle" or a "palace," and he is said to have an "empire." In *News on the March* he is compared directly to "the Pharaohs," and he is called both "America's Kubla Khan" and "an emperor of newsprint," while Leland speaks of Kane's having built his own "absolute monarchy." He reigns for a time uneventfully (#14) and prescribes laws (#15): Leland compares Kane's "Declaration of Principles" to "the Declaration of Independence, or the Constitution." In that Declaration, moreover, Kane quite explicitly cites his aspiration to be a hero, a "fighting and tireless champion" of the people. (It seems intriguing in my context that—although one almost needs a stop-frame projector to discern this fact—Kane's *second* sled, the one he is given as a boy by Thatcher for Christmas, is called "Crusader.")

Despite his aspiration (#16), Kane loses favor with the gods and/or his subjects—losing not only many of his newspapers and an election, but "the love of the people of this state." He is (#17) driven from the throne and city, becoming a recluse at Xanadu—just as Leland had predicted he would "sail away to a desert island, probably, and lord it over the monkeys" (we have seen the monkeys in the opening shots of the film). He dies (#18) a mysterious death—the entire film is, in a sense, an attempt to solve the mystery of Kane's dying utterance—at the top of a hill (#19), at the very start of the movie. His children (#20) do not succeed him; according to *News on the March*, his only son died in 1918. Kane does not match up with the last two items in Raglan's list, in which the hero is not buried (#21), while nevertheless having one or more holy sepulchres (#22).

I have awarded Kane all Raglan's points from #6 to #20, for a total "score" of 15, which is very high. Only the truly greatest heroes (Oedipus,

Moses, and so on) do any better, while Kane ties with Jason and even Zeus, and does better than Joseph, Elijah, and Apollo. Even if one were to argue with some of my decisions and deny him a couple of points here or there, he would still do quite well—at least as well as Robin Hood, say, at thirteen, or Siegfried, at eleven.

Like many a mythic hero before him—like, as well as unlike, Oedipus, or Arthur, or perhaps even Moses—Kane is after all a failure. Still, even Jed Leland, in his bitter old age, concedes, "I suppose he had some private sort of greatness."

"I might have been a really great man," Kane tells Thatcher. "The whole story is in that," Orson Welles has said.[12]

Yet not the whole story, surely. Recognizing parallels between Kane and traditional mythic heroes does not in itself resolve the mystery that remains regarding Kane and his character, any more than does the recognition of a correlation between Kane's life and Hearst's. Rather, the historical sources and the mythical correspondences work with and against each other. The resulting tensions between realism and myth convey the mystery, power, and illumination we feel as we see and hear the tale of Charles Foster Kane.

Notes

1. *Orson Welles: A Critical View*, trans. Jonathan Rosenbaum (New York: Harper and Row, 1979), 64, 65. See the present volume, 135.

2. See Welles's comments in Peter Bogdanovich, "The Kane Mutiny," *Esquire* 78 (October 1972): 184, and Toland's in "How I Broke the Rules in *Citizen Kane*," *Focus on "Citizen Kane"*, ed. Ronald Gottesman (Englewood Cliffs, N.J.: Prentice-Hall, 1971), 74.

3. Quoted in Juan Cobos, Miguel Rubio, and José Antonio Pruneda, "Orson Welles," trans. Rose Kaplin, in *Interviews with Film Directors*, ed. Andrew Sarris (New York: Avon, 1969), 551, hereafter cited in text as Cobos. See the present volume, 57.

4. See, in particular, Robert Carringer's "*Citizen Kane, The Great Gatsby*, and Some Conventions of American Narrative," *Critical Inquiry* 2 (Winter 1975): 307–25, reprinted in the present volume, 116–34.

5. *The Hero with a Thousand Faces* (New York: Pantheon, 1949), 30, 38.

6. Lord Raglan, *The Hero: A Study in Tradition, Myth, and Drama* (New York: New American Library, 1979), 174–75; hereafter cited in text as Raglan.

7. *Anatomy of Film* (New York: St. Martin's, 1978), 178.

8. For a fuller discussion of some of the arguments I make in this and the next paragraph, in an essay which also deals with others of Welles's films, see my "Where You Can't Get at Him: Orson Welles and 'The Attempt To Escape from Father,'" *Literature/Film Quarterly* 13 (1985): 2–9.

9. *The Myth of the Birth of the Hero and Other Writings*, ed. Philip Freund (New York: Vintage, 1964), 95.

10. Herman J. Mankiewicz and Orson Welles, *The "Citizen Kane" Book* (New York: Bantam, 1971), 181.

11. Quoted in Dilys Powell, "The Life and Opinions of Orson Welles," *London Times*, Sunday, 3 Feb. 1963; cited in Peter Cowie, *A Ribbon of Dreams: The Cinema of Orson Welles* (South Brunswick, N.J.: A.S. Barnes, 1973), 34.

12. Interview with Cobos et al., p. 551. See the present volume, 56.

Welles or Wells?—A Matter of Adaptation

HARRY M. GEDULD

T HE MOST sensational of all adaptations from literature, Orson Welles's Mercury Theatre radio version of H.G. Wells's *The War of the Worlds*, was broadcast over CBS on the evening of 30 October (Halloween) 1938. Recordings of the broadcast are extant and the radio script has been published in Hadley Cantril's *The Invasion from Mars* (1940) and Howard Koch's *The Panic Broadcast* (1970).[1] Historians, biographers and social psychologists have assembled the facts and explored every conceivable aspect of the panic created by the broadcast. They have discussed its demonstration of the nascent power of the mass media and underscored its importance in creating the fame (notoriety?) that brought Welles to Hollywood and to the making of *Citizen Kane*. In short, the scholarly focus has been on the impact and outcome of the radio program. Only cursory attention has been given to the script that created those consequences. Nonetheless, if we are to have a more complete understanding of what the original audience experienced on that memorable night in October 1938, we need to ask some long-overdue questions about the script. How innovative was it in comparison with other radio plays of the period? What sort of adaptation was it? How, precisely, did it diverge from its source? Why were the changes made? Above all, assuming that Welles is accorded main credit for the adaptation (an assumption that has been questioned and that will be considered later), to what extent did the broadcast express his concerns rather than those of H. G. Wells?

The *War of the Worlds* radio script was not, of course, written in a vacuum. It needs to be viewed in relation to two background factors: the conventions and limitations of 1930s radio drama and the influence of radio journalism. These factors were interrelated, but it will be convenient to examine them separately before dealing with the questions I have just raised.

THE CONVENTIONS AND LIMITATIONS OF 1930S RADIO DRAMA

The origins of radio drama in the United States have been traced to 1926, the year Henry Fisk Carlton presented an original sketch entitled "The Three Elevens." In the following year Carlton and William Ford Manley went on to write the first radio adaptations—a series of brief plays based on short stories by O. Henry. Radio drama was soon being adapted from a

This essay was written specifically for this volume and is published here for the first time by permission of the author.

wide variety of stage plays, novels, biographies, and short stories. By the mid-1930s the conventions of radio adaptation had become well established and were being promulgated in a profusion of handbooks on how to write for radio. The authors of these handbooks usually started by differentiating writing for different media—most frequently, for stage plays and radio plays. They generally agreed that there were substantial differences between those forms and that most differences were to the disadvantage of radio drama. Thus James Whipple, in his *How to Write for Radio* (1938), listed twelve means of presentation available to the stage dramatist, but only three (dialogue, sound effects, and music) for the radio dramatist. Whipple considered the radio dramatist to be seriously handicapped by his inability to use any kind of visual presentation, but claimed nevertheless that radio drama was a greater art form than the stage or screen because it offered greater challenges to and made greater demands on the dramatist for overcoming the limitations of his medium.[2]

Adaptation was considered to be no easier than writing original radio drama. Whether it was a stage play or prose fiction that was being adapted, the instructional guides seemed to be in general agreement with the observation of handbook author Sherman Paxton Lawton: "Very little that is written for another purpose is directly usable at the microphone. Most of it must be re-written."[3] A few handbooks actually recommended that the radio dramatist close the book being adapted and refrain from consulting it while writing the adaptation. But the majority advocated a different procedure known as "telescoping." They urged the radio dramatist to study his source carefully with the purpose of adjusting it to the limitations of the medium. This involved two reductive processes: economizing and scenarization. The first involved removing all secondary characters and stripping the plot to its bare essentials. The second required conveying all characterization and action through dialogue or sound effects. The radio dramatist was urged to keep the speeches of individual characters brief. It was believed that long speeches slowed up a play's dramatic action. The radio dramatist was also advised to refrain, as much as possible, from using narrators. It was maintained that extensive use of narrators (or any voices that sounded like radio announcers) discouraged the audience from suspending its disbelief. Dramatists were supposed to eliminate anything that reminded listeners that they were listening to radio. The microphone was expected to eavesdrop on scenes, not to advertise its presence.

The objective of this process—whether it involved an original radio play or an adaptation—was writing a script whose broadcast time (including commercial breaks) could not exceed forty-five minutes, and was usually limited to thirty. This time restriction was a concession to the supposed limited attention span of the radio audience. It frequently allowed for adequate treatments of short stories or one-act plays, but close adaptations of longer works, such as H. G. Wells's novel, were considered out of the question. However, fidelity to the source was never a serious objective of the radio adapters of the period. Their ideal was summed up by Katherine Seymour and John T. W. Martin in their book *Practical Radio Writing* (1938): "A radio adaptation is successful in so far as it has eliminated the non-essential elements, providing the writer's judgment has been sound in deciding which are the non-essentials, and providing, too, that he has been faithful in interpreting the spirit and quality of the original story."[4] We shall consider subsequently how the *War of the Worlds* adaptation measured up to this ideal.

THE INFLUENCES OF RADIO JOURNALISM

In his *Dos and Don'ts of Radio Writing*, Ralph Rogers, president of the Associated Radio Writers of America, reminded his readers, "Don't overlook the fact that the radio audience responds heartily to news broadcasts. Capitalize on this desire for news whenever possible."[5] His advice was sound. The problem for radio dramatists was how to apply news to their art form. News broadcasts were the most popular kind of program in the 1930s, but by 1937, the year Rogers published his book, only one producer had found a successful formula for combining news and radio drama. He was Roy Edward Larsen, later to become president of Time, Inc. In 1928 Larsen launched a series of ten-minute radio programs called "News Casts." They consisted of news bulletins based on items selected from the pages of *Time* magazine. In the following year Larsen replaced "News Casts" with a series entitled "News Acting." Instead of news bulletins, "News Acting" presented original five-minute radio plays on current events, performed by casts of professional actors. These short plays proved so successful that Larsen developed an even more ambitious series of news dramatizations under the title "The March of Time."[6] The first program was broadcast 6 March 1931, preceding the *March of Time* film series by four years. Ironically, the film series is now best known indirectly through Welles's brilliant parody at the beginning of *Citizen Kane*, and that parody in turn has obscured the fact that the radio series exerted a greater influence on Welles than the film series.

The radio "March of Time" was broadcast over CBS or NBC, sometimes once, sometimes three times a week, during 1931–35 and 1941–45. Welles was one of the professional actors who participated in the series, and among his colleagues were Agnes Moorehead, Paul Stewart, Ray Collins, and Everett Sloane, all of whom would be recruited by him for the Mercury Theater on the Air and would eventually appear in the cast of *Citizen Kane*.

The radio "March of Time" was the most popular news program of the 1930s. But as a news program it was an anomaly. As we have already noticed, it did not actually broadcast news; it broadcast dramatizations based on the news. It conveyed the semblance of authenticity rather than authenticity itself. Instead of presenting the recorded voices of celebrities, it employed actors to impersonate them in situations that might resemble the facts, or that might be purely imaginary. Like *Citizen Kane*, it repeatedly blurred the lines between fact and fiction, as well as between journalism and entertainment. In spite of that (or more probably because of it), radio audiences found "The March of Time" more exciting than regular newscasts and more credible than most radio plays. But the listener who got the most out of the series was Orson Welles. It suggested the kind of radio play he would go on to create and it exemplified how to create it. Larsen's series had turned ersatz news into radio drama. Welles's *War of the Worlds* adaptation would transform radio drama into ersatz news, using many of the techniques of "The March of Time."

The most important of those techniques was the use of dramatic voices that did not represent characters in the usual sense. They fell into two main categories. The first encompassed voices that belonged uniquely to radio, such as announcers, interviewers, newscasters, weather forecasters, wireless operators, and radio hams. Their presence in a radio drama had a purpose comparable to D. W. Griffith's use of authentic-looking historical recreations (such as Lincoln and his generals) in the context of a fictional narrative: that is, to transform fiction into apparent fact. Relevant sound effects, creating and sustaining what Evan William Cameron has called "a sense of a continuous and unbounded spatial environment,"[7] were also used in combination with these "nonfiction" voices to persuade radio audiences that what they were listening to was actually going on in the real world.

Here, without the sound effects, are two brief examples. The first is from the "March of Time" program of 28 January, 1937, which dealt with a natural disaster in the Midwest[8]; the second, from *The War of the Worlds* adaptation, is unmistakably an imitation of it:

(I)   3rd HAM
            W9AUH. W9AUH. Louisville, calling
            WHZG. Need medical supplies desperately.
            Also doctors, nurses and extra
            police . . . Send whatever you can.
            Situation desperate. 'Bye.

                                 4th HAM
            W9SQ calling WHZG. Fire has broken
            out. 20,000 threatened. (FADE). Rush
            dynamite, pumps, anything. Fire has got
            to be put out.

                                 WINDHAM
            Go ahead. I can't hear you. Repeat
            your call. Tell me where you are. Come in
            please . . . Come in. Come in . . .

(II)   OPERATOR ONE
This is Bayonne, New Jersey, calling Langham
Field . . . Come in, please . . . Come in,
please . . .

OPERATOR TWO
This is Langham Field . . . go ahead. . . .

OPERATOR ONE
Eight army bombers in engagements
with enemy tripod machines over Jersey Flats.
Engines incapacitated by heat ray. All
crashed. . . . Enemy now discharging
heavy black smoke in direction of—

OPERATOR THREE
This is Newark, New Jersey . . .
This is Newark, New Jersey . . .
Warning! Poisonous black smoke pouring in from
Jersey marshes. Reaches South Street. Gas masks
useless . . .

OPERATOR FOUR
2X2L . . . calling CQ . . .
2X2L . . . calling CQ . . .
2X2L . . . calling CQ . . .
Come in, please . . .

In addition to such typical radio voices, "The March of Time" used narrators extensively, in violation of one of the most hallowed conventions of the handbooks on writing radio drama. Many handbooks also maintained that dialogue increased the pace of a radio play, while narrators slowed it up. But the "March of Time" repeatedly disproved that notion by using narrators to create vivid sound montages, which heightened the pace of the dramatic action. A typical example is the following passage, from the same broadcast of 28 January, 1937:

VOICE OF TIME (OVER MUSIC)
And from all over the flood area, each hour brings
new tales of suffering and disaster; at Portsmouth
a house swirls down the river, its five occupants
screaming to helpless folk on the shore. A match
is thrown on oil-coated waters at Huntingdon, West
Virginia, and when the flames die out, a small boat
is found; in it the charred skeleton of a woman at
one end and at the other, the skeleton of a little
child, a blackened collie dog clasped in her arms.

At Cincinnati, a fireman, after a four-hour fire is
extinguished, is found standing rigidly, grasping
his still spouting hose, frozen . . . (Seymour, 135)

In such passages as I have quoted, "The March of Time" demonstrated that radio plays did not have to be restricted to the spatial and temporal frame of dialogue scenes. Narrators and various "nonfiction" voices could shift the focus of attention wherever or whenever the dramatist desired. They could create a multiplicity of scenes, interact with one another or with the dialogue episodes, and could offer the widest possible range of viewpoints or perspectives on any given situation. In short, they could provide the radio dramatist with the means of achieving aurally much of what cinema achieves through editing.

More and more radio dramatists in the 1930s took advantage of this liberation of radio from the limitations of stage drama. Among them was Archibald MacLeish, whose radio verse play, *Air Raid*, dealt with the bombing of a fictitious European town. The announcer (Ray Collins, on loan from the Mercury Theater) conveyed the impression of being omnipresent, and his vivid commentary was backed by an array of realistic sound effects. Yet the play's occasionally rhetorical text and its non-American location precluded any anticipation of the public reaction to the "War of the Worlds" broadcast. Nonetheless, one listener followed the program with especially rapt attention. It was Orson Welles. Macleish's play must have given him further confirmation of the dramatic effectiveness of the techniques of the radio "March of Time." Final confirmation would come only four days later, when he broadcast his adaptation of *The War of the Worlds*.

THE ADAPTATION

I have called it Welles's adaptation, but Welles's responsibility for the radio script of *The World of the Worlds* has been called into question by its publication—not once but twice—under the name of Howard Koch. Frank Brady notes that Welles was infuriated to find that Howard Koch was named author of the adaptation when it was first published in Hadley Cantril's *The Invasion from Mars* (1940). Welles wrote Cantril: "Now it's perfectly true that Mr. Koch worked on *The War of the Worlds* since he was at that time a regular member of my writing staff. To credit the broadcast version to him, with the implication that its conception as well as execution was his, is a gross mistake."[9] He pointed out that in addition to his own involvements with it, John Houseman and Paul Stewart had also made important contributions to the script. It should be noted that recordings of the original broadcast as well as the text of the play that Cantril published in 1940 make no mention of Koch's name. Both sources indicate that the show opened with the following statement:

> The Columbia Broadcasting System and its affiliated stations present Orson Welles and the Mercury Theatre on the Air in *War of the Worlds* by H. G. Wells.

Only in Koch's book, *The Panic Broadcast* (1967), does the script open with a statement—evidently inserted gratuitously at some date subsequent to the broadcast—to the effect that the play was by Koch. Koch's brief account of the writing of the script underscores the notion that he was its sole creator:

> At the time I was a young playwright doing my first professional job, which was writing the radio plays for the Mercury Theatre's Sunday evening programs sponsored by CBS and which were built around the name and talents of Orson Welles . . . Each week by rehearsal time I was responsible for sixty pages of script dramatizing some literary work—usually a novel or story—assigned to me by Orson or his co-producer, John Houseman, both of whom had pretty exacting standards . . . A day came when a novella was handed me—H. G. Wells's *The War of the Worlds*—with instructions from Houseman to dramatize it in the form of news bulletins. Reading the story, which was laid in England and written in narrative style, I realized I could use practically nothing but the author's idea of a Martian invasion and his description of their appearance and their machines. In short, I was being asked to do an almost entirely original hour-length play in six days. I called Houseman, pleading to have the assignment changed to another subject. He talked to Orson and called back. The answer was a firm no. This was Orson's favorite project . . . The six days before the broadcast were one nightmare of scenes written and rewritten between frantic telephone calls and pages speeding back and forth to the studio. (Koch, 12–15)

Although Koch's account mentions no other names as contributors, there is no reason to believe that the adaptation of *The War of the Worlds* was an exception to Welles's usual collaborative procedure of preparing scripts for the Mercury Theater on the Air. Koch makes it clear that he had no particular interest in *The War of the Worlds*. He considered it a "silly" story and "not particularly believable."[10] The adaptation was simply another assignment handed to him. At the same time, he indicates that the adaptation was "Orson's favorite project"—which would suggest that Welles gave it far more attention than usual. And this not only explains Koch's reference to "a nightmare of scenes written and rewritten between frantic telephone calls," but it also suggests that his original draft was extensively changed to conform to what Welles had in mind. More convincing than Koch's account is the following statement by Welles, in his letter to Cantril: "The idea for *The War of the Worlds* broadcast and the major portion of its execution was mine. Howard Koch was very helpful in the second portion of the script and did some work on the first, most of which it was necessary to revise."[11]

To sum up, the adaptation should be considered Welles's rather than Koch's because Welles's involvement with the project was at every stage as

much as or greater than Koch's. Welles conceived the project. He super-
vised the writing and rewriting of the script and contributed his own suggestions to it. Finally, he directed the play and acted in the lead role. It
was his adaptation just as *Stagecoach* was John Ford's film, even though
the screenplay was by Dudley Nichols. Koch's contribution to the *War of
the Worlds* broadcast was merely one among several.

Koch's claim with regard to the source of the adaptation is no less cava-
lier than the rest of his account. He insists that he was able to use "practically nothing" from H. G. Wells but the "idea of a Martian invasion and . . .
[Wells's] description of their appearance and their machines." Unlike the
rest of Koch's statement, this claim is not a matter for debate. It is demonstrably untrue. It should be noted that Orson Welles did not make a similar claim.

The broadcast version was, indeed, a free adaptation—but it was not as
free as Koch would have us believe. Comparison with the novel reveals
that the adaptation affected three different categories of material: what
was retained, what was eliminated, and what was changed. What was
retained includes not only what Koch mentioned, but also the following:

1. Direct quotation or paraphrase of passages from the novel, comprising much of the script's prologue and virtually the entire dialogue in
   the second half of the script—which is taken almost verbatim from
   Book 2, chapter 7 of the novel.

2. All the material in the script relating to the isolation of the main narrator, who believes for a while that he is the last man on Earth; his
   wanderings through a desolate and ruined landscape; his description of a deserted and ruined city; his discovery of the dead
   Martians; and his explanation of their deaths.

This amounts to a considerable borrowing from the novel. At the same
time, there are numerous omissions—as one might expect in a 60-page
script based on a work that runs to some 240 pages (the text of the standard, "Atlantic" edition of H. G. Wells's work). These omissions are mainly
matters of detail. But the script also omits (or fails to provide equivalents
for) two important episodes: an episode in which the narrator-hero and a
cowardly and a mean-spirited curate are trapped by the Martians,[12] and
the novel's lengthy description of Martian physiology.[13] Welles obviously
omitted the curate episode to avoid offending the religious sensibilities of
some of his listeners. The fascinating account of Martian physiology was
probably excluded for two reasons: it might have been too horrifying and
it would have turned the second half of the play into a virtual monologue.
Far more evident than the omissions are the script's changes. The novel
takes place in the south of England in the last years of the nineteenth century. The script updates the story to 1938 and transfers the setting to New
Jersey and New York City. With this relocation to the United States comes

an Americanization of some of the language, a shift of emphasis towards science and sophisticated military technology, and a diminution of the novel's moral and social concerns. When they land in the United States, the Martians are confronted by bombers and by highly mechanized field artillery. More significantly, the novel's single narrator, an anonymous philosopher, is replaced by a skeptical scientist (Professor Pierson, played by Orson Welles) who at first refuses to believe that living intelligence could exist on Mars but later witnesses the first Martian to land on Earth. His viewpoint is augmented by the perspectives of numerous secondary narrators (announcers, radio operators, eyewitnesses).

The updating and relocation of the story are keys to understanding Welles's objectives with regard to the adaptation. The subtext of H. G. Wells's novel was the Day of Judgement for British imperialism. It had taken its cue from a comment of Wells's brother, Frank. One afternoon during the 1890s the two brothers were strolling through the peaceful Surrey countryside discussing the extermination of the native Tasmanian population by British settlers, when Frank had a sudden thought: "Suppose some beings from another planet were to drop out of the sky suddenly, and begin laying about them here!"[14] Seizing on the idea, H. G. Wells wrote a novel that turned the tables on the colonialists with a vengeance. He depicted the British—not their colonial subjects—being exterminated by a superior technological power. It was a vision that had some validity in 1898, but in 1938 Orson Welles was far more concerned with the rising threats of fascism and Nazism than with the residual problems of the British Empire. A close adaptation of *The War of the Worlds* would have struck American listeners as nothing more than a quaint piece of Victoriana, but updating it allowed Welles to exploit the newfound possibilities of radio and to give the narrative a degree of topical relevance. These two objectives are evident in the structure of the broadcast, the script of which falls into two halves, separated by a commercial break during the actual broadcast. These two halves are distinctly different in form, style, and purpose.

The first half traces a series of events from the initial Martian landing to the obliteration of all human resistance. Overtly influenced by the radio "March of Time" style, it totally demolished the established notion that anything in a broadcast play that reminded audiences that they were listening to radio had the effect of undercutting dramatic illusion. This section of the "War of the Worlds" script used radio explicitly and reflexively for the purpose of creating verisimilitude. Contemporary newspaper commentaries and subsequent studies of the broadcast convey the impression that it was the program's flash bulletins that provoked the panic—that many listeners who tuned in to the broadcast after it had started mistook those bulletins for the real thing. In fact, the script clearly reveals that listeners were bombarded not only by flash bulletins but also by many other techniques that undoubtedly shaped their credulity. The most striking of those techniques were as follows:

1. Marshalling the entire spectrum of news broadcasting styles of the 1930s. Among these were the voices of a forecaster giving a weather report; familiar-sounding announcers interrupting regular programming to issue statements and flash bulletins; a mobile radio unit providing a field report; a roving commentator interviewing an eminent scientist; a public official delivering a proclamation; and a fighter pilot contacting ground control as he goes into action.

2. Using program interruptions, fades, and various sound glitches supposedly caused by atmospheric or on-location conditions.

3. Making direct allusions to the microphone. Typically, in the middle of his commentary an announcer would remark, "I'm pulling the microphone with me as I talk. I'll have to stop the description until I've taken a new position."

4. Indiscriminately referring to real and imaginary places, thereby deliberately blurring the distinction between fact and fiction.

One further technique was to have far-reaching developments in Welles's later work. This was fragmenting the narrative to remove the impression that a play was being broadcast. Although the story unfolds in a strictly linear fashion, this was not readily apparent from the mosaic of material that provides the narrative information. The objective of this fragmentation of narrative material was to convey the impression that a normal sequence of "non fiction" programming was in progress. The play opens with a factlike statement, tying what follows with the evening of 30 October 1938, the actual time and date of the broadcast. The play continues not with the introduction of characters and a dramatic situation, but with a weather report and the start of a concert of light music. The dramatic situation develops almost imperceptibly as events fall into place in the form of news annnouncements, bulletins, interviews and on-location broadcasts.

We can now see that this technique of using a multiplicity of voices to develop a single story from many perspectives was Welles's first embryonic attempt at the narrative form of *Citizen Kane*, which similarly develops out of a simulated news program.

The second half of the *War of the Worlds* script is in total contrast to what precedes it. This section focuses on the experiences of a single character, the same Professor Pierson who was interviewed when the first Martian cylinder landed. In a lengthy monologue, Pierson describes his wanderings through the ruins of New England, convinced that he is the last living human being. His monologue gives way to a dialogue when he encounters an aggressive Stranger with a plan for destroying the invaders and taking over the Earth. Repudiating the Stranger's plan, the professor continues his wanderings. There follows a second and final lengthy monologue in which Professor Pierson recounts his arrival in a deserted New York City and his unexpected discovery of the decaying corpses of the Martians: "They were killed by the putrefactive and disease bacteria against which their systems were unprepared." Pierson's monologue concludes with a vision of the Earth restored to normalcy.

This second part of the script contains none of the devices of radio journalism that characterize the first half. Since the setting is a ruined world in which radio has ceased to exist, Pierson's two monologues and his dialogue with the Stranger could not possibly have been "justified" as radio broadcasts. Except for the inordinate length of the monologues, the second half of the script was essentially a reversion to pre-"March of Time" radio drama, in which the microphone inexplicably eavesdropped on the situations it presented. The purpose of this section was mainly ideological: its centerpiece was a discussion of the survival of the fittest in the face of a ruthless enemy. Most of that discussion was derived from the novel, but, as we shall see, Orson Welles added one passage that expressed his own political fears.

As many commentators have observed, in updating the story and transferring its location from southern England to New England, Welles was exploiting American concerns with the ongoing crises in Europe and the Far East. Those concerns, associated with frequent news stories about developments in aviation, were simultaneously feeding growing fears of attacks on the United States from the air by invading armies. But in adapting H. G. Wells's novel, there was a further item on Welles's agenda. Throughout most of the 1930s Welles was disturbed by the possibility that American democracy might be subverted from within. Several years prior to the *War of the Worlds* project he had been involved in a number of memorable productions of the Federal Theater Project. One with which he was not involved particularly intrigued him. It was a stage adaptation of Sinclair Lewis's novel *It Can't Happen Here* (1935), which dealt with an imaginary fascist takeover of the United States. Lewis's work seemed topical to Welles when he saw the play in 1936, and it still seemed topical in 1939 when he tried, unsuccessfully, to persuade RKO to let him direct a film version of the novel. In the interim he had managed to insinuate the possibility of internal subversion into the script of "The War of the Worlds." The word "insinuate" must be emphasized. Whereas the first half of the play is dominated by the theme of alien invasion, the second half brings up the notion of an internal takeover at only one point. This occurs at the end of the dialogue between Professor Pierson and the Stranger. In Wells's novel the Stranger, identified as an artilleryman, outlines a daring plan for overcoming the Martians. The narrator (Pierson's equivalent) is initially impressed, but eventually goes on his way when he realizes that the artilleryman is not a man of action but merely a big talker. The radio script follows the novel up to the point where the Stranger envisages human beings seizing control of the Martian weapons (heat-rays). It then adds the following entirely new piece of dialogue, which underscores the kind of threat that might emanate not from any alien source, but from totalitarian elements within the United States:

STRANGER

Imagine having one of them lovely things
with its heat-ray turned wide and free! We'd
turn it on Martians, we'd turn it on men.
We'd bring everybody down to their knees.

PIERSON

That's your plan?

STRANGER

You and me and a few more of us we'd own the world.

PIERSON

I see.

STRANGER

Say, what's the matter? Where are you going?

PIERSON

Not to *your* world . . . Good-bye, Stranger . . .

However meaningful such additions were to Welles, the adaptation incensed the author of the novel. Its extensive changes must have reminded him of other liberties taken with his novel that had aroused his ire forty years earlier: In 1897 and 1898 two American yellow-press journals had published unauthorized versions of the novel, one relocating the action to New York City, the other to Boston.[15]

When details of the panic reached H. G. Wells in England, he ordered his New York representative, Jacques Chambrun (who had granted permission for a radio adaptation to be broadcast) to voice his protests to CBS. Chambrun told the CBS representatives, "It was not explained to me that this dramatization would be made with a liberty that amounts to a complete rewriting of *The War of the Worlds* and renders it into an entirely different story. Mr. Wells and I consider that by so doing the Columbia Broadcasting System should make a full retraction. Mr. H. G. Wells is personally deeply concerned that any work of his should be used in a way, and with totally unwarranted liberty, to cause deep distress and alarm throughout the United States." Orson Welles reacted to this statement by praising the novel on the one hand and insisting, on the other, that the broadcast "constituted a legitimate dramatization of a published work."[16] In his biography of H. G. Wells, David C. Smith comments:

The use of the book's title (and the transposed plot) was probably simply a misunderstanding. Wells was concerned that the radio show would hurt his message of the period (he had just been lecturing in America, and was on the way to Australia within a month) but in the event his stock was raised by the show, which traded on beginning fears in the U.S. of the German and Japanese menace.[17]

H. G. Wells's wrath was appeased by an apology and financial compensation from CBS, and he harbored no lingering resentment towards Orson Welles. Indeed, the two men had a cordial encounter in Texas in 1940 shortly before the writer published his novel *Babes in the Darkling Wood*, and about a year later, when Welles had become Hollywood's wunderkind, H. G. Wells sent him a telegram congratulating him on his masterly film, *Citizen Kane*. Regrettably, H. G. Wells seems never to have appreciated the fact that Welles's radio adaptation of his novel had, in its own way, been as revolutionary an achievement as the film. But in that respect he was no more lacking in percipience than most of the commentators who, over the years, have demonstrated far more interest in the panic than in the remarkable script that provoked it.

Notes

1. Hadley Cantril, *The Invasion from Mars: A Study in the Psychology of Panic* (Princeton, N.J.: Princeton University Press, 1940); Howard Koch, *The Panic Broadcast: Portrait of an Event* (New York: Avon Books, 1970); Koch hereafter cited in text.

2. James Whipple, *How to Write for Radio* (New York: McGraw-Hill, 1938), 9, 21.

3. Sherman Paxton Lawton, *Radio Drama* (Boston: Expression Company, 1938) 30.

4. Katherine Seymour and John T. W. Martin, *Practical Radio Writing* (London and New York: Longmans, Green & Co., 1938), 117; hereafter cited in text as Seymour.

5. Ralph Rogers, *Dos and Donts of Radio Writing* (Boston: Associated Radio Writers, 1937), 14.

6. On the radio "March of Time," see Raymond Fielding, *"The March of Time," 1935–1951* (New York: Oxford University Press, 1978), 8–18.

7. Evan William Cameron, *"Citizen Kane*: The Influence of Radio Drama on Cinematic Design," in *Papers of the Radio Literature Conference, 1977*, ed. Peter Lewis (Durham, NC, 1978), 93.

8. The "March of Time" excerpt is from Seymour, 134.

9. Quoted in Frank Brady, *Citizen Welles* (New York: Charles Scribner's Sons, 1989), 177; hereafter cited as Brady.

10. Quoted in Brady, 166.

11. Quoted in Brady, 177.

12. H.G. Wells, *The War of the Worlds*, Book 1, chapter 13, Book 2, chapters 1–5.

13. *The War of the Worlds*, Book 2 chapter 2.

14. *Strand Magazine* 59 (1920): 154. H. G. Wells dedicated the novel to Frank, for "the rendering of his idea."

15. See David Y. Hughes, *"The War of the Worlds* in the Yellow Press," *Journalism Quarterly* (University of Minnesota) 43 (1966): 639–46.

16. Quoted in Brady, 175.

17. David C. Smith, *H. G. Wells: Desperately Mortal* (New Haven and London: Yale University Press, 1986), 76.

The Director as Actor

JAMES NAREMORE

ORSON WELLES would never have been given an opportunity to direct in Hollywood had he not also been an actor. He was best known to the public as a radio personality, and he later became famous as the man who played Harry Lime in *The Third Man*. Throughout his career he depended on his star image in order to acquire financing for his favorite projects. He was, in fact, one of the few great auteurs who found it necessary to perform in almost every film he made. (*The Other Side of the Wind* is a notable exception to this rule; even in *The Magnificent Ambersons*, Welles is present as the omniscient narrator.) Perhaps he ought to be described as an amateur director and a professional actor, because he usually worked behind the camera for love and in front of the camera for money.

But if acting provided Welles with a source of income, it also affected his idea of directing in important ways. In the late 1930s, when he had become New York's most influential exponent of conceptual theater, he wrote an essay in which he speculated ironically on this phenomenon. The director, he noted, was a relatively new character in theatrical history; Shakespeare, for example, would not have recognized such a person, and nineteenth-century theatrical companies had relied on self-effacing stage managers. For hundreds of years the actors—and particularly the stars—controlled performances; then, in the period between the 1880s and the 1920s, a new fashion emerged, typified by the carefully designed spectacles of David Belasco and Hardin Craig, and by director-centered ensembles founded by Konstantin Stanislavsky and Vsevolod Meyerhold. The rise of the director, however, did not mean the death of the actor. "We are so proud of the fact that we don't allow old-time stars on the stage today," Welles remarked, "we forget that their influence from the fifth row center can be much more insidious."[1]

As a man who admired the "old-time stars," Welles managed theater and film in such a way as to keep his own conceptions and performing idiom at the center of our attention. He was the farthest thing from what we now know as an "actor's director," and as a performer he appeared in more bad films than anyone except Marlon Brando; even so, his acting technique was in many ways homologous with the narrative and audiovisual components of his work. To appreciate this point, we need only con-

This essay was written specifically for this volume and is published here for the first time by permission of the author.

sider the most famous close-up of his movie career: his first appearance in Carol Reed's *The Third Man*. The shot depends very little on makeup and not at all on Welles's celebrated voice, but as the critic Michael Anderegg has observed, it functions as a kind of signature, enabling Welles the star to enter the film in spectacular and witty fashion, like a rabbit from a hat.[2] The camera is tilted and angled downward, looking obliquely at his face in a style that roughly approximates the out-of-kilter effect of some of Welles's compositions; meanwhile Welles collaborates by lowering his head and turning to a three-quarter profile, so that he appears to be smiling back at the camera from a sidelong, under-the-lashes position. In the context of the narrative, the close-up is supposed to represent what Joseph Cotten sees, but it also allows Welles to engage in direct address to the audience. Shrouded in dramatic darkness, wearing a black hat and a topcoat that looks rather like a cape, he provokes a frisson of sinister unease mingled with a sense of amused recognition. Like Laurence Olivier as Richard III or Tony Perkins as Norman Bates, he plays the role of a theatrical villain who threatens his audience by looking at them. But unlike Olivier and Perkins, he is also himself—"your obedient servant," as he often said on the radio, shyly taking a bow.

Most of Welles's performances had something of the curious ambiguity or double purpose I am trying to describe in this close-up, and a similar doubleness carried over into the form of virtually all the dramatic shows he directed for radio, film, and television. Indeed, I would argue that Welles's major accomplishment as both an actor and director was his ability to synthesize two apparently contradictory forms of theatricality: On the one hand, he was a brilliant practitioner of what John Houseman called "magical effect," and he was clearly indebted to a romantic or gothic tradition of Shakespearean drama, grand opera, and stage illusionism; on the other hand, he was also a didactic, somewhat Brechtian storyteller whose cultural politics were shaped during the period of the Popular Front, and whose technique was visibly rhetorical and strongly dependent on direct address. The tension between these extremes—in other words, the tension between Welles as conjurer and Welles as narrator—accounts for many of the special qualities of his films in general.

The dialectical relation between the two important aspects of Welles's work can be seen most clearly in *F for Fake*, where he appears as a narrator-magician, and where he functions as a cross between a pedagogue and a con man. At the beginning of the film he makes a key disappear and reappear; but then, in his role as guide, he cautions us that the key isn't "symbolic of anything," because "this isn't that sort of movie." Later, he confesses to being "a charlatan," and he quotes the French magician Robert Houdin to the effect that "a magician is an actor who plays the role of a magician." Having expounded on the philosophical implications of trickery and forgery, however, he easily slips back into his illusionist's persona, fooling us with a cleverly edited, shaggy-dog story about Picasso.

In a sense, Welles's entire career as an actor was predicated on his ability to dazzle audiences while he was lecturing to them—a complicated purpose that was both enhanced and threatened by the machinery of mechanical reproduction. Thus in 1940, at about the time when he was beginning work on *Citizen Kane*, he delivered an unpublished lecture entitled "The New Actor," in which he theorized the need for an overtly rhetorical performing style that would run counter to both Stanislavskian aesthetics and the classic realism of Hollywood. He began the lecture by making a distinction between what he called "formal" and "informal" drama. The formal drama, he explained, belonged to rigidly hierarchical cultures, and was truly ritualistic (rather like a church service or a bullfight), inculcating little sense of actorly style or personality; the informal drama, in contrast, grew out of modern, relatively flexible societies, and produced idiosyncratic actors who treated the audience on a somewhat personal basis. In the informal tradition, which for Welles included all European theater from Shakespeare to the present, "it is impossible to be a great actor unless you deal with your audience."[3] Before the establishment of fully representational, proscenium theater, this "dealing" took specific forms: "We know that Chaliapin adored the gallery and loathed the expensive seats. The greatest moment for the Russian peasants was when Chaliapin sneered at the big people and played for the gallery when he played Boris Goudonof." But in more recent times, Welles argued, the situation had changed: "Even before the movies, actors stopped considering their audiences. It was the constant effort of people like Stanislavsky in a very serious way and John Drew in a frivolous way to pretend there is a fourth wall. This is death to acting style. It is practically impossible to create a new acting style which excludes the direct address to the audience."

Welles's insistence on immediate contact with the public cannot fail to remind us of Brecht, whom I have already mentioned. Let me quickly add, however, that Brecht and Welles should be kept somewhat distinct, because they had different politics and different cultural agendas. To be sure, Welles was for some time committed to a political theater, and like every left-wing intellectual in America during the 1930s, he knew about Brecht's writings. In fact, Marc Blitzstein's *The Cradle Will Rock*, which Welles directed in a famous impromptu performance, was dedicated to "Bert Brecht" (see the title page of the playscript in the Lilly Library archive), and was an attempt to apply the principles of *The Threepenny Opera* and *Mahagony* to an American situation. Richard Wilson was fond of recalling a memorable day in the late 1940s when Welles and Brecht actually met in New York. According to Wilson, Brecht appeared backstage after a matinee performance of the Mercury Theater production of *Around the World in Eighty Days*, puffing a cigar and effusively praising Welles's idea for the play.[4] During this period, Welles was under consideration as the director of *Galileo*, and not long afterward, according to Barbara Leaming, he inserted a series of complex allusions to Brecht's famous essay on Chinese acting into *The Lady from Shanghai*.[5] Nevertheless, throughout his career Welles remained a political liberal and a star; unlike Brecht, he did not encourage his audience to talk back to the spectacle, and his idea of the theater remained expressionist and "magical," in a secular, quasi-Freudian sense. All of his work was dependent on structures of fascination and illusion, and on his own role as manipulator. Perhaps for that reason he was regarded within the entertainment industry as a "showman"—albeit an uncooperative one.

These differences aside, Welles clearly shared certain attitudes with Brecht, especially a hatred of fascism, a love of pedagogy, and a critical attitude toward bourgeois realism. Both men favored types of drama that used a good deal of narration, and both were aware that the cinema and the radio inhibited direct address, erecting an invisible barrier between the actor and the audience. Welles loved the trickery inherent in the film medium, and he belongs to a line of cinematic magicians that begins with Georges Méliès; but at the same time he was a critic of the mass media's potential for demagoguery—a theme that preoccupied him in the "War of the Worlds" broadcast, in the uncompleted *Heart of Darkness*, and in *Citizen Kane*. As a result, his best work is both imaginative and cerebral, both oneiric and satiric.

Welles's attack on what he once called the "pallid" realism of mainstream American cinema was twofold, bearing traces of the different types of theatricality I have been discussing. In the first place, he experimented with complex forms of narration, some of which I shall mention in a moment. In the second place, he drew on a flamboyant and old-fashioned theatrical rhetoric, so that he often seemed anachronistic. He filled his appearances on the screen with signifiers of impersonation—wearing false noses, brandishing cigars, dressing in black, speaking in accents or deep Shakespearean tones—so that in later years he was regarded as a somewhat campy figure. In a similar fashion, he elicited unorthodox behavior from the people he directed. Stars like Rita Hayworth and Charleton Heston seemed to be participating in a masquerade when they worked for Welles, and everyone else became unusually animated or stylized. George Coulouris, who played Thatcher in *Citizen Kane*, once told an interviewer that "the scene in which we argue back and forth in the newspaper office is not conventional movie acting. With other actors or another director, it would have been 'brought down' a lot and lost a good deal."[6] In fact the entire Thatcher section of the film is a foreshadowing of a technique that would become increasingly important to Welles's later work; the players project their lines to a much greater degree than in an ordinary movie, ignoring the conventional idea that acting for the camera ought to be low-key. Agnes Moorehead, Ray Collins, and Dorothy Commingore are all a bit more wide-eyed and loud than they need to be; Collins, for example, underplays the villainy of Jim Gettys, but he stays in mind because he handles the quieter lines of dialogue almost like a stage actor, preserving the illusion of calm while speaking at a high volume.

The early episodes of *Kane* contain many subtle and deliberate echoes of Victorian melodramatics, but even the later scenes with Susan Alexander at Xanadu are particularly high-pitched, creating a sort of repressed hysteria. By the time Welles came to direct *The Lady from Shanghai* and *Touch of Evil* he began to push this rapidly paced, grotesquely exaggerated technique in still more radical directions. One could cite many examples, especially from the second film: Uncle Joe Grandi and his boys dashing through the early morning streets of Los Robles and squabbling like the Three Stooges; Menzies expressing grief over Quinlan by dropping his head flat down on a table and speaking in operatic despair; the hot-rod gang twitching and snapping their fingers like the chorus in a Michael Kidd dance number. But the most obvious instance is the performance of Dennis Weaver, whose role as the crazy Mirador Motel "night man" is even more weirdly distorted than the film's wide-angle photography. According to Weaver, Welles told him, "never let anyone get in front of you."[7] As a result, he plays every scene on a diagonal with the other actors, usually dashing about in quickstep, his head jerking from side to side in what Manny Farber called "spastic woodpecker effects." When he meets the Grandi gang he has an attack of the heebie-jeebies, and when he finds a leftover joint in Janet Leigh's room he literally screams in terror. Outside the motel after the rape scene, we see him in the most stylized pose of all, embracing a windblown tree and babbling like one of Shakespeare's fools.

Welles was almost alone among American moviemakers of his day in striving for a theatrical intensity—a "hot" style of acting that has more in common with Griffith or Eisenstein than with the tradition of American talking pictures. He relished the opportunity to use vivid character actors like Akim Tamiroff, Everett Sloane, or Glenn Anders, and he loved to people his films with international types in offbeat costumes who scurry about making broad gestures and yelling their lines. He had a lively sense of how these various bodies reacted against one another within the frame, and he moved them in eccentric fashion, producing a surreal comedy. As the director-star, he also had a keen awareness of his own acting range. A massive, fascinating presence, he often photographed himself from a low angle, using a fish-eye lens that made him look phallic. He was nevertheless somewhat graceless in movement, and his best performances were in the roles of very old men. As the young Charles Foster Kane, he usually plays scenes from a seated position; when he does move, as in the dance at the *Inquirer* party, his somewhat stilted, robotic behavior seems in keeping with the notion of Kane as a hollow man, and with the deterministic atmosphere of the film as a whole.

Welles's most impressive instrument was of course his voice, but in *Kane* and all his other films he delivers lines rapidly, almost throwing away phrases and then lingering over a word, as if he were trying to achieve a pastiche of ordinary, excited speech. A masterful stealer of scenes and in some ways a throwback to the nineteenth-century stage, he knew that if he glanced away from the person to whom he was speaking he would capture the audience's attention. This slightly distracted look, plus the gauzy photography he preferred for his own close-ups, gave his acting what François Truffaut called a "softly hallucinated" tone, a counterpoint to the nightmarish mood of his mise-en-scène. At the same time, however, his decentered rhetoric called attention to his status as the enunciator of the film, allowing him to engage in a kind of indirect address to the audience. In the language of Irving Goffman, we might say that Welles was employing a form of "disclosive compensation," allowing himself to narrate his role without much regard for the other characters.[8] There are many precedents of such techniques in Shakespearean theater, but as Michael Anderegg has pointed out, Welles's presentational style also reminds us of Brecht's idea that the actor should "make himself observed standing *between* the spectator and the text." In Welles's portrayal of Franz Kindler in *The Stranger*, for example, he repeatedly gives a sense of what Anderegg describes as "commentary in tandem with representation" (Anderegg, 76), as if the dialogue were meant to have the "quoted" feeling that Brecht favored in all his theoretical writings.

This style became especially noticeable whenever Welles acted in movies that were directed by other people. Late in his career, when he appeared in countless cameo roles, he almost always positioned himself in three-quarter profile, looking at a space somewhere between the camera and the other players. As he spoke he occasionally glanced sidelong at the person he was addressing, acknowledging their presence but at the same time making his dialogue sound rather like a soliloquy. He also assumed an unorthodox posture when he worked as a narrator in films. Most on-camera narrators look squarely into the lens, but Welles barely seemed to notice it, sometimes appearing lost in thought, occasionally behaving as if he were a public speaker confronting a group of people arrayed around the room. The technique is especially noticeable in *F for Fake*, and in TV shows like "Orson Welles's Sketchbook" and "The Fountain of Youth." In these cases, as in his dramatic impersonations, he made us unusually aware of the apparatus, creating an alienated style of address.

At virtually every other level of his later appearances in the media, Welles established a split between the performer and the role. I have elsewhere pointed out that his makeup in *Mr. Arkadin* is visible, so that we cannot know whether the star or the character is participating in a masquerade; in such films as *The Immortal Story* and *The Merchant of Venice*, he creates an even more unsettling effect, adopting theatrical makeup in order to set himself off from all the other players. In the 1960s, in one of his guest performances for the "Dean Martin Show" on American TV, he brought a makeup kit onto a bare stage and began telling the story of Shakespeare's *Merchant of Venice*, transforming himself into Shylock as he spoke about the play. When his beard, wig, and false nose were firmly in place, he launched into a rendition of the "Hath not a Jew eyes" speech.

Meanwhile, Welles's own productions were saturated with explicit forms of narration, becoming a sort of anatomy or typology of the various relations between showing and telling. In this regard, we should remember that Brecht and Piscator derived their concept of "epic" theater from Goethe, who used the word to describe a type of narrated drama. Nearly all of Welles's work is "epic" in precisely the sense Goethe intended. In *F for Fake*, for example, he not only provides a running commentary, but also appears with Oja Kodar in a dramatic episode in which both characters are posed abstractly against a cyclorama, as if they were narrating their respective roles. In *The Fountain of Youth*, his seldom-seen pilot film for an American TV series, he recounts most of the story and at the same time dubs his own voice in place of the characters, even speaking lines that are intended for the actress Joi Lansing.

Welles's detractors might argue that this strategy was prompted by budget limitations or by his hammy desire to play all the roles, but I believe it grew logically out of his fondness for parables and other forms of oral storytelling. His more expensive projects also contain instances of narrative *discours* alongside cinematic *histoire*: consider the series of narrators in *Kane*, or the brilliantly modern approximation of Victorian omniscience in *Ambersons*; consider also O'Hara's story about the sharks, Arkadin's parable of the scorpion and the frog (*Mr. Arkadin*), and Kafka's parable of the Law (*The Trial*). One of the most interesting applications of the technique is in the unfinished *Don Quixote*, in which Welles reads Cervantes to a child, sometimes dubbing his voice in place of the other actors and allowing his nondiegetic narration to lapse into moments of conversation with the dramatic characters.

Ultimately, Welles's experiments with complex narration can be traced back to his radio shows of the 1930s, especially to programs like "His Honor, the Mayor," which, as Jonathan Rosenbaum has noted, have a "neo-Brechtian" format.[9] Critics sometimes assume that narration is endemic to radio, but one reason why Welles seemed an innovative director was because he thought of the medium as narrative rather than dramatic. Most radio drama in his day—such as Cecil B. DeMille's popular "Lux Radio Theater"—treated the action as if it were taking place on a posh Broadway stage. "There is nothing that seems more unsuited to the technique of the microphone," Welles once said, "than to tune in on a play and hear the announcer say, 'The curtain is now rising on a presentation of . . .'" He wanted to eliminate what he called the "impersonal" quality of such programs; like Franklin Roosevelt, he thought of the radio as a piece of living-room furniture, and he sought to establish what he called an "individual" contact with the audience. "When a fellow leans back in his chair and begins: 'Now this is how it happened,'" he wrote, "the listener feels that the narrator is taking him into his confidence; he begins to take a personal interest in the outcome."[10]

The "personal" aspect of Welles's narration helped to reveal his distinctly populist and American upbringing, and it points to another feature of his work as an actor-director that I should like to emphasize in closing: Welles was justly famous for his hypnotic voice, but he was also skeptical about the power of rhetoric. After all, having produced the "War of the Worlds" broadcast, he knew firsthand how the public could be hoodwinked and controlled. He was one of the twentieth century's most dynamic public speakers, and on the screen he often played men who mesmerized audiences on formal public occasions—for instance, he was Charles Foster Kane delivering an election speech, Father Mapple giving a sermon, and Clarence Darrow summing up a case. (Most interestingly of all, he was almost Kurtz, the antihero of *Heart of Darkness*—a man whose voice, as Conrad tells us, "rang deep to the very last.") In many of his personal appearances as a movie narrator, however, he adopted an air of self-depreciating irony or playful seriousness that prevented him from seeming authoritarian. At this level, Welles the pedagogue had something in common with Welles the magician: in both forms he was capable of fooling us, but he liked to reveal his tricks. Perhaps the most important thing to say about him is that he never lost his democratic instincts. Even though he wanted to persuade us, he never let us forget that he was only an actor.

Notes

1. "The Director in the Theatre Today," lecture given to the New York Theatre Education League, 1939. Orson Welles Collection (box 4, folder 22), Lilly Library, Bloomington, Indiana.

2. Michael Anderegg, "Orson Welles as Performer," *Persistence of Vision* 7 (1989): 73; hereafter cited in text as Anderegg.

3. "The New Actor," typescript notes for a lecture, 1940. Orson Welles Collection (box 4, folder 26, 3), Lilly Library, Bloomington, Indiana.

4. Author's interview with Richard Wilson, February 1977, Santa Monica, California.

5. Barbara Leaming, *Orson Welles: A Biography* (New York: Penguin, 1986), p. 411.

6. Interview with Ted Gilling, *Sight and Sound* (Summer 1973): 42. The commentary here and in the next few paragraphs is derived from my book, *The Magic World of Orson Welles* (New York, Oxford University Press, 1978; rev. ed., Dallas: Southern Methodist University Press, 1989); hereafter cited as Naremore 1978.

7. Quoted in "Life Award to Orson Welles," American Film Institute, Los Angeles, California, 1975, 10.

8. For additional commentary on this phenomenon in the movies, see James Naremore, *Acting in the Cinema* (Berkeley: University of California Press, 1988), 68–82.

9. Jonathan Rosenbaum, review of *Orson Welles: A Bio-Bibliography*, by Brett Wood. *Film Quarterly* (Spring 1990): 62.

10. Welles's comments on radio for the *New York Times* are discussed more fully in Naremore 1978, 13–14.

Citizen Kane: From Log Cabin to Xanadu

LAURA MULVEY

ALTHOUGH THE idea of embarking on a new analysis of the most written-about film in film history is daunting, I am using *Citizen Kane* for a specific and experimental purpose. That is, I want to speculate about certain areas of overlap between psychoanalysis and history and use the film, as it were, as a guinea pig. I have two further excuses for this project. First, although the history in question here is primarily that of the United States, I have tried to approach that history from a European perspective which, I feel, illuminates aspects of the film that have been overlooked. Second, I am applying the film theory and criticism of my generation to this film, which has been put through the mill by each generation of critics since it appeared in 1941. The main influences on my thought have been psycho-analytic theory and feminism, and both have strongly inflected my analysis of *Citizen Kane*. Although the presence of feminism in this essay may not be obvious at first glance, the principles of feminist film theory have not only molded my way of thinking about cinema in general, but have necessarily informed my approach throughout this particular analysis. My approach is experimental in another way: it is a feminist analysis of a film that is not, on the face of it, appropriate for a feminist analysis.

However, *Citizen Kane* is about an enigma, and the enigma is refracted through a text that creates a strong appeal in its spectator to read clues and to decipher meanings. The film creates an active, self-conscious form of spectatorship and one that is not founded on a polarization of gender (that is, an active spectator positioned as masculine in relation to an eroti-cized feminine spectacle). One of the ways in which *Citizen Kane* seems strikingly anti-Hollywood is the absence of the glamour effect generated by a female star. Welles's own towering presence on the screen provides a magnetic draw for the spectator's eye and leaves little space for sexualized voyeurism. This displacement opens up a space for a different kind of voyeurism, that of curiosity—both the perhaps prurient desire to crack the secret of a life and also a kind of detective work, a reading of cinematic signs that carries on alongside and finally transcends that of the diegetic investigator. So, liberated from its conventional erotic obsession with the female figure, cinematic voyeurism—displaced—is replaced by a different currency of exchange between screen and spectator.

Feminist film theory has always been preoccupied with the question of decipherment—first and foremost, of course, the decipherment of uncon-

---

This essay was adapted for this volume by Laura Mulvey from material in her BFI monograph, *Citizen Kane* (1992), and is published here for the first time by her permission.

scious meanings invested in images of women. It is in this light that the appropriation of psychoanalytic theory by feminist film theory should be understood. Psychoanalytic theory is, itself, a means of decoding symptoms: symptoms that have evaded the processes of censorship in the conscious mind, with the original material then disguised by the unconscious mind through its own particular linguistic processes of condensation and displacement. Freud, searching for analogies to describe the language of the unconscious, cited the hieroglyph and the rebus. Without implying any literal identity between the cinema and the unconscious, critics have pointed out that the cinema, sliding between the visual and the verbal and in the very looseness of its "language," can also be compared to the hieroglyph and rebus. And meanings created through image, gesture, object, camera movement, and so on, can be transferred on to subsequent repetitions or similarities (of image, gesture, object, camera movement, and so on), displacing or condensing their resonances to forge links in the proverbial chain of sliding signifiers. *Citizen Kane* exploits these formal aspects of film in a story/scenario that is itself about its main protagonist's unconscious.

I have broken down the overlap between psychoanalysis and history into three separate levels:

1. *Citizen Kane*'s narrational strategy and its exploitation of the cinema's hieroglyphic potential to create a space for a deciphering spectator. I will argue that this form of spectatorship has historical and political significance.

2. The psychoanalytic content of the story, as reflected in its narrative structure, patterns, and symmetries. I will argue that these themes are organized around gender and also reach out to wider American mythologies that have a social significance for an immigrant society.

3. The historical background and the political crisis at the time when the film was made, refracted through a psychoanalytic frame of reference.

Citizen Kane's polemical edge was directed at contemporary politics. The film's politics were not only eclipsed over the course of the years, but were glimpsed only through innuendo and implication even at the moment of its release. And then, its critical reputation as one of the great films of all time detached it further from its politics and left it floating, as it were, in the discourse of pure film criticism. The Hearst references were understood, at the time and since, as personal and scandalous rather than as political. Not only will I be attempting to right this balance, but I will also argue that the film's politics include psychoanalysis, and that only through the application of psychoanalytic theory can its politics truly emerge into visibility. Then themes of Oedipal conflict and fetishism come into play, not only within the story itself, but to reflect back onto the historical conflicts from which the film emerged.

Psychoanalytically orientated critics may have been intimidated by Pauline Kael's famous and triumphant citation of Orson Welles's apparently dismissive description of the film's psychoanalytic themes as "dollar-book Freud." However, Welles' remark, taken in context, seems less dismissive.[1] At the time when *Citizen Kane* was attracting widespread attention as a portrait of newspaper tycoon William Randolph Hearst, Welles issued a careful press statement about his film. He drew attention to its psychological themes in an attempt to generalize the personal into the political. He discussed Kane's separation from his mother, his subsequent parenting by a bank, and the significance of the sled Rosebud, which "in his subconscious . . . stood for his mother's love which Kane never lost. In his waking hours, Kane certainly forgot the sled and the name which was painted on it. Case books of psychiatrists are full of these stories. It was important for me in the picture to tell the audience as effectively as possible what this really meant . . . The best solution was the sled itself . . . It was necessary that my character be a collector—the kind of man who never throws anything away."[2] Faced with the skepticism and, indeed, disappointment of the assembled press over this psychoanalytic emphasis, Welles made his infamous and oft-quoted remark about "dollar-book Freud." My intention here is to restore some of the depth inherent in the "Freud" and to take Welles, in the spirit of his own analysis beyond the level of the 'dollar book'. At the same time I shall try to unravel the intricate interweaving of the quite obviously factual references to Hearst with their by and large fictional psychoanalytic underpinnings and, finally, to speculate about the wider ideological significance of both.

Although I shall return to the film's politics at the end of this essay, I want to place the film historically before embarking on the theoretical sections of my analysis. Some dates: work started on the *Citizen Kane* script in February 1940, during the "phony war" period that followed the German invasion of Poland in 1939. While scripting continued in the spring and early summer, the German offensive moved across Europe; *Citizen Kane* went into production on 29 June, during the bleakest moments of the war, between the fall of France in May and the Battle of Britain, which stretched out, in a last stand against Hitler, from July to September 1940. As Europe appeared to be falling inexorably to fascism, the battle between involvement and isolationism was bitterly engaged in America. When *Citizen Kane* opened in New York in May 1941, Pearl Harbor was still six months away. Not only was the question of the war in Europe the burning public issue at the time, it was also of passionate personal importance to Orson Welles. He was deeply committed to Roosevelt, the New Deal, and the struggle against fascism, but was also deeply influenced by European culture. Hearst, on the other hand, had always been a major exponent of isolationism, particularly where Europe was concerned. He had broken with the Democrats over Wilson's involvement of the United States in World War I and with the Republicans over, among other things, Hoover's support for the League of Nations. Although the historical and political background is hardly visible on an explicit level, I shall attempt to argue that its presence is distinctly discernable through the film's imagery and in its metaphoric allusions.

1

Now: the inscription of a mode of spectatorship. The film—as has been often pointed out before—challenges conventional relations between screen and spectator. But, most crucially, it uses the language of cinema to create a mesh with the language of the psyche. The enigma in *Citizen Kane* goes beyond content level of the "Rosebud" mystery to a level of form, presenting the spectator with a film text that is aesthetically constructed around visual clues that appeal to an active, curious, spectator who takes pleasure in deciphering enigmas and interpreting signs. Music also plays its part. Bernard Herrmann wrote about the necessity for musical leitmotivs in *Citizen Kane*:

> There are two main motifs. One—a simple four-note figure in brass—is that of Kane's power. It is played in the very first two bars of the film. The second is the Rosebud motif. A vibraphone solo, it first appears during the death scene at the very beginning of the picture. It is heard again and again throughout the film under various guises, and if followed closely, is a clue to the ultimate identity of Rosebud itself.[3]

Curiosity has to have an object, an enigma to arouse it. In *Citizen Kane*, the central enigma of Kane himself is neatly encapsulated in, or displaced onto, Rosebud, which then becomes the focus of the journalist/investigator's quest. But the enigma is never solved for the characters within the fictional world on the screen, either through the protagonist's investigation or through the witnesses' testimony. Welles separates the spectator from the diegetic world of the screen and upsets our normal assumption that the story's resolution will be provided by its characters' transcendent understanding. In this way the film avoids the conventions of the hermetically sealed narrative usually associated with the Hollywood cinema. It opens up and marks another kind of narrational strategy, which breaks down the barriers between the screen and the auditorium, moving, as it were, out of the diegetically contained third person and into the second-person mode of address.

By its very use of inconsistency and contradiction, the film warns the audience against any reliance on the protagonists as credible sources of truth and, ultimately, deflects understanding, away from character, away from a dramatic interplay between people and their destinies. In *Citizen*

Kane the audience can come to their own conclusions, but only if they break through the barrier of character as the source of meaning and start to interpret clues and symptoms on the screen as might a detective or a psychoanalyst. Once the characters fall into place as just one element in an intricately patterned web, the film's own internal consistency and logic, independent of character, come clearly into focus. In this sense the film as a whole, as a text, sets up an enigma, and through its formal mode of address, through its use of the camera, it also sets up the clues to its decipherment. The clues spread through the story on the screen, hidden in the varied elements that make up a film: camera movements, objects, gestures, events, repetitions, mise-en-scène. Among these elements, the characters are only one more link in the chain, another piece in the jigsaw puzzle. So *Citizen Kane* upsets our usual sense of hierarchy in storytelling, in which the ratio between people and things tends to be organized along an anthropomorphic bias. The spectator is left to "figure out" what is going on (beyond, in Lucy's famous words to Linus, 'Rosebud's his sled') and to pick up hints at messages that are quite clearly not delivered by Western Union.

The film's opening sequence sets up the relationship between camera and spectator and invokes the spectator's investigative gaze through a collaboration with the investigation of the seeing camera rather than with the unseeing character. When the title "*Citizen Kane*" fades from the screen and the film's initial image takes its place, the audience is swept into the story with an interdiction and a camera movement. A sign saying "No Trespassing" can easily be seen through the murky lighting, and a wire fence fills the screen, barring the way forward. This sign, although rationalized through its place on the gate of the Xanadu estate, directly addresses the audience. Everyone knows that prohibited space becomes immediately fascinating and that nothing arouses curiosity more than a secret. And in response, after barely even pausing on the first image, the camera cranes up and over the top of the fence, moving forward through a series of lap dissolves and grounds of neglected grandeur, towards a fairytale castle on the top of a hill. There is no grounding of the camera here. It is freed from an establishing character's presence, literally approaching the gate on the ground. The space is simply that of the screen and the frame, and the gravity-defying movement of the camera.

The camera's movement functions both literally and figuratively. It establishes a place and a mystery but it also gives a visible rendering of the opening of a story as an opening of a narrative space. The space of the story is depicted as an enclosed place from which the audience is excluded, and the camera's effortless passage from outside to inside acts like a magic eye, opening a way into the storyteller's world and imagination. The end of the film reverses the camera movement, so the space that opened up the story is symmetrically closed, returning the audience to their original position, outside the wire fence, ultimately back into the auditorium, the same as they were, but different for having undergone the experience of the previous ninety minutes.

There is an echo, in this narrating camera, of the grand experiment that Welles had planned for his first Hollywood project, the adaptation of Conrad's *Heart of Darkness*. That project grew out of the Mercury Theatre's radio series "First Person Singular," in which novels built around a narrating "I" were adapted for dramatic performance and combined with the storyteller's "voiceover." *Heart of Darkness* had been one of these productions. To transform the first-person narration into the new medium, cinema, Welles wanted to shoot the film with the camera as the eye of the "I," using a subjective camera throughout, the kind later used by Robert Montgomery in *The Lady in the Lake*. The difficulties involved in shooting the film in this way greatly inflated the *Heart of Darkness* budget, and the project was shelved. The film was to have been introduced by a prologue in which Welles would give an an illustrated lecture on subjective camera and explain directly to the audience that the camera's point of view was also theirs. Robert Carringer, in his book *The Making of "Citizen Kane"* says:

> To Welles's explanatory narration, the camera would adopt the points of view, successively of a bird in a cage, a condemned man about to be electrocuted, and a golfer driving a ball. Then it would take Welles's point of view from the screen, looking into a movie audience made up entirely of motion picture cameras. In the final shot, an eye would appear on the left side of a black screen, then the equals sign, then the pronoun I. The eye would wink, and a dissolve would lead to the opening shot of the film.[4]

The opening of *Citizen Kane* offers an infinitely more sophisticated version of a subjective camera. Because the camera's look is not associated with a character, a literal first-person participant in the story, it takes on, rather, the function of narrator outside the world of the story. While it still assimilates and represents the audience's eye as they look at the screen, it also sets up an invocation to decipher. Later in the film the shadowy presence of Thompson, the investigating journalist, acts as a surrogate for the audience's curiosity, carrying the narrative forward and precipitating the film's flashbacks to the past. He is never, however, given the transcendent look that is marked by a character's assimilation to a subjective camera.

Because the overt solution to the Rosebud enigma only appears in the film's closing seconds, many important signs and clues set up earlier in the film will, more likely than not, have gone unnoticed in a first viewing. *Citizen Kane* has, built into its structure, the need to think back and reflect on what has taken place in the main body of the film as soon as it finishes. And when the camera tracks into the furnace and supplies the 'missing piece of the jigsaw puzzle', it throws everything that has led up to that moment into a new relief. Those whose curiosity has been truly engaged by the film find themselves wanting to see it again. The next and subsequent viewings are bound to be experienced quite differently from the first. There is, in a sense, a didactic metaphor at play here. The film's "active spectator" is forced to look back at and reexamine events as though the film were suggesting that history itself should be constantly subjected to reexamination. Not only should history never be accepted at face, or story, value, but also, from a political perspective, it should be detached from personality and point of view and be rediscovered, as it were, in its materiality and through the decoding of its symptoms. This inscribed return to the past to decode the film as history overlaps with the question of the unconscious and its enigmas.

The sled, for instance, functions as lost object and as screen memory, and, being literally buried in the snow, it is both hidden and preserved, perfectly in keeping with Freud's picture of memory within the unconscious. The little glass ball that contains the log cabin and snow scene makes three appearances, one at the very beginning of the film, Kane's death scene; one at the end, when Susan leaves him; and one in the middle, when they meet for the first time. Because the glass ball belongs to Susan, it first appears in the chronology of Kane's story when she does, that is, in the middle of the film, during Leland's turning-point narration. Kane meets Susan in the street, at a crossroad, and she stops, as it were, in its tracks, Kane's journey back into his past. He explains to her:

> "You see, my mother died, a long time ago. Well, her things were put in storage out West. There wasn't any other place to put them. I thought I'd send for them now. Tonight I was going to take a look at them. A sort of sentimental journey."

This scene includes the second of the only two times in the film that Kane mentions his mother. And this nostalgia for his past also reintroduces the theme of motherly love and ambition.

> SUSAN: I wanted to be a singer. That is, I didn't. My mother did . . .
> It's just—well you know what mothers are like.
>
> KANE: Yes. You got a piano?

(Susan herself comments perceptively at the end of her narration 'Perhaps I should never have sung for Charlie that first evening . . .') The glass ball is distinguishable on Susan's dressing table, to the left-hand side of her reflection in the mirror. Neither of the characters draws attention to it, nor does the camera, but there it sits, like a narrative time bomb awaiting its moment, the observant spectator to pick up and take note.

These are just some instances of the way in which the film links motifs through objects. The 'semiology' of the objects offers the spectator an aesthetic opportunity to return to and reread the text and to puzzle out its configurations retrospectively. The end returns the viewer to the beginning; there is both the formal symmetry (the camera's exit through the fence) and the unanswered questions that are left hanging in the smoke rising from Xanadu's chimney.

2

The next area of overlap between psychoanalysis and history lies inside the film, starting with the narrative structure of the film and its organization around thematic symmetries. The personalized nature of the flashbacks and their general adherence to chronology overshadow and disguise the film's underlying dramatic structure, which divides into two parts, cutting across the chronological biography and the narrations of the different witnesses with a broad, dominating, binary opposition. Kane's rise and decline separate the two parts narratatively, but his relation to male and female worlds separate the two parts thematically. The Thatcher and Bernstein stories tell of Kane's dramatic rise to triumphant success. Susan's and Raymond's flashbacks tell the story of his disgrace and withdrawal. The first two stories are set in the competitive, public, all-male world of newspaper reporting; Susan's and Raymond's narratives are set in the spectacular, cultural, and feminized world of the opera and Xanadu. The turning point comes in Leland's narration, which deals with Kane's love life and political life, and the increasingly inextricable relationship between the two. The turning-point effect is accentuated by the fact that the world of politics is sandwiched between Kane's meeting with Susan and their marriage.

Kane's defeat in his campaign for governor marks the apex of the rise-and-fall structure and switches the movement of the story. Kane invests all his financial and emotional resources into Susan's career in opera so that, in terms of the film's symmetry, the opera, *Salammbo*, balances the newspaper, the *Inquirer*. While the *Inquirer*'s triumph led to Kane's first marriage and to politics, *Salammbo*'s collapse leads to the claustrophobic grandeur of Xanadu. Kane's major enterprise is concentrated on buying and importing art treasures to construct an appropriate environment for his retreat into an isolated domesticity with Susan.

The scene of Kane's childhood separation from his parents could be described as the film's "primal scene." It enacts, in dramatic form, the two psychoanalytic motifs that determine the later development of the plot and divide it into its two parts: the child's closeness to his mother and his instinctive aggression against his surrogate father. The first, male-dominated section of the film tells the story of the radical, Oedipal Kane continuing to battle against his surrogate father. The second, Susan-dominated section of the film shows him isolated from public life and fetishistically amassing things, attempting to fill, as it were, the void of his first loss, his separation from his mother.

The Thatcher flashback covers, in three scenes, the whole span of Kane's career, from the first meeting in the snow, to Thatcher's rage at Kane's campaigns against capitalist corruption, to the stock-market crash and Kane's bankruptcy. The last lines in the sequence are:

THATCHER: What would you like to have been?

KANE: Everything you hate.

When Kane, as an old man, gives his uncompromising answer to Thatcher's question ("everything you hate"), this one line suddenly illuminates the Oedipal element in Kane's political behavior. The line, the last of the Thatcher episode, links back not only to Kane's violent reaction to Thatcher at their first meeting, but also to the *Inquirer*'s campaigns against everything for which Thatcher stands. To fight against Thatcher, the banker and old-fashioned capitalist, Kane espouses the cause of those who suffer at the hands of privilege, using as his weapon a new form of capitalist enterprise, that is, the mass-circulation newspapers known in the United States as the 'yellow press'. But, in implying that this radical stand has an unconscious, Oedipal origin, the film throws doubt on the altruism of Kane's politics and implies a personal agenda concealed behind the overtly political principles.

When Kane first attacks Thatcher, he uses the sled as a weapon; his aggression is directed at the adult male who is threatening to, and who will, separate him from his mother.

MOTHER: Mr. Thatcher is going to take you on a trip with him tonight, You'll be leaving on number ten.

FATHER: That's the train with all the lights on it.

CHARLES: You goin' Mom?

THATCHER: Oh no. Your mother won't be going right away, Charles, but she'll . . .

CHARLES: Where'm I going?

The scene is credible only from a psychoanalytic point of view. The characters' motivations and attitudes are not rational or explicable. Only the threatening nature of the doubled fathers, and their incompatible violences, give the scene cohesion.

This scene splits the image of the father into two opposed aspects, but both pose a threat to the child. While the biological father threatens the son with physical violence, the surrogate father threatens him with separation from his mother. The scene ends with the mother and son clinging to each other, the mother protecting her child against his father's violence, the child holding on to her love and staring resentfully offscreen at his substitute father, who proposes to introduce him to a new cultural and symbolic order. The child is suspended between two psychological phases, wavering on the threshold between a pre-Oedipal love for his mother and rivalry with his father and the post-Oedipal world in which he should take his place within society, thereby accepting separation from his mother and acknowledging the authority of his father. The scene is played with the irrationality and condensation of the unconscious. The characters act out their psychic roles without regard for verisimilitude, and the snow-covered landscape with its remote log cabin is an appropriate setting for this psychic moment. Kane never crosses the threshold between the pre- and post-Oedipal, remaining frozen, as it were, at the point of separation from his mother and, from then on, directing his Oedipal aggression at his surrogate father. The child, from then on, is in conflict with the Symbolic Order.

There is a symbolic father who represents the demands of culture and society and necessarily disrupts the mother and child's unity. A child's closeness to its mother creates a sphere of physical and emotional completeness, simultaneously an eden and a strangulation, a place of safety from which to escape, and, once escaped, a place of longing that cannot be regained. There is a before and an after. The sphere of maternal plenitude gradually gives way to social and cultural aspirations represented by the father's social and cultural significance. This process may never, as in the case of Charles Foster Kane, be satisfactorily achieved. If Mr. Kane represents a pre-Oedipal father, Thatcher personifies the father who should teach the child to understand the symbolic systems on which social relations rest and which replace the physical, unmediated bond between mother and child. Both money and the law are products of a social order based on abstract principles and symbolization. Money transcends the physicality of a literal exchange of objects and substitutes an abstract system of value. The law transcends the literal and physical relations between people and places them within a timeless system of morality. The scene inside the log cabin polarizes Kane's split father figures on each side of these symbolic systems. One represents poverty, failure, and ignorance, while the other represents wealth, success, and education. When Mrs. Kane signs her son away to the world of culture and social advancement by means of a legal agreement and in return for money, she seems to acknowledge the inevitability of a transition that only the mother, she seems to imply, can ever understand and, then, only mourn. The child's mourning returns, in the manner of the repressed, through symptoms that perpetuate an original trauma. He will become fixated on *things* and the accumulation of objects, rejecting the abstract complexities of capital, exchange, and the circulation of money.

The real father, who is left behind in the "before" that the log cabin stands for, complains, "I don't hold with signing away my boy to any bank as guardeen just because we're poorly educated." His speech and dress are rough and diametrically opposed to Thatcher, whose clipped legalistic language and dark suit come from a world without room for emotion. That world is about Order, both in the sense of regulation and hierarchy, without which money cannot become capital. Mrs. Kane's correct grammatical speech and her dark dress are iconographically closer to Thatcher than to her husband. She understands some abstract cultural necessity while her husband ('I want you to stop all this nonsense, Jim)' in his naïveté, does not. The scene in the log cabin places Thatcher and Mrs. Kane together on the right-hand side of the frame, sitting at the table with the documents, while Mr. Kane hovers anxiously, and unstably, on the left side. In this famous scene of deep-focus photography, Charlie is playing outside, as seen through the window—within the divide. Within the Oedipal conflict, it is the mother's role to give up her child. To hold on to him would be to keep him in the netherworld of infancy, cultural deprivation, and impotence, and would prevent his departure on the journey towards greatness, towards the White House, as it were. In *Citizen Kane*, the transition is too abrupt and painful, and is never resolved.

The last shot of the separation scene holds for a long time on the abandoned sled now covered by the snow, while a train's whistle sounds in the distance. As I mentioned earlier, in Freud's theory of the unconscious, a memory that is apparently forgotten is also preserved, to return, if called on, at a later date. The snow, with its connotations of both burying and freezing, perfectly evokes this metaphor. The memory can be recovered when something happens to make the mind delve into the depths of time and the unconscious, just as the memory of Rosebud is revived for Kane by the little glass snowstorm and log cabin he finds when Susan leaves him. The mise-en-scène is no more rational than the characters' actions. The remote, snow-covered countryside and the little log cabin create a phantasmic landscape that introduces American myth into the psychoanalytic metaphor, and the action combines melodramatic gesture with the rudimentary elements of Oedipal drama.

When the serial father figures who stood in his way—Thatcher, Carter and the *Chronicle* (the lawyer/banker, nonpopulist/liberal journalist, the yellow-press magnate)—have been defeated by the Kane *Inquirer*, there is a party/celebration that also marks Kane's passage from youth to maturity. At this point, towards the middle of the story, a triumphant happy ending seems to be a foregone conclusion. Happy endings are, in popular culture, immediately preceded by marriage, the rite of passage that marks a transition from youthful irresponsibility to patriarchal authority. The party, almost like a stag party (the original script included a brothel scene that was ultimately cut, at the request of the Hays office) leads immediately to Kane's engagement. When he appears with Emily Monroe Norton,

Bernstein's narration ends on a triumphant note. He understands that Kane's marriage opens the way for his next step up the ladder towards the presidency.

> MISS TOWNSEND (awestruck): She's the niece of the President of the United States!

> BERNSTEIN: President's niece, huh! Before he's through she'll be a President's wife!

Kane's campaign as Independent candidate for governor is a stepping-stone on the way to the White House. (The March of Time: "The White House seemingly the next easy step.") In American mythology, the iconography generated by the White House complements the iconography of Kane's childhood. In his trajectory from the poverty and obscurity of a remote Colorado log cabin to fabulous wealth one step from the White House, Kane encapsulates a populist cliché of the American political dream. Like a version of the old Whittingtonesque folktale of trans-class mobility, "from a log cabin to the White House" is a story cum icon of American mythology. The United States, as the land of equality and opportunity, promised to put the old folktale within reach of all the European rural and urban poor who crossed the Atlantic. William M. Thayer called his biography of President James Garfield *From Log-Cabin to the White House*[5] to emphasise the parallels between Garfield's trajectory and that of President Lincoln, both born to poor pioneer families "in the wilderness," both called to the highest office in the United States. In a short article[6] Freud suggested that the story of a young man's journey to seek his fortune could be the basic model of the daydream, but he also points out that it integrates the erotic fantasy with the ambitious fantasy. The young man achieves power and riches through marriage to the daughter of a an important man who will pass on his position to a worthy son-in-law. Kane's first marriage illustrates the close ties between the love or erotic element of this daydream story and the theme of power through marriage and inheritance through the wife. His marriage to Emily Monroe Norton, the president's niece, puts him, as it were, in line to succeed the president, just as, in Freud's bourgeois version, a father-in-law leaves a business to his daughter's husband or, in the folktale version, the hero is rewarded for his heroism with the princess's hand in marriage, thereby inheriting her father's kingdom.

But Kane himself, or perhaps more precisely Kane and his unconscious, sabotage the "happy ending". So, ruined by success, his future narrative path leads not from a log cabin to the White House, but from a log cabin to Xanadu. Susan and the theme of fetishism take over from Oedipal struggle. And although Kane tries for a while and with an increasingly rhetorical and empty sense of desperation, to turn Gettys into a father/monster, he lapses back into the personal, unable to come to terms with the symbolic implications of political and thus patriarchal power. The *Inquirer* and its campaigns fall into the background when Kane's personal struggle against Thatcher becomes subsumed into a circulation battle against the *Chronicle*, which, in turn, is subsumed into political ambition. In the sixteen years covered by the breakfast-table montage, the fairytale promises of Bernstein's narration fade away. The film and Kane's life then both reach a crossroads. By the time he starts on his political campaign, Kane's radical, Oedipal, populist politics are a thing of the past, and slogans about the "cause of reform" against Tammany Hall look increasingly like an investment in his own dictatorial personal power. Both Leland, explicitly, and Gettys, implicitly, accuse him of not being able to distinguish between the personal and the political.

It is during the *Inquirer* party that Kane's collecting mania is first mentioned, as if, once his struggle with his surrogate father has faded, this symptom could perpetuate the scene of separation in the snow in his unconscious. So this symptom, which in the future will take on manic proportions, appears chronologically before his relationship with Susan and before his self-exile from the male world of power and politics into the female world of fantasy and fetishism. This massive accumulation of "things" relates back, metonymically, to the original lost object, the sled, and the traumatic loss represented by the object, his mother. At the party Bernstein mentions, for the first time, Kane's new habit of collecting statues:

BERNSTEIN: Say, Mr. Kane, so long as you're promising there's a lot of statues in Europe you ain't bought yet—

KANE: You can't blame me Mr. Bernstein. They've been making statues for two thousand years and I've only been buying for five.

There is, however, an Oedipal as well as a fetishistic element here. Kane's collecting obsession fits in with his rebellion against the frugal principles of careful investment and return for which Thatcher stands. The third and last scene between Kane and Thatcher includes this dialogue:

THATCHER: Yes, but your methods. You know, Charles, you never made a single investment. You always used money to—

KANE: To buy things. To buy things. My mother should have chosen a less reliable banker.

The Protestant ethic of productive capitalism stands in diametrical opposition to the wasteful consumption of capital through the accumulation of useless things. Kane is not interested in productive capital (*'Sorry but I'm not interested in goldmines, oil wells, shipping, or real estate . . .'*) and the abstract, symbolic, concepts of money and exchange. He cashes in his capital and turns it into concrete objects. In the second part of the film, and especially in the construction of Xanadu, Kane takes spending to obsessive levels, being unable even to unpack the vast amount of stuff he accumulates. At the same time, as evidenced in the last scene at Xanadu, he has never thrown any object away. The "things" of a lifetime lie strewn about, higgledy-piggledy, and the camera tracks across them, allowing the audience to recognize particular objects that have figured in earlier scenes, and to find the original object, the sled "Rosebud." This massive accumulation of things is set in the context of a lifetime that has attempted to freeze and preserve a traumatic moment of loss. Held in the timelessness of the unconscious, the things relate to each other metonymically, reaching back, longingly and through displacement, towards the original lost object, which screens the memory of loss itself. Into the midst of these fetishized objects, the film introduces a personification of fetishism into its story line.

I argued earlier that the film does not entice the spectator into voyeuristic complicity by means of a depiction of femininity as spectacle. When Susan's erotic qualities and performing abilities enter the scene, the audience is not involved with Kane's gaze. Susan produces an effect of distanciation, and Kane's estimation of his love object is wildly at odds with reality. From the first moment that Susan sings at the parlor piano, the audience finds listening to her painful. But for Kane her voice is the source of true fascination. As he fetishizes Susan's inadequate voice into a precious and valued object, he blinds himself to what he knows and invests all his emotional and financial resources in a deluded belief. He transforms Susan into a highly stylized and produced object. For the opera, her small, inadequate, singing voice is dressed up and embellished in an elaborate costume crowned with two enormous blond plaits and a top-heavy headdress. Her legs move across the stage appearing incongruously vulnerable and detached from her body. Confusion swirls around Susan, the presentation of the opera, and the culture it attempts to mimic.

At the same time, the review Kane finishes for Leland indicates that, in some way, he perceives the situation realistically. Fetishism, according to Freud's theory, bears witness to the human psyche's ability to separate knowledge and belief. The woman's body may be traumatically misperceived as castrated, and thus the knowledge of sexual difference itself is disavowed, and belief in the missing "object" is then preserved by a substitute idealized object. Nevertheless, psychoanalytic theorists since Freud have argued that fetishism is a structure of which the castration model need only be one example. Fetishistic disavowal and substitution can represent other kinds of traumatic loss. In the Kane "case study," the child's separation from his mother is traumatic and need not be literally or mechanically tied to castration anxiety. However, the substitution of an object for the mother (the sled), and subsequent objects (Kane's "things"), and, finally, another woman (Susan), all bear witness to the structures of disavowal, substitution, and displacement.

Fetishism holds time in check. It is fixated on a thing that artificially resists the changes that knowledge brings with it. The object links back to the original scene and substitutes for it. Freud argues that the fetish functions as a screen memory. The fetish interjects an object between memory and the actual traumatic moment. At the same time the object also marks the place of the lost memory it masks. Freud describes a screen memory as a "witness, simultaneously precious and insignificant, where something that must never be lost may be hidden and preserved."[7] This image evokes the little sled (simultaneously precious and insignificant) buried in the snow (hidden and preserved).

The fact that Kane's collecting is directed exclusively towards European things brings a wider cultural and historical metaphor into the scene. The statues he collects are European in origin and imported into his collection. They prefigure the opera and its European origin, by means of which Susan is transformed into a living fetishized fantasy. Everything is then concentrated in Xanadu itself. And the scenario of the opera and the scenario of Xanadu, while being constructed out of culture and antiquity, end up as pastiches. Although they have a veneer of European antiquity and culture, they are empty, shell-like constructions that Kane never even attempts to understand.

3

I now want to introduce the third level of the overlap between psychoanalysis and history: the political context in which the film was made. It is here that the figure of William Randolph Hearst arises with full force as the main object of Orson Welles's attack. The question of Hearst, of course, added a further level of enigmatic encrustation to the film. Hearst himself contributed the first dramatic, public chapter of *Citizen Kane*'s extra-cinematic history in the vendetta waged by the Hearst press against the film just before and after its release. At the end of a private screening of the film, the columnist Louella Parsons, accompanied by her chauffeur and two Hearst lawyers, stormed out, furious at what she had seen; only the chauffeur stopped to say to Welles that he enjoyed the picture (Brady, 278). Hearst not only attempted indirectly to sabotage the release of the film but attacked Orson Welles politically. Welles's radio program "His Honour the Mayor" in CBS's "Free Company" series was reported in the Hearst press, sometime after the broadcast but coincidentally with the release of *Citizen Kane*, to have been condemned by the American Legion as "an appeal for the right of all subversive fifth-column groups to hold anti-American meetings in the public hall of an American city," and because "the name itself, "Free Company," sounds suspiciously Communistic."

Frank Brady, in his book *Citizen Welles*, describes the subsequent government surveillance:

> Welles never knew that a number of Hearst sympathizers began reporting
> Orson's activities to the FBI as potentially dangerous to the national interest.
> . . . In a report by a special FBI agent to J. Edgar Hoover, it was noted: "It
> should be pointed out that this office has never been able to establish that
> Welles is an actual member of the former Communist Party or the present
> Communist Political Association; however, an examination of Welles's activi-
> ties and his membership in various organizations reflects that he has consis-
> tently followed the Communist Party line and has been active in numerous
> 'front' organisations." (Brady, 292–93)

Welles fought back with reiterated denials that Hearst was the model
for Kane, responding politically to political attacks, with psychoanalytic
explanation to economic sabotage, and later through anecdote and
humor. One of the last denials appeared, strangely, in his introduction to
Marion Davies's book *The Times We Had*, published in 1975:

> Xanadu was a lonely fortress and Susan was quite right to escape from it.
> The mistress [Marion Davies] was never one of Hearst's possessions . . . she
> was the precious treasure of his heart for more than thirty years until the last
> breath of life. Theirs was truly a love story. Love is not the subject of *Citizen
> Kane* . . . If San Simeon had not existed it would have been necessary for the
> authors to invent it.[8]

In the face of the Hearst campaigns and their undoubted ability to damage Welles professionally, and to damage him through political *innuendo*,
there is no doubt that he had to deny the importance of the Hearst model
for Kane "after the event." Debate, however, continued over the origin of
the Hearst model in the context of rival claims over the authorship of
Citizen Kane. John Houseman describes Herman J. Mankiewicz's interest:

> Total disagreement persists as to where the Hearst idea originated. The fact
> is that, as a former newspaper man and an avid reader of contemporary his-
> tory, Mank had long been fascinated by the American phenomenon of
> William Randolph Hearst. Unlike his friends on the left, to whom Hearst was
> now an archenemy, fascist isolationist and a red baiter, Mankiewicz remem-
> bered the years when Hearst had been regarded as the working man's friend
> and a political progressive. He had observed him later as a member of the
> film colony—grandiose, aging and vulnerable in the immensity of his recon-
> structed palace at San Simeon.[9]

In the years before Welles went to Hollywood, Hearst's vast empire was
barely staving off financial collapse. In 1937 his financial affairs were
removed from his direct control and put in the hands of a Conservation
Committee, and he was forced to auction off some of his art collection. In

March 1939 his financial difficulties were the subject of a *Time* magazine cover story, and around the same time Aldous Huxley's Hearst novel, *After Many a Summer Dies the Swan*, was published. In *Citizen Welles*, Frank Brady describes a dinner, at which Welles was present, held to celebrate the publication of Huxley's book, and at which the model for the portrait and the consequent impossibility of turning the novel into a film were discussed. (Brady, 219). Hearst was, therefore, in the news during the months before the conception of *Citizen Kane*. It was when 'the miraculous contract had three and a half months to run and there was no film in sight' (in John Houseman's words) that the Hearst idea was floated somewhere between Welles and Mankiewicz. But when Welles, who was definitely on the left, decided in 1940 to use Hearst as the basis of his first film, he was interested in more than the story of a grand old man of capitalism who was running out of time and money.

Orson Welles had come of age, as it were, and had risen to be an outstanding figure in American theater at a time when extraordinary opportunities had been created by the New Deal's cultural policy, as orchestrated through the Works Progress Administration. Welles first attracted widespread attention with his production of *Macbeth* for the Negro Theater Project in Harlem, of which John Houseman was, at that time, a director. Welles and Houseman were later commissioned by the Federal Theater to run their own company, which they named after its WPA number, Project #891. Welles, returning to the United States from Europe in 1934 at the age of nineteen, was formed intellectually and professionally by the Popular Front and the theater of the New Deal. Welles and Houseman then founded their own, independent Mercury Theater and published their manifesto in the Communist party newspaper, the *Daily Worker*. Welles's growing reputation as an actor and director was established at a new level by his Mercury productions. Their success brought offers from CBS radio, for which Welles was already working, and the formation of the Mercury Theater of the Air. One of their regular Sunday evening radio adaptations, broadcast on Halloween 1938, "The War of the Worlds," put Welles on the front pages of newspapers across the United States, and led George Schaeffer of RKO to invite Welles and the Mercury company to Hollywood. In spite of his outstanding qualities as an actor and director, it is always possible that his career would not have taken off in such meteoric style if it had not been for the unprecedented, and unrepeated, opportunities offered by the WPA. This would add a personal element to Welles' political commitment to Franklin Roosevelt, borne out by Welles's continued support for him throughout the years, support the president publicly acknowledged. In 1944 Roosevelt chose Welles to run a radio campaign to sell war bonds, and that year Welles devoted himself to campaigning for the president's reelection; he was invited to the White House for the reelection celebration. In 1944 Roosevelt even encouraged Welles to stand as candidate for senator in California.

Hearst had moved from reluctant support for Roosevelt as the Democratic presidential candidate in 1932 (only at the last moment and under enormous pressure, when it became clear that his candidate, John Garner, had no hope of victory) to outright denunciation of him for the rest of the 1930s. Hearst was far from in retreat from political activity during the New Deal period. His hostility toward Roosevelt escalated critically regarding new tax legislation that penalized the super-rich in 1935 and union protection legislation that led to conflicts with his own editorial staff during the mid-1930s, after they organised through the American Newspapers' Guild. Hearst's increasingly vituperative move to the Right was also a symptom of a generalized political polarization during this period, instanced not only by Upton Sinclair's candidacy for the governorship of California but by the longshoremen's strike in 1934, the defeat of which Hearst contributed to through behind-the-scenes politics as well as newspaper pressure. But polarization in American politics was also marked by international association, both on the Left and the Right. Toward the end of 1934 the *San Francisco Examiner* published, without editorial comment or detachment, three articles by Nazi propagandist Goebbels. And the Hearst papers' red-baiting campaigns, prototypical of anti-Communist McCarthyism of the postwar period, escalated in the same year. In 1936 his antagonism toward Roosevelt put Hearst back in the Republican camp. He contributed $30,000 to the Republican campaign and said, "The race will not be close at all, Landon [the Republican candidate] will be overwhelmingly elected and I'll stake my reputation as a prophet on it."[10]

The Hearst papers were instructed to refer to the New Deal as the "Raw Deal." William Stott describes how the newspapers reached a low ebb of credibility:

> Throughout the early thirties the press managed to ignore or belittle evidence of a depression. In the 1936 Presidential campaign, more than 80 per cent of the press opposed Roosevelt, and he won by the highest percentage ever. During the campaign and for years after, many newspapers, including major syndicates, went beyond all legitimate bounds in an effort to disparage the President and the New Deal. And, as Roosevelt warned the editors, the press lost by it. Public opinion polls in the late thirties suggested that 30 million Americans, nearly one American in three, doubted the honesty of the American press.[11]

Hearst's deep involvement with public and political affairs during the 1930s, and his active support for the Right, present a problem for any attempt to analyze *Citizen Kane* in terms of Welles's own political position. Kane retires from politics after his personal disgrace and political defeat, and the film thus avoids almost any reference to the contemporary political scene and its immediate antecedents. Nonetheless, this apparent lapse has important implications. It allows the Hearst model to be molded into a narrative that has its own self-sufficiency, its own symmetries, and wider metaphorical significance. The split in the narrative between male and female spheres achieves sharp relief as an aesthetic structure in its own right; Kane retreats from public life into a private world of his own making. Furthermore, the psychoanalytic and metaphoric aspects of the film's themes gather a strength that moves beyond the individual into wider mythological issues. The Hearst model is, thus, of importance for *Citizen Kane* not only in its accuracy but in its deviations. In its accuracy it comments on a major and recognizable political figure of the far Right from the political perspective of the liberal Left. Mankiewicz used Ferdinand Lundburg's hostile biography *Imperial Hearst* for his source material so precisely that Lundburg brought a suit for plagiarism against *Citizen Kane* in 1948. The accuracies are obvious. They include the silver-mine fortune; concentration on political power through a popular press that exploited jingoism, sex, and violence; the Hearst papers' part in the Spanish-American War; Hearst's aspiration to the presidency and tangles with Tammany Hall; his collecting mania and his construction of San Simeon; his poaching of arch rival Pulitzer's staff from the *World*; his relationship with Marion Davies. The deviations are concentrated particularly at the beginning and end of *Citizen Kane*, in Kane's humble birth in a log cabin, his separation from his mother, and his relation with, and separation from, Susan Alexander. There was no precedent in the Hearst/Davies model for Susan's humiliating failure as an opera singer and attempted suicide, or in the breakdown of their relationship. Hearst and Davies lived happily together, unmarried, until his death in 1951. These deviational elements are the basis for a psychoanalytic reading of the film.

The insertion of a psychoanalytic explanation for the famous Hearstian puzzle makes *Citizen Kane* seem particularly iconoclastic. The fictional unconscious that the film constructs may well amount to nothing more than sophisticated mischief making on the part of the screenwriter and the director. It could be that it seemed amusing to find unconscious motivations for the eccentricities of a recognizable, aging, and reactionary public figure. After all, the political problem that Hearst represents, radical youth giving way to conservative old age, is a cliché in a society that pioneered adolescent revolt as a rite of passage into responsible citizenship. But the war in Europe and the alignment in the United States of Left and Right around isolation or involvement throw light both on the appeal that a Hearst-based script would have for Welles and on the wider implications of its psychoanalytic undertone.

By the time Welles and the Mercury players arrived in Hollywood, Hearst was a major opponent of the entry of the United States into the war in Europe. For the Left, the threat of fascism was actual and urgent. The Mercury Theater had staged a production of *Julius Caesar* in which Caesar was portrayed as a contemporary fascist surrounded by black shirts; the production was lit to create a Nuremberg look, in the aftermath of the infamous Nazi rally. In the eyes of the Left, the powerful tycoon's press campaigns to keep America from joining the struggle against fascism was tantamount to support for fascism. While he was vacationing in Germany in 1934, Hearst had visited Hitler, and the German press had quoted Hearst's approving and friendly remarks, which Hearst later claimed had been misquoted. But the famous lines spoken by Kane during an interview included in "News on the March" are the only trace of contemporary politics in *Citizen Kane*:

> I have talked with the responsible leaders of the Great Powers—England, France, Germany, and Italy. They are too intelligent to embark upon a project that would mean the end of civilization as we now know it. You can take my word for it, there will be no war.

And alongside the commentary:

> No public man whom . . . Kane himself did not support . . . or denounce. Often support . . . and then denounce . . .

the fictional newsreel shows Kane appearing on a balcony with Hitler. The penultimate draft of *Citizen Kane* links Kane more explicitly to fascism through his son, who grows up to become a Nazi and is killed in a raid on an armory in Washington, DC. So although the film is set in an earlier moment in American history, the choice of Hearst as the subject of Welles's film was still politically relevant in the late 1930s. Right-wing opposition to Roosevelt had emerged as a new and real threat in the context of fascism.

From the perspective of the New Deal and antifascist politics, Hearst presented an appropriate subject for the first Mercury production in Hollywood. However, the political references to Hearst are overshadowed by the psychoanalytic undertones of the fictional character Kane. But the condensation of the real-life political and fictional psychoanalytic traits carry their implications into a psychoanalytic attack on the politics of right-wing populism. This is where the film is daring. It could be that the furor over the question of whether or not the film was a portrait of Hearst distracted critics and commentators from what the film was implying about the political and personal bankruptcy of the American Right. The film continually reaches out towards a mythological level, appropriating quite obvious, even hackneyed, psychoanalytic tropes to cut corners between character and metaphor.

The image of Kane at the end of the film serves as an allegorical warning about the fate of European/American relations. As I noted at the beginning of this essay, the film was made during the bleakest period of the war, when Roosevelt was becoming more and more convinced of the need for America to get involved in the conflict. Welles's portrayal of Kane is an apt image of the destiny that isolationism would bring in its wake. Kane is shown as an old man, lonely and alone, literally isolated in the enormous, claustrophobic castle he has constructed as a fantasy world against the world outside, no longer involved with it, and incarcerated inside his own mausoleum. This image seems to represent the isolationist policies of the Hearst press; and Xanadu, through its blatant similarity to San Simeon, is one of the most transparent references to Hearst in the film.

Robert Carringer, in *The Making of Citizen Kane*, analyzes the designs of RKO's art director, Perry Ferguson, for Xanadu, showing how the Great Hall at Xanadu was based closely on a photograph of the Great Hall at San Simeon. Carringer notes:

> The Hearstian element is brought out in the almost perverse juxtaposition of incongruous architectural styles and motifs—Gothic along the far wall, Venetian Baroque in the loggia, Egyptian on the landing (including a sphinx on a plinth!), vaguely far Eastern figures along the staircase. (Carringer, 54)

Such a confusion of culture points to a confusion of history and the ordering of time—and also to the confusion of populist politics. If Kane, and by implication Hearst, is stuck in a fetishistic inability to understand or acknowledge the processes of history, the film seems to hint that this disorder has a psychoanalytic origin. And, also by implication, the isolationist stance is a sign of a repressed, unworked—through Oedipal trajectory that has been prematurely broken off, leaving the subject tied to a "frozen" memory of loss. In Freudian terms, a child's edenic relation to his or her mother may be represented metaphorically by antiquity, the place of ancient origin, the "old world." It is striking that no Hollywood genre, and relatively few individual films, deal with migration across the Atlantic. It is almost as if this passage, from the old to the new world, was a taboo subject in American popular culture. In *Citizen Kane*, however, the old world is presented ambivalently. It contains a threat of paternal violence within the "before" of the before/after divide between the mother's exclusive and dependable love and the child's Oedipal journey into the outside world of ambition. For both these reasons the 'old world' is in danger of lying outside history, subject to repression. At the moment of fascist threat, Welles seems to suggest a psychoanalytic metaphor to explain the dilemma facing the Euro-American collective psyche. At the same time, the film's formal appeal cuts across a purely psychoanalytic rhetoric and refuses only to represent its dilemma. The film addresses the discernment of those spectators who can figure out an enigma without the help of a narrator/commentator. The spectators, in the last resort, will piece together the history of the film's protagonist in its closing moments and then, if their curiosity has really been engaged, will review and retell the film by tracing and linking together the clues and symptoms that conceal, but preserve, its meaning.

In doing so, they would be directed not only towards the figure of the newspaper magnate and his hold over national narrative, but also towards their own ability to read cinematic images, and even, perhaps, towards the entanglement of contemporary politics with past, historical, trauma.

There is a kind of poetic justice in Welles's and cinematographer Toland's use of deep focus in a film that attacks Hearst. The magnate of newspapers and old-style movies is depicted in a new style of cinematography pioneered by the newspapers' new rival, the photo-magazines. And, on the level of sound, Welles made maximum use of his own experience in radio, the medium beloved by Roosevelt, to create a texture that had never been heard before in the Hollywood cinema. And although the deep-focus look had been previously pioneered in Hollywood, the politics of *Citizen Kane* juxtaposes it, perhaps even coincidentally, with the cinematic aesthetics of other Left cinemas of the 1930s and 1940s. In the view of André Bazin, the deep-focus cinematography of Jean Renoir's Popular Front movies in the 1930s in France returned in the Italian Neo-Realist and leftist cinema of the post-war period. For Bazin, engagement between spectator and screen in *Citizen Kane* was an effect of its composition, and formed a tryptich with the Popular Front cinema on the one hand and that of Neo-Realism on the other. Dramatic juxtapositions are composed within the frame, and a shot then lasts long enough for the spectator to work out the relationships between the characters and to extract the poetic and emotional implications of the scene. Bazin argued that this kind of composition gave the spectator's eye and mind an autonomy and freedom that both montage and the cutting conventions of commercial cinema (especially after the coming of sound) denied.

From my own, European, point of view, Bazin's inclusion of *Citizen Kane* in his political/aesthetic argument always seemed anomalous and to privilege aesthetics over politics. However, looking again at *Citizen Kane*, in the context of the New Deal in the United States and of the conflict between an extreme Right and an attempted Popular Front in both the United States and Europe, Welles's perhaps intuitive approach to cinema finally fits with Bazin's intuitive triptych.

Notes

1. Frank Brady, *Citizen Welles: A Biography of Orson Welles* (New York: Doubleday, 1989), 285, hereafter cited in text as Brady.

2. In Dilys Powell, "The Life and Opinions of Orson Welles," *London Times*, Sunday, 3 February 1963.

3. Bernard Herrmann, "Score for a Film," in Focus on "Citizen Kane", ed. Ronald Gottesman (Englewood Cliffs, N.J.: Prentice-Hall, 1971), 70.

4. Robert Carringer, *The Making of "Citizen Kane"* (Berkeley: University of California Press, 1985), 11; hereafter cited as Carringer.

5. William Makepeace Thayer, *From Log-Cabin to the White House: Life of James A. Garfield, Boyhood, Youth, Manhood, Assassination, Death, Funeral* (New York: J.B. Alden, 1883).

6. Sigmund Freud, "The Relation of the Poet to Day-Dreaming," in *On Creativity and the Unconscious: Papers on the Psychology of Art, Literature, Love, Religion*, translated by Joan Riviere et al. (New York: Harper and Row, 1958), 44–54.

7. Sigmund Freud, "Fetishism," in *The Standard Edition of the Complete Psychological Works*, vol. 21 (London: Hogarth, 1961).

8. Marion Davies, *The Times We Had* (New York: Bobbs-Merrill, 1975),

9. John Houseman, *Unfinished Business* (London: Chatto and Windus, 1986), 223.

10. W. A. Swanberg, *Citizen Hearst* (London: Longman, 1965), 477.

11. William Stott, *Documentary Expression in America* (London: Oxford University Press, 1973), 79.

Orson Unmasks Himself

HENRY JAGLOM

O RSON WELLES was the first person to see a rough cut of my film *Always*. As he sat in the dark of my cutting room, watching it, sitting behind me in the wide wheelchair that he travelled with for comfort, smoking his Monte Cristo cigar as I operated my KEM editing machine, his only discernible responses were frequent, intense outbursts of laughter, alternating with long, gentle, almost mournful sighs.

This was quite a contrast to the time, a year earlier, when we had undergone the same process for *Can She Bake a Cherry Pie? Then* he had stopped me every twenty seconds or so, suggesting, commenting, praising, insulting. It had been a wonderful, valuable, incredible experience, an amazing tour-de-force performance of filmmaking criticism that expanded from a discourse on acting, camera angles, editing, and dialogue to cover such widely divergent subjects as art, history, politics, psychology, sociology—the entire spectrum, in fact, of creative human endeavor. He had dazzled me, provoked me, taught me—and I had loved it and gained immeasurably from it, and expected more of the same now. But this time he was mainly sighs.

When we came to the end of the film and I pushed the stop button on the last reel, the silence behind me felt ominous. I knew he must have hated the movie, the most revealing movie I would ever make, and couldn't find the words to tell me. Orson could be silent like no one else, and it was so rare an event as to be quite unnerving. I turned and found him deep in thought, so completely impregnable that I waited for what seemed like an eternity. It must have been, in fact, a full three or four minutes before I finally asked him the inevitable, desperate, "Well?"

"I'm jealous," Orson murmured.

Thinking that I hadn't heard right, I asked, "*What*? What did you say?" I knew that, as it almost always was with us, the tape recorder was running, taking it all down for posterity, for the book of his memoirs that we were someday going to write together. But I had to hear it again, in the flesh, just to be sure I had heard correctly.

"I'm jealous," he repeated, still in a very gentle voice, seemingly more to himself than to me.

"What do you *mean*?" I asked, thinking for an insane, heady moment that he meant my film was so wonderful that he was jealous of *it*. "You

---

This essay was written specifically for this volume and is published here for the first time by permission of the author.

304

keep forgetting you're Orson Welles!" It was something I often teased him about, his surprisingly genuine and humble ability to entirely lose track of the significance of what he had accomplished in his life, of who he was to others, of what his name *meant* to the world. "How can *you* possibly be jealous? You've made six or seven of the greatest movies ever made. You've made the film most people consider the greatest one that will ever *be* made."

"Of course," he said with a dismissive wave of his hand. "That's not what I meant. I *do* like your film—a great deal—but that's not what I'm talking about. I was thinking about how I've always hidden behind a mask, every time I've been on screen. Now you've made a movie, I see a movie here, in which the filmmaker, for the first time I think, absolutely does not wear *any* mask at all. How astonishing! I'd like to do that just once in my life." He thought a moment, then smiled. "But I wouldn't *really* do it, would I? I'd disguise myself. I'd try to show them this or that, make them see me in some way or other. It's the difference in our generations, I guess. I wouldn't be capable of just exposing who I am, nakedly, the way you have, warts and all . . . " He drifted into thought, then almost whispered: "God, would I love to, just once, before I die. To truly drop the mask . . ."

Orson Welles's entire astonishing, chaotic, and brilliant career involved his hiding behind masks. It was practically impossible for me, as director of my first film, *A Safe Place*, in 1970, to persuade him to play his part without some kind of a mask. "What nose do you want?" was one of the earliest questions I remember him stumping me with. When I realized what he meant and told him, "No nose, *your* nose," he acted outraged, as if I was revealing the ignorance of my youth and inexperience. Two very unpleasant days followed before he summoned me up to his suite at the Essex House in New York City, where he triumphantly informed me: "Okay. You win. No nose. I'm growing a *beard*!" It was, in fact, the beard that he grew for the part of the lapsed Wonder-Rabbi spinning his Hassidic tails in *A Safe Place*, that Orson wore for the rest of his life. And it was, of course, a mask.

On stage as on screen, beyond the mask of his Makeup, he had always, quite naturally, hidden behind the mask of his Character. But it didn't stop there. In personal appearances, on talk shows, even in *life* when he found himself among strangers, he hid behind the mask of his outsized Persona, the one that seemed so overwhelming and intimidating to so many people: the erratic, outrageous, somewhat ferociously aging wunderkind.

Orson's lifelong attraction to the art that has as its very essence the blurring of the line between reality and illusion was another piece of this same puzzle: Nothing gave him as much consistent pleasure as teasing audiences, and himself, with the many masks of Magic.

Even his Physical Being, as represented by his ever-increasing weight, became a mask for him to hide behind, in some infinitely more complex way. And no matter how seriously he dieted, no matter how insistently he swam his laps, no matter how often he made *me* eat the gourmet meals he denied himself in order to have me describe each of the tastes to him, his Weight remained a mask that, once assumed, he was never able to drop.

More than anything else, Orson Welles was a mythomaniac, a person who invents himself. But in his case the combined image that came from all his disguises was the very thing that defeated him in the end. People drew the wrong conclusions about who and what he was and added those conclusions, layer by layer, onto the rapidly growing mythology that attached itself to him over the decades. As in the final scene of *The Lady from Shanghai*, it was ultimately impossible for the world to find the real Orson Welles among all the mirrored reflections he had so busily set up from very early in his life.

Who *was* this extraordinary, singular, unique creature whose immense and varied talents no one could ever comfortably define or neatly assess? Critics attempting to appraise him contradicted themselves in the most bizarre ways. One of the most prominent of them once referred to him as "a genius without talent," a grotesque and absurd oxymoronic phrase that he forever quoted and by which he was eternally disturbed, and at the same time, amused.

The financial powers who could have made it possible for him to make a film were too terrified of that which they did not understand. Orson was, quite simply, impossible to neatly categorize; and lacking predictability— one true sign of any major artist—is, of course, the single worst crime as far as Hollywood (and most of the world) has always been concerned. Therefore the last third of Orson's life was sadly spent receiving awards and honors, performing what he called his "dancing bear" act for prospective backers and their assorted hangers-on, and, over and over again, being denied the support necessary for him to do the work for which he never stopped preparing.

Because I had lunch with Orson once or twice a week for most of the last eight years of his life, and because I spoke with him almost daily, I was constantly amazed that the man I got to know so well in no way resembled the mythical mask-wearer that everyone else saw and believed him to be. I discovered an incredibly open, deeply warm, and profoundly human friend, one who was generous to an unbelievable fault, was caring and concerned, and vulnerable to the point of such fragility that he could be wounded terribly by the unaware, casual, critical statement of almost any outsider. I was always astounded by the way in which so many who did not know him viewed him as an arrogant, terrifying, egocentric ogre. They approached him with so much diffidence and fear as to set him up in such a way that his only possible response would be to satisfy their expectations. The Mask would win again. And while he hated the isolation that this response inevitably brought him, he was oddly comforted by playing the part that had been invented for him to act out, and did it with such force and style that it was captivating to watch, even as I would kick him under the table to try to get him to stop. His "Jewish Conscience," he called me, after they would leave, and roar with laughter.

When I started to prepare the film that followed *Always, Someone to Love*, I knew that one of the main things I wanted to accomplish in it was to have Orson, once and for all, be revealed for who he truly was, *without* any mask. But as we started to discuss his role, he immediately reached for the comfort that came from preparing to assume several complex emotional and dramatic disguises, despite his professed desire to do without them "just once." I realized that what I would have to do would be to essentially *trick* him into letting his masks down. And when I told him as much one day at lunch, I was surprised by his response to understand that he, in fact, *wanted* me to do just that. I said: "I want them to see you just the way you are, here, with me, the real, undisguised you." "It won't be of any interest to anyone," he responded, but in such a way that I knew he was going to *let* me "trick" him into finally allowing himself up on screen: No mask, no nose, no emotional armor, no theatrical invention, just Orson Welles in all his easy, witty brilliance, his complex, warm, informed charm, his stimulating, original, fluid mind, and—mainly—the sweet, supportive, deeply loving man that he truly was.

We succeeded, Orson and I. So much so that for many, many months after his death it was hard for me to really miss him, because on my editing machine, day after day, I was faced with Orson—the *real* Orson—simply, truthfully, magnificently being himself in a seemingly endless conversation with me and some of my friends, at the ultimate lunch at our corner table at Ma Maison, one that would never have to come to an end.

Ironically, strangely, happily, sadly—this turning out to be Orson's final film performance—we got him up there back where he had started, in The Theatre, saying his farewells, blowing us a kiss, uttering the most logical last word with which to cap his nearly half-century on screen—"Cut!"— then applauding his audiences across all the years in thanks for all the times that they, despite everything, had applauded him.

And finally, most importantly, I felt, having the last laugh—the biggest, most embracing, most magnificent last laugh I like to think in the history of cinema . . .

"Never expect justice in the world. This is not part of God's plan," Orson wrote in *The Dreamers*, one of the last films that he was never to make.

But the sound of Orson's laughter, for me, is a kind of justice that I can hold on to, and thankfully, share.

It is the justice of letting the world see him, at long last, free from all his masks.

Selected Bibliography

Bazin, André. *Orson Welles: A Critical View*. Translated by Jonathan Rosenbaum. Los Angeles: Acrobat, 1991. This work was originally published in France in 1972, and was very influential on later studies. Introduction by François Truffaut.

Bessy, Maurice. *Orson Welles: An Investigation into His Films and Philosophy*. New York: Crown, 1971.

Brady, Frank. *Citizen Welles: A Biography of Orson Welles*. New York: Doubleday, 1989. The most detailed biography in terms of Welles's career, less full for his personal life.

Carringer, Robert L. *The Making of "Citizen Kane"*. Berkeley: University of California Press, 1985. A fascinating and balanced study of the production of the film, as well as of the plans for the adaptation of Conrad's *Heart of Darkness*.

Comito, Terry, ed. *"Touch of Evil"*, Rutgers Films in Print. New Brunswick, N.J.: Rutgers University Press, 1985. Contains Welles's continuity script for the film, interviews with Welles and Charlton Heston, reviews, and critical studies.

Cowie, Peter. *A Ribbon of Dreams: The Cinema of Orson Welles*. 1973. Reprint. New York: Da Capo, 1983. A perceptive account of Welles's career, until *The Immortal Story*.

France, Richard. *The Theatre of Orson Welles*. Lewisburg, Penn.: Bucknell University Press, 1977. A Scholarly study of Welles's early career, before *Citizen Kane*.

Gottesman, Ronald J., ed. *Focus on "Citizen Kane"*. Englewood Cliffs, N.J.: Prentice-Hall, 1971. A very useful collection of early reviews, articles by Welles and others connected with the film, and critical essays. Includes a content outline of the film.

———, ed. *Focus on Orson Welles*. Englewood Cliffs, N.J.: Prentice-Hall, 1976. An excellent collection, with essays on most of Welles's major films.

Higham, Charles. *Orson Welles: The Rise and Fall of an American Genius*. New York: St. Martin's, 1985. Welles as self-destructive.

Howard, James. *The Complete Films of Orson Welles*. New York: Citadel Press, 1991. Contains a useful filmography and synopses (sometimes unreliable) of each film. Well-illustrated.

Kael, Pauline, and Herman J. Mankiewicz and Orson Welles. *The "Citizen Kane" Book*. New York: Little, Brown, 1971. Prints both the shooting script and the "cutting continuity" (the transcription of the final version), and Kael's controversial essay "Raising Kane."

Leaming, Barbara. *Orson Welles: A Biography*. New York: Viking, 1985. This is the authorized biography, with many quoted comments by Welles.

Lebo, Harlan. *"Citizen Kane": The Fiftieth-Anniversary Album*. New York: Doubleday, 1990. As its title suggests, more celebration than analysis, but readable and well-illustrated.

Lyons, Bridget Gellert, ed. *"Chimes at Midnight"* (Rutgers Films in Print). Includes the continuity script, interviews with Welles and Keith Baxter (who played Prince Hal), reviews, and critical essays.

McBride, Joseph. *Orson Welles*. New York: Viking, 1972. Like Cowie's book, this is a trend-setting early study.

———. *Orson Welles: Actor and Director*. New York: Harvest, 1977. Especially interesting when discussing Welles's work as an actor.

Mulvey, Laura. *"Citizen Kane"*. BFI Film Classics. London: British Film Institute, 1992. An excellent, detailed analysis of the film.

Naremore, James. *The Magic World of Orson Welles*. Dallas: Southern Methodist University Press, 1989. A revision of a fine study first published in 1978; covers Welles's entire career in detail.

Taylor, John Russell. *Orson Welles: A Celebration*. London: Pavilion Books, 1986. Good, illustrated overview of Welles's career; contains excellent filmography.

Welles, Orson. *Orson Welles on Shakespeare: The W.P.A. and Mercury Theatre Playscripts*. Edited by Richard France. New York: Greenwood Press, 1990.

Welles, Orson, and Peter Bogdanovich. *This Is Orson Welles*. New York: HarperCollins, 1992. Edited by Jonathan Rosenbaum. Records many conversations over a number of years between Welles and the younger filmmaker; an appendix includes Rosenbaum's "summary of the cuts and other alterations made in Welles' original version of *The Magnificent Ambersons*."

Wood, Bret. *Orson Welles: A Bio-Bibliography*. Bio-Bibliographies in the Performing Arts. New York: Greenwood Press, 1990. The most extensive bibliography of works by and about Welles; astutely annotated.

A Welles Filmography

1941 *Citizen Kane*

PRODUCTION COMPANY: RKO/Mercury

PRODUCER: Orson Welles

DIRECTOR: Orson Welles

SCREENPLAY: Herman J. Mankiewicz and Orson Welles

PHOTOGRAPHY: Gregg Toland

MUSIC: Bernard Herrmann

CAST: Orson Welles (Charles Foster Kane), Joseph Cotten (Jedediah Leland), Everett Sloane (Bernstein), Dorothy Comingore (Susan Alexander Kane), George Coulouris (Walter Parks Thatcher), Agnes Moorehead (Mrs. Kane), Ruth Warwick (Emily), William Alland (Thompson/narrator of newsreel), Harry Shannon (Mr. Kane), Erskine Sanford (Herbert Carter), Ray Collins (Jim Gettys), Paul Stewart (Raymond), Fortunio Bonanova (Matisti), Buddy Swan (young Charles Foster Kane), Sonny Bupp (Kane's son)

1942 *The Magnificent Ambersons*

PRODUCTION COMPANY: RKO/Mercury

PRODUCER: Orson Welles

DIRECTOR: Orson Welles

SCREENPLAY: Orson Welles, based on the novel by Booth Tarkington

PHOTOGRAPHY: Stanley Cortez (with additional scenes by Russell Metty and Harry Wild)

MUSIC: Bernard Herrmann (additional music by Roy Webb)

CAST: Orson Welles (narrator), Tim Holt (George Amberson Minafer), Joseph Cotten (Eugene Morgan), Anne Baxter (Lucy Morgan), Agnes Moorehead (Fanny Minafer), Dolores Costello (Isabel Amberson Minafer), Ray Collins (Jack Amberson), Richard Bennett (Major Amberson), Erskine Sanford (Roger Bronson), Don Dillaway (Wilbur Minafer), J. Louis Johnson (Sam), Gus Schilling (drugstore clerk), Charles Phillips (Uncle John), Dorothy Vaughan and Elmer Jerome (spectators at funeral), Olive Ball (Mary), Nina Guilbert and John Elliot (guests), Anne O'Neal (Mrs. Foster), Bobby Cooper (young George)

1944 *Journey into Fear*

PRODUCTION COMPANY: RKO/Mercury

PRODUCER: Orson Welles

DIRECTOR: Norman Foster (and, uncredited, Orson Welles)

SCREENPLAY: Joseph Cotten and Orson Welles, based on the novel by Eric Ambler

PHOTOGRAPHY: Karl Strauss

MUSIC: Roy Webb

CAST: Joseph Cotten (Howard Graham), Dolores Del Rio (Josette Martel), Orson Welles (Colonel Haki), Ruth Warwick (Stephanie Graham), Agnes Moorehead (Mrs. Mathews), Everett Sloane (Kopeikin), Jack Moss (Banat), Edgar Barrier (Kuvetli), Jack Durant (Gogo), Eustace Wyatt (Dr. Haller), Frank Readick (Mathews), Stephen Schnabel (Purser), Hans Conried (Oo Lang Sang, the magician), Robert Meltzer (steward), Richard Bennett (ship captain)

1944 **(released 1946)** *Jane Eyre*

PRODUCTION COMPANY: 20th Century Fox

PRODUCER: William Goetz

DIRECTOR: Robert Stevenson

PHOTOGRAPHY: George Barnes

MUSIC: Bernard Hermann

SCREENPLAY: Robert Stevenson, Aldous Huxley and John Houseman, based on the novel by Charlotte Brontë

CAST: Orson Welles (Rochester), Joan Fontaine (Jane), Margaret O'Brien (Adele Varena), Henry Daniell (Mr. Brocklehurst), Peggy Ann Garner (young Jane), Hillary Brooke (Blanche Ingram), Sara Allgood (Bessie), Agnes Moorehead (Aunt Reed), Elizabeth Taylor (Helen Burns)

1944 *Follow the Boys*

PRODUCTION COMPANY: Universal

PRODUCER: Charles K. Feldman

DIRECTOR: Eddie Sutherland

SCREENPLAY: Lou Breslow, Gertrude Purcell

MUSIC DIRECTOR: Leigh Harline

CAST: George Raft (Tony West), Vera Zorina (Gloria Vance), Charley Grapewin (Nick West), Charles Butterworth (Louie Fairweather), and guest stars (Orson Welles, Marlene Dietrich, the Andrews Sisters, Dinah Shore, Donald O'Connor, Peggy Ryan, W. C. Fields, Jeanette MacDonald, Sophie Tucker, Arthur Rubinstein)

1946 *Tomorrow is Forever*

PRODUCTION COMPANY: International

DIRECTOR: Irving Pichel

SCREENPLAY: Lenore Coffee, based on the novel by Gwen Bristow

PHOTOGRAPHY: Joseph Valentine

MUSIC: Max Steiner

CAST: Claudette Colbert (Elizabeth Macdonald), George Brent (Larry Hamilton), Orson Welles (Erich Kessler/John Macdonald), Natalie Wood (Margaret), Richard Long (Drew)

1946 *The Stranger*

PRODUCTION COMPANY: International

PRODUCER: S. P. Eagle [Sam Spiegel]

DIRECTOR: Orson Welles

SCREENPLAY: Anthony Veillers (and John Huston and Orson Welles, uncredited)

PHOTOGRAPHY: Russell Metty

MUSIC: Bronislaw Kaper

CAST: Orson Welles (Franz Kindler/Charles Rankin), Loretta Young (Mary Longstreet), Edward G. Robinson (Wilson), Philip Merivale (Judge Longstreet), Richard Long (Noah Longstreet), Byron Keith (Dr. Lawrence), Billy House (Mr. Potter), Martha Wentworth (Sarah), Konstantin Shayne (Konrad Meinike), Theodore Gottlieb (Farbright), Pietro Sosso (Mr. Peabody)

1946 (released 1948) *The Lady from Shanghai*

PRODUCTION COMPANY: Columbia

PRODUCER: Orson Welles (Executive Producer: Harry Cohn)

DIRECTOR: Orson Welles

SCREENPLAY: Orson Welles, based on the novel *If I Die Before I Wake*, by Sherwood King

PHOTOGRAPHY: Charles Lawton, Jr.

MUSIC: Heinz Roemheld

CAST: Orson Welles (Michael O'Hara), Rita Hayworth (Elsa Bannister), Everett Sloane (Arthur Bannister), Glenn Anders (George Grisby), Ted de Corsia (Sidney Broom), Gus Schilling (Goldie), Louis Merrill (Jake), Erskine Sanford (Judge), Carl Frank (District Attorney Galloway), Evelyn Ellis (Bessie), Wong Show Chong (Li), Harry Shannon (horse cab driver), Sam Nelson (Captain), Richard Wilson (district attorney's assistant), players of the Mandarin Theatre, San Francisco

1948 *Macbeth*

PRODUCTION COMPANY: Republic/Mercury

PRODUCER: Orson Welles

DIRECTOR: Orson Welles

SCREENPLAY: Orson Welles, based on the play by William Shakespeare

PHOTOGRAPHY: John L. Russell

MUSIC: Jacques Ibert

CAST: Orson Welles (Macbeth), Jeanette Nolan (Lady Macbeth), Dan O'Herlihy (Macduff), Edgar Barrier (Banquo), Roddy McDowall (Malcolm), Erskine Sanford (Duncan), Alan Napier (Holy Father), John Dierkes (Ross), Keene Curtis (Lennox), Peggy Webber (Lady Macduff), Lionel Braham (Siward), Archie Heugly (young Siward), Christopher Welles (Macduff's child), Brainerd Duffield (1st murderer), William Alland (2nd murderer), George Chirello (Seyton), Gus Schilling (Porter), Jerry Farber (Fleance), Lurene Tuttle (Gentlewoman), Robert Alan (3rd murderer), Morgan Farley (Doctor)

1949 *Black Magic*

PRODUCTION COMPANY: Edward Small

PRODUCER: Gregory Ratoff

DIRECTOR: Gregory Ratoff

SCREENPLAY: Charles Bennett, based on Alexandre Dumas's *Memoirs of a Physician*

PHOTOGRAPHY: Ubaldo Arata and Anchise Brizzi

MUSIC: Paul Sawtell

CAST: Orson Welles (Cagliostro), Nancy Guild (Marie Antoinette/ Lorenza), Valentina Cortese (Zoraida), Margot Grahame (Mme Du Barry), Charles Goldner (Dr. Mesmer), Berry Kroeger (Alexandre Dumas), Raymond Burr (Alexandre Dumas, *fils*), Frank Latimore (Gilbert), Stephen Bekassy (De Montagne)

1949 *Prince of Foxes*

PRODUCTION COMPANY: 20th Century Fox

PRODUCER: Sol C. Siegel

DIRECTOR: Henry King

SCREENPLAY: Milton Krims, based on the novel by Samuel Shella-barger

PHOTOGRAPHY: Leon Shamroy

MUSIC: Alfred Newman

CAST: Tyrone Power (Orsini), Orson Welles (Cesare Borgia), Wandra Hendrix (Camilla), Felix Aylmer (Verano), Everett Sloane (Belli), Katina Paxinou (Mona Zoppo), Marina Berti (Angela), Leslie Bradley (Esteban)

1949 *The Third Man*

PRODUCTION COMPANY: London Films/British Lion

PRODUCERS: Alexander Korda and David O. Selznick

DIRECTOR: Carol Reed

SCREENPLAY: Graham Greene, based on his unpublished short novel, subsequently published in 1950

PHOTOGRAPHY: Robert Krasker

MUSIC: Anton Karas

CAST: Joseph Cotten (Holly Martins; narrator in American version; in British version, the narrator is Carol Reed), Trevor Howard (Major Calloway), Alida Valli (Anna Schmidt), Orson Welles (Harry Lime), Bernard Lee (Sargeant Paine), Paul Hoerbiger (the porter), Annie Rosar (the porter's wife), Sigfried Breuer (Popescu), Ernst Deutsch (Kurtz), Erich Ponto (Dr. Winkel), Wilfrid Hyde-Whyte (Crabbin), Hedwig Bleibtreu (Anna's landlady), Herbert Halbik (Hansl)

1950 *The Black Rose*

PRODUCTION COMPANY: 20th Century Fox

PRODUCER: Louis D. Leighton

DIRECTOR: Henry Hathaway

SCREENPLAY: Talbot Jennings, based on the novel by Thomas B. Costain

PHOTOGRAPHY: Jack Cardiff

MUSIC: Richard Addinsell

CAST: Tyrone Power (Walter of Gurnie), Orson Welles (General Bayan), Jack Hawkins (Tristram), Cecile Aubry (Maryam), Finlay Currie (Alfgar), Henry Oscar (Friar Roger Bacon), Michael Rennie (King Edward), Herbert Lom (Anthemus), Bobby Blake (Mahmoud), Laurence Harvey (Edmond)

1952 *Othello*

PRODUCTION COMPANY: Mercury

PRODUCER: Orson Welles

DIRECTOR: Orson Welles

SCREENPLAY: Orson Welles, based on the play by William Shakespeare

PHOTOGRAPHY: Anchise Brizzi, G. R. Aldo, George Fanto, Obadan Troiani, Alberto Fusi

MUSIC: Francesco Lavagnino and Alberto Barberis

CAST: Orson Welles (Othello), Micheál MacLiammóir (Iago), Suzanne Cloutier (Desdemona), Robert Coote (Roderigo), Michael Lawrence (Cassio), Hilton Edwards (Brabantio), Fay Compton (Emilia), Nicholas Bruce (Lodovico), Jean Davis (Montano), Doris Dowling (Bianca), Joseph Cotten (senator), Joan Fontaine (Page)

1953 *Trent's Last Case*

PRODUCTION COMPANY: British Lion

PRODUCER: Herbert Wilcox

DIRECTOR: Herbert Wilcox

SCREENPLAY: Pamela Bower, based on the novel by E. C. Bentley

PHOTOGRAPHY: Max Greene

MUSIC: Anthony Collins

CAST: Orson Welles (Sigsbee Manderson), Michael Wilding (Philip Trent), Margaret Lockwood (Margaret Manderson), John McCallum (John Marlowe), Miles Malleson (Burton Cupples), Hugh McDermott (Calvin C. Bunner)

1953   *Si Versailles M'était Conté* [also known as *Versailles*]

PRODUCTION COMPANY: CLM-Cocinex

PRODUCER: Clément Duhour

DIRECTOR: Sacha Guitry

SCREENPLAY: Sacha Guitry

PHOTOGRAPHY: Pierre Montazel

MUSIC: Jean Francaix

CAST: Sacha Guitry (Louis XIV), Georges Marchal (young Louis XIV), Claudette Colbert (Mme de Montespan), Micheline Presle (Mme de Pompadour), Giselle Pascal (Louise de la Valliére), Lana Marconi (Marie Antoinette/Nicole Leguay), Fernand Gravey (Moliére), Jean Desailly (Marivaux), Bernard Dhéran (Beaumarchais), Jean-Claude Pascal (Alex de Fersen), Orson Welles (Benjamin Franklin), Jean-Pierre Aumont (Cardinal de Rohan), Gérard Philipe (D'Artagnan), Edith Piaf, Yves Deniaud, Jean Tissier, Pierre Larquey, Bourvil

1953   *L'umo, La Bestia e la Virtu*

PRODUCTION COMPANY: Rosa Films

DIRECTOR: Steno [Stefano Vanzina]

SCREENPLAY: Steno, Brancati, from the play by Luigi Pirandello

PHOTOGRAPHY: Mario Damicelli

CAST: Orson Welles (the Beast), Toto, Celia Matania, Franca Faldini

1954   *Three Cases of Murder*:
       Segment With Welles: Lord Mountdrago

PRODUCTION COMPANY: Wessex/London Films

PRODUCERS: Ian Dalrymple and Hugh Perceval

DIRECTOR: George More O'Ferrall

SCREENPLAY: Ian Dalrymple, from a short story by W. Somerset Maugham

PHOTOGRAPHY: Georges Perinal

MUSIC: Doreen Carwithen

CAST: Orson Welles (Lord Mountdrago), Alan Badel (Owen), Helen Cherry (Lady Mountdrago), André Morell (Dr. Audlin)

1954   *Napoleon*

PRODUCTION COMPANY: CLM

DIRECTOR: Sacha Guitry

SCREENPLAY: Sacha Guitry

PHOTOGRAPHY: Louis Née

MUSIC: Jean Francaix

CAST: Daniel Gelin (younger Napoleon), Raymond Pellegrin (older Napoleon), Michéle Morgan (Josephine), Orson Welles (Hudson Lowe), Sacha Guitry, Danielle Darrieux, Maria Schell, Corinne Calvet, Marcel Rey, Jean Gabin, Yves Montand

1955 *Trouble in the Glen*

PRODUCTION COMPANY: Republic/Wilcox-Neagle

PRODUCER: Herbert Wilcox

DIRECTOR: Stuart Robertson

SCREENPLAY: Frank S. Nugent, based on a story by Maurice Walsh

PHOTOGRAPHY: Max Greene

CAST: Orson Welles (Sandy Menzies), Margaret Lockwood (Marissa), Forrest Tucker (Lance), Victor McLaglen (Parlan), John McCallum (Malcolm), Eddie Byrne (Dinny Sullivan), Archie Duncan (Nollie Dukes)

1955 *Mr. Arkadin* [British title: *Confidential Report*]

PRODUCTION COMPANY: Mercury/Cervantes/Sevilla Studios/Film Organisation

PRODUCER: Orson Welles (Executive Producer: Louis Dolivet)

DIRECTOR: Orson Welles

SCREENPLAY: Orson Welles, based on his own novel

PHOTOGRAPHY: Jean Bourgoin

MUSIC: Paul Misraki

CAST: Orson Welles (Gregory Arkadin), Paola Mori (Raina Arkadin), Robert Arden (Guy van Stratten), Akim Tamiroff (Jacob Zouk), Michael Redgrave (Burgomil Trebitsch), Patricia Medina (Mily), Mischa Auer (the Professor), Katina Paxinou (Sophie), Jack Watling (Marquis of Rutleigh), Grégoire Aslan (Bracco), Peter van Eyck (Thaddeus), Suzanne Flon (Baroness Nagel), Tamara Shane (woman in apartment), Frédéric O'Brady (Oskar)

1956 *Moby Dick*

PRODUCTION COMPANY: Warner Brothers/Moulin

PRODUCER: John Huston

DIRECTOR: John Huston

SCREENPLAY: Ray Bradbury and John Huston, based on the novel by Herman Melville

PHOTOGRAPHY: Oswald Morris

MUSIC: Philip Stainton

CAST: Gregory Peck (Captain Ahab), Richard Basehart (Ishmael), Leo Genn (Starbuck), Harry Andrews (Stubb), Orson Welles

(Father Mapple), Bernard Miles (Manxman), Mervyn Johns (Peleg), Noel Purcell (Carpenter), Edric Connor (Daggoo), Joseph Tomelty (Peter Coffin), Philip Stainton (Bildad), Royal Dano (Elijah), Seamus Kelly (Flask), Friedrich Ledebur (Queequeg), Tamba Alleney (Pip), James Robertson Justice (Captain Boomer)

1957 *Man in the Shadow* **[British title: *Pay the Devil*]**

PRODUCTION COMPANY: Albert Zugsmith/Universal International

PRODUCER: Albert Zugsmith

DIRECTOR: Jack Arnold

SCREENPLAY: Gene L. Coon

PHOTOGRAPHY: Arthur E. Arling

MUSIC: Hans Salter

CAST: Jeff Chandler (Ben Sadler), Orson Welles (Virgil Renchler), Colleen Miller (Skippy Renchler), Ben Alexander (Ab Begley), Barbara Lawrence (Helen Sadler), John Larch (Ed Yates), James Gleason (Hank James), Royal Dano (Aiken Clay), Paul Fix (Herb Parker), Leo Gordon (Chet Huneker)

1957 *The Long Hot Summer*

PRODUCTION COMPANY: 20th Century Fox

PRODUCER: Jerry Wald

DIRECTOR: Martin Ritt

SCREENPLAY: Irving Ravetch and Harriet Frank, Jr., based on fiction by William Faulkner

PHOTOGRAPHY: Joseph La Shelle

MUSIC: Alex North

CAST: Paul Newman (Ben Quick), Joanne Woodward (Clara Varner), Anthony Franciosa (Jody Varner), Orson Welles (Will Varner), Lee Remick (Eula Varner), Angela Lansbury (Minnie), Richard Anderson (Alan Stewart), Sarah Marshall (Agnes Stewart), Mabel Albertson (Mrs. Stewart)

1958 *Touch of Evil*

PRODUCTION COMPANY: Universal

PRODUCER: Albert Zugsmith

DIRECTOR: Orson Welles

SCREENPLAY: Orson Welles, based on the novel *Badge of Evil* by Whit Masterson, and an earlier script by Paul Monash

PHOTOGRAPHY: Rissell Metty

MUSIC: Henry Mancini

CAST: Orson Welles (Hank Quinlan), Charlton Heston (Mike Vargas), Janet Leigh (Susan Vargas), Joseph Calleia (Pete Menzies), Akim Tamiroff ("Uncle" Joe Grandi), Valentin De Vargas (Pancho), Ray Collins (District Attorney Adair), Dennis Weaver (motel "night man"), Joanna Moore (Marcia Linnaker), Mort Mills (Schwartz), Marlene Dietrich (Tanya), Victor Millan (Manolo Sanchez), Lalo Rios (Risto), Michael Sargent (Pretty Boy), Mercedes McCambridge (gang leader in motel), Joseph Cotten (coroner), Zsa Zsa Gabor (owner of strip joint), Phil Harvey (Blaine), Joi Lansing (Zita), Harry Shannon (Gould), Rusty Wescoatt (Casey), Wayne Taylor, Ken Millar, Raymond Rodriguez (gang members), Arlene McQuade (Ginnie), Dominick Delgarde (Lackey), Joe Basulto (delinquent), Jennie Dias (Jackie), Yolanda Bojorquez (Bobbie), Eleanor Dorado (Lia), John Dierkes (policeman)

1958 *The Roots of Heaven*

PRODUCTION COMPANY: Darryl F. Zanuck Productions/20th Century Fox

PRODUCER: Darryl F. Zanuck

DIRECTOR: John Huston

SCREENPLAY: Romain Gary and Patrick Leigh-Fermor, based on the novel by Romain Gary

PHOTOGRAPHY: Oswald Morris

MUSIC: Malcolm Arnold

CAST: Trevor Howard (Morel), Juliette Greco (Minna), Errol Flynn (Forsythe), Eddie Albert (Abe Fields), Orson Welles (Cy Sedgwick), Paul Lukas (Saint-Denis), Herbert Lom (Orsini), Gregoire Aslan (Habib), André Luguet (Governor), Friedrich Ledebur (Peer Qvist)

1959 *Compulsion*

PRODUCTION COMPANY: Darryl F. Zanuck Productions/20th Century Fox

PRODUCER: Richard D. Zanuck

DIRECTOR: Richard Fleischer

SCREENPLAY: Richard Murphy, based on the novel and play by Meyer Levin

PHOTOGRAPHY: William C. Mellor

MUSIC: Lionel Newman

CAST: Dean Stockwell (Judd Steiner), Bradford Dillman (Artie Straus), E. G. Marshall (Horn), Orson Welles (Jonathan Wilk), Diane Varsi (Ruth Evans), Martin Milner (Sid Brooks), Richard Anderson (Max), Robert Simon (Lt. Johnson), Edward Binns (Tom Daly)

1959 *Ferry to Hong Kong*

PRODUCTION COMPANY: A. Lewis Gilbert/Rank

PRODUCER: George Maynard

DIRECTOR: Lewis Gilbert

SCREENPLAY: Vernon Harris and Lewis Gilbert, based on a novel by Max Catto

PHOTOGRAPHY: Otto Heller

MUSIC: Kenneth V. Jones

CAST: Curt Jurgens (Mark Conrad), Orson Welles (Captain Hart), Sylvia Sims (Liz Ferrer), Jeremy Spenser (Miguel Henriques), Noel Purcell (Joe Skinner), Margaret Withers (Miss Carter), John Wallace (Police Inspector), Roy Chiao (Johnny Sing-Up), Shelley Shen (Foo Shoo)

1959 *David and Goliath*

PRODUCTION COMPANY: ANSA

PRODUCER: Emimmo Salvi

DIRECTOR: Richard Pottier and Ferdinando Baldi

SCREENPLAY: Umberto Scarpelli, Gino Mangini, Emimmo Salvi, and Ambrogio Molteni

PHOTOGRAPHY: Adalberto Albertini and Carlo Fiore

MUSIC: Carlo Innocenzi

CAST: Orson Welles (Saul), Eleanora Rissi-Drago (Merab), Ivo Payer (David), Giulia Rubina (Michal), Massimo Serato (Abner), Pierre Cressoy (Jonathan), Edward Hilton (Prophet Samuel), Kronos (Goliath), Furio Meniconi (King Asrod), Luigi Tosi (Benjamin of Gaba), Dante Maggio (Cret), Ugo Sasso (Huro), Umberto Fiz (Lazar)

1960 *Austerlitz*

PRODUCTION COMPANY: Compagnie Française de Production Internationale/Societé Cinematographique Lyre Films/Galatea/ Michael Arthur Film/Dubrava Film

PRODUCER: Alexander Salkind and Michael Salkind

DIRECTOR: Abel Gance

SCREENPLAY: Abel Gance and Roger Richebe

PHOTOGRAPHY: Henri Alekan and Robert Juillard

MUSIC: Jean Ledrut

CAST: Pierre Mondy (Napoleon), Jean Mercure (Talleyrand), Jack Palance (General Weirother), Georges Marchal (Lannes), Jean-Marc Bory (Soult), Orson Welles (Fulton), Michel Simon (d'Alboise), Jean-Louis Horbette (Constant), Martine Carol (Josephine), Jean-Louis Trintignant (Segur), Leslie Caron (Mlle de Vaudey), Claudia Cardinale (Pauline), Rossano Brazzi (Lucien Bonaparte), Vittorio De Sica (Pope Pius VII)

1960 *Crack in the Mirror*

PRODUCTION COMPANY: Darryl F. Zanuck/20th Century Fox

PRODUCER: Darryl F. Zanuck

DIRECTOR: Richard Fleischer

SCREENPLAY: Mark Canfield, based on the novel by Marcel Haedrich

PHOTOGRAPHY: William C. Mellor

MUSIC: Maurice Jarre

CAST: Juliette Greco (Eponine/Florence), Bradford Dillman (Larnier/Claude), Orson Welles (Hagolin/Lamorcière), William Lucas (Kerstner), Alexander Knox (President), Catherine Lacey (Mother Superior), Maurice Teynac (Doctor), Austin Wills (Hurtelaut), Cec Linder (Murzeau)

1960 *The Tartars*

PRODUCTION COMPANY: Lux

PRODUCER: Richard Gualino

DIRECTOR: Richard Thorpe

SCREENPLAY: Sabatino Cuffini, Ambrogio Molteni, Gaio Fratini, Oreste Palella, Emimmo Salvi, and Julian De Kassel

PHOTOGRAPHY: Amerigo Gengareli

MUSIC: Renzo Rossellini

CAST: Orson Welles (Burundai), Victor Mature (Oleg), Liana Orfei (Helga), Arnoldo Foà (Chu-Ling), Bella Cortez (Samja), Folco Lulli (Togrul), Luciano Marin (Eric), Furio Meniconi (Sigrun)

1961 *Lafayette*

PRODUCTION COMPANY: Films Copernic/Cosmos Film

PRODUCER: Maurice Jacquin

DIRECTOR: Jean Dréville

SCREENPLAY: Jean-Bernard Luc, Suzanne Arduini, Jacques Sigurd, François Ponthier, Jean Dréville, and Maurice Jacquin

PHOTOGRAPHY: Claude Renoir and Robert Hubert

MUSIC: Steve Laurent and Pierre Duclos

CAST: Michel Le Royer (Lafayette), Jack Hawkins (General Cornwallis), Orson Welles (Benjamin Franklin), Howard St. John (George Washington), Vittorio De Sica (Bancroft), Edmund Purdom (Silas Deane), Jacques Castelot (Duc d'Ayen), Folco Lulli (Le Boursier), Wolfgang Preiss (Baron Kalb), Liselotte Pulver (Marie Antoinette), Albert Rémy (Louis XVI)

1962 *The Trial*

PRODUCTION COMPANY: Paris Europa/FI-C-IT/Hisa-Films

PRODUCER: Alexander Salkind and Michael Salkind

DIRECTOR: Orson Welles

SCREENPLAY: Orson Welles, based on the novel by Franz Kafka

PHOTOGRAPHY: Edmond Richard

MUSIC: Jean Ledrut, using the *Adagio* of Tomaso Albinoni

CAST: Anthony Perkins (Joseph K.), Orson Welles (Hastler), Jeanne Moreau (Miss Bürstner), Akim Tamiiroff (Bloch), Romy Schneider (Leni), Elsa Martinelli (Hilda), Arnoldo Foà (the Inspector),

Suzanne Flon (Miss Pittle), Madeleine Robinson (Mrs. Grubach), Wolfgang Reichmann (the courtroom guard), Thomas Holtzmann (Bert, the law student), Maydra Shore (Irmie), Max Haufler (Uncle Max), Fernand Ledoux (Clerk of the Court), Michael Lonsdale (the priest), William Chappell (Titorelli), Max Buchsbaum (Examining Magistrate), Maurice Teynac (Deputy Manager), Billy Kearns (first police officer), Jess Hahn (second police officer), Raoul Delfosse, Karl Suder, Jean-Claude Remoleux (executioners)

1962 *Rogopag*
[Segment with Welles: *La Ricotta*]
PRODUCTION COMPANY: Arco Film/Cineriz/Lyre Film
PRODUCER: Alfredo Bini
DIRECTOR: Pier Paolo Pasolini
SCREENPLAY: Pier Paolo Pasolini
PHOTOGRAPHY: Tonino Delli Colli
CAST: Orson Welles (the Director), Mario Cipriani

1963 *The V.I.P.s*
PRODUCTION COMPANY: MGM
PRODUCER: Anatole de Grunwald
DIRECTOR: Anthony Asquith
SCREENPLAY: Terence Rattigan
PHOTOGRAPHY: Jack Hildyard
MUSIC: Miklos Rozsa

CAST: Elizabeth Taylor (Frances Andros), Richard Burton (Paul Andros), Louis Jourdan (Marc Chapselle), Elsa Martinelli (Gloria Gritti), Margaret Rutherford (Duchess of Brighton), Maggie Smith (Miss Mead), Rod Taylor (Les Mangrum), Orson Welles (Max Buda), Linda Christian (Miriam Marshall), Dennis Price (Commander Millbank), Richard Wattis (Sanders), Ronald Fraser (Joslin), David Frost (Reporter), Robert Coote (John Coburn), Joan Benham (Miss Potter), Michael Hordern (Airport Director)

1964 *La Fabuleuse Aventure de Marco Polo* [U.S. title: *Marco the Magnificent*]
PRODUCTION COMPANY: Italica/SNC/Prodi Cinematografica/Avala Film/Mounir Rafla/Italaf Kaboul
PRODUCER: Raoul J. Lévy
DIRECTOR: Denys de la Pateliere and Noel Howard
SCREENPLAY: Raoul J. Lévy and Denys de la Pateliere
PHOTOGRAPHY: Armand Thirard
MUSIC: Georges Garvarentz
CAST: Horst Buchholz (Marco Polo), Anthony Quinn (Kublai Khan), Akim Tamiroff (Old Man of the Mountain), Robert Hossein

(Prince Nayam), Omar Sharif (Sheik Alaou), Elsa Marinelli (Lady with the Whip), Orson Welles (Ackermann), Gregoire Aslan (Achmed Abudullah), Massimo Giroti (Nicolo Polo)

1965 *Is Paris Burning?*

PRODUCTION COMPANY: Transcontinental/Marianne

PRODUCER: Paul Graetz

DIRECTOR: René Clément

SCREENPLAY: Gore Vidal and Francis Ford Coppola, based on the book by Larry Collins and Dominique Lapiere

PHOTOGRAPHY: Marcel Grignon

MUSIC: Maurice Jarre

CAST: Gert Fröbe (General Dietrich von Choltitz), Orson Welles (Consul Raoul Nordling), Bruno Crémer (Colonel Rol), Alain Delon (Jacques Chaban-Delmas), Pierre Vaneck (Major Roger Gallois), Claude Rich (General Jacques Leclerc), Jean-Pierre Cassel (Lt. Henri Karcher), Jean-Paul Belmondo (Morandat), Leslie Caron (Françoise Labe), Marie Versini (Claire), Wolfgang Preiss (Ebernach), Kirk Douglas (General George Patton), Glenn Ford (General Omar Bradley), Charles Boyer (Charles Monod), Anthony Perkins (soldier), Jean-Louis Trintignant (Serge), Simone Signoret (Café proprietress), Robert Stack (General Edwin Sibert), Yves Montand (Marcel Bizien), George Chakiris (soldier)

1966 *Chimes at Midnight* [also known as *Falstaff*]

PRODUCTION COMPANY: Internacional Films Española/Apine

PRODUCER: Emiliano Piedra and Angel Escolano

DIRECTOR: Orson Welles

SCREENPLAY: Orson Welles, based on plays by William Shakespeare and Raphael Holinshed's *Chronicles of England*

PHOTOGRAPHY: Admond Richard

MUSIC: Angelo Francesco Lavagnino

CAST: Orson Welles (Falstaff), Ralph Richardson (Narrator), Keith Baxter (Prince Hal), John Gielgud (Henry IV), Jeanne Moreau (Doll Tearsheet), Margaret Rutherford (Mistress Quickly), Norman Rodway (Hotspur), Marina Vlady (Kate Percy), Alan Webb (Justice Shallow), Walter Chiari (Silence), Michael Aldridge (Pistol), Tony Beckley (Poins), Fernarndo Rey (Worcester), Andrew Faulds (Westmoreland), José Nieto (Northumberland), Jeremy Rowe (Prince John), Beatrice Welles (Falstaff's page), Paddy Beford (Bardolph), Julio Peña, Fernando Hilbert, Andrés Mejuto, Keith Pyoft, Charles Farrell

1966 *The Sailor From Gibraltar*

PRODUCTION COMPANY: Woodfall

PRODUCER: Oscar Lewenstein and Neil Hartley

DIRECTOR: Tony Richardson

SCREENPLAY: Christopher Isherwood, Don Magner, and Tony Richardson, based on the novel by Marguerite Duras

PHOTOGRAPHY: Raoul Coutard

MUSIC: Antoine Duhamel

CAST: Jeanne Moreau (Anna), Ian Bannen (Alan), Vanessa Redgrave (Sheila), Orson Welles (Louis from Mozambique), Zia Mohyeddin (Noori), Hugh Griffith (Llewellyn), Umberto Orsini (postcard vendor), Erminio Spalla (Eolo), Eleanor Brown (Carla), Giabriella Pallota (girl at dance), Arnoldo Foà (man on train), Claudio De Renzi (Jeannot), Fausto Tozzi (Captain), John Hurt (John)

1966 *A Man for all Seasons*

PRODUCTION COMPANY: Highland/Columbia

PRODUCER: Fred Zinnemann

DIRECTOR: Fred Zinnemann

SCREENPLAY: Robert Bolt, based on his play

PHOTOGRAPHY: Ted Moore

MUSIC: Georges Delerue

CAST: Paul Scofield (Sir Thomas More), Robert Shaw (Henry VIII), Wendy Hiller (Alice More), Leo McKern (Thomas Cromwell), Orson Welles (Cardinal Wolsey), Susannah York (Margaret), Nigel Davenport (Duke of Norfolk), John Hurt (Richard Rich), Corin Redgrave (William Roper), Colin Blakely (Matthew), Cyril Luckham (Archbishop Cranmer), Vanessa Redgrave (Anne Boleyn)

1967 *Casino Royale*

PRODUCTION COMPANY: Famous Artists/Columbia

PRODUCER: Charles K. Feldman and Jerry Bresler

DIRECTORS: John Huston, Ken Hughes, Val Guest, Robert Parrish, Joe McGrath

SCREENPLAY: Wolf Mankowitz, John Law, and Michael Sayers, based on the novel by Ian Fleming

PHOTOGRAPHY: Jack Hildyard

MUSIC: Burt Bacharach

CAST: David Niven (Sir James Bond), Peter Sellers (Evelyn Tremble), Ursula Andress (Vesper Lynd), Orson Welles (Le Chiffre), Joanna Pettet (Mata Bond), Daliah Lavi (The Detainer), Deborah Kerr (Agent Mimi), Woody Allen (Jimmy Bond), William Holden (Ransome), Charles Boyer (Le Grand), John Huston (M), George Raft (as himself), Jean-Paul Belmondo (French Legionnaire), Peter O'Toole (Piper), Stirling Moss (driver)

1967 *I'll Never Forget What's 'is Name*

PRODUCTION COMPANY: Scimitar/Universal

PRODUCER: Michael Winner

DIRECTOR: Michael Winner

SCREENPLAY: Peter Draper

PHOTOGRAPHY: Otto Heller

MUSIC: Francis Lai

CAST: Orson Welles (Jonathan Lute), Oliver Reed (Andrew Quint), Carol White (Georgina), Harry Andrews (Gerald Sater), Michael Hordern (Headmaster), Wendy Craig (Louise Quint), Marianne Faithfull (Josie), Norman Rodway (Nicholas), Frank Finlay (Chaplain), Harvey Hall (Maccabee), Ann Lynn (Carla), Lyn Ashley (Susannah), Peter Graves (Bankman)

1967 *Oedipus the King*

PRODUCTION COMPANY: Crossroads/Universal

PRODUCER: Michael Luke

DIRECTOR: Philip Saville

SCREENPLAY: Michael Luke and Philip Saville, based on the play by Sophocles

PHOTOGRAPHY: Walter Lassally

CAST: Christopher Plummer (Oedipus), Lilly Palmer (Jocasta), Richard Johnson (Creon), Orson Welles (Tiresias), Cyril Cusack (Messenger), Roger Livesey (Shepherd), Donald Sutherland (Chorus leader), Alexis Mantheakis (Palace official), Demos Strenios (priest), Friedrich Ledebur (King Laius), Oenone (Antigone), Cressida Luke (Ismene), Costas Thomes, Paul Roche, Minos Argyrakis, Takis Emmanouel, George Dialegmenos (members of the Chorus)

1968 *The Immortal Story*

PRODUCTION COMPANY: ORTF/Albina Films

PRODUCER: Micheline Rozan

DIRECTOR: Orson Welles

SCREENPLAY: Orson Welles, based on the novella by Isak Dinesen

PHOTOGRAPHY: Willy Kurant

MUSIC: Eric Satie

CAST: Orson Welles (Narrator/Mr. Clay), Jeanne Moreau (Virginie Ducrot), Roger Coggio (Elishama Levinsky), Norman Eshley (Paul), Fernando Rey (merchant)

1968 *House of Cards*

PRODUCTION COMPANY: Westward

PRODUCER: Dick Berg

DIRECTOR: John Guillermin

SCREENPLAY: James P. Bonner

PHOTOGRAPHY: Piero Portalupi

MUSIC: Francis Lai

CAST: George Peppard (Reno Davis), Inger Stevens (Anne de Villemont), Keith Michell (Hubert Morillon), Orson Welles (Charles Leschenhaut), William Job (Bernard Bourdon), Maxine Audley (Matilde Vosiers), Pater Bayliss (Edmond Vosiers)

1968 *Fight for Rome* [also known as *The Last Roman*]
PRODUCTION COMPANY: CCC
PRODUCER: Artur Brauner
DIRECTOR: Robert Siodmak
SCREENPLAY: Ladislas Fodor
PHOTOGRAPHY: Richard Angst
MUSIC: Riz Ortolani
CAST: Laurence Olivier (Cethegus), Orson Welles (Emperor Justinian), Sylva Koxcina (Theodora), Honor Blackman (Amalaswintha), Robert Hoffmann (Totila), Harriet Andersson (Mathaswintha), Michael Dunn (Narses), Ingrid Brett (Julia), Lang Jeffires (Belisar)

1968 *The Southern Star*
PRODUCTION COMPANY: Euro Farance Films/Capitole Films/Columbia British
PRODUCER: Roger Duchet
DIRECTOR: Sidney Hayers
SCREENPLAY: David Purcell and John Seddon, based on the novel by Jules Verne
PHOTOGRAPHY: Raoul Coutard
CAST: George Segal (Dan Rockland), Ursula Andress (Erica Kramer), Orson Welles (Plankett), Ian Hendry (Karl Ludwig), Michel Constantin (José), Harry Andrews (Kramer), Johnny Sekka (Matakit)

1969 *Tepepa*
PRODUCTION COMPANY: Filmamerica/SIAP/PEFSA
DIRECTOR: Giulio Petroni
SCREENPLAY: Franco Solinas and Ivan Della Mea
PHOTOGRAPHY: Francisco Marin
CAST: Tomas Milian, Orson Welles (Colonel Cascorro), John Steiner, José Torres, Ana Mari Lanciaprima, Paloma Cela, Rafael Hernandez, Luciano Casamonica

1969 *Start the Revolution Without Me*
PRODUCTION COMPANY: Norbud Films
EXECUTIVE PRODUCER: Norman Lear
DIRECTOR: Bud Yorkin

SCREENPLAY: Fred Freeman and Lawrence J. Cohen

PHOTOGRAPHY: Jean Tournier

CAST: Orson Welles (himself, narrator), Gene Wilder (Claude Coupe/Phillipe Di Sisi), Donald Sutherland (Charles Coupe/Pierre Di Sisi), Hugh Griffith (Louis XVI), Jack MacGowran (Jacques Cabriolet), Billie Whitelaw (Marie Antoinette), Victor Spinetti (Duke d'Escargot), Ewa Aulin (Princess Christina)

1969 *The Battle of the River Neretva*

PRODUCTION COMPANY: Dobrovoljacka/Eickberg/Igor Film

PRODUCER: Steve Previn

DIRECTOR: Veljko Bulajic

SCREENPLAY: Ugo Pirro, Patko Djurovic, Veljko Bulajic, and Stevo Bulajic

PHOTOGRAPHY: Tomaslav Pinter

CAST: Yul Brynner (Vlado), Orson Welles (Senator), Curt Jurgens (General Lohring), Sergei Bondarchuk (Martin), Oleg Vidov (Nikola), Milena Dravic (Nada), Sylva Koscina (Danitsa), Hardy Kruger (Colonel Kartzner)

1969 *Michael the Brave* [also known as *The Last Crusade*]

PRODUCTION COMPANY: Romania Film

DIRECTOR: Sergiu Nicolaescu

SCREENPLAY: Titus Popovici

PHOTOGRAPHY: George Cornea

CAST: Orson Welles [uncredited], Amza Pellea, Irina Gardescu, Florin Persic, Septimiu Sever, Ilarion Ciobau, Sergiu Nicolaescu

1969 *The Kremlin Letter*

PRODUCTION COMPANY: 20th Century Fox

PRODUCER: Carter De Haven and Sam Wiesenthal

DIRECTOR: John Huston

SCREENPLAY: John Huston and Gladys Hill, based on the novel by Joel Behn

PHOTOGRAPHY: Ted Scaife

MUSIC: Robert Drasnin

CAST: Richard Boone (Ward), Bibi Andersson (Erika Boeck), Max von Sydow (Colonel Vladimir Kosnov), Patrick O'Neal (Lt. Commander Charles Rone), Orson Welles (Aleksei Bresnavitch), Ronald Radd (Potkin), Nigel Green (Janis), Dean Jagger (The Highwayman), Lila Kedrova (Madame Sophie), Barbara Parkins (B.A.), George Sanders (The Warlock), Raf Vallone (The Puppet Maker), Micheál MacLiammóir (Sweet Alice), Anthony Quinn (Kitai), John Huston (Admiral)

1970 *12 + 1*

PRODUCTION COMPANY: COFCI-CEF

PRODUCER: Claude Giroux

DIRECTOR: Nicolas Gessner

SCREENPLAY: Marc Beham and Nicolas Gessner

PHOTOGRAPHY: Ciuseppi Ruzzolini

CAST: Sharon Tate (Pat), Orson Welles (Markau), Vittorio Gassmann (Mike), Vittorio De Sica (Di Seta), Mylene Demongeot (Judy), Terry Thomas (Albert), Tim Brooke Taylor (Jackie)

1970 *Catch-22*

PRODUCTION COMPANY: Paramount

PRODUCER: John Calley and Martin Ransohoff

DIRECTOR: Mike Nichols

SCREENPLAY: Buck Henry, based on the novel by Joseph Heller

PHOTOGRAPHY: David Watkin

CAST: Alan Arkin (Yossarian), Martin Balsam (Colonel Cathcart), Richard Benjamin (Major Danby), Art Garfunkel (Captain Nately), Jack Gilford (Doc Daneeka), Buck Henry (Lt. Col. Korn), Bob Newhart (Major Major), Anthony Perkins (Chaplain Tappman), Paula Prentiss (Nurse Duckett), Martin Sheen (Lt. Dobbs), Jon Voight (Milo Minderbinder), Orson Welles (General Dreedle), Seth Allen (Hungry Joe), Robert Balaban (Captain Orr), Jonathon Korkes (Snowden)

1970 *Waterloo*

PRODUCTION COMPANY: Cinematografica/Mosfilm

PRODUCER: Dino De Laurentiis

DIRECTOR: Sergei Bondarchuk

SCREENPLAY: H. A. L. Craig, Sergei Bondarchuk, and Vittorio Bonicelli

PHOTOGRAPHY: Armando Nannuzzi

MUSIC: Nino Rota

CAST: Rod Steiger (Napoleon), Christopher Plummer (Wellington), Orson Welles (Louis XVIII), Jack Hawkins (General Picton), Virginia McKenna (Duchess of Richmond), Dan O'Herlihy (Marshal Ney), Rupert Davies (Gordon), Philippe Forquet (La Bedoyere), Gianni Garko (Drouot), Ivo Garrani (Soult), Ian Ogilvy (De Lancey), Michael Wilding (Ponsonby)

1970 *Upon this Rock*

PRODUCTION COMPANY: Marstan-Rock/Sheldon-Wilson/Stanley Abrams

DIRECTOR: Harry Rosky

SCREENPLAY: Harry Rosky

PHOTOGRAPHY: Aldo Tonti

CAST: Orson Welles (Michelangelo), Edith Evans (Queen Christina), Dirk Bogard (Prince Charlie), Ralph Richardson (Guide)

1970 *A Safe Place*

PRODUCTION COMPANY: BBS/Columbia

PRODUCER: Bert Schneider

DIRECTOR: Henry Jaglom

SCREENPLAY: Henry Jaglom

PHOTOGRAPHY: Dick Kratina

CAST: Tuesday Weld (Noah [Susan]), Jack Nicholson (Mitch), Orson Welles (Magician), Philip Proctor (Fred), Gwen Welles (Bari), Dov Lawrence (Larry), Fanny Birkenmaier (Maid), Rhonda Alfaro (girl in rowboat), Sylvia Zapp (young Susan)

1971 *Treasure Island*

PRODUCTION COMPANY: Massfilms/Les Productions FDL/CCC/Eguiluz Films

PRODUCER: Harry Alan Towers

DIRECTOR: John Hough

SCREENPLAY: Wolf Mankowitz and "O. W. Jeeves" [Orson Welles], based on the novel by Robert Louis Stevenson

PHOTOGRAPHY: Cecilio Paniagua

CAST: Orson Welles (Long John Silver), Kim Burfield (Jim Hawkins), Lionel Stander (Billy Bones), Walter Slezak (Squire Trelawney), Angel Del Pozo (Doctor Livesey), Rik Battaglia (Captain Smollett), Maria Rohm (Mrs. Hawkins), Paul Muller (Blind Pew)

1971 *Malpertuis*

PRODUCTION COMPANY: SOFIDOC/Les Productions Artistes Associés/ Societé d'Expansion du Spectacle/Artemis Films

PRODUCER: Pierre Levie and Paul Laffargue

DIRECTOR: Harry Kumel

SCREENPLAY: Jean Ferry, based on the novel by Jean Ray

PHOTOGRAPHY: Gerry Fisher

MUSIC: Georges Delerue

CAST: Orson Welles (Cassavius), Susan Hampshire (Nancy/Euryale/ Alice), Michel Bouquet (Dideloo), Mathieu Carrière (Yann), Jean-Pierre Cassel (Lampernis), Sylvie Vartan (Bets), Daniel Pilon (Mathias Krook), Dora Van Der Groen (Sylvie Dideloo)

1972 *Ten Days' Wonder* [*La Decade Prodigieuse*]

PRODUCTION COMPANY: Films La Boetie

PRODUCER: André Genovese

DIRECTOR: Claude Chabrol

SCREENPLAY: Paul Gegauff, Paul Gardner, and Eugene Archer, based on the novel by Ellery Queen

PHOTOGRAPHY: Jean Rabier

CAST: Orson Welles (Theo Van Horn), Marlene Jobert (Helene), Anthony Perkins (Charles Van Horn), Michel Piccoli (Paul Regis), Guido Alberti (Ludovic), Sylvana Blasi (woman), Giovanni Sciuto (moneylender), Ermanno Casanova (Viellard Borgne), Tsilla Chelton (Charles's mother), Eric Frisdal (young Charles), Vittorio Sanipoli (Police Inspector)

1972 *Get to Know Your Rabbit*

PRODUCTION COMPANY: Warner Brothers

PRODUCER: Steven Bernhardt and Paul Gaer

DIRECTOR: Brian De Palma

SCREENPLAY: Jordan Crittenden

PHOTOGRAPHY: John Alonzo

MUSIC: Jack Elliott

CAST: Tom Smothers (Donald Beeman), John Astin (Mr. Turnbull), Suzanne Zenor (Paula), Samantha Jones (Susan), Allen Garfield (Vic), Katharine Ross ("the terrific-looking girl"), Orson Welles (Mr. Delasandro), Hope Summers (Mrs. Beeman)

1972 *Necromancy* [also known as *The Witching*]

PRODUCTION COMPANY: Zenith Internationa

PRODUCER: Bert I. Gordon

DIRECTOR: Bert I. Gordon

SCREENPLAY: Bert I. Gordon

PHOTOGRAPHY: Winton Hoch

MUSIC: Fred Karger

CAST: Orson Welles (Mr. Cato), Pamela Franklin (Lori), Lee Purcell (Priscilla), Michael Ontkean (Frank), Harvey Jason (Jay), Lisa James (Georgette), Sue Bernard (Nancy), Terry Quinn (Cato's son)

1973 *F for Fake*

PRODUCTION COMPANY: Les Films de l'Astrophore/Saci/Janus Film

PRODUCERS: Dominique Antoine and François Reichenbach

DIRECTOR: Orson Welles

SCREENPLAY: Orson Welles and Oja Palinkas

PHOTOGRAPHY: Gary Graver and Christian Odasso

MUSIC: Michel Legrand

CAST: Orson Welles, Oja Kodar, Elmyr de Hory, Clifford Irving, Edith Irving, François Reichenbach, Joseph Cotten, Laurence Harvey, Richard Wilson, Paul Stewart, Howard Hughes, Sasa Devcic, Gary Graver, Andrés Vincent Gomez, Julio Palinkas, Christian Odasso, François Widoff, Peter Bogdanovich, William Alland

1977 *Voyage of the Damned*
PRODUCTION COMPANY: Entertainment/Associated General Films
PRODUCER: Robert Fryer
DIRECTOR: Stuart Rosenberg
SCREENPLAY: Steve Shagan and David Butler, based on the book by Gordon Thomas and Max Morgan-Witts
PHOTOGRAPHY: Billy Williams
MUSIC: Lalo Schifrin
CAST: Faye Dunaway (Denise Kreisler), Max Von Sydow (Captain Gustav Schroeder), Oskar Werner (Dr. Egon Kreisler), Malcolm McDowell (Max Gunther), James Mason (Dr. Juan Remos), Orson Welles (José Estedes), Katharine Ross (Mira Hauser), Ben Gazzara (Morris Troper), Lee Grant (Lili Rosen), Sam Wanamaker (Carl Rosen), Lynne Frederick (Anna Rosen), Julie Harris (Alice Feinchild), Helmut Griem (Otto Schiendick), Luther Adler (Professor Weller), Wendy Hiller (Rachel Weller), Nehemiah Persoff (Mr. Hauser), Maria Schell (Mrs. Miriam Hauser), Paul Koslo (Aaron Pozner), Jonathan Pryce (Joseph Manasse), Fernando Rey (President Bru), Donald Houston (Dr. Hans Glauner), Michael Constantine (Luis Clasing), José Ferrer (Manuel Benitez), Denholm Elliott (Admiral Canaris)

1979 *The Muppet Movie*
PRODUCTION COMPANY: ITC
PRODUCER: Jim Henson
DIRECTOR: James Frawley
SCREENPLAY: Jerry Juhl and Jack Burns
PHOTOGRAPHY: Isidore Mankofsky
MUSIC: Paul Williams and Kenny Ascher
CAST: Charles Durning (Doc Hopper), Austin Pendleton (Max), Scott Walker ("Snake" Walker), Lawrence Gabriel, Jr. (sailor), Ira F. Grubman (bartender), H. B. Haggerty (lumberjack), Bruce Kirby (gate guard), Tommy Madden (one-eyed midget), James Frawley (waiter), Arnold Roberts (cowboy), Edgar Bergen (himself), Milton Berle ("Mad Man" Mooney), Mel Brooks (Professor Max Krassman), James Coburn (owner of El Sleezo Café), Dom DeLuise (Bernie), Bob Hope (ice cream vendor), Madeline Kahn (El Sleezo patron), Carol Kane ("Myth"), Cloris Leachman (Lord's secretary), Steve Martin (waiter), Richard Pryor (balloon vendor), Orson Welles (Lew Lord)

1980 *The Secret of Nikole Tesla* [*Tajna Nicole Tesle*]
PRODUCTION COMPANY: Zagreb Film-Kinematografi
DIRECTOR: Kristo Papic
SCREENPLAY: Ivo Bresan and Ivan Kusan
PHOTOGRAPHY: Ivica Rajkovic

CAST: Peter Bozovic (Nikole Tesla), Orson Welles (J. P. Morgan), Strother Martin (George Westinghouse), Dennis Patrick (Thomas Edison), Oja Kodar, Boris Buzancic, Charles Millot, Ana Kavic

1981 *Butterfly*

PRODUCTION COMPANY: Par Par Productions

PRODUCER: Matt Cimber

DIRECTOR: Matt Cimber

SCREENPLAY: John Goff and Matt Cimber, based on the novel *The Butterfly* by James M. Cain

PHOTOGRAPHY: Eddy Van Der Enden

MUSIC: Ennio Morricone

CAST: Stacy Keach (Jess Tyler), Pia Zadora (Kady), Orson Welles (Judge Rauch), Lois Nettleton (Belle Morgan), Stuart Whitman (Reverend Rivers), James Franciscus (Moke Blue), Ed McMahon (Mr. Gillespie), June Lockhart (Mrs. Gillespie), Paul Hampton (Norton), Buck Flower (Ed Lamey), Ann Dane (Jane), Greg Gault (Bridger), John O'Connor White (Billy Roy), Peter Jason (Allen), Kim Ptak (Deputy)

1983 *Where is Parsifal?*

PRODUCTION COMPANY: Slederline

PRODUCER: Daniel Carrillo

DIRECTOR: Henri Helman

SCREENPLAY: Berta Dominguez D.

PHOTOGRAPHY: Norman Langley

MUSIC: Hubert Rostaing

CAST: Tony Curtis (Parsifal Kaltzanella-Boden), Cassandra Domenica (Elba Katzanella-Boden), Erik Estrada (Henry Board III), Peter Lawford (Montague Chippendale), Ron Moody (Baron Gaspard Beersbohm), Donald Pleasance (Mackintosh), Orson Welles (Klingsor), Christopher Chaplin (Ivan), Nancy Roberts (Ruth), Vladek Sheybal (Morjack), Ava Lazar (Sheila), Jay Benedict (Luke), Edward Burnham (Trofimov), Anthony Dawson (Ripple)

1987 *Someone to Love*

PRODUCTION COMPANY: International Rainbow

PRODUCER: M. H. Simonsons

DIRECTOR: Henry Jaglom

SCREENPLAY: Henry Jaglom

PHOTOGRAPHY: Hanania Baer

MUSIC: Diane Bulgarelli, Stephen Bishop, and Dave Frishberg

CAST: Henry Jaglom (Danny Speir), Orson Welles (Danny's friend), Andrea Marcovicci (Helen Eugene), Michael Emil (Mickey Sapir), Sally Kellerman (Edith Helm), Oja Kodar (Yelena), Stephen Bishop (Blue), Dave Frishberg (Harry)

Index